LASKER'S MANUAL OF CHESS

BY

EMANUEL LASKER

WITH 308 DIAGRAMS

DOVER PUBLICATIONS, INC.
NEW YORK

Published in Canada by General Publishing Com-
pany, Ltd., 30 Lesmill Road, Don Mills, Toronto,
Ontario.
Published in the United Kingdom by Constable
and Company, Ltd., 10 Orange Street, London
WC 2.

This Dover edition, first published in 1960, is an
unabridged republication of the work published
by David McKay Company, Inc., in 1947.

Standard Book Number: 486-20640-8

Library of Congress Catalog Card Number:
CD62-223

Manufactured in the United States of America
Dover Publications, Inc.
180 Varick Street
New York, N. Y. 10014

TO

MY DEAR WIFE

WHO SHARES WITH ME
MY CARES AND LABOURS
AND WHO LETS ME
SHARE IN HER JOYS

The Martha Lasker Estate wishes to express its thanks to Harold M. Phillips for his efforts in making possible the publication of the present edition.

EMANUEL LASKER: AN APPRECIATION

What can be said to be permanent in this fleeting world, if not our remembrance of the deeds of great men?—LUDWIG BAUER

It is a commonplace that great men are not really appreciated until death has removed them from our presence. Very few men, even very few great men, receive the homage that is rightly theirs during their lifetime. Emanuel Lasker was one of the few who become living legends; but in his case, it is a legend which is not easy to unravel. It is a legend which contains fact and fancy, unfair criticism and undiscriminating praise; a legend which depicts Lasker as shrewd and naive, as pessimistic and cheerful; a legend in which the obvious is mingled with the paradoxical.

Confronted with this confusing mass of material, it is not easy to answer the simple questions: How did Lasker become a great chess master, and in what did his greatness consist? Consider some of the difficulties: The frequently made claim that Lasker did not found a school (a claim made even by eminent masters) rests on a misconception and is in fact not true. How are we to reconcile the fact that although Lasker paid eloquent tribute throughout his life to Steinitz's theory of chess, Lasker himself followed a totally different theory? Many of Lasker's games have to this day not been properly explained, in some cases because of envy, in other cases because of the annotator's technical shortcomings. Yet Lasker himself frequently expressed dissatisfaction with attempts to explain the secret of his genius. Surely this is a ludicrous dilemma: how could Lasker have been World Champion for twenty-seven years without yielding up the secret of his mastery?

The best explanation of Lasker's genius appears in this very book. It is still another of the many Laskerian paradoxes that the highest flights of chess genius should have been described in a book for complete beginners!

When we meet great chessmasters, we are often disappointed by their narrowness, their limitations, their pettiness. Lasker was very definitely not a man of this type; he did not live for chess alone. The reader of this book does not need to be told that Lasker devoted years of study to mathematics and philosophy at the universities of Berlin, Goettingen, Heidelberg and Erlangen. The author of the *Manual* reveals himself not only as a philosopher in the technical sense, but as a man of philosophical temperament — a man who has lived in many lands, read much, reflected a great deal, observed carefully but not coldly — a man who knew suffering, pain, illness, disillusion, the loss of his worldly goods and the anguish of exile.

It is clear from the *Manual* that Lasker's character and experience are mirrored in his chess, and his chess is in turn reflected in his life. No other chessmaster has insisted so strongly on the resemblance between chess and life. Most chess books deal very strictly with technical chess data; no other chess book treats non-chess material in the way that the *Manual* does. To Lasker there was no contradiction here; the book took on the richness, the zest and variety of life.

It is this intimate connection between Lasker's life and his chess that tells us to look here for the secret of his chess genius. Lasker was a cheerful pessimist, or if you will, a moderate optimist. It was a lifelong outlook and it went into his chess. Because mathematics and philosophy played a large part in his life, they inevitably played a large part in his chess.

Lasker's theory of chess can best be understood by recapitulating his account of Steinitz's theory. Before Steinitz made his investigations, master chess had a *wilfully personal* character. A player with a dreary, uninspired style (the kind we see in the games of Staunton, Wyvill and other English masters of the mid-nineteenth century) produced dreary, uninspired chess. The great combinative geniuses (Morphy, Anderssen, Kolisch and their followers) produced delightful combinations whose artistry still gladdens us.

It was left to Steinitz to explain that advantages and disadvantages on the chessboard exist objectively and are conditioned by the situation actually on the board; that this situation, the relationship of forces, determines the proper plan to be followed; that the execution of this plan must make victory possible. As Lasker emphasizes in this book, planning is possible only on the basis of general rules — rules that sum up the lifetime experience of thousands of players. Without this inductive method, chess would sink back into the brute chaos of the physical world.

This *rational* quality of chess seems to have had a great fascination for Lasker. Again and again we find such statements in his book as "Reason which governs the world governs also the chessboard." (Here we see Lasker in the role of rather naive optimist. As a child of the nineteenth century, he could not resist the absurd thesis that in the long run, the world improves by a series of short-term catastrophes.)

"In Life," he says, "we are all duffers." In Life we are all checkmated, sooner or later; in chess, we can bring off many successes which are inherent in the rational nature of the game. So, "On the chessboard lies and hypocrisy do not survive long. The creative combination lays bare the presumption of a lie; the merciless fact, culminating in a checkmate, contradicts the hypocrite. Our little chess is one of the sanctuaries, where this principle of justice has occasionally had to hide to gain sustenance and a respite, after the army of mediocrities had driven it from the marketplace."

But it would be a mistake to think that Steinitz succeeded in giving chess an exclusively rational character. In an article in *Chess Review*, I once described Steinitz and his great contemporary Tchigorin in these terms: "These two geniuses had an unrivalled insight into the nature of chess. Whereas the popularizers think of chess as being amenable to order, logic, exactitude, calculation, foresight and other comparable qualities, Steinitz and Tchigorin agreed on one thing: that chess can be, and often is, as irrational as life itself. It is full of disorder, imperfection, blunders, inexactitudes, fortuitous happenings, unforeseen consequences. But whereas Steinitz strove with all his might to impose order on the irrational, Tchigorin went to the other extreme. Let us surrender to the irrational, he said in effect. Steinitz tried to banish the unforeseen. Tchigorin took delight in it. Steinitz sought order, system, logic, balance, broad basic postu-.

lates; Tchigorin wanted surprise, change, novelty, glitter, the lightning stroke from a clear sky."

In studying this contrast, we begin to sense the wide divergence between Lasker's praise of Steinitz and the way that Lasker played chess! Lasker wrote his tribute to Steinitz in so generous a mood that he omitted several failings of the Steinitzian system. Steinitz was above all a doctrinaire, a fanatic. He never took account of human weakness and imperfection. If an idea fitted into his system, it had to be right. If he lost a million times with the move, it was still right, but something else had gone wrong. Steinitz never pleaded his own physical weakness, his misery, his poverty, his loneliness as extenuating factors. They were ruled out by his system. Only what was on the board counted. He wanted general laws, he loathed the exceptions. It is doubtful whether in Steinitz's view there could be such a thing as an exception. Had Steinitz been told that much of his success was due to his passion for the game, his tenacity, his resourcefulness, his faith, his imagination — at all this he would have gaped.

Insisting so strenuously on the rule of reason in chess, Steinitz forgot that there is

in human beings, as in all living creatures, an irreducible element of irrationalism. It is, as we know, a force for great good as well as for boundless evil. Looking back to the description of Tchigorin, we can see that he exaggerated the role of the irrational as much as Steinitz overemphasized the power of reason.

When the work of Steinitz was continued by Tarasch, chess theory was both enriched and impoverished. Tarrasch took from Steinitz what particularly appealed to his own temperament: the formulation of broad concepts and their systematic application. Sometimes Tarrasch worked out these theories with a clarity and simplicity that to this day remain breathtaking in their large design and methodical execution. But there was something pallid about Tarrasch's method: it was most effective against weak opponents. Pit two players against each other who both have perfect technique, who both avoid weaknesses, and what is left? — a sorry caricature of chess.

Tarrasch the technician influenced a whole generation of chess players, but there was one man whom he never impressed. That man was Lasker! When the chess world was full of minor Tarrasches, Lasker went his own way, spoke his own mind, steered clear of sterile formulations, and gave the impression of being a complete anarchist in his chess style.

And yet Lasker's "anarchy" was clearly motivated: he combined the *objective laws* of Steinitz with the *subjective viewpoint* of Tchigorin. Whereas Steinitz and Tarrasch concentrated on the *exploitation* of weaknesses, Lasker was just as interested in the *defense* of weaknesses. To his contemporaries this was incomprehensible — and terribly laborious. To follow a general law without deviation is easy enough; to search for the unique qualities which exempt a specific position from a general law is very difficult. Such a task requires an open mind, serene self-confidence, great self-control, and an ever-active ability to accomodate one's views to changes in the situation on the board. Few people are capable of such creative skepticism: they are content to follow the obvious routes, to imitate a famous game, to accept the traditional, to learn a method rather than acquire a critical attitude.

Since most annotation was done by people who failed to fathom Lasker's views, he came off very badly in the books and magazines. The impression arose that he generally had a lost game, that

he "swindled" his way out at the end, that he did not know the openings, that his style was dull, and many other libels of similar content.

If we think of Lasker as a cheerful pessimist, we get a better insight into his games. Despite the naive optimism which crops up occasionally in his work, Lasker was basically a pessimist. But he was not the kind of pessimist who was wilted by his knowledge of evil: he was determined to make the best of things as he found them, he knew that many desperate situations can be saved by manly resistance, he knew that his opponents lacked his own poise. Prepared for the worst, he generally knew how to ward it off. (He remarks in the *Manual* that a player who starts off with a slight disadvantage is thereby stimulated to work harder and often achieves a good result; whereas a player with a slight advantage may overestimate it, become careless and get a really bad game.)

Lasker wanted his students to develop the same sturdy self-reliance which features his own games; he did not want to carry the reader on his back. Hence his notes are often short, mere hints: they point to the crucial factor in a situation, and the rest is left to the reader. Lasker's view of the openings follows the same line of reasoning. He did not believe in memorizing thousands of fashionable variations which would soon be out of fashion, replaced by other variations equally fashionable and equally transitory. If the reader learned to develop his pieces and to develop a feeling for maintaining the balance of power in apparently "bad" positions, Lasker was satisfied. Lasker's view of the openings was in line with his fundamental pessimism: in opening theory, the only certainty is change, flux, capricious taste. But most players prefer to have their choice of openings derived from dogmatic authority.

That Lasker was a great fighter is an observation which is common to all studies of his play. Nobody can estimate what enormous willpower went into Lasker's fighting ability; and yet at the core of this quality was his belief that each position is unique, that it has some hidden aspect which the skeptic, the man of resource, will finally unearth. But few people would have the self-confidence to agree with him when he writes, "Of my fifty-seven years I have applied at least thirty to forgetting most of what I had learned or read, and since I succeeded in this I have acquired a certain ease and cheer which I should never again like to be without."

This, it seems to me, is the great lesson of the *Manual*: Lasker teaches the reader not only to play chess, but he reveals something of his spirit of independence, of sincere striving for the truth, of faith in the humanities and heroic resignation in the face of what can't be cured and must be endured. He brings to the *Manual* not only the gifts of a great chessmaster but the qualities of a mathematician, a thinker and a poet. Where the modern specialist prattles glibly of right-angle forks in explaining a combination, Lasker reduces the combinative process to "the idea of superior force at a given point, and that of immobility." But "reduces" is not a good word to describe what Lasker does here. First he describes the combination clearly and precisely, as a mathematician or scientist might do it. Yet Lasker does not mean to disenchant the reader; he is trying to communicate to him the magic and exaltation of the combination, which is not only a technical process, but also the work of an artist.

So the above passage continues, "What is immobile must suffer violence. The light-winged bird will easily escape the huge dragon, but the firmly rooted big tree must remain where it is and may have to give up its leaves, fruit, perhaps even its life." Thus Lasker has described the combinative process in exact terms, but he has supplemented the description with a poetic figure which will always remain in the reader's memory. How is it, the reader asks, that the scientific description has been blended with an image which evokes Lasker's acute realization of the ever-present danger to which all living things are exposed? This mood often appears between the lines, as in the remark, "For the chessplayer the success which crowns his work, the great dispeller of sorrows, is named 'combination'."

But if there is tragedy beneath the surface, there is also humor; for, as we have seen, Lasker was a cheerful pessimist. In what other chess book will the reader find this sly dig in a discussion of Pawn promotion: "The Pawn has succeeded to the extreme of its possibilities until at its death it is rewarded with a new life — thus a Buddhist might put it — or, as we Westerners say, it is promoted to higher rank on account of the efficiency it has shown." No chess book is the worse for a chuckle or two.

It may help us to get a better insight into Lasker's style and methods if we consider some of his leading rivals. (We have already dwelt on the paradoxical relationship between the views of Steinitz, Tarrasch, Tchigorin and Lasker.)

For about fifteen years (between 1894, when Lasker won the World Championship title, and 1908, when he played Tarrasch), Dr. Siegbert Tarrasch was generally considered Lasker's leading rival. Tarrasch was a man of contrasting strength and weakness, of emphatically expressed likes and dislikes. I have already indicated that Tarrasch's strength resided in his ability to conceive broad general principles. When it came to executing the smaller details, Tarrasch was less successful. When it was a question of obtaining a "won game," Tarrasch was superb. When it came to winning it—against a Lasker or one of the other Titans — there Tarrasch often failed miserably.

How are we to explain this failing? Tarrasch has related in his *Dreihundert Schachpartien* that as a schoolboy, he excelled in every subject but mathematics. This tells us part of the story: a chess master who lacks a gift for mathematics may very well be deficient in specific chess qualities as well. Mathematics requires imagination *and* exactitude. Tarrasch was able to conceive the great plans, but he was inclined to be pedantic in execution. A great mathematician who had trouble with such simple matters as addition and subtraction could have an assistant take care of such menial tasks. In chess, however, "the battle is the payoff," and the master must be able to do everything for himself. To overcome the relatively weak resistance of lesser players was not an insoluble task for Tarrasch. To beat down the resistance of a Lasker was, however, too much for him.

Tarrasch's very facility in evolving enchantingly correct schemes of procedure eventually contributed to his failure! For these schemes began to degenerate into *schematicism*. As long as everything went according to plan, all was well. The minute that Tarrasch made a slip, or the game took an unexpected turn, Tarrasch lost heart. Lasker, on the other hand, benefited by not evolving far-reaching plans. Always ready for every emergency, never disheartened by unexpected obstacles, always determined to make the best of a difficult situation, he was in his element in positions that would have staggered a lesser man. *Where Tarrasch was dogmatic, Lasker was elastic.* The moral of Tarrasch's play, at its ideal best, inheres in its logic, and was therefore readily transmitted in books of instruction. The

moral of Lasker's play inheres in its ethics, *in Lasker's character*, and could therefore be passed on only to people who knew Lasker personally or could read the lessons of his play in his games. In the teaching process, the weaknesses of Tarrasch's character are cancelled out, while the strength of Lasker's character is what matters more than anything else. Most students have the intelligence to avoid Tarrasch's dogmatic excesses; but it requires nobility of character to be able to follow Lasker. Tarrasch teaches *knowledge*, Lasker teaches *wisdom*.

Had Pillsbury lived on into full maturity, he might have been the man to topple Lasker from his throne. Pillsbury left us no exposition of his theory of the game, so we can only piece together his views from his published games. Needless to say, this process of reconstruction is only subjective guesswork; every man is entitled to his own conception of Pillsbury's style.

Pillsbury, we know, was a disciple of Steinitz, hence he was a planner. But he avoided Steinitz's eccentricities; for him, chess was the art of the possible. But there was nothing dry or lifeless about this eminently common-sense view. Pillsbury was gifted with the imagination of a great artist. His plans were not beyond human grasp and execution (as Steinitz's so often were); they were clear, they were in the realm of the possible, they existed in the logic of the position. Yet they were plans which could be executed only by a great master.

For Pillsbury was dynamic. In his style imagination and energy were perfectly blended. Economy of means existed side by side with simplicity of design. The plans were on a grand scale, and they were carried out with an artistry which weaves its magic to this day. More than that: they were plans which were successfully executed not only against the outsiders and also-rans of the tournament world. Steinitz, Tarrasch, Maroczy, Schlechter, Janowski, Marshall and Lasker himself carried away many a bloody nose and a rueful countenance from their encounters with Pillsbury.

He was also a great fighter — perhaps not quite on the same plane as Lasker, but nevertheless a fighter in the grand manner. Thus we can say of Pillsbury that he was sound, aggressive and always a dangerous opponent. Of all the masters who were active in the period of Lasker's prime, he came nearest to being a worthy opponent of the Champion.

Pillsbury's great countryman Marshall was second to none in imaginative power, but it was an almost wholly undisciplined quality. He was a dangerous opponent to everyone, including himself. In the presence of a pretty combination, he was like a child to whom every toy is irresistible.

Lacking the ability to discriminate between the *attractive* and the *possible*, Marshall frequently overreached himself. Had he possessed this lacking quality, he could have reached the heights of chess mastery. His inability to discipline his imagination kept him out of the ranks of the first-rate.

With one or two exceptions, Lasker regularly beat Marshall in their individual encounters. Not only did Lasker beat him, but he did it in every conceivable way. Lasker crushed Marshall by refuting unsound combinations, by resorting to passive defense, by adopting simplification, by steering the game into channels distasteful to Marshall — and even by outcombining Marshall! But merely enumerating all these methods gives us a hint of Lasker's universality. What better proof of Lasker's greatness than his ability to outplay this richly endowed genius?!

Carl Schlechter was as far apart from Marshall as one could possibly imagine. It was Schlechter who in the end proved the most dangerous of Lasker's age contemporaries. Schlechter's growth as a chess master was slow, but he was all the greater when he reached maturity. All accounts of Schlechter paint him as an unusually good-natured and kindly man. He did not have that deeply imbued competitive instinct which is the mark of the immortals, and it was this defect which made him only a great master instead of one of the very greatest.

In Schlechter's character and style there were many paradoxical features. He was always known as the "Drawing Master," from his readiness to accept an offer of a draw. Many an opponent took advantage of his easygoing nature by suggesting a draw in a position where Schlechter had the advantage. But Schlechter was not a man who knew how to say "No!" Yet, despite this quality, he played many astonishingly beautiful games, and carried off a great number of brilliancy prizes.

Schlechter had an unrivalled knowledge of the book lines and opening theory, yet he generally played the initial stage with a freshness and simple, lucid originality which one would expect only from a natural player. In the beautifully written *Modern Ideas in Chess*, his disciple Richard Reti has paid eloquent tribute to the quality of *naturalness* in Schlechter's play; yet the most scholarly revision of the monumental Handbuch was the edition prepared by Schlechter!

One paradox after another: Reti tells us how Schlechter loved to refresh himself with the sights and smells of the lovely forests in the environs of Vienna; yet Schlechter spent most of his life in smoke-filled cafés!

And who is to explain the greatest paradox of all: how did the gentle Schlechter succeed in holding the mighty Lasker at bay? What a riddle for the psychologists! In their match in 1910, the Viennese master was at his best: he played questionable opening variations with great skill; he scored his only win in a game where he was unquestionably lost; he displayed courage and determination throughout. In fact, he missed winning the title of World Champion only by playing for a win in the last game of the match, when a draw would have given him the title!

Perhaps this is the key to the riddle, and a key as well to Lasker's greatness. May it not well be that Lasker, with his subtle instinct for the imponderables of combat and his flair for forcing his opponents to play out of character, deliberately led Schlechter into a wild position where placid play was out of the question? And so, in the last analysis, Lasker saved his precious title not by superior technical ability, but by fighting his opponent's *will*. It was a great triumph for Lasker's theories.

Janowski was a player who had much in common with Marshall. Janowski had the soul of a gambler, that quality of stubborn unreason which compels a man to choose the wrong course even though he knows better. Janowski was a thorough master of the middle game, a fine endgame player, a student of the openings. His defects were all personal: he was conceited, learned nothing from experience, never comprehended his strength and weakness. In Lasker's eyes, Janowski was a wilful child: he once remarked contemptuously that Janowski was merely a good position player gone wrong. For while Janowski could play positional chess beautifully and occasionally did, he suffered from the delusion that his forte was attacking play. He lost game after game with ridiculously headlong attacks; he never learned, and repeated the same faulty tactics again and again.

Lasker also remarked with his detached, penetratingly ironic insight that Janowski took so much pleasure in a won position that he could not bear to part with it and wind it up to a victorious conclusion. No wonder then, that Lasker simply toyed with Janowski in their matches. Janowski's irrational gambling instinct had nothing in common with Lasker's daring yet carefully weighed taking of risks. Janowski tried to batter down stone walls and ride ruthlessly over obstacles; he never bothered to appraise his opponents; he ignored technical difficulties. All these defects proved ruinous when he had to play Lasker.

Now we come to the man who succeeded in wresting Lasker's title from him: José Raoul Capablanca. In this one instance, Lasker's sure appraisal of his opponents failed him with catastrophic results. As soon as Capablanca achieved world-wide fame at the age of 21, by his overwhelming defeat of

Marshall, Lasker immediately recognized the appearance of a really dangerous rival. This was the one instance where Lasker was not true to his philosophy of struggle. He should have played a match while he was still in his prime; instead, he put off the battle as long as he could, finally agreeing to the match at an unfavorable time. Lasker played poorly and lost badly; yet, such was his reputation that to this day there are those who doubt that his inferiority was clearly demonstrated.

There is still one more riddle to be solved. Did Lasker found a school? The answer, in my opinion, is yes! But he was ahead of his time, and many years had to pass before his influence began to be noticeable. Among older players, Nimzovich and Alekhine paid their respects to Lasker repeatedly. As one surveys the contemporary masters, the spirit of Lasker's play reappears in the games of Botvinnik and Reshevsky — in their freedom from dogma, their tenacity in "bad" positions, their skill at finding resources hidden from lesser players. Lasker's school is not an easy one, and that is why he has had few disciples. To be a follower of Lasker, a player must have other qualities beside mere chess skill: he must have artistic integrity, he must be resilient, he must know when to lead and when to follow. It is a difficult course of study, but the rewards are great and lasting. It is a course for cheerful pessimists, who are reminded that this book ends with the hope that "also in these days of all-round mediocrity Reason is not wholly without partisans."

Fred Reinfeld

New York

August 23, 1946

DR. LASKER'S TOURNAMENT RECORD

Year		Prize	Played	Won	Lost	Drawn
1889	Amsterdam	2	8	5	1	2
1890	Graz	2	6	3	—	3
1892	London	1	11	8	1	2
1892	London	1	8	5	—	3
1893	New York	1	13	13	—	—
1895	Hastings	3	21	14	4	3
1895-6	St. Petersburg	1	18	8	3	7
1896	Nuremberg	1	18	12	3	3
1899	London	1	28	20	1	7
1900	Paris	1	18	14	1	3
1904	Cambridge Springs	2-3	15	9	2	4
1909	St. Petersburg	1-2	18	13	2	3
1914	St. Petersburg	1	18	10	1	7
1918	Berlin	1	6	3	—	3
1923	Maehrisch-Ostrau	1	13	8	—	5
1924	New York	1	20	13	1	6
1925	Moscow	2	20	10	2	8
1934	Zurich	5	15	9	4	2
1935	Moscow	3	19	6	—	13
1936	Moscow	6	18	3	5	10
1936	Nottingham	7-8	14	6	3	5
	Totals		325	192	34	99

DR. LASKER'S MATCH RECORD

Year	Opponent	Played	Won	Lost	Drawn
1889	Bardeleben	4	2	1	1
1890	Bird	12	7	2	3
1890	Miniati	5	3	—	2
1890	Mieses	8	5	—	3
1890	Englisch	5	2	—	3
1891	Lee	2	1	—	1
1892	Blackburne	10	6	—	4
1892	Bird	5	5	—	—
1893	Golmayo	3	2	—	1
1893	Vasquez	3	3	—	—
1893	Showalter	10	6	2	2
1893	Ettlinger	5	5	—	—
1894	Steinitz	19	10	5	4
1896-7	Steinitz	17	10	2	5
1907	Marshall	15	8	—	7
1908	Tarrasch	16	8	3	5
1909	Janowski	4	2	2	—
1909	Janowski	10	7	1	2
1910	Schlechter	10	1	1	8
1910	Janowski	11	8	—	3
1916	Tarrasch	6	5	—	1
1921	Capablanca	14	—	4	10
	Totals	194	106	23	65

CONTENTS

ANALYTICAL CONTENTS

FIRST BOOK

SECOND BOOK

THIRD BOOK

FOURTH BOOK

SIXTH BOOK

INTRODUCTION.

When I first saw the American edition of Dr. Lasker's Manual of Chess I was impressed by the value and importance of the book to chess players the world over.   Apart from the great influence which Dr. Lasker quite rightly has in the chess world, the book alone is epoch-making in the teaching of chess.   He touches lightly upon the non-essentials and devotes much instruction, much argument, and many illustrations to the things which he knows better than any other teacher to be indispensable to the making of the expert chess player.

He is imbued with the right chess spirit.   He looks upon chess not as a mere game but as a method of mind training.   In itself it is of no use, but so far as it is typical of struggle, of the desire for progress, of life itself, he recognises its part in the general scheme of things.

The most illuminating feature of the book is his grateful, respectful vindication of Steinitz, almost amounting to veneration.   I can well remember both of the Steinitz and Lasker matches and the impression I had at the time—the popular and consequently the uninformed impression—led me to believe that there was great animosity between the two principals.   It is clear to me now that this animosity only existed between the two factions, and was in reality confined to them.   Lasker admits that he was, and is, a pupil of Steinitz, the great master and the great original thinker.

I must leave the book to speak for itself. This present issue is neither a translation of the original German book nor a reprint of the American edition.   It is a thoroughly revised treatise containing the best of both books, with their errors of language and their typographical faults eliminated and their few chess errors corrected after further investigation and research.   Much new matter has also been embodied.   Many long months of unremitting labour have been bestowed upon this work, and I hope that the English speaking section of the chess world will welcome the book as the greatest treatise in all phases of the game that has yet been presented.

For my own part, I can only say that the proudest moment of my connection with the world of chess was when Dr. Lasker called upon me and proposed that I should both sub-edit and publish his book. I had flirted with the idea before that time, little thinking that ere I made up my mind to take definite steps I should be approached by the author himself.

It says much for Dr. Lasker's business abilities when I say that within a week the necessary formalities were concluded, and to mark the occasion he invited a number of well-known English and Continental Chess enthusiasts to a luncheon at which the project was formally launched. Although that event took place nearly two years ago, the whole of the intervening period has been devoted to perfecting the contents of the book, and I can only express the hope that the chess enthusiasts of the whole world will deem the time to have been well and successfully spent.

My final word is one of thanks to Dr. Lasker for his ready, kindly, and attentive assistance with the proofs, and his appreciative acceptance of suggestions and corrections; to Mr. A. H. E. Johnson for his thorough and painstaking vigilance in the matter of proof reading; and to the other players who have helped me so spontaneously in various stages of the work.

W. H. WATTS.

June, 1932.

PREFACE.

THAT I wrote this book, yea, that I wrote it with joy, will require, I trust, no more explanation than is supplied by its own contents and meaning. That after having written it in my mother tongue I should myself have re-written it in English does require explanation, even apology. Such, at least, is my sentiment, for I am by no means blind to the shortcomings of my diction, and I admire all languages in their purity and their noble life and love to see them used with the utmost art and sincerity and veneration.

But in the present case a difficulty arose. A translation by somebody foreign to the matter would have probably been, if conscientious, too literal. No translation, particularly no literal translation, can be accurate; it is in danger of reproducing the body, but not the essential thing, the soul, of the book. A book that has a history and has therefore been subjected to profound research may be translated, even so, only by a few masters of that difficult art; a book that has still to make

its history is bound to change considerably in translation. There is much in a good book that is not expressed nor expressible by means of words.

I had the option of sacrificing the elegance or the meaning of what I desired to say. And I made, I trust, the right choice in preserving what seemed to me of greater value. On the other hand, after having lived a good part of my life in English-speaking countries, I did not doubt that I should be capable of expressing myself definitely in the King's English.

In this book, principally I desire to explain and to extend the theory of Steinitz which originated while the master lived in England and in America. I desire to show that theory at work within and without the limits of Chess. Where the diction of this book may seem involved, let the reader be sure that I strove after simplicity, knowing full well that deep things are both simple and marvellous.

This book goes back to the " Handbook " of Staunton, with which it has in common the unbelief in compilation and the belief in the creative mind. I therefore trust that it will appeal to English readers.

In conclusion, I desire to thank both Mr. W. H. Watts and Mr. W. Winter, who have helped me in various stages of production, for their assistance and for the pains most conscientiously taken. Mr. Watts has thoroughly sub-edited the present edition, and all of the many corrections and alterations that he has made have my full approval.

EMANUEL LASKER.

LONDON, 1932.

PREFACE TO THE ORIGINAL GERMAN EDITION.

This Manual of Chess has aimed at system, at giving its object a structure. Is it not the first book of instruction written to represent the object of which it treats in the same way as an architect would try to erect a building? Ordinarily, books of instruction are written with an eye on the pupil, his wants, his views, his talents—in short, his p s y c h o l o g y, but not with the idea of showing the subject to be taught as a piece of architecture, as a harmonious unit, as a thing that has spiritual beauty in the way its parts are linked together so as to imbue the whole with one meaning. Ordinarily, therefore, books of instruction have no system: they merely put fragments by the side of other fragments; to change the order of these fragments, say in a book of Mathematics or Law, would do little or no harm. Not so in this Manual of Chess, unless my purpose has been defeated; there is a sufficient motive for every one of its parts, sometimes for every word, to stand where it stands, to read as it reads.

In a future, not far distant, man, I am convinced, will be very parsimonious with things of real value: with his work, with his time, with the substance that he offers to his mind. The man of this future will require that everything brought to his attention for him to retain in his mind should show a systematic structure. Of the books of instruction of the present day none will see that future.

What connects the parts of this Manual is the idea of Chess, wherewith I designate that force of mentality inherent in the game which has nourished it with the power of appealing to great masses and to many generations, so as to enable it to live through many centuries and to spread and to prosper. This idea is itself a structure of noble design. As if it were a valuable work of art buried among débris, it has here been searched for and laboriously u n e a r t h e d and brought to light by reviewing the history and reason and the life of the game. This idea is the idea of struggle, also of thy struggle

EMANUEL LASKER.

THYROW,
October, 1925.

LASKER'S MANUAL
OF CHESS

LASKER'S MANUAL OF CHESS

FIRST BOOK.

THE ELEMENTS OF CHESS.

THE game of Chess has a history that at all times has awakened interest but of which very little is known. We know some fables treating of the origin of the game, fables that are true to history only in so far as they lay the place of origin in Asia and the time of origin in a very distant past. Games similar to Chess have been discovered on Egyptian sculptures. Written documents, a thousand years old, referring to Chess, have been found. The game of Chess of those days was not, however, the game that we now know. No doubt, Chess has undergone many changes and who knows whether Draughts, or, more precisely, a game related to Draughts, was not a forefather of our Chess.

The European career of Chess began a thousand years ago. At that time it was an admired favourite in Spain, the game of the noble and the learned. In feudal castles and at the courts of princes it was cultivated; it was praised in artistic poems. For centuries it remained the aristocratic, noble, royal game, accessible only to a refined taste. Later, it penetrated through Italy and France, and at last it found a home wherever the foot of the white man trod.

Chess, as pointed out, has changed, but in its attire, in its forms only, by no means in its essence, its idea. That has remained unchanged all through the many centuries of its life. To discover this idea is therefore not difficult: at all times Chess has had the will, the intent, the meaning of picturing a war between two parties: a war of extinction, conducted

The Square

1

After Halving

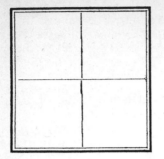

After Halving the Third and Last Time.

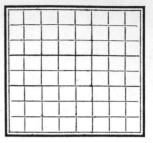

according to rules, laws, in a cultured manner, yet without clemency. This becomes evident from the rules of the game almost at first sight.

The Chess-board.

The most ancient and most enduring feature of Chess is certainly the board, the table upon which

After Halving a Second Time

it is played, the field of the Chess struggle. In consists of 64 parts every one a small s q u a r e, in their totality composing a large square. In eight rows and, perpendicularly thereto, in eight lines the 64 squares are ordered. Consequently one can draw a Chess-board by halving the side of a big square three times in succession as shown by the above diagrams.

The technical process of producing a Chess-board is therefore very simple, and the logical conception, neither is apprehension of the board complicated. The perception of the 64 squares by the eye is not so easy, but it has been facilitated by the use of colour. The squares are alternately coloured black and white, so that from time immemorial the Chess-board looks as follows:

It is of importance that the student of Chess should know the board very accurately; he should be able to visualise each square in its individual position as well as in its relations to its neighbouring squares. For this reason the board has been divided into three regions : the middle and the two wings. The left wing is composed of the first and second line to the left, the right wing in the same way by the two extreme lines on the right hand, and the middle is formed by the four remaining lines, the third, fourth, fifth and sixth. In the centre of this middle, four squares are situated, which form the intersection of the fourth and fifth line with the fourth and fifth row. These four squares in the centre of the board have, for strategic purposes, the greatest significance.

To describe the events on the Chess-board briefly and

exactly, a name has been given to every one of the 64 squares; in olden times a descriptive name, in our time, where the science of Nature and of Mathematics has become so prominent, a mathematical name. This mathematical name reminds us of a system of co-ordinates in the manner as introduced by Descartes. Accordingly, the eight "lines," running upwards, are successively designated by the letters a, b, c, d, e, f, g, h, and the eight "rows," running from left to right, are successively designated by the numbers 1, 2, 3, 4, 5, 6, 7, 8. The a line, b line . . . h line is therefore a certain line; the first row, second row . . . eighth row a certain row. Since each square belongs to one line and to one row only, it is unambiguously designated by its line and row. For instance, b5 is that one square on the b line that belongs to the fifth row. According to custom the letter precedes the number; one writes b5, never 5b. Thus this notation has the advantage of naming each square without ambiguity.

Of the other notation, the descriptive one, which is in use in many countries and also in the Anglo-

Saxon world, we shall speak more fully later on.

In the mathematical notation, the divison of the b o a r d described a b o v e would read as follows : the left wing a and b line, the right wing g and h line, the middle c, d, e, f line, the centre d4, d5, e4, e5. The boundary of the board is formed by the a line, the h line, the first row, t h e eighth row. The corners are a1, a8, h1, h8.

The student should endeavour to acquire the habit of designating the squares and of visualising their position. There are many Chess-players who f a i l m e r e l y from their incapacity to master this geometrical task, not suspecting its value.

The Pieces.

T h e armies combating each other on the board consist of Black and White pieces. The White pieces form the one side, the Black pieces the antagonistic side. The two sides are briefly called White and Black. The colouring of a piece therefore determines i t s obedience and fidelity, unconditionally. A piece never deserts to the enemy, nor does it ever rebel; it is faithful unto death. True, if it

falls in the combat, it wanders from the board merely into a box where the captured pieces are kept until the next game; then it celebrates a merry and hopeful resurrection.

White and Black have equal forces. Each has a King, a Queen, two Rooks (or Castles), two Bishops, two Knights, and eight Pawns. Either party, therefore, counts sixteen pieces. The pieces stand on the board until they are captured, each piece on one square, no two pieces on the same square. At the start of the game the pieces are placed in a determined position shown hereafter, and then they are moved, the players moving alternately. Thus a struggle of the Chess pieces takes place according to determinate rules, until the King of a party is captured by force or the contestants agree upon a drawn issue.

The pieces are usually carved of wood. The King has the appearance of a crowned m o n a r c h, the Q u e e n bears a smaller crown, the Rooks or Castles suggest sturdy castles, the Bishops have a characteristic h e a d - d r e s s, the Knights show a horse's head, and the Pawn is like a man without distinction, a man of the crowd, a common soldier.

King :

Queen :

Rook or Castle :

Bishop :

Knight :

Pawn :

The move consists in transferring a piece from one square to another. White "moves" a white piece, B l a c k a black one. Sometimes two pieces are thus put into motion, namely, when a hostile piece is "captured," i.e., removed from the board, or in "C a s t l i n g," or in "Queening" a Pawn, terms which will be explained later. All of this is executed according to fixed rules which the player is constrained to obey.

The Rules for Moving.

The King moves from its square to a neighbouring square, the Rook in its line or row, the Bishop diagonally, the Queen may move like a Rook or a Bishop, the Knight jumps in making the s h o r t e s t move that is not a straight one, and the Pawn moves one square straight ahead. But such moves are permitted only if the square upon which the piece lands is empty or occupied by a hostile piece. Moreover, the Rook, Bishop and Q u e e n a r e obstructed in their motion as soon as they strike an occupied square. T h u s, a Bishop on c1 may go to any square in the diagonal c1, d2, e3, f4, g5, h6 unless one of these squares is occupied; if e3 is occupied, f4, g5, and h6 are obstructed and the Bishop may not be moved there. The Rook, Bishop or Queen, however, can "capture" the obstruction, provided it is a hostile piece, by putting the moving piece on the square occupied by the obstruction and removing the latter into the box. Also, the other pieces, King, Knight and Pawn, may capture hostile men; the King or the Knight, w h e n e v e r they have the right to move to the square held by the hostile man, the Pawn, however, not thus but with a diagonal move forward to a neighbouring square. All pieces are subject to capture except the King. Its life is sacred, the player must defend it, it perishes only when no possible resource can save it from capture. Whenever that occurs the game is at an end; the player who cannot save his King from capture, is "Checkmate" and loses the game.

These rules are not complete, besides they are too brief so that the reader cannot be expected to obtain a clear conception through them, but they serve as an initial step in that they produce a vivid impression of the Chess struggle. We shall now consider them in detail and at length in order to illuminate the various logical consequences that come thereby into play.

The King.

The King may move from the square it occupies to any square satisfying the following conditions:

1. A neighbour to the square of occupation.

2. Not occupied by a man of its own party.

3. Not menaced by any hostile piece.

Once during the game the King may violate the first of these rules, namely, in Castling, otherwise never. In Castling, the King is moved TWO squares to the Right or Left, as the case may be, and the Rook towards which the King has moved is then placed upon the square which the King jumped over. But this move is not permitted when

1. The King is in "Check," i.e., menaced with capture.

2. The King or Rook has already made a move.

3. The move of the Rook is obstructed.

4. The King or Rook after Castling would be exposed to capture.

What has been said here in dry words may now be presented pictorially.

The White King placed on c2 has only ONE possible move, to wit, to b2. It may go there, because firstly, that square is neighbour to c2; secondly it is not occupied by a man of its own party but a hostile one; and thirdly, the square b2 is not menaced by any enemy, neither the Black King nor the Black Rook, nor the Black Pawn in their present positions being able to capture a piece on b2. On the other hand, the White King could make no other move; it cannot move to b1, d1, on account of the Black Rook, nor to b3, d3, on account of the Black Pawn, nor to d2 because of the White Pawn standing there, still less to c1, where two slayers would await it, nor to c3, which is menaced by Bishop b2 and obstructed by a White Pawn besides. To other squares it cannot move since they are not neighbours to its present residence.

The reader may demonstrate that in the above position also the Black King has only one possible move, namely, to g7.

Black to move. His King is "Checked" because menaced by the White Queen. The King cannot capture the Queen since g7 is threatened by Pawn f6; the King can go nowhere else for the White Queen threatens its place of refuge; the White Queen can be captured by no Black

piece. The King can therefore not be saved, the "Check" is a "Mate," "Checkmate"; Black has lost the game.

Castling *

The two Kings and the four Rooks still stand where they stood at the commencement of the game. Let us suppose that hitherto none of these pieces has moved. White, if he has the move, can Castle with Rook h1 by placing it on f1 and *simultaneously* jumping with King to g1; or he can Castle with Rook a1 by placing it on d1 and jumping with King to c1. Black, if it is his turn to move, can Castle with Rook a8, whereby King and Rook occupy the squares c8, d8 respectively. But he cannot Castle with Rook h8,

* In practice the player will be well advised always to move the K first and then his R when making this move.

because the White Queen would attack the Rook after Castling and therefore Castling is illegal.

squares of the second row: h2, f2, e2, d2, c2, g1, g3, g4, g5, g6, g7, g8.

The Rook or Castle *

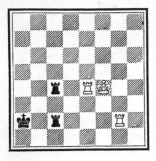

The Bishop.

The Rook c2 has the following possible moves: to b2, d2, e2, f2 and capture of g2. It cannot go to c1 or c3 because it is under obligation to guard its King against the White Rook g2. The Rook c4 can go to a4 or b4 or d4 or capture e4 but cannot capture f4 because Rook e4 is an obstruction; it may also go to c8 or c7 or c6 or c5 or c3 but not to c2 or c1 owing to the obstruction of Rook c2. The Rook e4 has only two squares open to it, d4 and c4, and the Rook g2 no less than 12 squares, any square of the g line and all but two

In this position three Bishops are on the board, c3, c4, f6; also three Rooks, c1, d2, f7, and of course the two Kings—the Kings never being captured —on a1 and g8. Since the Bishops move diagonally, Bishop c3 can capture f6, and vice versa. But the Bishop c3 cannot capture Rook d2 because the Bishop is forced to protect its King against Bishop f6 by obstruction. The Bishop c4 can capture Rook f7; this piece is immobile since it is pinned by the Bishop c4. The number of squares to which in the above position the Bishops might move, is

* The name "Castle" is rarely if ever used in modern chess literature for this piece.

therefore found to be for
$c4 = 10$ (a2, b3, d5, e6, f7,
b5, a6 d3, e2, f1); for $f6 = 9$
(h8, g7, e5, d4, c3, e7, d8,
g5, h4); for $c3 = 4$ (b2, d4,
e5, f6).

The Queen.

In this position two
Queens, a Rook, a Bishop
and the two Kings are on
the board. The Black
Queen a4 which can move
like a Rook or like a Bishop
has the following moves at
its disposal: to b4, c4, d4,
capture on e4, a1, a2, a3,
a5, a6, a7, a8, b5, c6, d7,
b3, capture of c2. The
White Queen, however, has
a very limited range, be-
cause it is pinned by the
Rook e8. If the pin would
be released it could go to
h7 and there, supported by
the Bishop c2, Checkmate
the King; as it is, the
Queen must either capture
the Rook e8 or suffer capture by that piece.

The Knight.

Here are four Knights on
the board, and a Rook and
a Bishop and the two
Kings. Two of the Knights
are immobile, Knight e2
on account of the Bishop h5
and the Knight g7 because
of the Rook g3: they must
protect their Kings. The
Knight f5 can move to one
of the following squares:
e7, d6, d4, e3, g3 (whereby
it captures the Rook) h4,
h6. The shortest jump on
the Chess-board is, namely,
to take two squares (in the
air) in a line or row and one
s q u a r e perpendicularly
thereto. That movement
allows to Knight f5 eight
possibilities, but in the
above position one of these,
on the square g7, is taken
away by the obstruction of
a Kt partisan to Knight f5.
The Knight f6 has eight
possible moves: it threatens
the hostile King, "gives
Check," "Checks," and the
King will have to fly, for

instance, to f7, in order to save himself.

The Pawn.

Here you see 16 Pawns, therefore all that were in the box, and two Rooks, one Bishop, one Knight, the two Kings besides. At the beginning of the game the White Pawns are placed on the second row and the Black Pawns on the seventh row; thence they move or capture ahead towards the enemy, the White Pawns from below upwards, the Black Pawns in the opposite direction. For instance, Pawn d4 may capture e5 and conversely, because the Pawns, though moving ahead in their file, capture obliquely, always advancing towards the enemy

The above position shows three immobile Pawns, "blocked" Pawns: g3, g4, f7. Pawn g3 is blocked by g4, because the Pawn does not capture straight ahead

but obliquely. T h e position shows nine Pawns standing on the squares where they stood at the start of the game: a2, b2 e2, f2, h2, a7, b7, c7, f7; they have not moved yet; the other seven Pawns have advanced during the progress of the game. The Pawn d4 has two possible moves: to advance to d5 or to capture e5. The Pawn c3 has only one possible move: to advance to c4.

Now the rule was introduced about four centuries ago that Pawns in their initial position and which are not blocked may advance one or two steps according to the plan of the player. This rule made the game more lively, and therefore the Chess world accepted it in time. For instance, Pawn a2 may advance to a3 or to a4 in one move.

With this rule a difficulty arose. Its object was to accelerate the pace of the Chess events and to add to their variety, but it betrayed sometimes the obvious rights of the opponent. To illustrate this point, observe the two Pawns f2 and g4. The Pawn g4 stands on guard over f3. If f2 advances to f3, g4 can capture it; thus it had been for many centuries; after the introduction of the new rule Pawn f2 could evade Pawn g4 by advancing at once to f4 and could then molest Black unpunished. Naturally, the Pawn g4 on guard felt itself deceived, when the hostile Pawn crept through the advance posts. There were scenes of hot dispute. It could not be the meaning of the innovation to make the advancing Pawn immune. And finally justice was victorious: the Pawn standing on guard was acceded the right of capture, just as if the Pawn trying to slip through had advanced one step only; but the Pawn on guard cannot defer this movement but must execute it without loss of time as an immediate reply to the attempted advance. If, for instance, in the above position White moves f2—f4 Black may answer g4 × f3, thus executing his original intention of capturing the Pawn on f3. This species of capture is named "capture in passing" or, with the French expression capture "en passant." If the Pawn, after f2—f4, is not immediately captured by g4 "in passing," it stays unmolested on f4 and has thereafter to contend only with the hostile Pawns of the f and e line.

The Pawns only advancing ahead arrive, in advancing row by row finally to the eighth row where according to the rule they would come to a barrier and would be immobile. Should this signify their death? Should they now become useless after having done their duty and fought their way through the ranks of the enemy? That would not be in keeping with justice. Since in a struggle it is honourable to draw upon oneself the fire of the enemy and to do him harm, the Pawn advancing to the last row is rewarded by becoming an "officer" in its army; it is changed for a Queen, Rook, Bishop or Knight, according to the will of the player; it is promoted to a higher rank since officers have much more mobility and value than Pawns.

If it is White's turn to move here, he may advance Pawn e7 to e8, change it for a Queen and call Mate

If it is Black's turn to move, he can advance f2 to f1, demand a Knight and Checkmate White.

The Initial Position.

From time immemorial the men are placed at the beginning of the game in the order shown above, and White makes the first move. In the corners stand the Rooks, on the first row the White officers in the order R, Kt, B, Q, K, B, Kt, R; the corner to the right of White is white; in the second row stand the White Pawns, in the seventh row the Black Pawns and in the eighth row the Black officers, every one opposite to a White officer of its own kind, the Queen opposite the Queen, the King opposite the King, and so forth. The White Queen is placed on a white square, the Black Queen on a black square, the Queen therefore on a square of its own colour —a remnant of feudal gallantry.

The End of the Game: Checkmate (Mate), Stalemate, Draw.

With a Checkmate the game is decided, but not every game ends with a Mate.

If he whose turn it is to move can make no legal move and yet his King is not Checked he is not Checkmated though the game necessarily is at an end. Such a conclusion of the game is called a Stale mate, a useless, a false, an unproductive Mate, briefly "Stalemate." He who is Stalemated does not lose the game nor win it either, because loss of the game is suffered only by him who is "Checkmated," and an essential condition therefore is that the King should be in Check, whereas in a Stalemating position the King is not in Check.

Again when neither of the opponents believes he has the power to end the g a m e by administering Checkmate, the game is undecided, " drawn," by mutual agreement. This agreement may be voluntary or compulsory. Compulsory when the two opponents repeat their moves, going backwards and forwards without changing their position, compulsory also when for fifty moves in succession no essential change, no advance towards the final goal can be demonstrated by either player. This demonstration, such is the accepted law, is achieved when during these fifty moves no capture nor the advance of a Pawn has been performed, for these are, by common consent, the outward, the visible signs of an essential change.

Here White is to move, Black menaces Checkmate in two ways, either by Qh3 captures h2 or plays to g2. White cannot defend the threat, he therefore tries to attack the opponent by giving Check with Qb6—a6. Black is forced to reply K a8–b8. Now Qa6–b6 again checking. The pinned Pawn cannot capture, hence Kb8 —c8 or —a8. Again Qb6— a6, Ka8 (c8)—b8. And the Checks have no end, the game is drawn by "Perpetual Check."

The Function of Strategy.

Herewith the rules and laws of the game are laid down; according to the very same rules play the beginner and the veteran, the duffer and the master. Whoever does n o t follow these rules does not play Chess; whoever follows them belongs to the community of Chess-players that counts many millions.

What distinguishes the Chess-players, all of whom follow the same rules, is called strategy: the plan, meaning, intent, force, briefly the reason of their moves.

This reason is no different from all reason, but a part of it, grown on its body, possessed of its force a n d conditioned by its pains. On the same tree where a little branch hangs, called the logic of Aristotle, there hangs another branch named Strategy in Chess.

The Descriptive Notation.

Since reason, to be communicated, needs a system of expression, a kind of language, the Chess community has invented and propagated technical words and a notation of squares and moves. True, many nations follow the notation by co-ordinates described and used above: e2—e4 signifies the move that places the piece at e2 on e4; yet with many nations a descriptive notation arising from the life of the Chess community in those countries has been preferred. This notation refers to the initial position; it calls the Rooks a1 and a8 the "Queen's Rooks," Knights b1, b8 "Queen's Knights," Bishops c1, c8, "Queen's Bishops," Bishops f1, f8, "King's Bishops," Knights g1, g8, "King's Knights," Rooks h1, h8 "King's Rooks," Pawns a2, a7, "Queen's Rooks' Pawns," Pawns b2, b7 "Queen's Knight's Pawns," and so on. The squares of the board, when it is White's turn to play, are called according to the line and row, e4, for instance, "King's fourth," a5, "Queen's Rook's fifth," and when it is Black's turn to play the squares are named according to Black's point of view. For Black, who is sitting before the eighth row, that eighth row is his first row, and K4 signifies for him e5, and QR5 signifies for him a4. In short, Black and White are treated in this notation as enjoying the same privileges, either having a right to his point of view. Thus,

whereas in the algebraic notation in the initial position the two usual moves to start the game e2—e4, e7—e5 are denominated in a different way, in the descriptive notation they would read White P—K4, Black P—K4, and hence they are denominated in the same way. The descriptive notation goes down to and accentuates the reason for these moves, which are identical, the algebraical notation only states the geometry of the Chess-board and therefore distinguishes between various geometrical regions of the board without heeding in any way the meaning of Chess strategy.

Either notation has its advantages, and it is useful to know both of them. For the use of a people that notation will of course be preferred that has its root in custom, tradition, history of the national Chess community. And therefore in what follows only the descriptive notation will be employed.

A few signs are international. A Capture is indicated by the oblique cross ×, a Check by the straight cross +, Checkmate by ±, Castling K side by o—o, Castling Q side by o—o—o.

Our Task.

In adopting the above rules and style of speaking and of writing, it will be our task to make visible the Reason of the game of Chess. According to the manner and law of Reason that task will oblige us to start from simple questions, ever to advance to more complicated questions by l o g i c a l deduction, and finally to unearth all the different sources of Reason as manifested in Chess and to draw our final conclusions.

On the Advantage of a Plus in Pieces.

First Proposition : The Plus of a Rook suffices to win the game.

When one is Checkmated the pieces that are inactive onlookers of the disaster, however m a n y they might be, are of no avail. Pieces that cannot aid in staying a danger are of no value. Let us, however, consider the question of a Plus in pieces under a certain condition that from the learned of the Middle Ages has received the curt name of " *ceteris paribus.*" Advantages and disadvantages being equal, being evenly balanced—that is the meaning of this condition. The above proposition is certainly not valid in all situations.   As a proposition in Euclid, the above thesis would be a rank failure, but *ceteris paribus* it is as true as gold.

Now the method of Euclid would do no good in Chess. Reason in Chess —we shall see that the more clearly later on—is not of t h e mathematical order. Chess is no certainty. And when it becomes one, Chess will have ceased to be useful.   To enable the Chess players to follow an argument, the i d e a of the learned of the Middle Ages embodied in the curt Latin *ceteris paribus* is indispensable.

By means of the *ceteris paribus* we are within our rights to suppose that all the other pieces, being of equal force and value, have fought a drawn battle, at the end of which they, like the two lions that devoured each other up to the two tails, have emigrated from the Chess-board into the box, thus leaving the stronger side with Rook in a safe position and the K i n g, against the bare King.

If the stronger side has the Move, we can demonstate that Rook and King against King can always force a Checkmate. This demonstration is mathematical. It is founded upon a certain process, by which the weaker side is eventually shorn of its mobility, its King being confined in a prison with ever narrowing walls, and finally forced into a Checkmate. The demonstration begins by showing that with the pieces available certain Mating positions exist and continues by making evident that the weaker side, in the course of the above process, may be driven into one of these Mating positions.

As long as the King is in the middle of the board, it cannot be Mated by King and Rook. For let us suppose that the two aggressive pieces have arrived at their position of strongest effect. Then the two Kings will stand opposite each other and the Rook will give Check on line or row, and thus the besieged King will be Checked and have five squares of its domain cut off by the enemy. This is easily seen.

Strongest Effect of King versus King.

Here the Kings stand as near to each other as possible since they must not expose themselves to capture, not even to capture by the opposing King.

They stand in "Opposition," they prevent each other from moving on any one of the three squares White's Q3, Q4, Q5.

Strongest Effect of King plus Rook versus King.

The Kings are in Opposition, the Rook Checks and deprives the hostile

King of the three squares adjoining those dominated by the White King. Thus the King placed on the Bishop-line is driven to-wards the Knight-line, a line nearer to the boundary than the one the King held previously.

Mating Position with King on Border.

Mating Position with King in Corner.

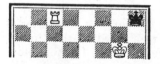

The stronger side forces the hostile King to the border and if need be into a corner by proceeding as the fisherman who drives fish into his net and then draws the net, narrowing down the space available to his prey until finally no room is left to the victim.

But there is a point that needs further elucidation. After all, the above picture does not come true to reality. Let us consider the following position:

The King in the Net.

True, the Black K on his QB5 cannot get over the Q file nor his fourth row as long as the White Rook, protected by its King, stands on guard on Q5. But how is the net to be drawn tighter? If the Black King should refuse to move, the tightening of the net would be impossible.

The fish in the net of the fisherman might refuse to move, not so the King in the net of the Rook. The *right* of moving in Chess is at the same time an *obligation*. In by far most instances the right to move is of great value, but there are cases, as shown above, where to move is disadvan-tageous. Yet, rightly or wrongly, the laws of Chess do not permit a free choice in this respect: you have to move, whether you like it or find it irksome. The constraint to move is usually called by a German word, "*Zugzwang*," that has become international in its usage.

Let us return to the above position, White to move. White plays King from K6 to Q6. If Black replies King from B5–Kt5, or Kt6, the Rook will follow it up with R–QB5, thus cutting off the QB file; and if Black replies King from B5–B6, the White King will get into Opposition, King from Q6 to B5, and the play might further proceed methodically King from B6 to Kt6, R from Q5 to Q4, King from Kt6 to B6, King from B5 to Q5, King from B6 to B7, King from Q5 to B4 and so on. To drive the King by means of the *Zugzwang* on to the border and there to give it the Checkmate is, after all that has been said, an easy task.

S e c o n d   Proposition : King and Bishop or King and Knight against the bare King make a Drawn game.

Let us deliberate according to the above method. We soon find that a Checkmate with King and Bishop or King and K n i g h t against King is impossible even when the weaker side has its King placed in the most unfavourable position, the corner. Should the aggressive King stand even in o p p o s i t i o n to the cornered K i n g, the besieged party will yet have one s q u a r e of escape; should that be taken away by Bishop or Knight, the King in the corner will not be Checked and therefore a Stalemate will result; conversely, if t h e cornered King is Checked it is driven only on more favourable ground. The task of Checkmating with the above force is unsolvable.

Third Proposition : King and two minor pieces against the bare King will force the Checkmate unless both the minor pieces are Knights.

On account of the lesser force of Bishops or Knights as compared with the Rook or Queen the two latter officers are called the "major" pieces, the former officers the "minor" ones. With the aid of two minor officers and the King Mating positions can always be constructed, for instance, the three that here follow :

net. When the hostile King is aimed at, systematic progress is possible only in the direction of a diminution of the mobility of that piece. The direction of the process being thus determined, the final aim being one of the Checkmating positions, the problem is clearly put and its solution requires little pains.

With two Bishops it is easy to imprison the hostile King by putting the two Bishops alongside of each other. They then dominate two neighbouring diagonals and thus divide the board into various parts separated from each other, so that the hostile King, caught in one of these compartments, is unable to enter into another.

But it is impossible to arrive at all such Mating positions by a systematic process, in a methodical fashion. And, since Chess is not to be played at haphazard for any length of time, that circumstance is highly significant. Hence, we must distinguish between those of the above Checkmates that can be arrived at by force and those that can be gained only through intervention of the error or hastiness or bad judgment of y o u r opponent.

A systematic process is always, this way or that, the drawing in of a logical

Here the Black King is restricted to the compartment b o r d e r e d by the squares QR7, QR6, QKt6, QKt5, QB5, QB4, Q4, Q3, K3, KB3, KKt3, KKt4,

KR4 and KR5. The King
cannot move on to any
square of this border and
therefore cannot reach any
square outside of its compartment. With the ap-
proach of the White King,
it will be easy to draw the
net together and to Checkmate the Black King.

With two Knights the
Checkmate cannot be
forced. For let the Black
King be driven into a cor-
ner, the task of forcing the
Checkmate still fails.

This is a critical position.
In order to achieve the
Checkmate the King must
be driven into the corner.
Therefore, its escape, KB1,
must be cut off. If to this
end Kt from K5 to Q7 and
Black replies K–R1, the
Black King will return to
Kt1, because that square
must not now be cut off by
either Kt to B6 or Kt from
Q5 to K7 on account of the
law of Stalemate. Return-
ing, the King will again
threaten to escape via B1

and thus keep one of the
Knights busy such as the
one on Q7. And no further
progress can be achieved.
Only a manifest blunder
will enable White to bring
about   t h e   Checkmate,
namely, by
    1. Kt from Q5 to B6ch.,
K to R1.
Obviously, this move is
a grave mistake, for thus
B l a c k voluntarily goes
where White wants to drive
it; the move K–B1 would
Draw.
    2. Kt from K5 to B7
Mate.
With Bishop, Knight
and King versus King, the
Checkmate is attainable,
but in a complicated man-
ner. The principle of the
hunt for the King is this:
the King, the Bishop and
the Knight in their effort
to chase the adverse King
into a corner, must apportion *different* tasks to each
other, thus aiding each
other; they must not per-
form any task doubly which
would amount to an un-
necessary competition be-
tween each other and would
be a useless effort. Each one
of these pieces must therefore cut off squares to the
hunted King that are not
cut off by the other pieces,
each one must have its own
allotted share of squares to
guard and must not tres-
pass. With this principle

in view, it is not hard to drive the King into a corner. But now another difficulty arises. The adverse King must be driven into one of those corners that the Bishop can assail, as mate cannot be *forced* in either of the other corners. If the Bishop moves on white squares, it is limited to these white squares, for diagonals running through a white square comprise white squares only; and with black squares it is the same. Hence, the hunted King will be prudent to allow itself to be driven towards a corner unattainable to the Bishop and to shun either corner of the colour assailable by the Bishop. On the other hand, the assailant, having driven the King into the safe corner, is confronted by the problem of driving it into one of the unsafe corners.

This latter task has to be studied in detail. The play runs as follows:

1. K from R6 to Kt6
   K from R square to Kt square
2. K from Kt6 to B6
   K from Kt square to R square
3. Kt from K7 to Q5
   K from R square to Kt square
4. Kt from Q5 to B7
   ....

Thus the corner is cut off.

4. ....
   K from Kt square to B square
5. B from Q4 to R7
   K from B square to Q square
6. Kt from B7 to Q5
   K from Q square to K square

Black makes an attempt to gain more freedom of movement.

7. K from B6 to Q6
   K from K square to B2
8. Kt from Q5 to K7
   K from B2 to B3
9. B from R7 to K3
   ....

The net holds tight, the attempt of the Black King is frustrated.

9. ....
   K from B3 to B2
10. B from K3 to Q4
    K from B2 to K square
11. K from Q6 to K6
    K from K to Q square

12. B from Q4 to Kt6ch.
    K from Q square to K
    square

Now the Knight has to cut off the square K8.

13. Kt from K7 to B5
    K from K to B sq.

14. Kt from B5 to Q6
    K from B sq. to Kt2

15. K from K6 to B5
    K from Kt2 to R3

16. B from Kt6 to Q8
    K from R3 to R4

17. Kt from Q6 to K8
    K from R4 to R3

18. B from Q8 to Kt5ch.
    ....

The Black King dares not return, else it is Checkmated at once.

18.   ....
    K from R3 to R2

19. K from B5 to B6
    K from R2 to Kt sq.

20. K from B6 to K7
    K from Ktsq. to R2

21. K from K7 to B7
    K from R2 to R sq.

22. B from Kt5 to R6
    K from R sq. to R2

23. B from R6 to B8
    K from R2 to R sq.

24. B from B8 to Kt7ch.
    K from R sq. to R2

25. Kt from K8 to B6
    Mate.

Fourth Proposition: The Plus of a Pawn does not always suffice to force the win, but in the majority of cases it does.

In considering this proposition, one must accentuate the c o n d i t i o n of

ceteris paribus very strongly. The plan of "exchanging" the hostile pieces one by one, until the extra Pawn beside the two Kings remains alone on the board, is often difficult and perhaps impossible to be carried through. But, for all that, let us consider this task solved and let us now inquire into the concluding stages of that contest.

First, let the Pawn fight the adverse King unaided. Will the Pawn be able to advance unharmed on to the eighth row, there to be Queened, afterwards to Checkmate the King? Or will the King approach the Pawn meanwhile and capture it? The question is one of pure mathematics. While the Pawn advances one square the King approaches one s q u a r e. Hence, the Pawn having to advance by Pawn steps until it Queens, the King to approach by King steps to the square where the Pawn Queens, all depends on the relation of the two members Pawn steps and K i n g steps. If the number of Pawn steps is less than the number of King steps, the Pawn will Queen. If they are equal, or if the number of Pawn steps is greater than the number of King steps, the King will capture. For instance, if the

White Pawn is on K6, White to move, the Black King must stand at a distance of two squares from White's K8, or the Pawn, t h o u g h unaided, will Queen. The Black King m u s t therefore in that moment stand upon one of the squares QB1, QB2, QB3, Q1, Q3, K1, K2, KB1, KB3, KKt1, KKt2, KKt3 to stop the Pawn. The Black King must stand within a certain rectangle formed by two squares, which have the line White's K6, K7, K8 as a side. Each one of these squares is commonly spoken of as "the square of the Passed Pawn." The P a w n is "passed" because it has escaped the perils of opposing Pawns and is now free to advance to the eighth row unhampered by hostile pawns.

As an exercise show that if the Black King stands here on Q4, K4, or KB4, White having the move, it cannot stop the pawn.

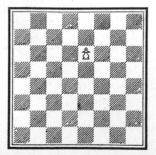

In the next diagram, the B l a c k King stops the Pawn, but the White King aids it. Will the Pawn now advance? Far from it! The King will first gain room for the Pawn by *Zugzwang* a n d therefore use the Opposition.

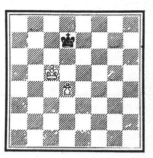

White to move wins by
1. K—Q5   K—K2
2. K—B6   ....
Thus the White King has gained the power over Q7, a point over which the Pawn will have to march.
2. ....   K—Q1
3. K—Q6   K—B1.
4. K—K7   ....
Now the White King also guards Q8. No matter what Black may do, the Pawn will safely advance to Q5, Q6, Q7 and Queen on Q8.
Black to move will draw.
1. ....   K—B2
Now the B l a c k King fights the White one, preventing its advance.
2. P--Q5   K—Q2

The Pawn on Q5 is a hindrance to its own King by preventing it from taking the Opposition against the adverse King.

3. P—Q6   K—Q1

The best move! If 3 .... K–B sq. instead, White would gain the Opposition with 4. K–B6 and win with 4 ...., K–Q sq.; 5 P–Q7, K–K2; 6 K–B7.

4. K–B6   K—B1
5. P–Q7ch.   K—Q1
6. K–Q6

White is forced to make this move or he loses his Pawn, but now Black is stalemated and the game Drawn.

If it is Black's turn to move here, White wins. If White to move, the game is uselessly prolonged or ends in a Stalemate as shown above.

From these considerations the strategy of play of King plus Pawn versus King can be deduced. But the Pawn on the border-lines makes an exception; in its case the Opposition has no value. Assume White Pawn QR5, White King QR6, Black King QR1. Black moves K–Kt sq., and White, not being able to advance on to the seventh row, has gained nothing. The boundary protects Black. White can never drive the King out of the corner. If White cuts off the mobility of the Black King, it flies to the corner and is there Stalemated.

This play in the corner and round the corner is of interest. To illustrate it, we append two instructive positions.

White to move can only Draw, because his King then remains imprisoned, the Black King moving to B2 and to B sq. alternately.

Neither the Bishop nor the King nor the Pawn can drive the Black King from its corner. The King moves out of it and into it until being Stalemated, the game is Drawn.

On the Advantage of the Attack against an Unprotected King.

If the King is exposed to continual Checks and cannot soon find protection behind its own pieces, it is hopelessly lost. The action of Queen, Rook, Bishop against the King is so strong that obstructions are needed to keep the King from being Checkmated. And even if the King is helped by some obstructions, when strong and varied pieces are conducting the attack the obstructions might prove too weak and the King might therefore easily be caught in the meshes of a "Mating net."

The Black pieces stand apart from their King. They are powerful for attack but seem to have forgotten their duty of defence. The White army, weak in numbers but well placed, succeeds in a quick thrust.

  1. Q—R6ch. K—Kt1
  2. Q—Kt6ch. K—R1
  3. R—R3 Mate.

Black has exposed his King. Black on the move might procure a safe retreat for the King to Kt2 by advancing P—Kt3. If White is to move, he wins.

1. R—Kt6ch. K—K2
2. R—R7ch. K—K1
              (best)
3. R—Kt8ch. Q—Q1
4. R × Qch. K × R
5. R—R8ch. K moves
6. R × R and wins by plus of pieces.

White has left the first row unprotected and Black can therefore drive the White King into a Mating net by co-operation of Rook, Knight, and Pawn on KB5.

1. — — —   R—R8ch.
2. K—R2   R—R8
              Mate
or 2. K—B2 R—B8
              Mate

In order to see more clearly why a series of Checks is so dangerous, let us analyse the defences against a Check.

A Pawn that Checks forces the opponent to capture the Pawn or to withdraw the King.

A Checking Knight must be captured or the King must fly.

A Bishop or Rook or Queen that Checks must be captured or the line of assault must be obstructed or the King must fly.

Against a "Double-Check," a Check given by two pieces simultaneously, there is only one possible defence: flight.

If therefore the King has no mobile aggressive partisans to help it by capture or obstruction of offenders, it must fly continually and has only the hope of finally joining its own forces and finding a place of safety. But against an assailant who knows what he wants and goes about his business deliberately, the task of the deserted King is a very hard one.

For Checkmating suffice a few pieces provided their force is used up to its extreme limit. Here follow a few instances of maximum work.

A Queen all by itself Checkmates the King hemmed in by its Rooks.

The King, in the middle of the Board and unobstructed, therefore very mobile, is Checkmated by the slight force of Queen, Knight, Pawn.

And here in the middle of the board a Checkmate administered by Rook and two Bishops.

Against the cornered King, Rook and Knight alone are sufficient.

Numerous are Mating positions of a few pieces provided that the hunted King is hemmed in by some of its own pieces which thus obstruct its flight. For instance, the "Smothered Mate" executed by a lone Knight.

And now a Mate by Double Check.

The two White pieces struggle against an overpowering number, but a Double Check saves them and wins the day.

1. R—B8 mate

In these six positions the White K is not shown as he takes no part in administering the mate.

From all the foregoing it is apparent that the attack against an exposed King is full of promise provided it can be pursued by several pieces of which one is a major officer.

On the Advantage brought about by a Simultaneous Attack upon Several Objects.

But also when the assailant has no superiority in pieces nor an exposed King as object of attack he has a multitude of aims to achieve which would procure him an advantage, for the capture of any officer or even of the modest Pawn may be of great value; to capture is, *ceteris paribus*, a gain if the opponent cannot recapture, as we know from our first proposition.

True, to threaten an officer is rarely opportune, because the officer is either " guarded," i.e., defended by its comrades in that they dominate its square and therefore threaten w i t h capture any and every piece capturing the officer—or else the officer, being very mobile, simply takes to flight. But that is not so when several attacks of this nature take place at one and the same time. According to the fundamental rules, the players may m o v e only one piece at a time; except w h e n castling, hence, in case of a simultaneous attack on several p i e c e s, not all of the assailed pieces can fly at the same moment; some must therefore tarry and suffer the consequences. To save them requires an extraordinary effort, principally a hurried counter-attack by the flying officers themselves against the adverse King or on valuable pieces of the opponent, so as to prevent him from capturing one of the pieces that have fallen into his power and to make possible their flight; and this great effort has to be made very quickly and with energy, else a catastrophe is imminent.

When a Bishop, Rook or Queen attacks a piece which by its flight would expose a comrade, possibly the King, to capture, the defender is in the same predicament, since flight may be out of the question. In that case the attacked piece has to be fortified as far as possible or else, if the defence fails, has to sell its life as dearly as possible. If the piece protects the King, whose life is precious before all else, the piece is incapable of flight, it is pinned and must fight desperately. Worse still, if the King itself is assailed, it cannot defend by obstruction, unless one of its officers can aid the King by obstructing the attack of the enemy or, better still, by slaying the aggressor, the King must fly and abandon such piece as might be exposed by his flight.

Black plays P–R8 Queens; White replies by Queening his Pawn and Checking the Black King, which has to fly and thus to open the road for the capture of his Queen.

White, checked by the Black Queen, interposes the Bishop and thereby pins the Checking piece which stands on the same diagonal as the Black King.

White plays R × Bch., assailing the Queen at the same time. Black saves his Queen by replying Q × R. Then R–R7ch., winning the Queen that stands on the seventh row.

Black to move, White wins.

Bishop Kt2 is pinned by R at Kt3. A pinned piece obstructs but is hampered in its capacity of capture or guarding. Therefore, White with impunity captures the P with Q. This Pawn is guarded by the Bishop only in appearance, not really. The pinned Bishop is now twice attacked, by R o o k and Queen, and Black is unable to guard it the second time, except by Q–B3, which is futile on account of Q × Q.

White Checks Q–QKt8 King moves on to second row, then Q–R7ch., attacking the Rook simultaneously and thus winning it.

S h o w that Kt–K7ch. which would win the Queen is contrary to the fundamental rules of the game.

White plays P–Q4 and simultaneously a t t a c k s Bishop and Knight. He "forks" B i s h o p and Knight.

W h i t e on the move "Discovers C h e c k" by moving his Rook, preferably with R × P. B l a c k might now attempt R–B3 though that would not avail him much. If he replies K –Kt1 instead, the White Rook returns to Kt7 with Check, drives the King into the corner and " Discovers Check " thereafter by R × KtP. Show that White in this fashion would finally win the QR.

The Bishop p i n s the Knight inasmuch as the Bishop could capture the Queen but for the obstruction of the Knight. This pin is, however, not unconditional. If the Knight moves while attacking the adverse King, the pin is wholly illusory. Hence, Black plays Kt–K5, Checking and assailing the dangerous Bishop at the same time and thus winning it.

B l a c k pins the White Knight on KB3 by his QB. But the pin is conditional. Can White execute a strong t h r e a t by moving the Knight? Indeed, he can. He captures the KP with the Knight, thus attacking the Bishop with his Queen. And if B × Q, the threat of White against the King is executed : B × Pch., K–K2 ; Kt–Q5 Checkmate. This motive recurs often. In an opera called the " Seekadett " (" The Cadet at Sea ") a short game of Chess is played on the stage and it is this motive that is used on that occasion.

On the Use of Superior Power at Decisive Points.

If a pinned piece incapable of movement or a blocked Pawn is assailed, a fight ensues on that spot, since the piece under attack under conditions as above described cannot take to flight ; the only way to save the piece is by hurrying supports to it. As soon as the assailant, and were it only for a moment, obtains the superiority at the point of contest, he is at liberty to capture the piece and to hold on to the advantage thus gained. The rule by which i t i s determined which side has the advantage on a given spot is very simple : two pieces which dominate the spot are stronger than one a n d weaker than three and keep the balance to two hostile pieces on that spot. And so it is in general, even the King making no exception to this simple piece of arithmetic.

will not let me gain and to obtain my purpose I must support that Pawn or that piece upon the point aimed at by units in number superior or at least equal to those of the defender.

Here White intends P–Q4. That point is dominated by Queen, Knight on KB3 and Pawn on QB3, it is defended by Bishop on QB4, Knight on QB3, Pawn on K4. The units being equal in number, White is safe in advancing the Pawn.

The Rook on Q5 is immobile because pinned by the White Bishop. White attacks it by Kt–K2. Now it is twice attacked and guarded only once. Black keeps the balance by R–R5. Now White plays Kt × R, so as to immobilise the other Rook. Black may reply R × Kt, but only to lose that rook, since White assails it anew by K–K3, thus gaining the superiority of two against one upon the disputed point Q5.

The idea of superiority is of frequent use. I intend, for instance, to put a Pawn or a piece upon a point of vantage that my opponent

Though the rule as above stated holds unexceptionally good, it needs a corollary in that the "value" of the pieces engaged in the contest have to be taken into account. Generally it would be foolish to post a Queen, however well defended, upon an empty spot assailed by a hostile Pawn. To place a very valuable piece upon a contested point cannot be my intention, unless I obtain thereby a very valuable compensation.

The question becomes very much more complicated as soon as several points are under contention simultaneously. To obtain the superiority upon the spot A, I may attack one of the defenders of that spot situated on B, and even though my opponent have superiority on B, that attack may serve me to gain superiority on A.

The Rook is twice assailed and twice defended, hence on White's Q4 the forces are even; in s p i t e of this the Rook is lost, b e c a u s e the defending Queen is assailed. White plays Q × Qch. Now the Rook cannot save itself either by R–Q8 ch., or by R–Kt5ch., because Black is in Check. Black replies Kt × Q. After this interlude, White has gained the superiority on Q4 and captures the Rook gratis.

Also pins have to be taken into consideration.

Here the Black Queen is pinned, the White Queen also. Though the Rook on B2 seems to be defended twice and a s s a i l e d no oftener than twice, it is lost. White simply captures it with Bishop, since neither King nor Queen can r e c a p t u r e. Black must answer K–B1, White continues with B–K7ch., forces K × B and wins the Queen. All this complication arises because the squares adjacent to the spot KB2, also the spot KKt1, where the Black King stands, enter into the turmoil.

White is under no menace. He proceeds to attack and selects the QP as his object. The first step is to block it with R–Q4. The QP is pinned, as long as the Black Rook tries to defend it. If Black replies K–B1. White proceeds to assail the pinned and blocked Pawn anew by P–QB4. P×P is unplayable because of R×Rch. So Black must abandon the Pawn and seek compensation elsewhere, preferably by R–Kt1, in counterattack upon a weak White pawn.

On Q4, where the Black QP stands, attack and defence are in balance. To obtain the superiority White forces the protecting piece, the Black King, from the scene of action. To this end he uses his "Passed Pawn," the RP. By advancing it, he threatens to Queen it within five moves. Evidently, the Black King must stop that dangerous Pawn. By the sacrifice of

the Passed Pawn the White King will be enabled to gain the QP, then the KP and will finally guide his BP to the eighth row, to victory. Therefore, t h e game proceeds 1. P–R4, K–K3; 2, P–R5, K–Q3; 3 P–R6, K–B3; 4, P–R7, K–Kt2; 5 K×P, K×P; 6 K ×P and wins by superiority.

On the Exchange— Value of the Pieces.

In the course of the contests above described the aggressor may often, if he so chooses, capture hostile men at the price of sacrificing some of his own men. To capture a piece of the enemy and in compensation to give up a piece therefor is called an "exchange." You exchange Bishop for Knight, if your Bishop captures the Knight and is recaptured. You exchange Pawn for Pawn, Queen for Queen, Rook for Rook in the same way. But if you capture Rook for Knight or Bishop, you are considered to have made a good bargain, you have "won the exchange." Some Chessfriends prefer the Knight to Bishop, others the Bishop to Knight and they make e x c h a n g e s accordingly Who is in the right? Or is there neither right nor wrong in these proceed-ings; are they, maybe, under the rule of an incomprehensible hazard?

In the games of most Chess lovers such a hazard seems to dominate; even though this law of chance, or whatever it might be, cannot be considered truly incomprehensible, s i n c e Psychology may assist us in deciphering it, it is sufficiently difficult of explanation as to balk the human stupidity that we proudly call "intellect." But it is not this difficulty that we are trying to assail at the present. We rivet our attention on the games of the experienced, the thinking, the strong players, preferably the strongest of them, the masters, and among them certain regularities s h o w v e r y plainly. T h e experience derived from games played between such as deserve the title of masters, during centuries has proven these regularities. Hence, we know that *ceteris paribus* Knight and Bishop are even, either is *ceteris paribus* worth three Pawns, Rook *ceteris paribus* as strong as K n i g h t or Bishop and two Pawns, Queen very nearly as strong as two Rooks or three minor pieces.

The supposition implied in the term " *ceteris pari-* *bus* " is, however, of importance. " All other circumstances being equal," that is the meaning of *ceteris paribus.* In strict Logic, the other circumstances are never equal. The supposition is that we consider them of equal weight or import. A n d the " we " in no wise refers to the inexperienced player. The nearly perfect player—say the master—is he who judges. We erring mortals, try to guess his judgment. While in this we are doing our level best, we modestly keep him in mind and seek to approach his efficiency a n d h i s methods. To l e a v e the *ceteris paribus* o u t o f reckoning would plunge us into the claws of Nonsense that would reduce our proud intellect to blundering romanticism akin to madness. To give an instance, here is a position where a Pawn is stronger than a Knight and a Queen and a Rook.

White with the move plays P × Kt, calls for a Knight, says Check, simultaneously attacks Queen, then captures Queen and thereafter the immobile and helpless Rook. Mark the exceeding value of the right to move. Black to move would have an enormous superiority.

Ceteris paribus notwithstanding, t h e exchange values of which a few are set down above, are therefore always somewhat problematical. For all that, they are to the Chess-player a most needed compass. If he conscientiously follows them, his ship n e a r l y always, even though only after many moves, runs safely into port.

We are not without a method to probe the above values a n d to discover others. All we have to do is to build simple positions, in which the values under discussion, s a y R o o k against Bishop and Pawn, with due regard to the *ceteris paribus* are set to fight each other and carefully to analyse the course of that fight. Of the application of this method a few examples are here given.

Rook versus Bishop and Pawn. The *ceteris paribus* condition is here fairly fulfilled, both sides having besides two blocked Pawns each. True, the W h i t e King has a very advantageous position, but such an advantage can be forced by methodical play as soon as the advantage of Rook versus Bishop and Pawn is conceded. This position represents the final stages of the contest. White has all the initiative, he is the aggressor. He assails the QP twice. It is guarded twice, but by assailing the King White can drive that protection away and thus attain the superiority on Q6. 1 R–R7ch., K–Q1 ; 2 K–K6. Thereafter R–Q7 and R × P. The advantage of t h e " exchange " is abandoned, since Bishop may now capture Rook, but King recaptures and holds now advantage of position in that it attacks the Black Pawns while the hostile

King is inactive and must suffer the destruction of its army of Pawns. Then White wins at his leisure.

The Queen is weaker than two Rooks if the hostile King is protected against Checks, otherwise it may be stronger. *Ceteris paribus*, it would appear, the Queen is a trifle weaker than two Rooks.

White plays here R–QB3, then R (R1)–QB1, thus doubling the Rooks to assail the BP and winning it. To win the RP would, it is true, be difficult, because the Rooks have to protect the King against Checks. It is evident, however, that the Rooks have the initiative and that Black's hope is merely to Draw by Perpetual Check.

Even one Rook is sufficient to make a hard fight against the Queen, provided that the Rook has not to lend its help to other pieces, for instance, to weak Pawns, but has a little protection from elsewhere to lean upon.

White Draws by moving his Rook from B3 to QR3 and back to B3 unless forced to move the King, which clings to the vicinity of its Pawn. Thus White is never in *Zugzwang* and his pieces are never unprotected.

A Rook without any support loses against the Queen *ceteris paribus*. If it stays under the protection of its King it is at last driven off by *Zugzwang*. The following instance will illustrate sufficiently:

If Black to move, the Rook must move away from the King and soon gets lost by White Checking and attacking Rook simultaneously, thus 1 R–QR7; 2 Q–Kt5ch., K–R8; 3 Q–R6ch. The Rook can never go to KR7 on account of the Checkmate by Queen on first row. 3 ...., K –Kt8; 4 Q–Kt6ch., K–R7; 5 Q–R7ch., K–Kt8; 6 Q–Kt1 or Kt8; Checks and wins the Rook.

If White to move, he can easily manœuvre so as to bring about the same or a similar position with Black to move. For instance 1 Q–Q4ch., K–R8; 2 Q–R8ch., K–Kt8; 3 Q–R4.

It is not difficult to multiply researches of the above type concerning the exchange-value, and such exercises are of exceeding use to the student. What has been said is sufficient to guide him in this work, which I should recommend to him most earnestly.

THE THEORY OF THE OPENINGS.

SECOND BOOK.

The Chess fraternity had reached an understanding of the foregoing points centuries ago. Proof: the stories dealing with Chess in olden times speak of the above stratagems; words that from usage in Chess play have crept into common usage such as to "Check" an opponent, to "Mate" him, to make a Drawn game, originate from this sphere of mentality; in olden times a King to whom a son was born at the exact moment that he attacked King and Rook with his Knight called the newly born prince "Shak-Ruk," meaning "Check-Rook"; and this Prince, we are told, became a brave hero. The above considerations and observations are the elements of all Chess strategy, just as intelligible to every Chess player, as is his mother-tongue. And five centuries ago these elements embodied the whole of Chess science. But then a novel idea entered into the plan, setting a problem which stirred the Chess fraternity passionately and which even now excites it greatly.

In abstract terms the problem may be stated as follows: how and according to what rules must the pieces from the initial position, where they stand ineffective and obstructive, be marched into efficient battle array?

For hundreds of years Chess players had started their games in a happy-go-lucky fashion. After a few such chance moves, complications arose and in these complications skill and sagacity were displayed; they considered that the start of the game, compared to the importance of the hand-to-hand fight which ensued afterwards, was insignificant. Then one day some genius, now unknown to us, began to pay attention to the different ways of opening the game. And if he has done no more—and probably he did not—than to record some of the methods of starting the game and to designate these "Openings" by the names of the eminent players who preferred them, his performance was most estimable. Suddenly, in the fifteenth century, we find Openings provided with

Hwell

well-known n a m e s and analysed in books written to that end, and peculiar terms are coined and introduced such as " Gambit " or " G i u o c o P i a n o." Furthermore, from that day the problem of Openings becomes the point upon which attention has been centred and remains so, one may say, even to the present day.

To visualise the beginning of this evolution we may surmise that at an ancient date, when players of original talent, whom to-day we would call " natural " players, predominated over all others, some unknown genius, with a penchant for collecting information, made notes of the beginnings of g o o d g a m e s, compiled them, classified them, and exhibited his work to a few friends. As a natural consequence, some of the industrious and intelligent learners would, in the first dozen moves, overcome superior players of that day, by employing the tactical manœuvres gleaned from the manuscript o f their compiler-friend. One can imagine the surprise of spectators and the wrath of the defeated masters as they observed newcomers, without natural talent, waging a s t r o n g fight

purely with the aid of a book of compiled information.

Their wrath evaporated of course, but the cause of it endured. Since those days we have continued to have compilers of " variations," players who fight according to the book, and those with natural talent who, however, can no longer climb to the summit.

There is justification for the compiler. B u t can a player hope to become a master merely by studying a compilation ? No. That were possible if the number of the different lines of play were small. In Chess, however, t h a t number, no matter how critically one may select and how many feeble lines of play one may reject, goes into many millions. The brain cannot encompass them by a process of mere compilation. One must therefore search for rules, laws, principles capable o f comprising within their compass the result of a thousand, nay of ten thousand different variations.

That, naturally, has been done. The process is common to all investigation which aims at comprehending a bulk of matter too large to be comprehended in detail. Probably, the players with natural talent thus tried to offset the efforts of book players. In the eighteenth century they announced their first rule: *"Sortez les pieces"*— "Get the pieces out." The meaning of this brief sentence is clear. The pieces obstruct each other in their initial position, the Chess-board in the middle is unoccupied, let the pieces get out so as to obtain dominance over a fair share of the unoccupied territory. And let the pieces fight the opponent in his endeavour to lay his hand on too much of that territory. And, if you have mobilised your pieces sooner than he, assail him quickly, before he can throw his undeveloped and therefore inefficient force into the action.

It took a hundred years before a new rule was announced. Anderssen, the winner of the first International Tournament, that of London, 1851, said: "Move that one of your pieces, which is in the worst plight, unless you can satisfy yourself that you can derive immediate advantage by an attack." One may guess the reasons for this rule. If you cannot successfully carry through an ambitious enterprise, it is sufficient to get your house into order and to improve the worst spots. In the initial position the KP, the QP, the two Knights, occupy the weakest positions, because they obstruct the most; hence, Anderssen's rule points out the necessity of moving these four men from their initial positions. But later the same rule applies again and again.

A few decades went by, tournaments became of frequent occurrence, and the masters, coming together oftener than before, evolved a "public opinion." That tended towards the rule: Avoid the moves of Pawns in the Opening as far as possible. The distrust of Pawn moves was founded on experience in tournament play. If one was worsted in the Opening, one could almost invariably point to a Pawn move as the original offence. The reason is that time is valuable in Chess as it is everywhere else. There are Pawn moves that are effective, for instance, such as lay hold on important points in the centre of the board or remove an obstruction; but there are very many Pawn moves that really are not effective. Distrust a pawn move, examine carefully its balance sheet: this was the sentiment of the masters a few decades after 1851, and, with slight modifications, this sentiment is still very strong and likely to last unchanged.

I have added to these principles the law : Get the Knights into action before both Bishops are developed. The advantage obtained in following this law is certainly not great, yet it is distinctly perceptible.

By means of rules, laws, principles of the above kind, players with natural talent could dispense with compilations and the memorizing of them. But games played by them were again and again analysed and compiled and memorised, so that at last, no matter how they tried to vary from the " book " they had to play against themselves, and, of course, they could not successfully do that. All of which shows that nobody can wholly escape the dire necessity of compiling variations and of examining and memorising them. And therefore such a compilation, though a brief one, is correctly included in a Manual of Chess.

Here follows a collection of variations essential in Opening play. They are selected from the million of possibilities as possessing character, importance, and value as instruction to a

marked degree. A number of variations are slightly indicated, some only hinted at, so as to provide the reader with matter for his own research and to accustom him to independent judgment and to initiative.

The Petroff Defence or Russian Game.

1 P–K4, P–K4; 2 Kt–KB3, Kt–KB3; Black replies to the attack on his KP by counter-attacking the White KP. 3 Kt × P, P–Q3. It would not be advisable to answer with 3 ....
Kt × P immediately, viz. :
4 Q–K2, Q–K2; 5 Q × Kt, P–Q3; 6 P–Q4, P–KB3; 7 Kt–QB3 with an obvious advantage. 4 Kt–KB3, Kt × P; 5 P–Q4, P–Q4. Now White wants to drive off the Black KKt. Black will fight to maintain it in its position. 6 B–Q3, Kt–QB3. Rather faulty would be 6 ...., B–Q3; 7 O–O, B–KKt5; 8 P–B4, O–O; 9 Kt–B3, and White has the superiority in the centre. 7 O–O. To bring the King into safety before the centre by exchange of Pawns is opened to the officers. 7 .... B–K2; 8 QKt–Q2. The Knight avoids B3 so as to keep the QBP mobile. 8 ...., P–B4; 9 P–B4.

Position after White's ninth move.

Position after White's tenth move.

9. ....   B—K3

If 9 ...., Kt–Kt5, White retreats 10 B–Kt1.

10. P × P   B × P
11. R—K1   ....

White has attained his object of driving off Black's Knight on K5. But White may also continue :—

10. R—K1   P × P
11. Kt × Kt   P × B
12. Kt—B5   B—Q4
13. B—Kt5 with attack.

Again

9. ....   Kt × Kt
10. B × Kt   O—O
11. Q—Kt3, and White has the best of it.

All in all, the early advance of the KBP does not seem advisable.

8. ....   B—KB4
9. R—K1   Kt × Kt
10. Q × Kt   ....

Black may here play 10 ...., B × B or B–Kt5. White has retained the advantage of the first move, no more. As an instance 10 ...., B × B; 11 Q × B, O–O; 12 B–Q2, B–B3; 13 Kt–K5. Or else 10 ...., B–Kt3; 11 Kt–K5; or 10 ...., B–Kt5; 11 Kt–K5. Inadvisable seems 10 .... Q–Q2 because of 11 B–Kt5.

Returning again to the main variation, let Black retreat his advanced post.

8. ....   Kt—B3
9. P—B3   O—O
10. Kt—K5

And now White will fortify his advanced Knight or force Black to exchange it and will then be able to recapture with QP and to assail the adverse King by a mass of Pawns. White has the initiative. White may also follow another plan. 3. Kt × P, P–Q3; 4. Kt–KB3, Kt × P; 5. Q–K2,

Q–K2; 6. P–Q3, Kt–KB3;
7. B–Kt5, Q × Q ch (or B–
K3, or QKt–Q2); 8. B × Q,
Kt–Q4. A very compli-
cated Ending will ensue,
where the minor pieces pre-
dominate.

A principal variation,
where White tries for too
much

5. P—Q4   P—Q4
6. B—Q3   Kt—QB3
7. O—O   B—K2
8. R—K1   B—KKt5

Black can reply by
counter-attack. If 9. B ×
Kt, P × B; 10. R × P, B
× Kt; White cannot reply
11. P × B on account of 11
........., P–B4; (12. R–B4?
O—O; 13. P–Q5, B–Kt4
and regains at least his P).

9. P—B3   P—B4
10. P—B4   B—R5

Black obtains counter-
attack, since White has
made too many Pawn
moves.

11. B × Kt   QP × B
12. P—Q5   O—O

with advantage rather for
Black.

The Hungarian Defence.

1. P—K4   P—K4
2. Kt—KB3   Kt—QB3
3. B—B4   B—K2
4. Kt—B3   Kt—B3
5. P—Q3   P—Q3
6. P—QR3   ....

in order to guard the KB
against exchange by Kt—
QR4.

6. ....   B—K3
7. B—K3   O—O
8 O—O   Kt—KKt5
9. Kt—Q2   ....

*Position after White's ninth
move*

White predominates on
Q5. Or else 8 ...., P–
Q4; 9 P × P, Kt × P; 10 Q–
Q2. White is well devel-
oped.

Philidor's Defence.

1. P—K4   P—K4
2. Kt—KB3   P—Q3
3. P—Q4

If the White pieces are
to penetrate into the centre, it is necessary to force
the Black KP to submit to
exchange.

3. ....   P—KB4

A bold answer, to get the
White KP out of the way.

4. B—QB4   ....

White retaliates by aiming against the Black King which will have difficulty to obtain a safe position.

4. ....   BP × P

Black insists on forming a mass of Pawns in the centre.

5. Kt × P   ....

White destroys the mass of Pawns by giving up a piece in order to assail the King.

5. ....   P × Kt

There is no help for it, since Kt–B7 as well as Q—R5 ch are threatened.

6. Q—R5 ch   K—Q2

Of course if 6. .... P–Kt3; 7. Q–K5 ch gains the Black R

7. Q—B5 ch   K—B3
8. Q × KP   ....

Position after White's eighth move

Black will not be able to secure his King except at great expense. For instance 8 ...., P–QR3; 9 B–K3, Kt–B3; 10 Kt–B3 (threatening P–Q5 ch), B–KKt5; 11. P–KR3, B–Q3; 12. Q–QR5 (threatening B–Kt5 ch), P–QKt3; 13. Q–R4 ch, P–Kt4; 14. Kt × KtP.

The sound plan for Black is not counter-attack but patient defence as follows:

3. ....   P × P
4. Kt × P   ....

Also Q × P may be played since the Queen cannot easily be driven from this strong post. If 4. .... Kt–QB3; 5. B–QKt5.

4. ....   Kt—KB3
5. Kt—QB3   B—K2
6. B—K2

With the intention of advancing P–B4, in order to get a grip on point K5 and to strengthen the points K4, Q5 later on by KB–B3.

6. ....   Kt—B3
7. O–O   O—O
8. P—B4   R—K1
9. B—B3   B—Q2

The threat of White was 10. Kt × Kt followed by 11. P–K5.

10 K—R1

As preparation for P–QKt3, and B–Kt2 which at present would be venture-

some because of the reply
10. .... P–Q4; 11. P × P,
B–QB4; 12. P × Kt, B × P;
13. Kt–K2, B × B followed
by R × Kt or similar lines
of play.

Position after White's tenth move.

White has the Initiative

If Black tries to keep his
KP in its place on K4,
Hanham's variation results.

1. P—K4   P—K4
2. Kt—KB3   P—Q3
3. P—Q4   QKt—Q2

If 3. .... Kt–QB3; 4.
P × P, Kt × P; 5. Kt × Kt,
P × Kt; 6. Q × Q ch, K × Q.
The Black King is not well
placed.

4. B—KKt5   B—K2
5. B × B   Q × B
6. Kt—B3   KKt—B3
7. Q—Q2   O—O
8 O—O—O

Position after White's eighth move.

White has gained in
space, but the position of
Black presents few assailable points.

Another important varia-
tion of Hanham's defence:

4. B—QB4   P—QB3

To secure the point Q4
and to obtain mobility for
the Queen.

5. B—KKt5   Q—B2

If 5. ...., Q–Kt3; 6
B–Kt3, and the B l a c k
Queen stands somewhat ex-
posed.

6. P—B3   KKt—B3

To gain a Pawn move by
6. .... P--KR3; 7. B–R4
seems hardly to the point,
since the Pawn, at least for
the present, seems better
left at home.

7. QKt—Q2   ....

Position after White's seventh move

It will not be easy for Black to institute a counter-attack. True, a certain menace might develop in 7 ...., P × P and attack on KP or by the hazardous manœuvre 7 ...., P–KR3 followed by 8 ...., P–KKt4.   .

The Two Knights' Defence.

1. P—K4   P—K4
2. Kt—KB3   Kt—QB3
3. B—B4   Kt—B3
4. Kt—Kt5

The idea of this move which sacrifices develop-ment in the interest of at-tack is to disturb the de-velopment of Black by assailing the weakest point in the Black camp, KB2.

4. ....   P—Q4
5. P × P   ....

That the attack of White is reasonable appears from the consequences of 5. ...., Kt × P. Then White m a y obtain a n advantage by the sacri-fice 6. Kt × BP, K × Kt; 7. Q–B3 ch, K–K3; 8. Kt–B3, Kt–K2; 9. P–Q4, P–B3; 10. B–KKt5, soon to be followed by Castling Queen's side. Black can-not get his King into safety, the White Rooks very soon become active, for instance, 10. ...., P × P; 11. O–O–O, P × Kt; 12 KR–K1 ch, K–Q2; 13. KB × Kt, P × Pch.; 14. K–Kt1. Or 10. ...., P–KR3; 11. QB × Kt, B × B; 12 O–O–O, R–B1; 13. Q–K4. Or else, 8. .... Kt–Kt5; 9. Q–K4 as recommended by Leon-hardt. 9. .... P–B3; 10. P–Q4. The sacrifice of the piece against some Pawns, in view of the in-secure position of several of the Black pieces, appears to be well founded.

5 ....   Kt—QR4
to retain attack Black abandons a Pawn for the present.

6 B—Kt5 ch   P—B3

To hold on to the attack. If 6. .... B–Q2; 7. Q–K2.

7 P × P   P × P
8 B—K2   P—KR3
9 Kt—KB3   P—K5
10 Kt—K5   ....

The Knight wants to stay in the centre supported by the White Pawns. White has nothing to fear from 10. .... Q–Q5; 11. P–KB4,

B–QB4; 12 R–B1 since then the White Pawns will soon drive the Black pieces off with P–B3, P–Q4 or P–QKt4.

10. .... B—Q3
11 P—Q4 Q—B2
12 B—Q2 !

Thus White takes advantage of the bad position of Black Knight on R4. If 12. .... B × Kt; 13. P × B, Q × P; 14. B—QB3; White has an excellent position.

12 .... Kt—Kt2
13 Kt—B4

Position after White's thirteenth move

 B × P
14 B—K3 B—B5
15 Kt—B3 ....

A position full of life. White has an advantage in development.

Black may follow another line of attack.

5 .... Kt—Q5
The Knight goes into the centre and therefore re-

nounces immediate attack against the White KB.

6 P—QB3 P—Kt4 !
The Knight defends its good post. If it gives way at once, White proceeds with 7 P—Q4

7. B—B1 ....
The precious KB does not desire to be exchanged for the exposed Black Knight (Leonhardt).

But 7. P × Kt, P × B; 8. P × P, Q × P; 9 O—O, B–Kt2; 10. Kt–KB3, Kt–Q2; 11. Kt–B3 is not without merits.

7 .... Kt × P
8 P × Kt Q × Kt
9 P × P Q × P ch
10 Q—K2 Q × Q ch
11 B × Q P—QB3

A difficult End Game, White probably has a slight advantage.

Position after Black's eleventh move

Continuations where White instead of making an immediate attack is satisfied with placid development, are numerous. One is 4. P–Q3, leading up to a firm but unaggressive position. More energetic is 4 P–Q4. After

4 P—Q4	P × P
5 O—O	Kt × P
6 R—K1	P—Q4
7 B × P	Q × B
8 Kt—B3	

Black best secures his Queen in placing it far out of the reach of minor pieces.

8	Q—QR4
9 Kt × Kt	B—K3
10 QKt—Kt5	O—O—O

Not 10 ...., Q–Q4 on account of 11 Kt × BP.

11 Kt × B	P × Kt
12 R × P	Q—KB4

Position after Black's twelfth move

Black has a sound development. As an instance of what might follow. 13. Q–K2, B–Q3; 14. B–Kt5, QR–B1; 15 R–Q1, P–KR3; 16. B–B1, K–Q2; 17. R–K4, R–K1; 18 R × R, R × R; 19. Q–Q3, Q × Q; 20 R × Q, Kt–Kt5; 21. R × P, Kt × BP; whereupon Black has the initiative on the Queen's side.

The Centre Game and The Centre Gambit.

1 P—K4	P—K4
2 P—Q4	

Black frustrates the simple threat to gain a pawn most easily by capturing the assailant Pawn.

2	P × P
3 Q × P	....

The early exposure of the Queen allows Black to gain a move by attacking it.

3	Kt—QB3
4 Q—K3	....

The Queen might also go to R4, but on K3 it has better opportunities for attack on the King's side.

4	Kt—B3
5 Kt—QB3	

White must not attack prematurely as, for instance, by 5. P–K5, Kt–KKt5; 6. Q–K4, P–Q4!; 7. P × P in passing, B–K3, and Black is so well developed that the Pawn minus is more than compensated for.

5	B—Kt5
6 B—Q2	O—O
7 O—O—O	P—Q3
8. Q—Kt3	Kt—K4

*Position after Black's
eighth move*

But 3 ...., P × P may be
played, to reply to 4 P–K5
with 4 ...., P–Q4.

4 Kt—KB3   ....

With 4. P × P, QKt × P;
5. B–Kt3, B–B4; 6. P–
KB4, QKt–Kt5; 7. P–E5,
Kt–B7; 8. Q–K2, Kt–Kt1:
White brandishes his sword
in vain and gets hurt himself.

4 ....   P × P
5 O—O

Black menaces now 9
........., B × Kt followed by
10 ...., Kt × P, also 9
........., Kt–R4. All in all,
he is well prepared for the
ensuing struggle.

White can play a verit-
able Gambit—the above
line of play is one in name
only—by abandoning his
Pawn for the time being.

3 P–QB3   P—Q4
To capture the Pawn
would develop White so
rapidly as to give him
sufficient compensation for
the loss in material.

4 KP × P   Kt—KB3
5 Q × P   Q × P
6 Kt—B3   Kt—B3
Black is well developed.

King's Bishop's Opening.

1 P—K4   P—K4
2 B—B4   Kt—KB3
Black develops aggres-
sively.

3 P—Q4   Kt—B3
Black now develops while
defending at the same time.

*Position after White's
fifth move.*

This position that can
arise in a variety of ways
leads to a variety of continuations, and is therefore
of conseqeunce.

Black may choose be-
tween 5 ...., B–B4,
which allows the Max
Lange attack that is treated
under this heading later on,
and 5 ...., Kt × P, that
has been treated of in the
section of the Two Knights'
Defence. Also 5 ...., P–
Q3 or 5 ...., B–K2 are
good enough to develop
Black, for instance, 5 ......,

B–K2; 6 P–K5, Kt–KKt5;
7. R–K1, P–Q3; 8 P × P,
Q × P; 9. P–KR3, Kt–B3;
or 6. R–K1, P–Q3;
7. Kt × P, O—O, where-
upon Black is well enough
developed.

White may, of course,
choose a slow development,
for instance, by 3. P–Q3,
Kt–B3; 4. Kt–QB3, B–
Kt5; 5. Kt–K2, P–Q4; 6.
P × P, Kt × P; 7. O–O, B–
K3; but then Black has no
difficulties to overcome.

Max Lange's Attack.

1	P—K4	P—K4
2	Kt—KB3	Kt—QB3
3	P—Q4	P × P
4	B–QB4	Kt—B3
5	O—O	B—B4

Black tries to maintain
the advantage of the Pawn
plus, White aims at throwing the Black pieces into
disorder.

*Position after Black's
fifth move.*

6 P—K5   P—Q4

This counter-attack de-
velops QB and Queen but

abandons the King's side.
Steinitz, consequently, proposed 6 ...., Kt–KKt5.
If White, analysing super-
ficially, then tries an impetuous attack, the weak
troupe of the aggressor is
soon repulsed, viz., 7. B ×
P ch, K × B; 8. Kt–Kt5 ch,
K–Kt1; 9. Q × Kt, P–Q4;
10. P–K6, Q–B3.   Again
7. P–KR3, KKt × KP; 8.
Kt × Kt, Kt × Kt; 9. R–K1,
P–Q3; 10. P–B4, P–Q6
ch; 11. B–K3, P × P; 12.
Q × BP, Q–R5; 13. Q–B2,
Q × Qch.; 14. B × Q, B × B
ch; 15. K × B, B–K3. Black
has no difficulty in over-
coming such premature
assaults and thereby gaining an advantage.   The
right plan for White is to
play safely. 7 B–B4. Now 8.
P–KR3 is menaced. Hence
7. ...., P–Q3; 8. P × P,
P × P; 9. R–Kch., K–B1.

*Position after Black's ninth
move in Steinitz' variation*

10	P—KR3	Kt—B3
11	QKt—Q2	B—B4
12	Kt—Kt3	Q—Kt3

The possibilities are numerous. White can hardly claim an advantage.

The Max Lange attack is provoked by Black's sixth move. 6. .... P–Q4.

7 P × Kt   P × B
8 R—Ksq ch. B—K3

B l a c k may answer 8 ...., K–B1, but the King remains there exposed a long time, for instance, after 9. B–Kt5. The strategy of B l a c k should be to try for safety a n d counter-attack b y means of Castling Queen's side.

9 Kt—Kt5   ....

If 9. P × P, R–KKt1 ; 10. B–Kt5, B–K2 ; 11. B × B, Q × B ; 12. Kt × P, R–Q1 ; 13. P–QB3, R × P ; Black is well developed.   14. Q–R4 ?, K–B1 ! whereupon the KKtP is weak. After the Knight move, on the contrary, the development of Black is hampered, since 10. Kt × B followed by 11. Q–R5 ch winning the Bishop is a menace.   By this threat White retains the attack.

9 ....   Q—Q4
10 Kt–QB3   Q—B4
11 QKt—K4   B—KB1

The right move since the King's wing needs support. If 11 ...., B–Kt3, Black's Quen's wing remains very strong, but at the expense of giving up resistance on the King's side, wherefore the Black King then cannot obtain a safe post.   White would reply to 11. ...., B–Kt3 by 12. P × P, R–KKt1 ; 13. P–KKt4, Q–Kt3 ; 14 Kt × B, P × Kt ; 15. B–Kt5, thus p r e v e n t i n g Castling Queen's side and forcefully menacing 16 Q–B3. A celebrated game—White : Marshall ; Black : Dr. Tarrasch, took the following course, 11. ...., O—O—O ; 12. Kt × QB, P × Kt ; 13. P–KKt4, Q–K4 ; 14. P × P, KR–Kt1 ; 15. B–R6, P–Q6 ; 16. P–QB3, P–Q7 ; 17. R–K2, B–Kt3 ; 18. K–Kt2. In the long run the Black Pawn on Q7 is untenable. The Knight on K4, soon supported by P–B3, dominates the centre.   Therefore, the retreat of the Bishop 11....... B–KB1 is well founded.   Apparently 12. P–KKt4 refutes the move, but in reality no. Black would defeat the attempted refutation by 12. ...., Q × Pch ; 13. Q × Q, B × Q ; 14. P × P, B × P ; 15. Kt–B6 Double Check, K–B1 ; 16. Kt × B, P–KR4 ! Taken all in all, White can hardly do better than

12 Kt × BP   K × Kt
13 Kt—Kt5 ch   K—Kt1
14 R × B   P × P
15 P—KKt4   Q—Q4

Not 15. ...., Q–Kt3 on account of 16. Q–B3.

16 R × P   P—KR4
17 R—Kt6 ch   B—Kt2
18 Kt—K6   K—B2

*Position after Black's
eighteenth move*

White to play.

There is plenty of play in it on either side.

The Ponziani Opening.

1 P—K4   ....
2 Kt—KB3   P—K4
3 P—B3   Kt—QB3

Black will do best to attempt neither gain of a Pawn nor to sacrifice a Pawn, but rather to strive for continued development.

3 ....   Kt—B3
4 P—Q4   Kt × KP

Now 5 ...., P–Q4 is possible; hence White is forced to attempt a counter-move.

5 P—Q5   Kt—Kt1

The Knight must not go to K2 where it would block Bishop and Queen.

6 Kt × P   ....
Or else 6. B–Q3, Kt–B4.

6 ....   B—B4
7 Kt—Q3   B—Kt3
8 B—K2   O—O
9 O—O   P—Q3
10 Kt—Q2   Kt × Kt

The Knight is captured, because it threatens to exchange the valuable KB via QB4.

*Position after Black's
tenth move*

Black will now complete his development by Kt–Q2, R–K1, Kt–B1.

Black is by no means restricted to the above line of play. He may, for instance, very well play

4 ....   P × P
5 P—K5   ....
Or 5. P × P, P–Q4, whereupon Black is secure.

5 ....   Kt—Q4
5. .... Kt–K5 would be speculative, not to say hazardous. 6. Q–K2, P–B4; 7. P × P in passing,

P–Q4. Still, White's task is by no means simple. For instance, 8. KKt–Q2, Q × P; 9. P–B3, P–Q6; 10. Q–K3, Q–Kt4 and White has had his trouble for next to nothing.

| 6 P × P | B—Kt5 ch |
| 7 QKt—Q2 | P—Q3 |

or 6	P—Q3
7 Kt—B3	B—K3
8 B—QKt5	B—K2
9 P × P	P × P

All in all, the difficulties that Black encounters in this Opening are not considerable.

The Vienna Opening.

| 1 P—K4 | P—K4 |
| 2 Kt—QB3 | .... |

The best reply, according to the rules laid down above, would seem to be

| 2 .... | Kt—KB3 |
| 3 B—B4 | Kt × P |

Now 4. B × P ch is not to be recommended, because White, after giving up his developed pieces, cannot follow up the attack; viz., 4. .... K × B; 5. Kt × Kt, P–Q4. Also with 4. Kt × Kt, P–Q4; 5. B–Q3, P × Kt; 6. B × P, Kt–Q2; Black has rather the better of it.

| 4 Q—R5 | Kt—Q3 |
| 5 Q × KP ch | .... |

If 5. B–Kt3, Black has the choice between safe

development with 5. .... B–K2 and an attempt at a promising attack with 5. .... Kt–B3; 6. Kt–Kt5, P–KKt3; 7. Q–B3, P–B4; 8 Q–Q5, Q–K2; 9. Kt × Pch., K–Q1; 10 Kt × R, P–Kt3.

| 5 .... | Q—K2 |

In the ensuing End Game, White has the advantage in mobility but hardly sufficient objects of attack.

A variation often employed by Mieses strengthens the pressure on the point Q5 as follows:

3 P—KKt3	P—Q4
4 P × P	Kt × P
5 B—Kt2	Kt × Kt
6 KtP × Kt	Kt—B3

In this way Black gets over the danger of having his QP shut in and has now a fair development. Again:

5 KKt—K2	Kt—QB3
6 B—Kt2	B—K3
7 O—O	Q—Q2

Black threatens Castling Queen's side and to institute an attack against the White King by advancing P—KR4—KR5. Black has a promising game.

White may try to get the Black KP out of the way.

3 P—B4	P—Q4
4 P × KP	Kt × P
5 Q—B3	Kt—QB3

Black defends by counter-attack. If 6 Kt × Kt Black counters with 6 ...., Kt–Q5.

6 B—Kt5   Kt × Kt
7 KtP × Kt   Q—R5 ch

Placid development 7. ...., B–K2; 8 P–Q4, O–O; 9 B–Q3, P–B3; 10 Q–R5, P–KKt3; 11 B × P. P × B leads to Draw by Perpetual Check.

8 P—Kt3   Q—K5 ch
9 Q × Q   P × Q

Position after Black's ninth move.

Black threatens 10. ...., B–Q2 followed by 11 ...., Kt × P. A difficult position, where Black need not fear to be at a disadvantage.

The Scotch Opening.

1 P—K4   P—K4
2 Kt—KB3   Kt—QB3
3 P—Q4   ....

The idea of this Opening is to open the centre to the pieces as soon as possible.

3 ....   P × P

Thus, it is almost obvious, the question of how to meet the assault upon the KP is most readily answered.

4 Kt × P   Kt—B3
5 Kt—QB3   B—Kt5

It is not so easy now to guard the KP. For instance, 6 P–B3 , O–O and soon P–Q4.

6 Kt × Kt   KtP × Kt
7 B—Q3   ....

Or 7 Q–Q4, Q–K2; 8 P–B3, P–B4; 9 Q–B2 (not Q–K3 because of the impending P–Q4–Q5), O—O; 10 B–Q2, P–Q4. Black is well developed.

7 ....   P—Q4
8 P × P   ....

Not 8 P–K5 which would be premature as an old game proves : 8 .... Kt–Kt5; 9 O–O, B–QB4; 10 P–KR3, Kt × KP; 11 R–K1, Q–B3; 12 Q–K2, O–O; 13 Q × Kt, Q × Pch; 14 K–R1, B × P; 15 P × B, Q—B6 ch; 16 K–R2, B–Q3 and wins. True, 10 P–KR3 is inferior, but also 10 B–KB4, P–Kt4; 11 B–Kt3, P–KR4; 12 P–KR3, P–R5; 13 B–R2, Kt × B; 14 K × Kt, B–Q5; 15 Q–K2, P–Kt5; 16 P × P, Q–Kt4 leaves the initiative to Black.

8 ....   P × P
9 O–O   O–O
10 B—KKt5   P—B3

White has now some attack, Black, in compensation, a fine Pawn in the centre.

11 Q—B3   B—K2
12 R—K1   R—K1

Position after Black's twelfth move.

Black will be able to drive the advanced White pieces off and to build up a firm position, for instance, 13 Q–Kt3, Kt–R4; 14 Q–R4, B × B; 15 Q × Kt, P–KR3.

The Opening takes a wholly different turn if White attempts to delay Black's Castling. To that end he must forego furthering his own development by 5 Kt–QB3 and harass Black as much as possible.

5 Kt × Kt   KtP × Kt
6 B—Q3   ....

The sudden assault 6 P–K5 would fail if Black keeps cool. Black replies 6 .... Q–K2; 7 Q–K2, Kt–Q4. If White continues in the same hazardous style, 8 P–QB4, B–R3; 9 P–B4, Black ob-

tains the advantage by 9 ...., Q–Kt5ch. If White slows down, Black can placidly proceed with his development, say with P–Q3, B–Q2, Castling Queen's side, or perhaps P–Kt4 and B–Kt2, disturbing the opponent on his part.

6 ....   P—Q4
7 Q—K2   B—K2
8 P—K5   Kt—Q2

To push 9 P–K6, whereupon 9 ...., Kt–B3, obviously causes no inconvenience to the opponent.

9 O—O   O—O

so as to reply to 10 P–KB4 with 10 ...., P–KB4. Black stands prepared.

While these variations are not unsatisfactory to the second player, he may try to obtain even more than above by assuming the aggressive at once.

4 ....   B—B4
5 B—K3   ....

The impertinent attempt 5 Kt–B5 can be punished by 5 ...., P–Q4; 6 Kt × Pch., K–B1; 7 Kt–B5, P × P; 8 Q × Qch., Kt × Q; 9 Kt–Kt3, P–B4; and Black is better developed than White.

5 ....   Q—B3
6 P—QB3   ....

Instead of this defensive move Blumenfeld has proposed the attackng move 6 Kt–Kt5. Obviously, White thereby gets his KP doubled so that the point K5 becomes easily accessible to the opponent. Black will first of all exchange the Bishops 6 .... B × B ; 7 P × B, then weaken the points KR6 and KB6 by 7 .... Q–R5 ch ; 8 P–Kt3 and finally defend his QBP with 8 ...., Q–Q1. Now White will resume the attack with 9 Q–Kt4, bearing down upon the KtP which has to serve as protector of the KKt that is bound to establish itself on B3. A good and safe reply to this is 9 ...., K–B1. Now 10 Q–B4, P–Q3 ; 11 B–B4, Kt–B3 ; 12 O–O, P–KR4 ! which provides the needed outlet for the KR while it threatens to engage the White KtP by P–R5 and thus to enlarge the scope of the Rook still further.

Position after Black's twelfth move in the Blumenfeld variation

Black is well developed. After :—

13 QKt–B3, Kt–K4 ; 14 B –Kt3, P–B3 ; 15 Kt–Q4, P– R5 the task of White would be a hard one.

The main play proceeds

6 .... KKt—K2

Now 7 B–QB4 is not to be recommended, because Black counters by 7 ...., Kt–K4. The aim of Black to advance P–Q4 is hard to prevent.

7 B—K2	P–Q4
8 B—B3	B × Kt
9 P × B	P × P

thus isolating the QP which will soon be a target for a Black Rook.

Paulsen proposed as preparatory to 8. Kt–Kt5.

7. Q—Q2	P—Q4
8 Kt—Kt5	B × B
9 Q × B	O—O

Black sacrifices the BP with good reason. 10 Kt × BP, R–Kt1 ; 11 Kt × P ?, Kt × Kt ; 12 P × Kt, Kt– Kt5 ! with terrible threats against the exposed White King. Better 11 Kt–Q2, P × P ; 12 Kt × P, Q–K4 ; 13 Kt–QKt5, Kt–B4 ; 14 Q– K2, P–QR3 ; 15 Kt–R3, P –QKt4. The sacrifice of the Pawn is manifestly justified.

| 10 Kt—Q2 | B—K3 |

Position after Black's tenth move in Paulsen's variation

In view of the splendid development of Black, no danger threatens from the attack of the Knight against the QB7. White will have his hands full to maintain the balance.

Again, another turn is given to the Opening if White defers or foregoes altogether the recapture of the Pawn he has given up.

4 B—QB4   B—B4

The move 4 Kt—B3 leads to the Max Lange attack or the Two Knights' Defence as previously outlined.

5 P—B3   ....

To attack at once before additional force is brought into play would be rather weak, even though a Pawn may thus be regained 5 Kt–Kt5, Kt–R3; 6 Kt × BP, Kt × Kt; 7 B × Kt ch, K × B; 8 Q—R5 ch, P– Kt3; 9 Q × B, P—Q4 ! whereby Black

assumes the aggressive 10 P × P, R—K1ch. If 11 K–B1, P–Kt3. White is in very bad shape.

5 ....   P × P

Instead of this Black can decline the proffered bait and proceed with 5 ...., Kt–B3 turning into a main line of play of the Giuoco Piano; but to accept a sacrifice and see the attack through is also good strategy.

6 Kt × P   P—Q3
7 B—KKt5   Q—Q2

Black must safeguard the point KB2.

8 Q—Q2   P—KR3
9 B—R4   KKt—K2
10 O—O—O

Position after White's tenth move.

The task for Black is no easy one. One of the possibilities runs as follows :

10 ....   Kt—Kt3
11 B—KKt3   P—R3
12 Kt—Q5   P—Kt4
13 B—Kt3   B—Kt2
14 K—Kt1   O—O—O

15 R—QB1

It would be difficult to foretell the chances of the fierce combat that is evidently approaching.

The King's Gambit

| 1 | P—K4 | P—K4 |
| 2 | P—KB4 | .... |

The intention of the proffered sacrifice is to remove the Black KP from its strong post and to open the KB file to the Rook.

| 2 | .... | P × P |
| 3 | Kt—KB3 | .... |

To hinder the Check of the Black Queen.

| 3 | .... | P—KKt4 |

To hold fast to the Pawn plus.

| 4 | P—KR4 | P—Kt5 |
| 5 | Kt—K5 | P—Q4 |

Black having m a n y Pawns at stake must strive for rapid development so as to be able to strike hard blows with his pieces.

| 6 | P—Q4 | .... |

White also must get quick action.

6	....	Kt—KB3
7	B × P	Kt × P
8	Kt—Q2	B—K3

Hereby Black guards the weak Pawn KB2 and fortifies himself.

Position after Black's eighth move.

White may regain the Pawn, but only at the expense of giving up his advance in development.

| 9 | Kt × Kt | P × Kt |
| 10 | Kt × KtP | B—Q3 ! |

Striking the vulnerable spot, White's KKt3. Or else

10	B—B4	B × B
11	Kt × B	Kt—B3
12	P—Q5	Kt—Kt5
13	Kt—K3	B—B4
14	P—R3	B × Kt
15	B × B	Kt × P
16	Q—Q4	O—O
17	B—R6	Q—B3
18	Q × Q	Kt × Q
19	B × R	K × B
20	R—KB1	Kt—Q4
		or K—K2

Black holds on to his two Pawns for the exchange though the two Rooks with best play will be able to Draw. And again

12	P—B3	Q—Q4
13	Kt—K3	Q—QKt4
14	Q—Kt3	Q×Q
15	P×Q	B—Q3
16	B×B	P×B
17	Kt×P	P—B4
18	Kt—K3	Kt—K2

A difficult Ending rather favourable for Black.

This interesting line of play, initiated by White's fifth move, was first analysed by Kieseritzky, a Polish master, and bears his name.

Another defence to it runs as follows:

5	....	B—Kt2
6	P—Q4	Kt—KB3
7	B—B4	P—Q4
8	P×P	Kt—R4

Here the Knight stands safe and menacing. Black wants to Castle soon.

| 9 | Kt—QB3 | O—O |
| 10 | Kt—K2 | .... |

To neutralize the Knight on R4. If 10 Kt×KtP, Kt–Kt6; the King's file is opened to the advantage of Black. 11 R—R2, Q—K2 ch; 12 Kt—K5, B×Kt; soon to be followed by R—K1.

| 10 | .... | P—QB4 |

In order to open up the centre.

Position after Black's tenth move.

If now 11 P×P in passing, 11 ...., Kt×P, Black gets quick development. After 11 QKt×P, Kt ×Kt; 12 B×Kt, P×P; the Kt loses its support 13 Q× QP, Kt–B3; 14 Kt×Kt, P×Kt.

| 11 | P—B3 | P×P |
| 12 | P×P | Kt—Q2 |

(This line of play originated in a game—Steinitz against Zukertort, Vienna tournament, 1882.) Black is well developed.

Instead of the Kieseritzky Gambit, White may choose the bolder line of the Allgaier Gambit.

5	Kt—Kt5	P—KR3
6	Kt×P	K×Kt
7	P—Q4	....

White must not lose time taking Pawns. 7 Q×P?, Kt–KB3; 8 Q×BP, B–Q3; and the attack goes over to Black.

7	....	P—Q4
8	B×P	Kt—KB3
9	Kt—B3	B—K3

Position after Black's ninth move

How White should neutralize the loss of the piece by his two Pawns plus is not evident. For instance,

10 Q—Q3	Kt—B3
11 O—O—O	P × P
12 Kt × P	Kt × Kt
13 Q × Kt	Q—Q4

or 12 Q—K3   Kt—K2

Taken all in all, neither the Kieseritzky Gambit nor the Allgaier Gambit seems wholly satisfactory. It appears, therefore, advisable to put off 4 P–KR4 which though shaking the mass of Black Pawns endangers White's King side too much. A later opportunity may arise for that advance. From this point of view arise the Gambits bearing the names of Salvio, Muzio, and Philidor.

1 P—K4	P—K4
2 P—KB4	P × P
3 Kt—KB3	P–KKt4
4 B—B4	....

The defence of Philidor is

4	B—Kt2
5 P—KR4	P—KR3
6 P—Q4	P—Q3
7 P—B3	Kt—QB3

Black attempts to maintain his Pawn plus and makes it hard for White to shake the Black Pawn mass.

Position after Black's seventh move

8 O—O   Q—B3

In order to continue with KKt–K2. White is now forced to essay hazardous onslaughts.

9 P—KKt3?   B—R6

or 9 P—K5?   P × KP

10 P × KP   Q—Kt3

Another line of play.

7 Kt—B3   Kt—QB3

Now 8 ...., P–Kt5 threatens the QP.

8 Kt—K2   Q—B3

White's attack is not convincing. The Russian master Tschigorin, one of the greatest connoisseurs of

Gambits, made use of the KKtP, not of the KRP, in order to break the chain of Black Pawns.

5	O—O	P—Q3
6	P—Q4	Kt—QB3
7	P—B3	P—KR3
8	P—KKt3	P—Kt5
9	Kt—R4	**P—B6**

Position after Black's ninth move in Tschigorin's line of play

White has here the opportunity of a large number of attacks without having to resort to the sacrifice of a piece. If 10 Kt–Q2 Black can hardly reply 10 ...., KKt–K2 on account of 11 QKt × P and will therefore have to develop the Kt to B3. The position is difficult for either side.

Black may attempt to meet Tschigorin's plan by an endeavour to Castle early.

5	O—O	P—Q3
6	P—Q4	P—K̃R3
7	P—B3	Kt—K2
8	P—KKt3	P—Kt5
9	Kt—R4	P—B6

But then

10	P—KR3	P—-KR4
11	B—Kt5	....

and the position is rather unbalanced. The White QB is too powerful.

All in all, Tschigorin's line of play seems to be appropriate and far more convincing than any other.

But Black may abandon the idea of maintaining his Pawns and rather use them for an assault against the King. The game then takes a wholly different turn. Thus results the Gambit of Salvio.

1	P—K4	P—K4
2	P—KB4	P × P
3	Kt—KB3	P—KKt4
4	B—B4	P—Kt5
5	Kt—K5	Q—R5 ch
6	K—B1	Kt—QB3

Now development is all important.

| 7 | P—Q4 | .... |

If 7 Kt × BP, the development of Black becomes overwhelming. 7 ...., B–B4; 8 Q–K1, P–Kt6; 9 Kt × R, B–B7; 10 Q–Q1, Kt–B3. Now Black will attempt to force P–B6, for instance, by P–Q4 and B–Kt5 and will overrun White.

7	Kt×Kt
8 P×Kt	B—B4
9 Q—K1	Q×Q ch

To force the attack by 9 ...., P–Kt6 is unjustified because the White Knight would soon occupy the strong post KB3.

10 K×Q	Kt—K2
11 B×P	Kt—Kt3

Position after Black's eleventh move

12 P—KKt3	B—Q5

Black has the best of it. If 13 Kt–B3, Kt×P; 14 Kt–Kt5, Kt×B. And if 13 P–B3, B×KP; 14 R–B1, P–KB3. Or

12 R—B1	Kt×B
13 R×Kt	B—K6

threatening 14 ...., B–B8, White has a hard game.

At all times White has tried to escape such difficulties by bold sacrifices. Thus arose the Muzio Gambit.

1 P—K4	P—K4
2 P—KB4	P×P
3 Kt—KB3	P—KKt4
4 B—B4	P—Kt5
5 O—O	P×Kt
6 Q×P	Q—B3

To throw the Queen thus early into the fray is necessary in view of the multitude of threats directed against the King. The strongest piece though most vulnerable to attack is also the one that can defend and counterattack the most effectively.

7 P—K5	....

To force the Queen out of relative safety and to open the King's file for the Rook and the square K4 for a Knight.

7	Q×P

The KP is too strong, it must be captured.

8 P—Q3	B—R3

To mass the obstructions against the attack on KB2.

9 Kt—B3	Kt—K2
10 B—Q2	QKt—B3

White makes ready for attack on the KKt, Black hurries supports.

11 QR—K1	Q—KB4

Here the Queen guards the points KB2, KB3, KB5 and is fairly safe.

(See diagram next page)

12 K–K4, apparently formidable, exposes the Rook too much. Black replies 12 ......, O—O, and thus threatens 13 ......, P–Q4 too strongly.

Position after Black's eleventh move

The results of painstaking analyses by many of the foremost masters are embodied in the following moves:

12 Kt—Q5   K—Q1
13 Q—K2   ....

The idea is if 13 ....
Kt × Kt; 14 B × Kt, Q × B;
15 B–B3.

13 ....   Q—K3
14 Q—B2   Q—Kt5

With best play Black appears to hold the advantage in the Muzio Gambit also.

In former times it was quite the fashion to play Gambits. Other Openings were then rated as dull. In those days numerous lines of play were tried that are hardly essayed at the present time.

The Cunningham Gambit.

1 P—K4   P—K4
2 P—KB4   P × P
3 Kt—KB3   B—K2
4 B—B4   B—R5ch.

It is best to submit calmly to loss of Castling.

5 K—B1   ....

In compensation White has the better development. For the moment he is master of the centre.

5 ....   P—Q3
6 P—Q4   B—Kt5
7 Kt—B3   ....

Position after White's seventh move.

Here White dominates the centre and with best play should always succeed in maintaining that advantage. Of course, the possibilities are numerous and it would be hard to strike what may be regarded as a perfect line of attack and defence.

To make a suggestion

7	Kt—QB3
8 B×P	B—K2
9 P—KR3	B—R4
10 P—KKt4	B—Kt3
11 P—Q5	Kt—Kt1
12 Kt—Q4	B—Kt4
13 Q—Q2	Q—B3
14 Kt—B5	

and White keeps his hold on the centre.

The Cunningham Gambit has gone wholly out of fashion.

The King's Bishop's Gambit.

1 P—K4	P—K4
2 P—KB4	P×P
3 B—B4	....

meeting the threat of the Check by evacuating a square for the King.

3	Q—R5ch.
4 K—B1	P—Q4

Necessary to support the attack. Unless aid comes immediately forward, the Queen is soon repulsed, for instance, 4 ...., P–KKt4; 5 Kt–QB3, B–Kt2; 6 P–Q4, Kt–K2; (or 6 ...... P–Q3; 7 P–K5, P×P; 8 Kt –Q5); 7 P–KKt3. This is an analysis made about sixty years ago. 7 .... P×P; 8 K–Kt2, Q–R3; 9 P×P, Q–KKt3; 10 Kt–B3, P–KR3. Matters for Black grow now rapidly from bad to worse. 11 Kt– Q5, Kt×Kt; 12 P×Kt,

O–O; 13 P–Q6, Q×QP; 14 B×P, P×B; 15 Q–Q3. R–K1; 16 Q–R7ch., K– B1; 17 B×P with a slashing attack.

5 B×P	....

White will try to keep the diagonal of the Bishop open. True, also 5 P×P has certain advantages, for instance, the opening of a file for the Rook and restriction of the Black QKt, but they are of minor importance.

5	P—KKt4

Now the advance 6 P– KKt3 is answered by 6 ...., B–R6ch.

6 Kt—QB3	B—Kt2
7 P—Q4	Kt—K2
8 Kt—B3	Q—R4
9 P—KR4	P—KR3
10 Q—Q3	

in order to liberate the KKt.

Position after White's tenth move

10	P—QB3
11 B—Kt3	B—Kt5
12 P—K5	Kt—B4
13 Kt—K4	Kt—Q2

The game is complicated, but Black keeps at it. He menaces Castling Queen's side.

| 14 | K—Kt1 | B × Kt |
| 15 | P × B | O—O—O |

In order to reply to 16 P × P, Q—Kt3; 17 QB × P with 17 ...., Kt × KP. And the answer to 16 Kt–Q6ch., Kt × Kt; 17 P × Kt would be 17 ...., Q–Kt3; 18 Q × Q, B × P ch. White has over-rushed matters.

However, Black has no need, should he fear those complications, to assume the aggressive, but may safely play for development.

3	....	Kt—QB3
4.	Kt—KB3	Kt—B3
5	Kt—B3	B—Kt5
6	P—K5	Kt—Kt5
7	Kt—Q5	O—O

threatening 8 ...., KKt × KP.

8	Kt × B	Kt × Kt
9	P—Q4	P—Q4
10	B—Kt3	P—KB3

Should White forego the early advance of the KP, Black will easily get an even position.

6	O—O	O—O
7	P—Q3	B × Kt
8	P × B	P—Q4
9	P × P	Kt × P
10	B × Kt	Q × B
11	B × P	Q—B4ch.
12	K—R1	Q × P
13	B × P	B—Kt5

These are some of the principal variations of the accepted King's Gambit. But Black may safely decline it though possibly a minute advantage will then accrue to White.

The King's Gambit Declined.

1	P—K4	P—K4
2	P—KB4	B—B4
3	Kt—KB3	P—Q3

The logical plan for White is to take advantage of the position of the Black KB for winning a move by 5 P–Q4.

4	P—B3	Kt—KB3
5	P—Q4	P × P
6	P × P	B—Kt5ch.
7	B—Q2	B × Bch.
8	QKt × B	P—Q4
9	P—K5	Kt—Kt5
10	B—Q3	P—KB4

Position after Black's tenth move

Black will be able to maintain the balance.

Black will have even fewer difficulties if White goes slowly.

4	Kt—B3	Kt—QB3
5	B—B4	Kt—B3
6	P—Q3	B—K3
7	Kt—Q5	Kt—Q5

Position after Black's seventh move

White will be unable to hold his advance posts. For instance, 8 P × P, P × P; 9 B–Kt5, P–B3; 10 Kt × Kt ch, P × Kt; 11 B–R4, B × B; 12 P × B, R–KKt1. Or 11 B × B, Kt × B; 12 B–R4; R–KKt1; 13 P–KKt3, R–Kt3. Black has by no means the worst of it.

The Falkbeer Counter-Gambit.

Aggressive players love to hoist an opponent with his own petard. They have invented the Counter-Gambits. To refute a proffered sacrifice by declining it and offering one themselves is their pleasure.

1	P—K4	P—K4
2	P—KB4	P—Q4
3	P × QP	P—K5

With 3 .... P × P the game would be balanced, but the advance of the Pawn, though perhaps not entirely sound, is worth some study. The player who chooses this variation evidently considers his KP worth more than the rather misplaced White Pawn on B4.

4	P—Q3	Kt—KB3
5	P × P	Kt × KP
6	Kt—KB3	B—QB4
7	Q—K2	B—B4

The idea of White, though tempting, is wrong. He plays for 8 P–KKt4 but cannot do it, since Black Castles and obtains a smashing attack 9 P × B, Q × P; 10 B–K3, Kt–QB3; 11 B × B, Q × B. The Black Rooks get too active.

| 8 | Kt—B3 | Q—K2 |

Black has a good game.

Much superior to the above line of play is the steady attack on the advanced Pawn.

4	Kt—QB3	Kt—KB3
5	Q—K2	B—Q3
6	P—Q3	O—O
7	P × P	Kt × KP
8	Kt × Kt	R—K1
9	Q—B3	B—KB4
10	B—Q3	B × Kt
11	B × B	P—KB4
12	Kt—K2	P × B

*Position after Black's
twelfth move*

*Position after Black's
eighth move*

9 P—KR3   ....

Necessary as safeguard
for 10 B–K3 as well as preparatory for 10 P–KKt4.

9	P—QR3
10 P—KKt4	P—QKt4
11 B—Kt3	Kt—QR4
12 B—B2	P—B3

Black has some little
attack because the QP is
exposed and the KP exerts
some pressure but White is
a Pawn to the good.

White will for a long time
constantly threaten attack
on the King's side. To decide whether from the be-
ginning of the sacrificial
combination the outlook for
Black was more favourable
than for White, gold scales
would be needed.

It is well to analyze these
variations, so as to form
position judgment, but the
King's Gambit is irretriev-
ably out of fashion.

Alternatively Black may
use his KB for attack.

6	B—B4
7 O—O	P—Q3
8 K—R1	O—O

Danish Gambit.

1 P—K4	P—K4
2 P—Q4	P × P
3 P—QB3	P × P
4 B—QB4	Kt—KB3
5 Kt × P	Kt—B3
6 KKt—K2	....

in order to Castle even if
6 ...., B–Kt5.

6	B—K2
7 O—O	P—Q3
8 P—B4	O—O

But it is questionable
whether the Bishop may
not be needed to support the
King. At some moment
White will play P–B4–B5
and eventually by B–KKt5

will gain the upper hand on the square Q5.

Giuoco Piano or Italian Opening.

1 P—K4	P—K4
2 Kt—KB3	Kt—QB3
3 B—B4	B—B4

The continuations 4 Kt-B3 or 4 P–Q3 lead to placid developments, for instance,

4 P—Q3	Kt—B3
5 Kt—B3	P—Q3
6 B—K3	B—Kt3
7 P—KR3	B—K3
8 B—Kt3	P—KR3
9 O—O	....

The task of detecting a good line of play becomes complicated only when the question arises where to Castle and after the opponent has arrived at his decision. But, after all, it seems that this decision, however arrived at, does not in itself constitute the turning point of the game provided the contestants continue to play up to the mark until the end.

The Giuoco Piano presents problems in abundance as soon as White assumes the aggressive in trying to build a centre of Pawns. In that case he has to discard the quiet continuation 4 Kt–B3 or 4 P–Q3 and has to attempt to push the QP to Q4 supported by the BP.

This end can be accomplished only by immediately playing 4 P–B3. If White Castles first, the attempt comes too late, because Black replies Kt–B3, attacks the KP and never yields another opportunity for White to obtain the supremacy in the centre.

4 P—B3	....

Now the Black KP, in view of the threatening attack by White's 5 P–Q4, can be held in position only with 4 .... Q–K2. But thereby Black loses a valuable move. White might follow up with 5 O–O, P–Q3; 6 P–Q4, B–Kt3; 7 Kt–R3, Kt–B3; 8 B–Q5 and eventually Kt–B4 with pressure on the KP and the King's file.

4	Kt—B3

This is the move that keeps a perfect balance.

5 P—Q4	P × P
6 P × P	B—Kt5ch.

Black must not lose any time, the QP strives to advance to Q4 in order to break up the White centre.

7 B—Q2	....

Also 7 Kt–B3, which involves the sacrifice of a Pawn, must be considered. But against other moves, such as K–B1, Black has no real difficulties to surmount.

7	B × Bch.

If 7 ......, Kt × KP Black must lose time moving his King about; 8 B × B, Kt × B; 9 B × P ch; K × B; 10 Q—Kt3 ch, P–Q4; 11 Q × Kt, R–K1; 12 O–O. Black has nothing better than K–Kt1, whereupon 13 Kt–B3 and White has an advantage.

8 QKt × B   P—Q4

Black can here break the centre by 8 .... Kt × KP, but White continues 9 P–Q5, Kt × Kt; 10 Q × Kt, Kt–K2; 11 P–Q6, P × P; 12 O–O. White, having the better development, easily wins the two weak Queen's Pawns and retains an advantage.

9 P × P   KKt × P

Position after Black's ninth move

10 O–O   O—O
11 R—K1   QKt—K2
12 R—QB1   ....

Although White is ahead in development he has an isolated QP which may become an object of attack and Black has a strongly posted Kt at Q4.

If, for instance, 12 .... P–QB3; 13 P–KR3 to prepare for Kt–K4, White has the superiority on some Black squares such as K5 and QB5 and perhaps also on Q6.

The Opening becomes very lively if White sacrifices a Pawn by

7 Kt—B3   Kt × KP
8 O—O   ....

One of the oldest variations and a very fine one runs as follows: 8 .... Kt × Kt; 9 P × Kt, B × P; 10 Q–Kt3, B × R; 11 B × P ch, K–B1; 12 B–Kt5, Kt–K2; 13 Kt–K5, B × P; 14 B–Kt6 and wins easily. Similarly 13 .... P–Q4; 14 Q–KB3, B–B4; 15 B–K6.

8 ....   B × Kt

If 8 .... Kt × Kt; 9 P × Kt, P–Q4; 10 P × B, P × B; 11 R–K1ch, Kt–K2; 12 Q–K2, B–K3; 13 Kt–Kt5, Q–Q2; 14 Kt × B, P × Kt; 15 Q × BP, Kt–Q4; 16 P–QR4, O–O; 17 B–Q2. The Ending is presumably even.

9 P–Q5   ....

the Mœller attack.

Position after White's ninth move

9 ....   B—B3

Another good move is 9........., Kt–K4; 10 P × B, Kt × B; 11 Q–Q4, P–KB4!, 12 Q × Kt, P–Q3; 13 Kt–Q4, O–O; 14 P–B3, Kt–B4; 15 R–K1, K–R1. White has a firm position, particularly with Knight on Q4, and will therefore be able to stand the Pawn minus, but he is far from having an advantage. All other moves for Black such as 9 ...., Kt–K2 or 9 .... O–O are appreciably weaker.

10 R—K1   Kt—K2
11 R × Kt   P—Q3

If Black Castles, the QP is sacrificed, as is the rule in such cramped positions. After 11 ...., O–O; 12 P–Q6, P × P; 13 B–B4, B × P; 14 B × P, Kt–B4; 15 B × R, B × R; 16 Q–Q5, Kt –R3 (the only move); 17 B –K7 followed by 18 B–B6 and wins.

Again 15 .... P–Q4; 16 Q × P with advantage. Or 13 .... B–K4; 14 Kt × B, P × Kt; 15 Q–Q6, Kt–B4; 16 Q × KP, P–Q3; 17 Q–Kt5 with the better End-game. At last 13 .... P–Q4; 14 B × P, B × P; 15 R–Kt1, Kt × B; 16 Q × Kt, B–R6; 17 R–Kt3, B–K2; 18 QR–K3 and wins.

12 B—Kt5   B × B
13 Kt × B   O—O

If 13 .... B–B4; 14 Q–B3

14 Kt × RP   K × Kt

Not 14 .... B–B4; 15 R–R4, Kt–Kt3; 16 R–R5.

15 Q—R5ch.   K—Kt1
16 R—R4   P—KB4
17 Q—R7ch.   K—B2
18 R—R6   R—KKt1
19 R—K1   Q—B1

White can now only at best obtain a draw. Rubinstein in *Lärobock i Schack* demonstrates the following line of play.

20 B—Kt5   R—R1
21 Q × R   P × R
22 Q—R7ch.   K—B3
23 R × Kt   Q × R

24 Q × RP ch, with Perpetual Check.

The Evans Gambit.

1 P—K4   P—K4
2 Kt—KB3   Kt—QB3
3 B—B4   B—B4
4 P—QKt4   ....

The idea of this Gambit, the discovery of Captain Evans, is to win a move for the formation of the centre, provided t h e proffered Pawn is taken.

Black is by no means forced to accept the sacrifice. If 4 .... B–Kt3, the Bishop is there safe and strong. A furious attack by White undertaken with the rejected Pawn would fail 5 P–Kt5, Kt–R4; 6 Kt × P, Kt–R3, and now Black menaces many attacks, 7 P–Q4, P–Q3; 8 B × Kt, P × Kt; 9 B × P, R–KKt1. White wins only Pawns while Black develops pieces continually. 10 B × P ch, K × B; 11 B × P, Q–Kt4; Black will c o n t i n u e the attack by 12 ...., Q × KtP or Kt–B5 and by force of his superior development will win with ease. On the other hand, if the B i s h o p , being attacked by 5 .... Kt–R4, gives way with the object of keeping Kt on R4 captive. 6 B–K2, P–Q4 !, 7 P × P, P–K5. A blockade of the Black Knight cannot be efficiently carried through, since Black by his energetic onslaught gives White many other things to think of.

Although the immediate attack by 5 P–Kt5 fails, there are several quiet con-tinuations w h i c h allow White a fair game. But the most important point is whether the Gambit may not be accepted with advantage.

| 4 .... | B × P |
| 5 P—B3 | .... |

The Bishop may retire to B4 or to R4—not so well to K2, where it would hinder the Queen from protecting KB2 if the need arise. In the last century many masters to name only the foremost : Anderssen, Zukertort, Tschigorin, most diligently analyzed these variations. The following continuations were discovered :—

5	B—B4
6 O—O	P—Q3
7 P—Q4	P × P
8 P × P	B—Kt3
9 P—Q5	Kt—R4

Not 9 ...., Kt–K4; 10 Kt × Kt, P × Kt; 11 B–R3.

| 10 B—Kt2 | Kt—K2 |

in order to use the open line should B × P.

| 11 B—Q3 | O—O |

White will now operate so as to advance the King's side Pawns P–B4—B5, etc., whereas Black will attempt to bring his Queen's side Pawns to bear. Whichever side is the first to arrive with the Pawns at the enemy's gate will win.

Again a wholly different picture.

9 Kt—B3	Kt—R4

Not 9 ...., Kt–B3, because 10 P–K5, P × P and again 11 B–R3.

10 B—Kt5	P—KB3
11 B—B4	Kt × B
12 Q—R4ch.	

and White stands firmly entrenched in the ntre.

And again, but not so strong

9 B—Kt2	KKt—K2
10 Kt—Kt5	P—Q4
11 P × P	Kt—R4
12 P—Q6	Kt × B
13 P × Kt	Q—Q4
14 Kt—QB3	Kt × B
15 Kt × Q	Kt × Q
16 KR × Kt	P—KR3

These various attacks may or may not succeed, but for the purpose of judging the value of the Gambit they are unfortunately not the measure. Black, by accepting the Gambit and then giving up his Pawn plus voluntarily, can strike a good bargain, because he thus escapes all peril and possibly gains a slight advantage over White.

7	B—Kt3

If White wants to change Queens, he can regain his Pawn. If not, Black will hold on to the Pawn, while refusing to exchange the KP. And thus White will

be blocked by the QBP and be without avenues of attack. If White foregoes 8 P × P, P × P; 9 Q × Q ch; Kt × Q; 10 Kt × P, which would allow Black a good Ending, he cannot set into motion his chain of King's side Pawns, since the presence of the Black KP would prevent it at its very inception.

This line of play is of account also in the variation

5	B—R4

If White wants to avoid the above defence, he cannot proceed with 6 O–O, P–Q3; 7 P–Q4, since then 7 .... B–Kt3 as above, and therefore he must immediately advance with the QP.

6 P—Q4	....

If Black now captures the Pawn with Pawn, White obtains the attack because the weak point KB2 can be guarded only by the Queen and in view of the many mobile White pieces the Queen in its turn becomes an object of attack, thus: 6 ...., P × P; 7 O–O, P × P; 8 Q–Kt3, Q–B3: 9 P–K5, Q–Kt3; 10 Kt × P, KKt–K2; 11 B–R3. Black will have to liberate himself, even at the expense of a pawn 11 ...., P–Kt4; 12 Kt × P, R–QKt1; 13 Q–R4; or 11 .... P–Q3; 12 P × P, P ×

P; 13 QR–Q1, O–O; or else Black will have to forego Castling, 11 .... B × Kt; 12 Q × B, P–Kt3; 13 KR–Q1, B–Kt2; 14 QR–B1, but all of this is rather unsatisfactory, undefined, aimless, as dancing upon a tight rope from which the dancer may easily fall (for instance, 14 .... Kt–R4; 15 B–Q3, Q–R4; 16 Q × P, B × Kt; 17 B–K2 wins). And during nearly the hundred years that the above position has been analysed, no final conclusion has been arrived at, which is significant of the validity of the position. For this reason the conscientious analyst is driven to recommend

6 ....   P—Q3

with the intention of turning into the variation discussed above.

If White wants to evade this line of play, he must immediately attack; the only target for attack at present is Black's KB2. Hence

7 Q—Kt3   Q—Q2

Not 7 ...., Q–K2, nor Q–B3 because of 8 P–Q5. In the position arrived at Black will have time to develop by means of Kt–B3, and O–O, etc., provided he is ever ready to give up his plus of a Pawn in the interest of rapid development.

On account of this readiness the masters, during the last thirty years, have little by little ceased the playing of Gambits.

Four Knights' Game.

1 P—K4	P—K4
2 Kt—KB3	Kt—QB3
3 Kt—B3	Kt—B3

This opening leads to no complications unless Black forces them. True, the latter strategy is perilous.

4 B—Kt5   ....

Herewith White obtains some pressure on K5.

4 ....   P—QR3

This reply is appropriate, since White must now make the decision—which diagonal the Bishop is to abandon or whether the Bishop should be exchanged.

5 B × Kt   ....

With 5 B–R4 White turns into variations of the Ruy Lopez. Black is then able to develop 5 ...., B–K2 or B–B4 without any disadvantage.

5 ....   QP × B
6 P—Q4   ....

Perhaps the strongest move. White would not obtain much by 6 Kt × P, Kt × P; 7 Kt × Kt, Q–Q5; 8 O–O, Q × KKt; 9 P–Q4, Q–KB4! because White

cannot get the Queen into
action. 10 R–K1, B–K3; 11
B–Kt5, P–R3, in order to
force the Bishop from one
of the two long diagonals
that it dominates. Now 12
Q–Q3 is beating the air,
since Black parries the
threat 13 Kt–Q6ch. simply
by 12 ...., K–Q2,
developing the QR at
the same time. Better
12 B–R4. True, Black
must be cautious here.
With 12 ...., P–KKt4?,
13 B–Kt3, O–O–O he
gets into trouble by 14
B–K5, R–Kt1; 15 Kt–B6,
R–Kt3? 16 P–KKt4. But
12 .... B–Q3 is all right;
13 P–KKt4, Q–QR4. A
decisive advantage cannot
be gained by White, 14 Kt
× Bch, P × Kt; 15 P–KB4,
P–KKt4; 16 P–B5, P × B;
17 P × B, P × P 18 R × Pch.
K–Q2; 19 Q–K2, QR–K1;
20 R–K1, Q × Rch. The
forced attacks leave White
weakened at the end.

6 ....   P × P

Black may also play 6
........., B–QKt5. Then 7
P × P, Q × Qch.; 8 K × Q,
B × Kt; 9 P × Kt, B × BP;
10 P–B3. White has a
slight initiative.

7 Q × P   Q × Q
8 Kt × Q   B–QKt5
9 P—B3

White has here the better
Pawn position, but Black

has two strong Bishops.
The Black Knight will
strive towards K4 or QB5.
White may have a slight
initiative, but that is in
order.

*Position after White's ninth
move*

Black may follow an alto-
gether different plan. He
may follow the moves of the
opponent, but, well understood, always on guard and
ready, if need be, to vary.

4 ....   B—Kt5
5 O—O   O—O
6 P—Q3   P—Q3
7 B—Kt5   ....

Up to this point every-
thing has gone the way of
undisturbed development,
but now 8 Kt–Q5 is threatening. Black must not
imitate White too long.
7 .... B–Kt5; 8 Kt–Q5,
Kt–Q5; 9 Kt × B, Kt × B;
10 Kt–Q5, Kt–Q5; 11 Q–
Q2. Thereby 12 B × Kt
followed by 13 Q–R6 is
menaced. 11 ......, Kt × Kt
ch; 12 P × Kt, B × P; 13 P–
KR3! First White moves

the King to safety.   13
.... K–R1; 14 K–R2,
R–KKt1; 15 R–KKt1, P–
B3; 16 Kt × Kt, P × Kt; 17
B–R4, R–Kt3; 18 Q–K3,
B–R4; 19 P–KB4 and
White should win.

7 ....   B × Kt
8 P × B   Q–K2

If 8 ...., Kt–K2;
9 Kt–R4, White easily
s u c c e e d s in advancing
P–KB4 a n d obtains a
lasting attack. A celebrated game, Schlechter
versus Duras, played at the
San Sebastian tournament
ran the following course : 7
........., Kt–K2; 8 Kt–KR4,
P–B3; 9 B–QB4, Kt–K1;
10 P–B4, B × Kt; 11 P × B,
P–Q4; 12 B–Kt3, P–B3; 13
P × KP, P × B; 14 R × Rch.
K × R; 15 Q–B3ch., K–
Kt1; 16 R–KB1, Kt–B2;
17 Q–B7ch., K–R1.
Schlechter here gave
his opponent a chance with
18 P × P, so changing the
order of the moves. 18
Q–B8ch., Q × Q; 19 R ×
Qch., Kt–Kt1; 20 P × P,
P × P; 21 Kt–B3. White
threatens to throttle Black :
21 ...., B–K3; 22 R ×
R, Kt × R; 23 Kt × P, Kt–
B2; 24 Kt × B, Kt × Kt; 25
B × P, and White won the
Ending.

9 R—K1   Kt–Q1
10 P–Q4   ....
White wants to open the
lines for his Bishops; Black
resists.

10 ....   Kt—K3
11 B—QB1   P—B3
12 B—B1   ....
Otherwise the Bishops
are in the way.

12 ....   Q—B2
13 P—Kt3   ....
(Rubinstein in *Lärobock
i. Schack.*)

13 ....   R—Q1
Black will have to play
patiently and guardedly.
He can take the initiative
with B–Q2, QR–B1, P–
QB4.
In recent years there have
been new and important
evolutions by Rubinstein,
Bogoljubow, Svenonius.
Rubinstein improved upon
an ancient variation.

4 ....   Kt—Q5
In hard-fought contests
with Rubinstein the following opinions were arrived
at :

5 Kt × P   Q–K2
Not 5 ...., B–B4 on
account of 6 B–K2, P–Q4;
7 Kt–Q3, B–Kt3; 8 P–K5,
Kt–K5; 9 O–O, P–QB3; 10
Kt–R4, and White liberates himself and maintains
his material advantage.

6 P–B4   Kt × B
7 Kt × Kt   P—Q3
8 Kt—KB3   Q × P ch
9 K—B2   Kt—Kt5 ch
10 K—Kt1   ....

Bogoljubow essayed too boldly, 10 K–Kt3. Then Black answers 10 ...., Q –Kt3, and the attack of Black becomes too strong. But after the text move the White King by P–KR3 finds a place of safety and then White obtains domination over the King's side and gains the initiative.

The idea of Svenonius is a very sound one. After 4 B–Kt5, B–Kt5; 5 O–O, O–O; 6 P–Q3, he moves 6 .... B × Kt; 7 P × B, P–Q4. Consequently, a complication arises in the centre.

8 B × Kt	P × B
9 Kt × P	Q—Q3
10 B—B4	R—K1
11 Q—B3	....

If 11 P × P, R × Kt; 12 P–Q4, R—K8; 13 B × Q, R × Q; 14 KR × R, P × B; 15 P × P, the following position arises.

Black to move

With 15 ...., B–K3 Black apparently has a defensible game, say 16 QR–Kt1, K–B1, 17 R–Kt7, R–B1.

11	P × P
12 P × P	R × Kt
13 QR—Q1	....

Not 13 KR—Q1 since this Rook has to guard the King. The sequence would be 13 ...., B–Kt5; 14 Q–Kt3, B × R; 15 B × R, Q–Q7.

13	B—Kt5

Position after Black's thirteenth move

14 Q—Kt3	....

14 R × Q leads to an easy Draw.

14	Kt × P
15 Q × B	Q—K3

(with equality)

The Ruy Lopez.

1 P—K4	P—K4
2 Kt—KB3	Kt—QB3
3 B—Kt5	....

The most logical of all Openings arising from the double step of the two King's Pawns. The attack directs itself against K5 anew.

The oldest defence is 3
.... P–Q3, which is the
most direct one. Surely a
sound and substantial one,
though it may not appeal
to the high-flown fancy.

3 ....   P—Q3
4 P—Q4   B—Q2

If 5 B × Kt, B × B; 6 P ×
P, B × P.

5 Kt—B3   Kt—B3
6 B × Kt   B × B
7 Q—Q3   ....

Black must now decide
what to do with his KP.
Obviously Q–K2, blocking
the Bishop, is doubtful, as
is Kt–Q2, which limits the
action of QB. However,
an unpretentious move suffices.

7 ....   P × P
8 Kt × P   B—Q2

Black desires to keep the
two Bishops and to guard
the point KB4.

*Position after White's
eighth move*

8 .... P–KKt3 is
tempting, but the Queen's
side is threatened. 9 Kt ×
B, P × Kt; 10 Q–R6, Q–
Q2; 11 Q–Kt7 winning a
Pawn. 8 .... B–K2
however may be ventured,
provided one keeps cool
under fire, 9 Kt–B5, O–O;
10 B–Kt5. Possibly 10
.........R–K1 would suffice.
11 O–O–O, B–B1 soon to be
followed by B–Q2, to drive
off some of the assailants.
Taken all in all, 8 ....
B–Q2, as above, seems ob-
vious.

9 P—KR3   B—K2
10 B—K3   O—O

White may now try O–
O–O, but then Black ob-
tains a target for attack in
proceeding with P–B3,
P–QKt4, etc. The game
seems evenly balanced.

Aggressive players have
often tried to start an immediate attack by

3 ....   P—B4

But White, who would
be unwise to play 4 P × P
allowing 4 .... P–K5,
which starts immediate
development.

4 Kt—B3   ....

and retains thereby an advantage. The continuation
might be

4 ....   Kt—B3
5 P × P   ....

White must not be too
fearful of attacks by Pawns

unsupported by pieces. The advancing Pawns of the opponent are soon attacked by Pawns and thereby work to the advantage of the player who has the greater number of pieces developed.

5 ....   P—K5
6 Kt—Kt5   Kt—Q5
7 P—Q3   ....

White will be able to keep the Pawn.

A defence which well satisfies the rules of development laid down at the beginning of this chapter is

3 ....   Kt—B3

whereby the White KP is threatened, neutralizing White's pressure upon the Black KP. White may proceed slowly, for instance, with Kt–B3, but if he desired to give motion to the game, to play a sharp, a biting game. he must not pause to parry this menace, but must find some new threat. In this position, Castling is suggestive of such threat for it liberates the Rook for use on the King's file.

4 O—O   Kt × P

The important Pawn is captured. Now not R–K1 at once; this move must be reserved until it carries a definite menace. It is more urgent to combat the minor pieces which would obstruct the Rook after its taking the field.

5 P—Q4 !   ....
If now 5 ...., P × P, 6 R–K1 is very dangerous.

5 ....   B—K2
To block the King's file.

6 Q–K2   ....
To use the Rook on the Queen's file if desirable.

6 ....   Kt—Q3
Defence as well as counter-attack.

7 B × Kt   KtP × B
The QP must safeguard the Queen against the Rook. If 7 ...., QP × B; 8 P × P, Kt–B4; 9 R–Q1, B–Q2; 10 P–K6, P × P; 11 Kt–K5 which threatens also Q–R5ch.

8 P × P   Kt—Kt2

Position after Black's eighth move

So far the attack of White has taken a logical course and results in the cramping of the Black pieces. But now they are out of immediate danger and ready to mass themselves for a counter-thrust. Evidently, White, who has conducted his attack with an astonishingly small number of troops, must now hurry to develop his reserves.

9 Kt—B3 O—O
10 R—K1 Kt—B4

White hinders P–Q4, Black attempts to force it.

11 Kt—Q4 ....

Now that the Black Knight blocks the KB, the White Kt. may safely occupy this central spot.

11 .... Kt—K3
12 B—K3 Kt × Kt
13 B × Kt ....

Even now 13 ...., P–Q4 is prevented, since in reply thereto White with 14 Kt–R4 would get permanent control of the square QB5, thus blocking the doubled Pawn.

13 .... P—QB4
14 B—K3 P—Q4

At last! Black will now fight offensively.

15 P × P e.p. B × P
16 Kt—K4 B—Kt2 !

Not 16 ...., B × Pch., 17 K × B, Q–R5ch., etc., because then the White Bishop would become too strong.

17 Kt × B ....

The QBP cannot be captured, viz., 17 B × P, B × B; 18 Kt × B, B × P; 19 K × B, Q–Kt4 ch.

17 .... P × Kt
18 QR—Q1 Q—B3
19 P—QB4 KR—K1
20 Q—Kt4 R—K3

Position after Black's twentieth move

If 21 B—Kt5, R × R ch; 22 R × R, Q × P; 23 Q–Q7, P–KR3. And if 21 B–B4, then 21 .... QR–K1.

A great many questions arise as soon as Black by

3 .... P—QR3

challenges the intentions of the White Bishop.

4 B—R4 ....

Of course, this is not forced. White might reply 4 B–B4 or B–K2 without getting into peril. And 4 B × Kt is quite playable as will be shown hereafter. But the above move is the most aggressive one, since it preserves the Bishop for future

action against the King besides maintaining the pressure on the square K5.

4 ....   Kt—·B3
5 Kt—B3   ....

A strong move—but it
has the disadvantage of
blocking the BP and thus
limiting the action of the
KB.

5 ....   B—B4
6 Kt × P   ....

6 P–Q3 is also good, but
the natural tendency of
White is to develop a field
of action.

6 ....   Kt × Kt
7 P—Q4   B—Q3
8 P × Kt   ....

This is the main varia-
tion. White has, however,
another move at his dis-
posal that is worth considering : 8 P–B4, Kt–B5 ; 9 P–
K5, O–O ; 10 O–O, P–Q
Kt4 ; 11 B–Kt3, B–Kt2 ; 12
P × B, P × P ; 13 P–B5.

*Position after White's
thirteenth move in the
sub-variation*

Black will here probably
proceed with 13 .... P–
R3. White has gained
much room but has driven
his Pawns relentlessly forward leaving at their rear
many spots that have to be
defended by the pieces only,
should Black succeed in obtaining the attack. There
is both profit and peril in
such impetuous advances.
The student, of course, has
to try them and to seek their
lesson.

The main play proceeds
8 ....   B × P
9 Kt—K2   ....

*Position after White's
ninth move in main
variation.*

White threatens P–KB4.
He evidently holds the
upper-hand in the centre,
though Black, with P–QKt4
and P–QB4 and B–Kt2 will
provide for the present
emergency.

Black does better by far to proceed safely.

5 .... B—K2

White has now little drive except against the KP. Of course, not 6 B × Kt, QP × B ; 7 Kt × P, Kt × P !. First the preparation.

6 O—O P—QKt4
7 B—Kt3 P—Q3

White will now challenge the Pawn at QKt5.

8 P—QR4 R—QKt1

This move seems yielding, but B l a c k, being initially on the defensive, is justified in that attitude. A premature attack may easily prove a boomerang, viz., 8 ...., B–Kt5; 9 P × P, Kt–Q5; 10 R × P, thus keeping the Black Queen busy, which therefore cannot get to QB in time to support the onslaught. For instance, 10 ...., R–QB1; 11 P–Q3 followed by 12 B–K3, supporting the King at the right moment.

Again, if 8......... P–Kt5; 9 Kt–Q5, Kt × P; 10 P–Q4, the lines are opened to the heavy artillery of White, 10 .... O–O; 11 R–K1, Kt–B3; 12 Kt × B ch, Q × Kt; 13 B–Kt5 threatening 14 B–Q5.

9 P × P P × P

Position after Black's ninth move

White has hardly any a d v a n t a g e. 10 P–R3 seems necessary, to limit the range of the Black QB.

But White can proceed sharply and thus contrive to give life and vigour to the game.

5 O—O Kt × P
6 P—Q4 P—QKt4
7 B—Kt3 P—Q4
8 P × P ....

The aggressive move 8 P–QR4 is aggressive at the wrong spot, as Schlechter demonstrated in his match against me. Black replies 8 .... Kt × QP; 9 Kt × Kt; P × Kt; 10 P × P (10 Q × P, B—K3), B–QB4; 11 P–QB3, O–O; 12 P × P, B–Kt3 with an even game.

8 .... B—K3
9 P—B3 ....

in order to make room for the cramped KB and to obtain a support for the Knight on Q4

9 .... B—K2

Position after Black's ninth move

Black is now ahead of White in development, so White must hasten to catch up.

10 QKt—Q2   O—O

10 .... Kt-B4; 11 B-B2, P-Q5; 12 Kt-K4 would leave the important point K5—and therefore the centre—at the command of White.

11 B—B2   P—B4
12 P × P e.p. Kt × P(B3)
13 Kt—Q4   ....

Thus White obtains some superiority on Q4 and a slight advantage in consequence.

In the diagrammed position many plans were essayed, among others that of an attack without preliminary development. This adventure gave rise to the "Breslau" variation.

10 R—K1   O—O
11 Kt—Q4   Kt × P

To guard with 11 ...., Q-Q2? loses deservedly by 12 Kt × B followed by 13 R × Kt. At all times where an opponent launches an impudent attack with an insufficient number of pieces, one must not retreat but counterattack, even at the price of a sacrifice. Black, for the rest, has here no choice. With 11 .... Kt-R4; 12 B-B2, P-QB4; 13 Kt × B, P × Kt; 14 B × Kt, P × B; 15 Kt-Q2, P-K6; 16 R × P, B-Kt4; 17 R-K1, B × Kt; 18 Q × B; Black gets nowhere.

12 P—B3   B—Q3
13 P × Kt?   ....

White should not play to win. He should be content with 13 B-KB4. Then 13 ...., P-QB4; 14 B × Kt, proposal of peace, 14 ...., P × Kt, which is accepted (if 14 ...., B × B; 15 P × Kt, P × Kt; 16 KP × P, White has the best of it); 15 B × P. Now the QB stands ready to guard the points KB2 and KKt1, and Black will have to ponder whether to extend his punitive expedition any farther. After 15 .... Kt-B4 White still stands weak on the King's side, but he can with impunity reply 16 Kt-Q2 and save the day.

The Breslau variation, however, is the continued

attempt by White to play to win until the bitter end.

13	....	B—KKt5
14	Q—Q2	Q—R5
15	P—KR3	....

Kt–Q6 was threatened.

| 15 | .... | P—QB4 |

Black has now a strong position however White may proceed. And he always remains a little stronger than White no matter what the first player may attempt or invent. For instance, 16 R–K3, P × Kt; 17 BP × P, Kt–B5; 18 B × Kt, QP × B; 19 P–K5, B–B2; 20 P × B, B–Kt3; 21 Q –Q1, QR–Q1; 22 R–K4, P–B4; 23 P × P in passing, KR–K1. The above position has been analysed many thousands of times, without conclusive results; t h e prevalent opinion is that Black has the advantage and, with best play, should win the game.

The following valuable variation is by Rubinstein

16	Q—KB2	Q × Qch.
17	K × Q	B—Q2
18	Kt—B5	B × Kt
19	P × B	Kt—Q6ch.
20	K—B1	Kt × R
21	K × Kt	KR—K1ch.
22	K—B2	R—K4

with decided advantage.

An altogether different turn is given to the game if Black abstains from the capture of the KP and in- stead aims at development. Two developing moves are effective.   Firstly

5	....	P—Q3
6	R—K1	P—QKt4
7	B—Kt3	Kt—QR4
8	P—Q4	Kt × B
9	RP × Kt	B—Kt2
10	B—Kt5	....

Herewith White exerts some pressure.

Position after White's tenth move

Secondly

5	....	B—K2
6	R—K1	P—QKt4
7	B—Kt3	P—Q3

The two modes of development are interchange- able.

| 8 | P—B3 | .... |

in order to guard the KB against exchange

8	....	Kt—QR4
9	B—B2	P—QB4
10	P—Q4	Q—B2

White's problem is whether to prevent Black

pinning his Kt by 11 ...., B–Kt5 or whether he may safely allow it. Shall he play 11 P–KR3 now, or should he have played it before? To me it seems better not to lose time with such slow, defensive moves so early in the game.

Position after Black's tenth move

Judging the position, it appears that the White QKt aims at the square KB1 whence it can go to K3 or Kt3, the White QR desires to occupy QB1 the QB has not made up its mind whether to go to Kt5, K3 or perhaps Kt2. Black, on the other hand, desires to take possession of the QB's file, to exert pressure on Q5 and to use his QB, which stands mobile and efficient, for m a n i f o l d threats.

The possibilities are many and diverse. For instance,

11	QKt—Q2	Kt—B3
12	P—Q5	Kt—Q1
13	Kt—B1	O—O
14	P—KR3	Kt—K1
15	P—KKt4	P—B3
16	Kt—Kt3	Kt—B2

Black will play P–Kt3 and Kt–Kt2; White will try to force an entrance for his Rooks on the KKt's file by posting his Knight on B5. Again

11	QKt—Q2	Kt—B3
12	Kt—B1	BP × P
13	P × P	B—Kt5
14	P—Q5	Kt—Q5
15	B—Q3	Kt—R4
16	Kt—Kt3	Kt—B5
17	B—B1	P—Kt4
18	B—K3	....

All in all, in this variation the law of action is rather dictated by White. But Black, by abstaining from this demonstration on his QB4 can choose a simpler line of play.

| 8 | .... | O—O |
| 9 | P—Q4 | B—Kt5 |

Position after Black's ninth move

Black plans something like this: 10 B–K3, R–K1; 11 QKt–Q2, P–Q4. The question is only, if 10 B–Kt5 would not give the game a turn, since after the exchange of that Bishop for Knight the move B–Q5 would threaten to hamper the Black Knight greatly. Also 10 P–QR4, which would keep the Black Queen busy, is effective. Enough, there are still problems to be solved; the whole truth in Chess is not by any means all known yet —*fortunately*.

Finally, White may follow the plan to lose no time whatever and accordingly even give up his precious KB.

4	B × Kt	QP × B
5	P—Q4	P × P
6	Q × P	Q × Q
7	Kt × Q	....

Black must not refuse this simplification, otherwise he loses too much space. Now White has four Pawns against three on the King's side, Black has a Doubled Pawn on the Queen's side and therefore difficulties in obtaining a Passed Pawn except with the aid of his pieces. But he has efficient pieces and need have no apprehensions in entering upon the struggle.

7	....	B—Q3
8	Kt—QB3	B—Q2
9	B—K3	O—O—O
10	O—O—O	....

White and Black, of course, are at liberty to choose other lines of play. To determine whether this plan is a little superior to that plan or not, we have discovered, as yet, no means but patient and repeated trial.

Significant is it, however, that the move P–KB3, ordinarily weak becomes very effective after the exchange of the hostile KB. This observation is due to Steinitz. Dr. Bernstein has applied it happily in the above question, in recommending against 5. Kt–B3 the defence 5 ...., P–B3 in this " Exchange " variation.

The Ruy Lopez Opening will continue to set tasks and offer fertile suggestions to Chess masters for a long time to come. This Opening is dearest and nearest to the spirit of the old game —that spirit, which dislikes rigid dogmas but, on the contrary, loves motion and struggle.

The Half-Open Games.

If White or Black on the first move advances P–K4, whereas the opponent holds the KP back, one-half of the board is open to the play of pieces whereas the other half abounds with obstructions.

An accurate theory of these Openings does not as yet exist. One can only say that White should strive to hold the centre without advancing Pawns until he has his Rooks ready; then he may push his Pawns with the intention of opening lines for these powerful pieces. The defence should resist the opening of lines, at least until it has exchanged a hostile Bishop. The attack must lose no time, the defence no space.

The Nimzowitsch Defence.

1 P—K4   Kt—QB3

White will now desire to make P–K4 difficult.

2 P—Q4   P—Q4

Black thus disputes with White the possession of the centre. If now 3 P–K5 Black may develop 3 .... B–B4 and fight for the point K5, particularly should White push P–KB4. To be sure, White would have no bad game after 3 P–K5, B–B4; 4 B–K3, P–K3; 5 B–Q3, KKt–K2; 6 Kt–K2, but nothing to boast of. To maintain mobility is the better strategy.

3 Kt–QB3   P × P
4 P—Q5   ....

None of the squares to which the Kt can go can be conveniently supported so he best retreats.

4 ....   Kt—Kt1
5 Kt × P   P—K3

Alternatively Black may try 5 .... P–K4.

6 B—QB4

The centre is opened; hence, pieces must hurry into it.

6 ....   Kt—KB3
7 B—Kt5   B—K2
8 B × Kt   B × B
9 P × P   B × KP
10 Q × Qch.   B × Q
11 B × B   P × B

White has a slight advantage. Black would have done better with 6 ...., B–K2, but White has advantage also then by making the capture at K6. If 6 ...., Q–K2; 7 Q–K2.

The Nimzowitsch Defence is quite playable. It is an opening which suits that kind of temperament which can defend patiently and at times assail surprisingly and fiercely.

White may turn it into a branch of the Centre Counter treated later.

The Fianchetti.

1 P—K4   P—KKt3
The King's Fianchetto
1 P—K4   P—QKt3
The Queen's Fianchetto.

Ancient Openings, presumably invented at a time before our rule of Castling was introduced, and when another form of Castling, a jump of the King over two squares was lawful. These were sane rules, and it would have been better if they had not been changed. After that unfortunate change, the Fianchetti lost their original purpose of providing a safe square for the King and developing the Rooks. To-day they present a weakness in that they leave the centre of the board in the control of the enemy. True, they do not present targets in the centre either, but a fighter is used to being a target as well as a shot.

One can only conjecture the course of the game, since rigid analysis of the multitude of possibilities is out of the question.

1 P—K4   P—KKt3
2 P—Q4   B—Kt2
3 Kt—KB3   P—Q3
4 Kt—B3   Kt—Q2

So far White has had no serious problems, but now it becomes difficult to find a weak point in the Black camp that can be assailed.   Well, it may be worth while to aim for the Black KB that defends the points KB3 and KR3.

5 B—K3   KKt—B3
6 P—KR3   ....

It is necessary to safeguard the QB, otherwise White's plan can be stopped by 6 .... Kt-Kt5.

6 ....   O—O
7 Q—Q2   P—K4

Now Black has his KR in play and therefore advances in the centre.

8 B—Q3   P × P
9 B × P   R—K1
10 O—O—O   ....

White Castles Queen's side because he has a target for his KR in view by advancing P—KR4—KR5; also he thus develops his QR. White has the freer game.

Similarly, the Queen's Fianchetto.

1 P—K4   P—QKt3
2 P—Q4   B—Kt2
3 Kt—QB3   Kt—KB3
4 B—Q3   P—K3
5 Kt—B3   ....

White must be careful not to advance Pawns beyond the fourth line before he has his Rooks ready.

5 ....   P—B4
To lay hold on the point K4

6 O— O   P—B5
Very problematical.
7 B × P   Kt × P
8 Kt × Kt   B × Kt
9 R—K1   B—Kt2
10 P—Q5   ....

Once the position is
opened, White will hold
the advantage.

Alekhin's Defence.

1 P—K4   Kt—KB3
This Opening is the re-
fuge of all those wishing to
get out of the books.   It
also has the advantage of
variety. On the other hand,
it is not altogether logically
satisfying.

2 P—K5   ....

The indicated move,
since otherwise Black, not
White, would assume the
initiative.

2 ....   Kt—Q4

White cannot permit the
Knight to stay in the
centre; it is best to ask it
at once where it wishes to
lodge.

3 P—QB4   Kt—Kt3
4 P—Q4   P—Q3
5 P—B4   ....

These moves are pre-
scribed if White desires to
maintain his central Pawn
formation. The idea un-
derlying this defence is on
the other hand to allow this
formation and then to proceed to break it up.

5 ....   P × P
6 BP × P   Kt—B3

Black makes this move
with a divided mind. He
would like to advance 6
........., P—QB4, but for the
present this counter-thrust
is easily parried by 7 P—Q5.
If 6 ...., P—K3; 7 Kt–
QB3 again prevents 7
........., P—QB4, Black certainly bears constantly in
mind the idea of advancing
the QBP, that shall break
the chain of White Pawns.

7 B—K3   ....

Not 7 Kt–KB3 because
of 7 ...., B—Kt5, and
the Knight is embarrassed,
since the Pawns on B4 and
Q4 are under pressure. The
advance 8 P–K6 fails on account of 8 .... P × P
followed by the counter-
sacrifice 9 .... P–K4; 10
P–Q5, Kt–Q5; and a speedy
P–K3.

7 ....   B—B4
8 QKt—B3   P—K3
9 Kt—B3   ....

*Position after White's ninth
move*

Here Black must come to a decision whether he wishes to resume his plan of P–QB4, mentiond on preceding page, or whether he should rather put pressure on the QP and play for development. The attack 9 ……… Kt–Kt5; 10 R–B1, P–B4; 11 B–K2 is undertaken by a minority of pieces and should lead to nothing but trouble. Black will scarcely be able to do better than

9 ………   Q—Q2
10 B—K2   O—O—O

White's threat by 11 B–Kt5 is only apparent, for though the KBP is weak White's QP is equally so. In reality Black is threatening 11 ……… P–B3.

11 Q—Q2   P—B3

If first 11 ………, B–K2; 12 R–Q1, the advance of the KBP is no longer so powerful.

12 P × P   P × P
13 O—O   ………

The situation has cleared. White, his BP and QP holding the central position is assured of the initiative remaining in his hands. He is strong also on the KB's file. Black has the KKt's file. This is no position in which the master may take a nap. It is a breeding-ground for combinations. True, White seems to have the stronger position, but this may not be the judgment of History. We must thank Alekhin for his discovery of the possibilities latent in 1 ……… Kt–KB3.

The From Gambit.

1 P—KB4   P—K4
2 P × P   ………

To capture the Pawn is better than to decline the offer by 2 P–Q3 or 2 P–K4.

2 ………   P—Q3
3 P × P   B × P
4 Kt—KB3   ………

Black's attack formerly ran 4 ………, Kt–KR3; 5 ………, Kt–Kt5; and 6 ………, Kt × P. To spoil this plan Lipke invented the defence 5 P–Q4, 6 Q–Q3, 7 Q–K4 ch. which is sufficient.

4 ………   P—KKt4

I played this in my match against Bird, in 1890.

5 P—Q4   P—Kt5
6 Kt—K5   B × Kt
7 P × B   Q × Q ch
8 K × Q   Kt—QB3
9 Kt—B3   B—K3
10 B—Kt5 !   ………

in order to prevent 10 ……… O–O–O (Rubinstein).

10 ………   Kt × P
11 Kt—Kt5 !   K—Q2
12 K—K1   B—B5
13 R—Q1 ch   K—B3
14 Kt—Q4 ch   K—Kt3
15 P—K3   P—KB3
16 B—R4   R—KB1

White now has the initiative. To develop the Black KKt is no easy task. True, the White KP is weak, but, all in all, to counter the Openng 1 P–KB4 with a Gambit is not wise; the simple 1 ...., P–Q4 is stronger.

Caro-Kann.

| 1 | P—K4 | P—QB3 |
| 2 | P—Q4 | P—Q4 |

The idea of Black's first move is to prepare for his second. His QP is thoroughly secured, and is a menace to White's KP.

After 3 P–K5 Black could develop all his pieces at his ease by B–B4, P–K3, QKt –Q2, and if occasion arises P–QB4, etc. Black has difficulties only if 3 P × P or 3 Kt–QB3 or possibly 3 P–KB3.

| 3 | P × P | .... |

If 3 .... Q × P Black's first move seems almost wasted. Therefore

| 3 | .... | P × P |
| 4 | P—QB3 | .... |

To secure the QP and to give the Q access to the Q side.

4	....	Kt—QB3
5	B—Q3	Kt—B3
6	P—KB4 ?	....

Hereby White becomes strong on K5 but weak on K4.

6	....	B—Kt5
7	Kt—B3	P—K3
8	O—O	B—Q3
9	Q—Kt3	Q—B2
10	Kt—K5	B—KB4

Black thus dominates K5 and is safe.

6	Kt—B3	B—Kt5
7	QKt—Q2	P—K3
8	O—O	B—Q3
9	R—K1	O—O
10	Kt—B1	....

Position after White's tenth move

A calm position, Black has a target for attack in the Pawn at QB3 which he can seek to engage by P–QKt4–Kt5, in order to open lines for his Rooks and possibly to weaken the White QP. White can make this plan illusory by P–QR4. Besides, he has chances on the King's side. Taken all in all, the position is exceedingly balanced.

3 P—KB3 ....

with the intention of holding the centre. Black

cannot reduce this plan *ad absurdum* simply by 3 ...., P×P; 4 P×P, P–K4, because White then develops rapidly with 5 Kt–KB3, P×P; 6 B–QB4.

3 ....   P—K3
4 Kt—B3   P—QB4!

This is the best counter to White's plan.

5 P×QP   KP×P
6 P×P   P—Q5
7 Kt—K4   P—B4

Not 7 ...., B×P; 8 Kt×B, Q–R4ch., as the German edition mistakenly has it, because of 9 P–B3!

8 Kt—Q6 ch B×Kt
9 P×B   Q×P

Black has a point of invasion at K6 where he might try to post a Knight. White's third move now proves a hindrance to his own development and is therefore useless.

The strongest line of play is

3 Kt—QB3   P×P
4 Kt×P   Kt—B3
5 Kt×Kt ch ....

5 Kt–QB3 is possible, but not 5 Kt–Kt3 which is met by 5 .... P–K4.

5 ....   KP×Kt

Thus White has the advantage on the Queen's side, although Black, by virtue of his rapid development and his Pawn plus on the King's side, has enough force to make counter-play.

6 B—QB4   ....

Here White dominates the important points Q5 and K6.

6 ....   B—Q3
7 Q—K2 ch   B—K2

Black had better avoid the exchange of Queens, since White has advantages for the Ending while Black has opportunities for attack against the King.

8 Kt—B3   O—O
9 O—O   R—K1
10 R—K1   Kt—Q2
11 P—B3   Kt—Kt3
12 B—Kt3   ....

In a celebrated game, Forgacs *versus* Dr. Bernstein, White in this position, followed the plan B–Q3, P–QKt3, P–QB4.

12 ....   B—KKt5
13 B—Q2   ....

Position after White's thirteenth move

White's plan is to make his Queen's side Pawns tell and to undertake no offen-

sive on the King's side.
Black will try to provoke
White to move one of his
King's side Pawns which
will then be a mark of attack
for his Pawn majority on
the K side. With first class
play, say in a correspon-
dence game between masters
White may be found to hold
a minute advantage.

The Centre Counter Opening.

1 P—K4   P—Q4

An essentially sound
idea. Black disputes the
centre from the very start.
It is his aim to neutralize
each piece. White de-
velops by opposing to it an
equivalent piece and to proceed with his own development as rapidly as possible.
To give an instance:

2 P×P   Q×P
3 Kt—QB3   Q—QR4
4 P—Q4   P—K4
5 Kt—B3   B—KKt5
6 P×P   Kt—QB3
7 B—K2   B—Kt5
8 O—O   KKt—K2

The Pawn cannot be
saved. The later it is captured, the better.
To meet this plan of
campaign White must
avoid exchanges of minor
pieces. Then the Black
Queen will at last become a
target. Such is also the

meaning of the following
play:

4 Kt—B3   Kt—QB3
5 B—K2   B—Kt5
6 P—KR3   B—R4
7 O—O   Kt—B3
8 P—Q3   P—K3
9 B—Q2   ………

Black finds it difficult to
discover a secure place for
his Queen. Note that KR4,
which would be advantag-
eous, is blocked by the QB,
hence the move 6 P–KR3,
that otherwise would be
questionable. Possibly this
move might have been post-
poned to a later stage with
equal effect.

*Position after White's
ninth move*

It remains for us to con-
sider the attitude White
should adopt if Black does
not at once recapture the
Pawn. In this case it is
hardly advisable to hold on
to it since Black would then
get a rapid and efficient
development. By his wil-

lingness to abandon the Pawn plus, White may get an even better development than in the preceding variations.

2	Kt—KB3
3 P—Q4	Q × P
4 Kt—QB3	Q—QR4
5 Kt—B3	....

and now 5 .... P—K4 is out of the question. And if

5	B—Kt5
6 P—KR3	B—R4
7 P—KKt4	B—Kt3
8 Kt—K5	....

and the Queen is assailed at once, whereby White gains another move, because a developing move, such as 8 .... QKt—Q2, would be answered by 9 Kt–B4, Q–R3; 10 P–Q5, whereby the Queen is shut in. Therefore

8	Kt—K5
9 B–-Kt2	Kt × Kt

10 O–Q2 with favourable development. And if

3	Kt × P
4 P—QB4	Kt—KB3
5 Kt—KB3	....

White has a phalanx of Pawns in the centre and has thus far the best of it.

The Sicilian Defence.

1 P—K4	P–-QB4
2 Kt—KB3	P–-K3
3 P—Q4	P × P
4 Kt × P	....

Thus White, not Black, dominates the point Q4.

4	Kt—KB3

Black prevents P–QB4 which would control Q5 as well as QKt5, hampering the Black Pawns.

5 Kt—QB3	....

It cannot be helped the QBP must be blocked.

5	Kt—B3

Whether this Knight should rather aim for Q2 is a question. Presumably, either variation is playable.

6 Kt × Kt	KtP × Kt

Otherwise, White, without having to run risks, would have a slight advantage by exchanging Queens.

7 P—K5	Kt—Q4
8 Kt—K4	Q—B2
9 P—KB4	....

thus a game of mine against Lipschutz.

9	P—KB4
10 P × P e.p.	Kt × P(B3)
11 Kt × Kt ch	P × Kt
12 Q—R5 ch	K—Q1

Position after Black's twelfth move

White has an attack against the King, but the position is very difficult inasmuch as Black has strong Pawns and good mobility. As an instance

13 B—K3   P—Q4
14 O—O—O   Q—KKt2
15 B—B4   B—Q2

and the attack against the King has considerable difficulties to overcome.

White's better plan is

13 B—Q2   P—Q4
14 O—O—O   ....

with eventually P—B4 to loosen the array of Pawns.

The tempting

5 ....   B—Kt5

is probably weaker. White simply develops.

6 B—Q3   ....

and now threatens an attack against the King's side, for instance,

6 ....   P—Q4
7 P—K5   KKt—Q2
8 Q—Kt4   ....

whereupon Black must weaken the King's side. And if

6 ....   Kt—B3
7 Kt × Kt   KtP × Kt
8 P—K5   Kt—Q4
9 Q—Kt4   P—Kt3
10 O—O   ....

and Black can win the Pawn only by giving away his fine KB, whereupon Black is in trouble on the Black squares, particularly after White plays B–R3.

Immensely more difficult becomes the game if Black plays to hold on to his KB and also keeps his QP back

2 Kt—KB3   P—K3
3 P—Q4   P × P
4 Kt × P   Kt—KB3
5 Kt—QB3   P—Q3
6 B—K2   B—K2
7 O—O   O—O
8 B—K3   Kt—B3
9 P—B4   Q—B2
10 Q—K1   P—QR3

in order to push P–QKt4 and to obtain for the QB a favourable diagonal.

11 B—B3   Kt—QR4
12 R—Q1   Kt—B5
13 B—B1   ....

Position after White's thirteenth move

White has covered his weaknesses well and also threatens an attack by Q–Kt3 or P–KKt4, but Black has counter-play on the Queen's side and also in the centre, where he can advance P–K4 under many conditions.

Black can also Fianchetto his KB, but then he must not move the KP, thus keeping the QB free and continuing to guard KB3 with a Pawn.

2	Kt—QB3
3 P—Q4	P × P
4 Kt × P	Kt—B3
5 Kt—QB3	P—Q3
6 B—K2	P—KKt3
7 O—O	B—Kt2
8 B—K3	O—O

Not 8 ...., P–Q4 because of 9 B–QKt5.

9 K—R1   ....

Position after White's ninth move.

White will attempt to get an opening by P–KB4. Again Black has chances on the Queen's side and in the centre. For instance: 9 ...., P–Q4; 10 Kt × Kt, P × Kt; 11 P–K5. The attempt to convert the Sicilian Defence into a Gambit is feeble.

1 P—K4	P—QB4
2 P—QKt4	P × P
3 P—QR3	P—Q4
4 P × QP	Q × P
5 B—Kt2	P—-K4

and Black is well developed.

All in all, the Sicilian Opening is full of tension.

The French Defence.

1 P—K4   P—K3

A very logical move, developing, and at the same time preparatory to 2 .... P–Q4 which engages the White KP and forces White to a far-reaching decision.

| 2 P—Q4 | P—Q4 |
| 3 Kt—QB3 | .... |

In case of the exchange 3 P × P, P × P, the game tends to a draw of which the symmetrical variation 4 Kt–KB3, Kt–KB3; 5 B–Q3, B–Q3; 6 O–O, O–O; 7 B–KKt5, B–KKt5; 8 P–B3, QKt–Q2; 9 QKt–Q2, P–B3; 10 R–K1, Q–B2; 11 Q–B2, KR–K1 furnishes a frightful instance. To produce a tension only two ways seem practicable—the advance P–QB4 or Castling Queen's side, but in either case the peril seems greater than the gain, so that such an enterprise hardly seems justified, least of all for the second player.

3 ....   Kt—KB3

With 3 .... P × P Black would leave the point K5 to White, but even then he would have a sound position.

4 B—Kt5   ....

If 4 B–Q3, P–B4!; 5 Kt–B3, P × QP; 6 KKt × P, P–K4; 7 Kt–B3, P–Q5; and Black has nothing to fear.

4 ....   B—K2
5 P—K5   KKt—Q2
6 P—KR4   ....

For Black to accept this sacrifice is hazardous and hardly advisable; he will be unable to bring his plus to bear upon the struggle, even if he survives the attack. From the immense multitude of possibilities an instance—alas! only one out of so many—may be given here : 6 .... B × B ; 7 P × B, Q × P; 8 Kt–R3, Q–R3 ; 9 P–KKt3, P–R3 ; 10 P–B4, and White has an excellent development and many targets for attack besides.

6 ....   O—O

If 6 .... P–QB4; 7 Kt –Kt5, P × P?; 8 Kt–Q6 ch, K–B1; 9 Q–R5 appears to win. And if 7 .... P–B3; 8 B–Q3 initiating a powerful attack.

7 B—Q3   R—K1
8 Q—R5   Kt—B1
9 R—R3

My brother, Dr. Berthold Lasker, has demonstrated that 9 ...., P–QB4 would lose. The analysis is a master-piece. It runs as follows : 9 ...., P–QB4; 10 R–B3, Kt–Kt3; 11 Kt–R3, Kt–Q2; 12 R × P!, K × R; 13 B × B!, K × B; 14 Q × P. Black is a R ahead and yet White obtains the advantage, no matter how Black may defend or attack. For instance, 14 ...., Kt–R1; 15 Q × Pch., Kt–B2; 16 Kt–KKt5, R–B1; 17 Kt × P. Black has no valid defence if 17 ...., R–KKt1; 18 Kt × Pch. is decisive. Similarly 14 ...., KKt × KP; 15 P × Kt, R–KKt1; 16 P–B4, Q–B1; 17 O—O—O. The position is full of finesse. For instance 17 ...., K–Q1; 18 Kt–KKt5!, Q × Pch.; 19 K–Kt1, R–K1; 20 Q × P, Q × RP; 21 Kt–Kt5 wins. Or 18 ...., Kt–Kt3; 19 P–B5, P × P; 20 P–K6, K–K2; 21 R–K1. Black is unable to obtain development. 21 .... R–R1 22 Q–Kt6, R–R3; 23 Q –B7ch. Or 21 ...., P–Q5; 22 Kt–Q1, Kt –Q4; 23 R–K5. And again 17 Kt–Kt3; 18 P–B5, P × P; 19 Kt–B4.

Black may seek counter-attack. 14 ...., Q–Kt3; 15 Q × Kt, Q × P; 16 K–Q2 !, Q × R; 17 Kt–KKt5 threatening mate in three. 17 ...., K–Q1; 18 Kt–Kt5 with an overwhelming attack.

The reader may himself complete the analysis of 14 ...., Q–Kt3. Black has other resources left, say 18 ...., R–K2 or 18 ...., Kt × P, but they are insufficient.

Again 14 ...., Q–R4; 15 Q × Kt, P × P; 16 Q–Kt5 ch., K–B1; 17 Q–B4ch. K–K2; 18 Q × P. White has two Pawns for the exchange and positional advantage. If 18 ...., Q–B2; 19 Kt–QKt5. Or 15 ...., K–Q1; 16 Q–Kt5 ch., R–K2. If 16 ...., K–B2; 17 P–R3, so as to menace P–QKt4 either at once or after P × P. 17 Kt–B4, Kt–B1; 18 P × P, P–Q5; 19 O–O–O.

The main variation was on

9 ....   QKt—Q2
10 R—B3   Kt—KKt3
                 or P—KB4

The resulting position is complicated and problematical.

Again

8 Q—Kt4   P—KB4
9 Q—R5   Kt—B1
10 P—KKt4   B × B
11 P × B   P—KKt3
12 Q—R6   P—B3

Position after Black's twelfth move

It is not easy to force an entrance into the Black camp. Black needs only to place a Rook on KKt2, in order to prevent the sacrifice of a Knight on KR4 or KKt3. Black can take the initiative on the extreme Queen's side. The QB dominates K3 and prevents a sacrifice on KB4.

In the French game the older masters, when playing White, used to open the square Q4 in order to occupy it with a Knight which thence exerts strong pressure. There are many ways to this goal, for instance, the one preferred by Steinitz.

1 P—K4   P—K3
2 P—Q4   P—Q4
3 Kt—QB3   Kt--KB3
4 P—K5   KKt—Q2
5 P—B4   P—QB4
6 P × P   Kt—QB3

Better than 6 .... B × P; 7 Q–Kt4; whereupon

Black must make some weakening move such as K–B1 or P–KKt3. One must not think, however, that this mistake would require Black to pay for it with the extreme penalty of losing.

7	B—K3	Kt × BP
8	Kt—B3	B—K2
9	B—Q3	O—O
10	Kt—K2	....

White secures Q4 even against P – K 3 as he simply captures. The game then slows down. As compensation f o r White's strong point in the centre Black has the QB's file.

The advance 3 P–K5 is not to be recommended unless White does so without losing a move thereby. Since the P on K5 is easily assailable, the QP must aid it and itself becomes a target. The White officers hardly get a fair chance in all this. Still, this line of play has also an advantage, namely, in White's gain of space. To give an instance,

2	P—Q4	P—Q4
3	P—K5	P—QB4
4	Kt—KB3	Kt—QB3
5	P × P	B × P
6	B—Q3	KKt—-K2
7	O—O	Kt—Kt3
8	B × Kt	RP × B
9	QKt—Q2	B—Q2
10	Kt—Kt3	B—Kt3
11	P—QR4	....

and again

4	....	Q—Kt3
5	P—B3	Kt—QB3
6	B—K2	P × P
7	P × P	KKt—K2
8	Kt—R3	Kt—B4
9	Kt—B2	B—Kt5 ch
10	K—-B1	P—KR4

These modes of development, which are numerous, are not aggressive. Still they do not lead to dead losses, but may, by good luck, produce good contests occasionally.

What a pity that the first player has it in his power to reduce the French game to a sterile and lifeless position almost certain to end in a draw! Otherwise, it would provide many a problem which would gladden the heart of every genuine Chess-lover.

English Opening or Sicilian on the First Move.

1	P—QB4	P—K4

Since the Sicilian yields a fair game to the second player, one is tempted to think that it should be proportionately stronger when essayed by the first player, who has all the advantages of that Opening and a move into the bargain.

2	Kt—QB3	Kt—KB3
3	Kt—B3	Kt—B3
4	P—Q4	P × P
5	Kt × P	Kt × Kt

A very unpretentious line of play which, however, seems sufficient.

6 Q × Kt	B—K2
7 P—KKt3	O—O
8 B—Kt2	P—Q3
9 O—O	Kt—Q2
10 Kt—Q5	Kt—Kt3

White has more room than Black but the Black position is free of weak spots.

Again

4 P—K3   ....

Shall Black now advance 4 ...., P–Q4? But after 5 P × P, Kt × P; 6 B–Kt5, the move which White is ahead gives him a far superior game than Black could obtain in the equivalent variation of the Sicilian.   Must Black play 4 .... P–Q3? White will then advance PQ4 and fare rather well, as for instance,

4	P—Q3
5 P—Q4	B—K2

If 5 ...., P × P; 6 Kt × P, and the White Knights are well posted.

6 B—K2	O—O
7 O—O	B—B4
8 P—QKt3	R—K1
9 B—Kt2	K—Q2

It is difficult for Black to obtain the initiative because White is in command of Q5 where the QKt can occasionally effect an entrance or where the QP may advance accordingly as White plans an attack by advancing his Pawns on the Queen's side or by concentration of pieces against the King.

If Black desires to do more than patiently wait for the initiative that White might be disposed to take, he will do well to keep the game closed and to imitate at first the moves of White.

1 P—QB4	P—QB4
2 Kt—QB3	Kt—QB3
3 Kt—B3	Kt—B3
4 P—Q4	P—Q4

If now 5 P–K3, then P–K3. But Black must be resolute enough to go on his own way, as, for instance, in the following variation:

5 B—Kt5	P × QP
6 KKt × P	Q—Kt3
7 KKt—Kt5	P × P
8 B × Kt	KtP × B
9 Kt—Q5	Q—R4 ch
10 Q—Q2	Q × Q ch
11 K × Q	B—R3 ch
12 P—K3	O—O
13 B × P	R—Q1
14 K—K2	B—Kt2
or 7 B—K3,	P—K4
8 Kt × Kt	Q × P

The above first four moves of Black are sound: that much is fairly certain. All the rest is speculative and is meant to be so and must in no way be considered as having gone through the mill of criticism and experience. The ground trodden above is yet rather new, and you may explore it as well as anybody else.

The Close Openings.

It is not so long ago that a game in which neither player advanced P-K4 was a rarity. Now such games, at least in the contests of masters, have become the rule.

Many causes have contributed thereto. The other Openings are already well known, and to try to introduce winning innovations into them has become a very risky business. In the Close Openings, on the contrary, not only is our knowledge limited, but even our analytical research has failed so far to produce definite and incontrovertible conclusions, for the results become perceptible only after many moves in a long drawn-out ending.

The methods which operate in these Openings are based not on "combination" but on " positional." play. These terms, their meanings, and their laws will be explained in the chapters that follow. In the meanwhile, not very much can be said on the theory of the Close Openings.

The Queen's Gambit.

1 P—Q4	P—Q4
2 P—QB4	....

To accept the Gambit is feasible, but it must not be done with the intent of holding fast to the Pawn.

2	P × P
3 Kt—KB3	....

Not 3 P–K3 on account of 3 ...., P–K4; 4 B × P, P × P; 5 P × P, B–Q3; whereupon Black's pieces are untrammelled.

3	P–K3

If 3 .... P–QKt4; 4 P–QR4, P–QB3; 5 P × P, P × P; 6 P–QKt3 regaining the Pawn easily with the superior game.

4 P—K3	Kt—KB3
5 B × P	P—QR3

in order to obtain development by P–QKt4

6 P—QR4	....

the Black QB shall not get an outlet.

6	P—B4
7 O—O	....

in order soon to be able to use the KR on the Queen's file.

7	Kt—B3
8 Kt—B3	B—K2
9 Q—K2	O—O
10 R—Q1	P × P
11 P × P	Kt—QKt5

*Position after Black's
eleventh move*

White has the initiative, Black is cramped. A method of development for Black is Q–R4, R–Q1, B–Q2, B–K1, QR–B1. Another one would be KKt–Q4, P–B4, P–QKt3. The pieces then are mobile, but the KP would be very weak.

Standard play is to decline the Gambit and to guard the QP by a Pawn.

2 ....   P—K3

This move protects as well as develops.

3 Kt—KB3   P—QB4

This move is worthy of consideration because Black thereby strengthens his centre so as to maintain the balance there. Its drawback is that the lines are opened very rapidly which benefits the first player more than the defence.

4 P × QP   ....

Herewith White wishes to create a vulnerable point in the Black camp whereas his own position on Q4 remains very strong.

4 ....   KP × P
5 Kt—B3   Kt—QB3
6 P—KKt3   ....

in order to exert pressure on Q5. With 6 B–Kt5, B–K2!; 7 B × B, KKt × B; 8 P–K3 (with 8 P × P, P–Q5, Black gains space whereas the Pawn plus cannot be long maintained); 8 ...... Q–Kt3; 9 Q–Q2, P × P; 10 P × P the game is equalized.

6 ....   Kt—B3

To play to exchange the QB by 6 ...., B–Kt5 would be weak. White would reply 7 B–Kt2 and be glad to give his Knight for the very mobile Bishop.

7 B—Kt2   B—K2
8 O—O   O—O
9 B—Kt5   B—K3

The QP requires this protection although the Bishop would otherwise be better off on B4 or Kt5.

10 P × P   B × P
11 R—B1   B—K2
12 Kt—Q4   Kt × Kt

in order to preserve the QB.

13 Q × Kt   Q—R4

These moves form a logical chain although their order may be changed.

*Position after Black's
thirteenth move*

I append a few further moves from a game, Marshall *versus* Rubinstein.

14	P—QKt4	Q—R6
15	Q—Q3	Q × KtP
16	B × Kt	B × B
17	Kt × P	B × Kt
18	B × B	QR—Q1

whereupon White has an advantage by his powerful well-supported Bishop.

1	P—Q4	P—Q4
2	P—QB4	P—K3
3	Kt—KB3	Kt—KB3
4	Kt—B3	QKt—Q2

Even though Black does not advance his QBP at once, he is well advised to keep himself ready to do so and therefore not to block the Pawn.

| 5 | B—Kt5 | B—K2 |

Also 5 .... P—B3 may very well be played. After 6 P—K3, Q—R4; 7 Kt–Q2, B–Kt5; 8 Q–B2, O–O; 9 B–K2, P × P; 10 B × Kt,

Kt × B; 11 Kt × P, Q–B2; Black may obtain play by his two Bishops, though in the centre White has a counter-balancing advantage.

6	P—K3	O—O
7	R—B1	R—K1
8	Q—B2	P—B3

White, having no other developing move to make, is now almost forced to play the KB.

9	B—Q3	P × P
10	B × P	Kt—Q4
11	Kt—K4	....

If 11 B × B, Q × B; Black may attempt to obtain an open game by Kt × Kt followed by P–K4.

| 11 | .... | Kt—B1 |

*Position after Black's
eleventh move*

Black will now slowly gain ground and beat back any attack since his position is void of weak spots.

1	P—Q4	P—Q4
2	P—QB4	P—QB3
3	Kt—KB3	Kt—KB3
4	Kt—B3	P × P

This is playable although White, with best play, always keeps the initiative.

5 P–K3   ………

If 5 P–QR4, B–B4 ; 6 P–K3, Kt–R3 ! ; 7 B × P, Kt–QKt5 ; the excellent position of the QKt gives Black a chance for a strong fight.

5	………	P—QKt4
6	P—QR4	P—Kt5
7	Kt—R2	P—K3
8	B × P	B—K2
9	O—O	O—O
10	Q—K2	QKt—Q2
11	R—Q1	P—B4
12	P—QKt3	Q—Kt3
13	B—Kt2	B—Kt2
14	Kt—B1	KR—Q1
15	Kt—Q3	………

Position after White's fifteenth move

White has a weak spot on QB3 that gives Black hope for counter-action.

Other defences to the Queen's Gambit, although playable, are difficult and cramped or not wholly sound.

Other Q.P. Games.

1 P—Q4

Black as well as White may vary from the above in manifold ways. White may play his QB to KB4 or to QKt2 or to Q2, Black may keep back his QP or advance it no farther than Q3 and develop his KB to Kt2. These lines of play, however, are not so vigorous as those treated above. They have variety, but not much point. A few instances must suffice.

1	………	P—Q4
2	B—B4	Kt—KB3
3	P—K3	P—B4
4	Kt—KB3	Kt—B3
5	B—Q3	P—K3
6	O—O	B—K2
7	P—B3	Q—Kt3
8	Q—B2	

And again

1	………	Kt—KB3
2	Kt—KB3	P—KKt3
3	P—B4	B—Kt2
4	Kt—B3	O—O
5	P—K3	P—Q3
6	B—Q3	QKt—Q2
7	O—O	P—K4

Now the game is "half open. See page 86.

| 8 | Q—B2 | R—K1 |
| 9 | B—Q2 | ……… |

White will place his
Rooks on K1 and Q1 with
the intention of then opening a line or two. He has
a firm and strong position.

To speak at length of
these lines of play would be
futile at this point. The
best way to become ac-
quainted with them is to
study them according to the
principles to be dealt with
in the chapters which follow. Besides, these variations are merely side issues.

Zukertort or Reti Opening.

1 Kt—KB3	P—Q4
2 P—QB4	....

A spiritual Opening
which possesses, it is true,
not so much force as
variety, but which is ex-
ceedingly plastic and therefore susceptible of being
turned into many wholly
different shapes.

Black is not bound down
to any particular defence.
He may for instance,
continue 2 .... P ×
P, or P–QB3 or P–K3
or PQ5: all these
moves are quite playable.
Black must not, however,
advance Pawns incautiously
or exchange centre Pawns
too readily for wing Pawns.

2	P—K3
3 P–QKt3	Kt—KB3
4 B—Kt2	P—B4
5 P—Kt3	Kt—B3
6 B—Kt2	P—QR4

In thus opening a way for
the QR, Black escapes the
necessity of providing an
exit for the QB. If
7 P × P Black might
will respond with 7 ....,
Kt × P; and though the
White QB exerts pres-
sure and perhaps forces P–
B3 Black has a good
centre. If White does not
play 7 P × P, the Black QP
may finally slip past and
establish a rather formidable wedge of Pawns.

2	P—QB3

White can now follow the
regular lines with 3 P–Q4
or else leave the centre open
for a while longer.

3 P—KKt3	Kt—B3
4 B—Kt2	B—B4

Herewith Black aims to
dominate K5 and to develop
the QR. But Black must
be careful not to permit
White to exchange the
Bishop by Kt—KR4. In
reply to that move, the
Bishop must be ready to
sidestep the attack with
B–K5 or B–Kt5 so long as
no safe retreat is provided
for it with P–KR3.

5 O—O	P—K3
6 P—Q3	QKt—Q2
7 P—Kt3	B—Q3
8 B—Kt2	O—O
9 QKt—Q2	P—K4

It is time to open the
centre, the Rooks are ready
for action.

*Position after Black's
ninth move*

Black is firm enough in the centre and can make play on the Queen's side by P—QR4.

A Summary.

In looking back upon the lines of play we have discussed, and which have evolved through the co-operation of many masters in many trials, we discern, in the web of variations, a certain trend, a certain rule or law.

FIRSTLY: It is of great value for either side to dominate *points*. Hence, not only the gain of material, pieces or Pawns, is important, but also the holding in hand of space. The more space you dominate, the less space for the opponent in which to move his pieces about, the more restricted the number of moves with which he may threaten you or guard himself against your threats.

SECONDLY: He who dominates central squares is better off than the ruler over wing squares. The squares have not an equal value. Those of the centre are the most important ones because thence Queen, Bishop and Knight command the largest number of squares. In the centre the important lines intersect. The struggle in the Opening turns therefore essentially round the domination of the centre proper K4, K5, Q4, Q5, and the extended centre from QB3, QB6 to KB3, KB6.

THIRDLY: He will have gained the advantage in the Opening who first succeeds in bringing Pawns and pieces to dominate the extended centre, and in such a way as not only to command as much area as possible, but to cramp the opponent.

FOURTHLY: To fix the exchange value of the Pawns and pieces and the move, in order to decide whether we may sacrifice a Pawn for so many moves gained in development and similar questions, the following table will be found to be a fairly accurate guide:

The Value

of the first move	$=1$
of the second move	$=\frac{4}{5}$
of the third move	$=\frac{3}{4}$
of the fourth move	$=\frac{2}{3}$
of the fifth move	$=\frac{1}{2}$
of the KP or QP	$=2$
of the KBP or QBP	$=1\frac{1}{2}$
of the KKt or QKtP	$=\frac{5}{4}$
of the KRP or QRP	$=\frac{1}{2}$
of the Kt	$=4\frac{1}{2}$
of the KB	$=5$
of the QB	$=4\frac{1}{2}$
of the KR	$=7$
of the QR	$=6$
of the Q	$=11$

These are, of course only estimates based on experience. The numbers given are obviously only approximate. But even though the position is complicated, they can still be of service in helping to determine whether one may venture upon sacrificing a piece for two Pawns, and in elucidating similar thorny problems.

Such a table, if it were possible, ought to include the values of dominating squares also, but I am not sure whether the table thus extended would retain its original form, whether it would not necessarily be more complex, whether it would not have to work with pairs of numbers and groups of squares. The virtue of the original table, however, is just its lack of complication. It is better, therefore, to go no farther but to stop right here and use only arithmetic. It is better to breed within yourself a sound judgment concerning the value of the squares. Practice and intelligent criticism will help you to develop it. The acquisition of such judgment is a hundred times more precious than the mere learning of a table of values just as in Life it is more important to breed than to learn. This practice you will find to be splendid discipline for you.

It is enough to understand and, from the foregoing variations, to be able to prove that for the purpose of the domination of the squares—well understood, not for the attack against the King—the centre is the most important space.

Also the attack against the King is important in the Opening, as well as the manner in which the squares are dominated.

Thus, pressure against the squares surrounding the Castled King is advantageous. But this is an inferior advantage because he who dominates the centre can combat menacing pieces by obstruction or exchange. Again it is important that you are able to place on the dominated squares pieces of minor value which are safe there and whence they have a wide range. At times open lines of Rooks and Bishops may have a value equivalent to that of a few Pawns.

But here we encounter no problems further concerning the Opening. These we shall have to examine very accurately later and from wholly different points of view.

THE   COMBINATION.

After these researches which have been enriched by the work of many generations and varied minds and which, therefore, cannot be, as yet, homogeneous, we now turn to systematic investigation. This must not be a mosaic, heterogeneously composed though in every detail beautiful; it has to be a unit, made so by reason, the business of which is not beauty but truth. To this end we begin by illuminating a concept which has to throw l i g h t upon the modern period of Chess evolution.

In every situation one easily discovers moves of violent, forceful and immediate effect. Their purpose is to produce a change in valuation, so as to humiliate that which is strong and to put into the foreground that which had been but slightly esteemed. Such moves are a Checkmate, the capture of a piece, the promotion of a Pawn, simultaneous attacks, Checks to King or Queen—in short, all moves which contain a menace sudden and brutal.

Such violent moves are opposed by moves equally violent. Attack and parry and counter-attack form therefore a chain. If in this chain link joins link in simple sequence, it is called a " variation " or a " variant." But the chain has often branches, connecting in points where two or more threats or parries continue the sequence. In that case, one speaks in the plural— " variations," and usually of a "maze" of variations.

In his analysis of the position the Chess-player has to see through the maze of variants in order to ascertain whether or not by forceful moves the game may be brought at once to a conclusion. He makes these investigations often, he makes t h e m always when the hostile forces have approached each other for mortal combat. Otherwise, he might let slip a favourable opportunity or fail in vigilance and lose thereby in a moment of inattention what he has gained in an hour of concentration. Nevertheless, ordinarily his work is merely prophylactic. Ordinarily, his labour remains a mere attempt, his investigation is ordinarily not made visible by his deed. The move that he chooses reflects none of his preparatory work because it is seldom that the net of variants contains a satisfactory solution.

In the rare instances that the player can detect a variation or net of them which leads to a desirable issue by force, the totality of these variations and their logical connections, their structure, are named a "combination." And he who follows in his play such a chain of moves is said to "make a combination."

Let us elucidate this concept by a variety of examples.

1

White to Play.

1.—White makes a combination consisting of but one variation. It starts with P—B6 threatening Mate. Only one parry is possible, P—Kt3. Hereupon Q—R6, a new threat of Mate which cannot be guarded, because neither Queen nor Rook can cover the point KKt2. Black has only the useless Q × Pch. to delay the Mate and is lost.

2

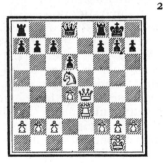

White to play

2.—White, though the exchange behind, can force a win by a combination which has two variants. It begins with 1 Kt—K7ch. If the Knight is captured the Queen recaptures and White wins by superiority. And if 1 ...., K—R1; 2 Q × Pch., K × Q; 3 R–R3 Mate. This second variant embodies the "idea" of the combination, the sacrifice of the Queen.

3

White to play

Capablanca to play

4.—White makes a combination by which he gains an important Pawn.

1 Kt—B3	R—B4
2 Kt—K4	R—Kt4
3 Kt(K4)–Q6	R—B4
4 Kt—Kt7	R—Kt4
5 Kt(Kt7) × P	

3.—White would here calculate the sequence of moves beginning with 1 Q × R. If then 1 ...., R × Q; 2 R—K8ch., forcing a Checkmate shortly. This is one variant, but there are others to be taken into consideration. Perhaps Black replies with a counter-thrust? 1 ...., Q—Kt1 ch.; 2 K moves or P–Kt3. Thereupon 2 ...., R × Q. Now 3 R—K8ch. Here again the variation splits into two variants, either 3 ...., Q × R—which would be bad—and finally 3 ...., R–B1, whereupon the calculation soon comes to an end. Shall White enter upon this course? The combination forces exchange of Rook and Queen. It depends upon his judgment whether he considers the combination worth making or not.

Black to play   5

5.—Black saves this apparently hopeless position by a combination

1	Q × Pch.
2 K × Q	Kt × Rch.
3 K moves	Kt × Q
4 B—Q4	Kt × P
5 B × Kt	

and White cannot drive the King out of the corner. The game ends in a Stalemate or a Draw.

Already these few instances prove that a combination must always have a "point," an "idea." One may recognise this idea by the surprise which it causes the spectator and by the feeling of freedom which its conception gives to the player. The idea solves a riddle at *one* stroke.

6

White to play

6.—White sees e a s i l y that after 1 Kt—B7ch. the Rook must not capture the Knight and therefore the King is driven into the diagonal of the Queen. By moving the Knight Check by discovery of the Queen is given, but since the Queen is attacked by the hostile Queen no Check by discovery would avail except a Double Check. 2 Kt –R6, whereupon again K–

R1. So far so good, but how can White win? Certainly, after 3 Kt–B7ch., King must again move to Kt1; this, however, leads only to a Draw by Perpetual Check—or no? Suddenly White grasps an idea and, delivered from the pain of laborious search, he jubilantly announces a Checkmate in four moves. The idea is to block the only square where the Black K i n g could escape, by offering a surprising sacrifice. 1 Kt–B7ch., K–Kt1; 2 Kt–R6 dbl. ch., K–R1; 3 Q–Kt8ch., R × Q (forced); 4 Kt–B7 Mates.

Morphy   7

Louis Paulsen

7.—Young Morphy, in the New York tournament of 1857, playing against Louis Paulsen, has t h e move. He had blocked the QP with his Queen and thus cramped White's QR and QB, but now White attacks that Queen and proposes to exchange. He ponders. Shall I exchange? but no! for I should then have to provide against B–Kt4 which would afterwards deprive me of my fine QB. Shall I protect the Queen with Rook so as to block with Rook? The Rook might be driven off by that Bishop. And the King looks weak. A pity that Q × Rch. won't finish the game right off. Maybe B × Pch. goes? No, King takes and unfortunately I have no diagonal Check with Queen so as to drive the King into the open. But there ought to be something, I feel it. How about Q × B? Why, there would be a Check with the Rook and B–R6, he cannot guard the threatened Mate by R–Kt1, of course—well, I should like to see him stop that attack. Morphy does not cogitate further, the rest of the combination with him is a matter of intuition.

Paulsen, surprised by the combination, does not render the strongest resistance. The game proceeds

1	Q × B
2 P × Q	R—Kt3ch.
3 K—R1	B—R6
4 R—Q1	

Not the best defence! True, 4 R–KKt1 was out of the question, because of 4 ...., R × Rch., 5 K × R,

R–K8ch., and mate next move.

There was, however, another method to parry the threat, namely, by attacking the formidable Rook on Kt3 with 4 Q–Q3. If then 4 ...., B–Kt7ch.; 5 K–Kt1, B × Pch.; 6 Q × R, RP × Q; 7 P—Q4, R—K5; 8 P—R3 and White would win therefore: 4 ...., P–KB4. After this not 5 Q–B4ch., K—B1! (preventing 6 Q–B7) but 5 R–Q1, B × P; 6 Q—B1 and White can still struggle; or 5 ...., B–Kt7ch.; 6 K–Kt1, B × Pch.; 7 K—B1, B × R; 8 Q–B4ch.; K–B1; 9 P–Q4, whereupon Black would surely win the ending with 9 ...., B–K7ch.; 10 Q × B, R—Kt8ch., etc. But in any case, White should have made it harder for Black.

4	B—Kt7ch.
5 K—Kt1	B × Pch.
6 K—B1	B—Kt7ch.

Still stronger 6 ...., R—Kt7, whereupon White is driven into a " Mating net."

7 K—Kt1	B—R6ch.
8 K—R1	B × P
9 Q—B1	B × Q

and Morphy won easily.

The consideration of forcible moves is necessary because in this way a short road to victory, provided it is on the board, can be discerned. The method is also practical because it eliminates all consideration of the immense multitude of non-violent moves and concentrates the attention upon a few possibilities which the human mind can easily digest. If a combination forcing a win has been found, nothing avails the opponent, for the demonstration of the win can be grasped. In Life it is different. There the struggles are not so indubitably terminated as in a game. The game gives us a satisfaction that L i f e denies us. And for the Chess-player the success which crowns his work, the great dispeller of sorrows, is named " combination."

The combination is born in the brain of a Chess-player. Many thoughts see the light there—true and false, strong and weak, sound and unsound. They are born, jostle one another, and one of them, transformed into a move on the board, bears away the victory over its rivals.

D o e s a Chess-master really cogitate as just outlined? Presumably so, but with detours and repetitions. However, it matters not by what process he conceives an idea; the important point to understand is that an idea takes hold of the master and obsesses him. The master, in the grasp of an idea, sees that idea suggested and almost embodied on the board. An idea does not arise accidentally in the mind of the master, who dominates the material, but has its *raison d'etre* on the board.

It is not enough to know that a combination is a sequence of forcible moves; one must be able to give a reason for the existence of that combination. If in the position, examined by the master, a combination is hidden, there is a reason for its existence; and again, if there is no such combination to be found, a reason for this non-existence can be detected. For instance, you will try in vain to Checkmate a mobile King safeguarded behind Pawns and defended by a few well-posted officers, without employing many moves. If in such position you insist upon searching for a combination which will Mate in a hurry, you will only lose time a n d brain-power. Again, simultaneous attacks are possible only under certain restricted conditions, namely such as are *geometrical*, as, for instance, when King and Queen stand in the same rank or file or diagonal or on points controlled by the same Knight. To execute such simultaneous attacks, not only must these geometrical conditions be satisfied, but also some very mobile and very threatening pieces are required. Even from these two instances it is sufficiently manifest that the conditions for the existence of a combination are circumscribed. And it is these conditions which give rise to the ideas in the mind of the master. Only when the hostile King has little mobility and little protection does the master make the attempt to find a combination which aims at a forced mate, because he knows that only then can the position contain the idea of a mate. And so it is with other ideas.

An idea must therefore have a motif or a net, a web of motifs, which is clearly discernible from the position.

Let us now consider the various motifs, one by one.

The most usual of all motifs is the weakness of a piece of little or no mobility. Such a piece invites attack. The imagination of the player is immediately stirred by the sight of an immobile piece. He is forced to seek for a combin-

ation which will finally break down the defence and secure the prey. Often a Bishop is assailed by a chain of Pawns and deprived of all mobility as in the following faulty Opening: 1 P–K4, P–K4; 2 Kt–KB3, Kt–QB3; 3 B–Kt5, P–QR3; 4 B–R4, P–Q3; 5 P–Q4, P–QKt4; 6 B–Kt3, Kt×P; 7 Kt×Kt, P×Kt; 8 Q×P? (better B–Q5), P–QB4; 9 Q–Q5, B–K3; 10 Q–B6ch., B–Q2; 11 Q–Q5, P–B5. Often a piece that has strayed too far into the hostile camp is cut off and falls helplessly. Often many hostile pieces concentrate their attack upon a blocked Pawn and win it by force of numbers. Often a pinned piece, often the King itself, after having been surrounded and made immobile, becomes the target for the united effort of the enemy's pieces.

To name this motif, let us emphasize the two ideas underlying it: the idea of superior force at a given point, and that of immobility. What is immobile must suffer violence. The light-winged b i r d will easily escape the huge dragon, but the firmly rooted big tree must remain where it is and may have to give up its leaves, fruit, perhaps even its life. Let us

name it the motif of encircling, since in this term the
two ideas of violence and of
immobility are blended.

A second motif, also very
common, may be deduced
from the rules of the game,
since it originates in the
geometry of the Chess-
board and of the moves of
the pieces. We name it
briefly the "geometrical"
motif.   This motif inspires
the player to seek for simultaneous attacks and de-
fences.

8

White to play

8.—Here the Black King
and Queen are on the same
diagonal and the Black
Queen is unprotected. Can
White take advantage of
this situation?   That is
possible only by giving
Check upon that diagonal.
But how can this be done?
Because the King could
capture the White Queen if
it checked on the diagonal,
namely. on QR3. But is it
impossible?   Thus do one's

thoughts work and the winning combination is dis-
covered.   Two motifs co-
operate to suggest it :—
firstly, the geometrical one ;
secondly, the motif of encircling the Black King.

9.—Another instance of
the geometrical motif is the
obstuction of a Rook by a
Bishop or vice versa. That
is quite artistic if this obstruction is forced upon the
opponent by the occupation
of the point where the two
lines of mobility, the dia-
ognal one and the straight
one, intersect.   A fine instance of this which we may
call the Intersection motif
follows.

By Troitzki   9

White to play and win

The Bishop from R6
can hold the White BP and
the White KtP from B5 ;
the Rook can hold the BP
from KB4 and the KtP
from QKt4. Black can thus
stop both Pawns, one with
the Bishop, the other with

the Rook. In order to make the Black pieces obstruct each other and thus frustrate their plans. White utilises his apparently useless pieces, the Knight and the Pawn on QKt3. 1 Kt–Q3. If now 1 ...., B–R6; 2 P–Kt4, and the Bishop is eliminated and White Queens a Pawn. Hence 1 ...., R × Kt. Now White threatens strongly by 2 P–B7. If 2 ...., R–B6; 3 P–Kt7, and 3 ...., B–B5 is ineffective because it obstructs the Rook. Again, if 2 ...., B–R6; 3 P–Kt4, B × P; 4 P–Kt7, and again the Bishop obstructs the Rook.

10.—Another instance, illustrating the Intersection motif.

10   *By Troitzki.*

White to play and win

The solution begins with brutally forceful moves 1 P–B7, B–R6; 2 P × P. Now the RP threatens to advance; hence, the Rook, unable to stop the RP, must stop the BP so as to relieve the Bishop which then will be able to stop the RP. But 2 ...., R–B7 is prevented by the King; therefore 2 ...., B–Kt5 ch.; 3 K–B1, B–B4; 4 P–R7, R–B7ch.; 5 K–Q, B–K5. Black has attained his end: the Bishop stops the one Pawn, the Rook the other; he seems saved. The Knight, however, places itself upon the intersection of the file and the diagonal, 6 Kt–B6. If the Rook captures, the Bishop is obstructed and P–R8 wins; if the Bishop captures, the Rook is obstructed and P–B8 wins. Black is lost.

The motif of obstruction, the geometrical effect of which we have just considered, is founded upon a principle applying to all contests. In every contest the forces opposing each other naturally strive for untrammelled activity. This aim is defeated by obstruction or by pinning. Often a friend obstructs the fighter. In a dispute you remind your opponent of his own assertion; will he now deny it? He is obstructed by his own former arguments. In Chess one of your men is often obstructed by your other men. You would like to remove them, so as to free your game, but the opponent now obstructs or pins the obstruction and does not allow it to move.

11   *Kagan*

White, Post, to play

11.—White, who has the material advantage, desires to win in a few moves and makes a combination by which he obstructs the Black pieces. The Bishop obstructs the QR, the QP obstructs the Bishop; hence, if the QP is forcibly kept back Black's QR will for a long time be out of play. The QP can be blocked by a move which also keeps the King in the centre and exposed. Hence, the first move of the combination is strongly suggested by the position

1 B—Q6   P × B

Black seeks compensation for his loss in mobility by laying his hand upon material force.

2 Q—Q2   ....

threatening Q and K by 3 R–K1

2 ....   Q—R3
3 R—K1ch.   K—Q1
4 B—B4!   ....

Black is given no time to bring his KR into action, an instance of the assault motif. The Bishop makes room for the Queen on Q6, so that the Black Queen must guard that spot. If now 4 ...., Q–KKt3; 5 Kt—Kt4! threatening 6 Kt –K5. Black cannot capture the Knight, as the Black Queen has to prevent Q–Q6. Black is lost, for instance 5 ...., R–K1; 6 Kt–K5, Q–K3; 7 Q–Q6; Q × Q; 8 Kt × P ch., K–B2; 9 B × Qch. and wins the Rook. Therefore

4 ....   Q—QB3
5 B—Q6   P—B3
6 Q—B4   ....

which threatens 7 B–K7ch., followed by 8 B × Pch.

6 ....   R—K1
7 B—B7ch.   Q × B
8 R × Rch.   K × R
9 Q × Q wins

The motifs of a combination, in themselves simple, are often interwoven with each other. What is it that unites the multiplicity of motifs? We call it the "idea." Motifs, as, for instance, a simultaneous attack against several pieces or the encircling of the hostile King, are tricks of the trade, technicalities. The idea which links the motifs is artistic, it creates something that had never before been there. Motifs can be taught, ideas must be discovered by original effort. Ideas come from nowhere, they are sudden inspirations; the place of motifs is definite: the memory.

Even the few simple m o t i f s above discussed breathe art when they are used in a manner to conquer points apparently in the firm grasp of the opponent. As an instance, let us consider the following study by L. Kubbel (from "150 Endspiele" by that artistic composer).

12

White to play and win

12.—The Knight c a n Discover Check; but where shall it move? It has no permanently safe retreat. The Queen which has to attack the King cannot spare the time to guard the Knight, and no other White piece is available for the purpose. The only help is the motif that King and Queen in the same line are weak. Therefore, t h e Knight dares to take a post in the line of the Black Queen but far away from that Queen so that, should the King capture the Knight, the Black Queen would be lost. And on this idea the first part of the combination is based. It is composed of a web of motifs which reveals the idea of the author.

1 Kt—K3ch.   K—Kt6
                        (best)
2 Q—Kt4ch.   K—B7
                        (best)
3 Q—B4ch.   K—K7
                        (best)
4 Q—B1ch.   ....

The Knight is guarded, as it were, because the King must not capture it or the Queen is lost by 5 Q–K1ch.

4 ....   K—Q7
5 Q—Q1ch.   K—B6
6 Q—B2ch.   K—Kt5

If 6 ...., K–Q5 ; 7 Kt–B5ch. wins the Queen.

7 Q—Kt2ch.   Kt—Kt6
                        (best)
8 Q—R3ch.

winning Queen or the Knight Mates on B2.

13.—Another instance, a simple one, which might easily occur in actual play, not, like Kubbel's study, the result of artistic invention.

13

White to play

Apparently the Knight cannot be saved except by premature exchange of Queens; actually, t h e Knight is safe at R8, where its support is indirect, thereafter, by Kt–Kt6, it has a firm foothold and can dispense with the aid of the Queen.

14

White to play

14.—This motif if of frequent occurrence in end games where a passed pawn is used to protect distant pieces or pawns.

The Knight cannot protect the Pawn by 1 Kt–B3 or 1 Kt–B7 for long, but the Pawn can protect the Knight by 1 P-Kt6. For, if 1 ...., K × Kt; 2 P-- Kt7, and Queens next move. Therefore Pawn and Knight do protect each other allowing the White King to approach the Black Pawn to capture it and then to decide the battle.

This illustrates a motif of g r e a t importance — the motif of "function." The power, the domain of force of a piece is decreased as soon as that piece has a certain task to do, as, for instance, in above position the power of the Knight is decreased by its having to watch the passed Pawn. A task or a multitude of tasks, such as, for instance, to obstruct a Rook or to parry the threat of a mate, if to be done by a certain piece, may be called the "function" of that piece, an expression borrowed from Biology. By studying the various functions of the hostile pieces and the effects these functions have of impeding those pieces we discern new motifs for combinations.

15

15.—Black's Pawn on his KKt2 has the task of guarding the RP as well as the forking check of the White Knight threatened on B6. Therefore, White wins an important Pawn by 1 Q × P. The Black KtP cannot successfully perform both his tasks.

16   *Hirschfeld*

White, Steinitz, to play and win

16.—The function of the Black Knight on KB3 is to guard the Queen. If attacked, it cannot budge. Steinitz foresaw this situation and prepared an attack which is overwhelm-

ing because the Knight is twice assailed and is threatened with capture with Check. 1 Kt–R5, and Black resigned. Black should have thought twice before he confided to a Knight so insecurely placed, a task so important as guarding the Queen.

17

Black, Mayet, to play

Lowenthal

17.—Point Q5 seems a certain conquest for the White Bishop. White seems about to triumph, but the White Queen has the function of protecting the KR and tries to pin the black knight on K5 also. This is attempting too much. To get the White Queen to relinquish its task is worth a whole Rook, so

1 ....   Kt—B3

and now Black wins easily.

18   *Tschigorin*

White, Steinitz, to play

18.—It is the function of the Black King to guard the BP, the black rook has to protect the P on Kt4. These two pieces having functions to fulfil are sensitive to disturbance. Black obviously desires to get his inactive Knight into play by Kt–K3; this, therefore, is the moment to disturb the Black pieces. Besides, P–QB5 is threatened. Is 1 P–B4ch. possible? Certainly, because after 1 ...., K×P; 2 R–R4ch. profits by the geometrical motif. White thus wins.

19   *L. Kubmann.*

White, Alekhin, to play

19.—The Black King has only one flight-square and little protection. The motif of encircling tells us that such a piece is a target. Kt–B6 would be Mate except for the Black Queen. In other words its function of guarding against the Mate deprives the Black Queen of any mobility outside the third rank.

1. Q–Kt5ch. ....

The White Queen, as above pointed out, is attacked only in appearance, but not in fact. The Check attacks the Knight simultaneously.

1. ....   Kt—Q2

Now 2 ...., Q×Q is threatened, since the Knight, as soon as it is unpinned, guards the Mate. But White sees to it that this protection becomes illusory by throwing another formidable piece into the combat.

2 KR—K1   ....

The obstruction 2 ...., B–K2 is of no avail since White, having a superior force in action, terminates the struggle by mere force. There follows 3 Kt(K4)–Q6 ch., K–B1; 4 R×B, Q×Q; 5 R×Pch., K–Kt1; 6 Kt–K7 or R6 Mate. Black is hopelessly beaten.

20

Meitner

White, Steinitz, to play

20.—The Black BP has the function of covering the King against the Check on R5; the QP has to obstruct the Queen's line and thus hamper the White Rook on Q1. On the other hand, the White Pawn on K5 obstructs both the Rook on K1 and the QB. Hence the move

1. P—K6   ....

suggests itself as an attack on two Pawns weighted down by functions and as the removal of an obstruction. If now 1 ...., BP × P; 2 Q × Pch. wins the Knight; if 1 ...., QP × P; 2 B × BP brings the Rook on Q1 into immediate action. Black might still try a feeble resistance 2 ...., Kt(R4)–B3; 3 B–Kt5, K–B1; 4 B–Q6 threatening 5 B × Kt, P × B; 6 Kt–B5.

Black is helpless. Finally if 1 ...., Kt × B; 2 P × BP ch., Q × P; 3 Kt–B5, and the open King's file is decisive.

21

Dr. Schmid

White, Prof. Berger, to play

21.—The Black Knight on K5 obstructs the KR, the KBP guards that Knight, the Bishop on R4 pins the White KKt. In consequence of this web of functions, the Black KBP and the Black QB are targets. Hence, the move 1 P–KKt4 is indicated. The game proceeded

1 P—KKt4	B—Kt3
2 P × BP	B × P
3 B × Kt	B × B
4 Kt—B3	B × Kt
5 Kt × Q	B × Q
6 Kt × Pch.	K—B2
7 Kt × R	B—B6

8. P × P, and White won.

22

White to play

23

Black to play

22.—The Black King has the function of guarding the Queen; its domain is therefore decreased; it cannot go to B1 nor to B2. The Black Queen has to guard against two Mates. Therefore, 1 B–B7ch. wins the Queen or forces mate.

23.—Sometimes a piece, without intending to, performs a task favourable to the opponent. For instance, it obstructs a passed pawn that w o u l d otherwise Queen; or it renders a too feeble resistance and threatens to fall an easy prey. Such pieces are possessed of a veritable fury of aggression. T h e y r u n "amok." They are desperadoes. The "desperado" motif is very frequent.

In diagram 23 the Rook is desperado.

As long as it stays on QR8 merely protecting QR7 everything is in danger. Therefore it seeks a target, the most valuable to the opponent, the King.

1 ....   R—B8ch

and Black wins.

24

Black, Duras, to play

Forgács

24.—The Queen on Q3 is desperado because on its account R × Q is not playable and the Rook on K7 is in danger. It therefore annihilates the strongest adversary that happens to be within its reach. 1 .... Q × B and wins.

25

Black, Marco, to play

v. Popiel

25.—The Black Bishop on Q5 is pinned! if it moves, the Rook is lost. It is also assailed by overpowering numbers. It looks for something to attack. It can indeed threaten, the greatest threat of all, namely, Checkmate by B–Kt8. Marco did not see the move and resigned a game that he should have won.

26

White, v. Oppen, to play

26.—The White Knight obstructs its own Rook which otherwise would be able to strike a death-blow by R(K1)–K7. It is desperado and makes the furious attack 1 Kt–Q5. Black replies P × Kt. Now 2 R(K1)-K7 would have won, but 2 R × Pch., K × R; 3 Q–R5ch., K–Kt1; 4 R–K7 is still more conclusive.

27

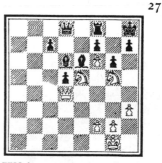

White to play and win

27.—The Knight on K5 and the Pawn on B6 obstruct their own Queen. The Pawn on B6 is blocked by the Black Pawn on B2, which guards the QB and the KtP. That KtP is also guarded by the RP, which has to protect the King against Q–KR4. The Knight on K5 is in desperado mood. Is that Black KtP guarded at all? All functions considered, no! Hence 1 Kt × KtP ch., K–Kt1; 2 Q–KR4 and wins.

28
Black, Em. Lasker, to play

Tarrasch

28.—To understand the motifs of this combination one must dig deep. White is attacking Queen and Rook with his KP; hence, both are desperados: they look for checks, for an attack on the Queen, for captures, for strong threats regardless of the sacrifice involved. 1 ...., R–Q8 ch. suggests itself, but that check is adequately guarded by the White Queen. Here is the function motif holding the White Queen. The White Queen guards t h e BP, w h i c h also is guarded by the KtP; and that KtP has to guard against the Check of the Black Queen. Considering the functions of the White Queen and KtP, the White KBP is n o t defended at all. Hence

1 ....   R × KBP

and everything else follows easily. Black wins.

Even after the Chessplayer in trying to detect the combination latent in a position has recognized the motifs at his disposal and by them has been led to unearth the various forcible moves which promise success, he has often still to determine the *order* in which these violent blows should be struck. To choose this order indifferently may permit a defence that, with p r o p e r discrimination, would not have been possible.

Englund, Jacobson, Nyholm, Olson.

29

White, Bogoljubow, Reti and Spielmann, to play

29.—The attack on KB7 has been beaten back, but White contemplates a move that attacks several things at once, namely, R–K7. This move cannot be prevented if preceded by R(B1)–K1 or by Q–K3.

On the other hand, White has a weak QP and Black threatens, after QR–Q1 to force the exchange of Queens. Against 1 R(B1)–K1 the reply QR–Q1 would force 2 P–Q5, P × P, and Black would breathe, possibly win. There remains 1 Q–K3. Of course, the reply QR–K1 would fail because of 2 R(B1) × P, since the Black KR would be overburdened with functions. But how about 1 ...., QR–Q1 ? Then 2 R–K7 fails on account of 2 ...., Q × P, and White has no time for 3 R(B1) × P before exchanging Queens, nor afterwards because of 4 ...., R × B.

This being the state of affairs, everything depends on timing the various moves rightly. Thus the idea occurs to *precede* R–K7 by R × BP. And now t h e combination is discovered.

1 Q–K3	QR—Q1
2 R × BP	R × R
3 R–K7	....

If now 3 ...., Q × P ; 4 Q × Q, and 5 R–K8 Mate.

3	Q—B1
4 R × R	K—R1
5 R × KKtP	

and the Black King, uncovered on the seventh row, is soon checkmated.

By A. Troitzki   30

White to play and win

30.—Here White has two strong moves to choose from, both hampering the mobility of Black greatly, namely, Q–Kt4ch. or B–R7 ch. The more forceful move is the check with the Bishop which permits only *one* reply, 1 .... K–Q5. After this reply the Check with the Queen comes in strongly, again permitting but one reply, namely 2 ...., K–Q4. Now a Queen Check would not avail, but 3 B—Kt8ch. develops the geometrical motif on two diagonals and one file. 3 ...., Q × B ; 4 Q–Kt3, or 3 ...., K–B3 ; 4 Q–R4, or 3 ...., K–K4 ; 4 Q–K1.

By far the largest number of combinations that play a part in the drama of a game do not actually occur, though they aid in determining the course of events nevertheless. It is sufficient that they be recognized as *intentions*, as possibilities with w h i c h players must reckon.

An intended combination is named a " *threat*." A threat becomes an attack unless the threatened party parries, defends, prevents, forestalls, defeats the intention. Ordinarily, this can be done in a multitude of ways from among which the defender has the choice.

It is good policy to assign the defence to a threat to an *inactive* piece. If, however, no reserve force is available, one has to choose the piece that is least burdened. If a piece has too many tasks to perform all at once, its force will be found insufficient and the structure erected by the defence will crumble.

31   *Burn*

White, Dr. Tarrasch, to play

31.—Black threatens to win a piece by P–QB4, since the Knight has to

guard the Bishop on Kt3, he also threatens R–K1 which would attack Queen and Rook simultaneously. How can the menaced Rook on K1 move and prevent P–QB4 at the same time? 1 R–K3 does not help, because 1 ...., R–K1 then makes the double attack with the same effect. Perhaps 1 R–QB1 But then 1 ...., R–K1 ; 2 Q–B6, R–K8ch. ; 3 K–B2, Q–Q7ch. ; 4 K–Kt3, Kt–R4ch. If the Rook moves, the square Q2 must be guarded. There remains 1 R–Q1.   1 ...., P–QB4 will have to be defeated by counter-attack for which purpose, it is true, the Queen is now released. Thus 1 R–Q1, P–QB4 ; 2 Q–K7 (pinning the QBP), R–KB1 ; 3 Kt–K6, Kt × Kt ; 4 B × Kt, P × B (Q × BP ; 5 Q × P3 ; 5 Q × KPch. K–Kt2 ; 6 Q–K7ch., R–B2 ; 7 Q–K5ch. Draws. Or else 2 B × Pch. followed by 3 Kt–B6. The move by which White can parry all threats is therefore indicated

1 R–Q1

B l a c k should have studied the situation carefully and would then have seen that his threats had indeed been warded off. In reply to his 1 .... P–QB4 he should have considered the effect of 2 B × Pch (for

2 B–Q5 would, after 2 ...., R–K1 lead to the consolidation of Black's game). His correct move was 1........., Kt–K1, giving a flight square to his King and protecting the weak square KB3 as well as his QBP. He, however, still thinks in the same channels as before, though the position has been materially changed by White's defence. In fact, the game proceeded

1 .... P—QB4?
2 B × Pch. K × B
3 Kt—B6 Q—Kt6??

B l a c k lost his head. 3 ...., Q–Kt4 was indicated, although also then White had the best of it.

4 Q—K7ch. K—Kt1
5 R—Q8ch. R × R
6 Q × Rch. K—B2
7 Kt–K5ch. K—K3
8 Q–Kt8ch. and wins the Queen.

32
Black, Capablanca, to play

Dr. Tartakower

32.—After 1 ...., R × B White would win by 2 Q –R4ch. But Black has a victorious alternative. He protects the KB and attacks the King at the same time.

1 .... Kt—Q4

If now 2 B–B4; 2 ...., Q—B3, whereupon again 3 .... Kt–K6ch. is threatened.

Suchting 33

White, John, to play

33.—Black's threat is R × Kt followed by Q–B6. The parry with P–B3 would be weak because the KBP has the function of safeguarding the second row. In fact, if 1 P–B3; Q–R6 would be annihilating. If 1 Kt–K4 the square KB3 is abandoned and Black can continue, as indeed he did, by 1 ...., Q–B6; 2 Q–R5, R × Kt; 3 P–QB4, R × P and White resigns. The correct defence was 1 QR–K1 which utilises an inactive piece. Then 1 ...., R × Kt is met by 2 Q×R, Q–B6; 3 R–K4. And 1 ...., QR –K1 by 2 Kt–K4! Q–B6; 3 R×R, R×Kt; 4 P×R, and the game should be a draw.

Of the above motifs, some occur often, some rarely. The reason for this difference in frequency is the initial position. There the pieces have certain prescribed p o s i t i o n s; the struggle in which they engage, though very varied, still follows a certain trend, and therefore certain types of combinations tend to recur.

1.—As a natural outgrowth of attacks against the Castled King, pressure on the Pawns round the King a n d sacrifices of pieces for them are frequent.

2. Again as a means of attacking the King, control of the 8th rank where the Queen or Rooks might Check the King becomes often the object of a combination.

3. F o r attacks against the King and also against Pawns the seventh rank is often utilised efficiently by Rooks and Queen.

4. The Knights on QB3 or KB3 a r e frequently

pinned by Bishops and a contest ensues round the pinned pieces.

It is not that combinations of the above type differ logically—not at all— only the frequency of such combinations causes us to pay them particular attention.

34

Baucher

White, Morphy, to play

34.—1 R—R3   ....
intending R × Pch., f o l- lowed by Q–R5 Mate. ·If Black defends with 1 .... B–K1, the Knight on K6 retains its dominating post undisturbed. Thus Baucher was induced to play

1 ....   P—R3

whereupon

2 Q—Q2   ....

threatens R (or Q) × Pch., and wins with ease.

35 *Black, Morphy, to play*

A. de Riviere

35.—1 .... Kt—B6ch.
depriving the RP of its
only efficient protection.

  2 P × Kt   Q—R5
  3 R—R1   B × P

Thus the White King is
held fast.

  4 B—Q2   R—B3
White resigns

36   *Amateur*

White, Steinitz, to play

36.—
  1 Kt × Bch.   Kt × Kt
  2 R × Pch.   K × R
  3 Q—R6ch.   K—Kt1
  4 Q—Kt5ch.   K—R1
  5 Q × Ktch.   K—Kt1
  6 Q—Kt5ch.   K—R1
  7 P—B6   R—KKt1
  8 Q—R6 and wins.

37   *Bauer*

White, Em. Lasker, to play

37.—
  1 B × Pch.   K × B
  2 Q × Ktch.   K—Kt1
  3 B × P   K × B
  4 Q—Kt4ch.   K—R2
  5 R—B3   P—K4
  6 R—R3ch.   Q—R3
  7 R × Qch.   K × R
  8 Q—Q7 and wins.

This motif: that of tear-
ing away the safeguards of
the hostile King at the expense of some pieces occurs
frequently.

38
Black, Bolte, to play

Steneberg

38.—Here the White King is principally defended by the RP and the KtP hence :—

1	B × Pch.
2 K × B	Q—R5ch.
3 K—Kt1	B × P
4 K × B	....

(or 4 P—B3, R–KKt1).

4	R—Kt1ch.
5 B × R	R × Bch.
6 K—B3	Q—K5 mate.

True, White's position was weak. Black could equally have won with 1 ...., Q–R5.

39

From a game at odds

White, Steinitz, to play

39.—The Black Rook on Kt4 must guard against mate in three moves, and is therefore bound to the Kt file.

| 1 Q—Q5ch. | K—R1 |
| 2 R—Q8ch. | .... |

White won differently but this was the most direct way.

| 2 .... | R × R |
| 3 Q × Rch. | B × Q |
| 4 R—K8ch. |

illustrating a combination in which the 7th and 8th ranks are exploited.

40

Owen

White, Boden, to play

40.—Black threatens R × B followed by Q × Pch. White forestalls him in the task of taking the King by storm.

1 R × P	R × B
2 Q—R5ch.	P × Q
3 R × P double ch.	K—Kt2
4 R—R7ch.	K—B1
5 P—K7ch.	K— K1
6 B—Kt5ch.	Q—Q2
7 B × Qch.	K × B
8 P × R	R—Kt5
9 R—R8	R—K5

10 P—Kt4 and Black resigned.

41   *Steinitz*

White, Albin, to play

41.—An attack on KKt7 is indicated. To get the obstructions out of the way is White's first objective.   1 P–R6 would be far from serving the purpose; in fact, would defeat it, because Black would refuse to exchange Pawns by pushing P–KKt3, whereby both files would remain closed. Either the obstructing P must first be blocked and then attacked by P—R6 or it must be forced away at the cost of a piece.   The former is too slow so

| 1 B—B6! | .... |

If now

1	P × B
2 P—R6	R × P
3 Q—Kt7ch.	Q × Q
4 P × Qch	K—Kt1
5 R—R8ch	K—B2
6 P—-Kt8=Q and wins.	

If Black defends the square KKt1 with 2 ...., Kt–K2 the combination proceeds as above except 6 R–B8 Mate.

The RP gathered an enormous strength by the sacrifice of the Bishop. This combination of Albin's has, it is true, a very common motif: the tearing down of a safeguard of the hostile King; but it compensates for this by joining with this motif others artistically interwoven with it: opening of files, power of the passed pawn and a clever mate.

L. Paulsen   42

White, Kolisch, to play

42.—

1 Kt KR4	P—KR3
2 Kt—B5	B × Kt
3 Kt—Q5	....

A typical attack on a pinned Knight.

3	Q—Q2
4 B × Kt	B—K3
5 Q—R5	K—R2

or 5 ...., B × Kt; 6 B ×
B, P × B ; 7 Q—Kt6ch. with
a safe Draw and the opportunity of getting a Rook
into action by K—R1 and
P—KB4.

6	K—R1	B × Kt
7	P × B	Kt—Q5
8	P—KB4	....

With a variation some-
thing as follows in mind :—
8 .... P × B; 9 P × P,
BP × P; 10 R–B6.

| 8 | .... | Q—B4 |

Offering exchange of
Queens, the typical defence
to heavy attacks against the
King.

9	Q × Q	Kt × Q
10	P × P	Kt—K6
11	B—K7	Kt × R
12	R × Kt	QR—K1

The BP had to be defen-
ded. White has evidently
the advantage.

So easy does it seem to
concentrate pieces against
the King and to sacrifice a
piece or two for its safeguards, but this device can
be easily met. The defen-
sive power of the King
must not be underrated. If
the hostile King retains
mobility, and if the hostile
pieces are protected, and
thus are not an easy prey to
a simultaneous attack, combinations of the above type

will fail. The hostile King
will simply flee and finally
reach a point of compara-
tive safety. Then Queens
will be exchanged and the
attack fade away.

Steinitz   43

White, Zukertort, to play

43.—White has a difficult
game, but could attempt to
make a fight by 1 Q–R3, P
–KKt3; 2 R × Rch., R × R ;
3 B × B, P × B; 4 Q—Q7.
Instead of a patient and
conscientious defence, he
essays a sacrificial attack
without accurately probing
it and thus violates the
ethics of the Chess-master.

1	B × Pch.	K × B
2	Q—R5ch.	K—Kt1
3	R—R3	P—B3
4	Q—R8 ch	K—B2
5	Q—R5ch.	K—K2

In fact, Steinitz did not
make this move at once but
repeated several times K–
Kt1, Q—R8ch., K–B2, Q–

R5ch. for purely technical reasons, having to consider the time allowed for deliberation and measured by a clock devised for the purpose.

6	R—K3ch.	K—B1
7	Q—R8ch.	B—Kt1
8	B—R6	R—K2
9	R × R	K × R
10	B × P	Q—KB4

The fight is now decided. The sequence was

| 11 | R—K1ch. | K—B2 |
| 12 | B—R6 | Q—R2 |

and White soon after resigned.

44.—These combinations occur in large numbers. Precious, artistic combinations are not of this type. They are individual, occurring only once and not to be duplicated. Compare with the above combination the one that follows, which has length, complication, force, and individuality.

44   *Ed. Lasker.*

White, Em. Lasker to play

| 1 | Kt × P | B × P |
| 2 | Kt × P | .... |

making use of the weakness of Q5,

2	....	B—K3
3	Kt—Kt5	B—B5
4	B—Q3	R—Q1
5	R—B2	Kt—B5
6	B × Kt	Q × B
7	Kt—R3	Q—K4
8	B × Bch.	Kt × B
9	Q—K2	....

Now a short respite in which the task of driving off the Black Knight, a vital question for White and Black, becomes the principal motif.

9	....	R—Q5
10	P—B3	QR—Q1
11	QR—B1	B—B4
12	K—R1	B—Kt5

The Knight is intended to make a desperate inroad

| 13 | P—QKt3 | Kt—Q7 |

If the Knight retreats, White exchanges a Rook by 14 R–B8 and soon relieves the pressure.

| 14 | Kt—K3 | .... |

The threat is 15 R–Q1 and 16 P–R3. Black seeks compensations for the Knight which is cut off but, while it lives, a terrible menace.

14	B—R6
15 R—Q1	B—Kt5
16 P—R3	....

Now commences a turmoil of attacks and parries.

16	B—R4
17 P—QKt4	B—B2
18 P—B4	Kt × P
19 K—R2	R × R
20 Kt × R	Q—K2

Only here I did not terminate the combination as I should have. I played 21 R × B, whereupon a difficult Ending ensued. The appropriate move was

21 Kt(Q1)–B2	R—Q5
22 Q—K3,	winning a

piece, for if

22	B—Kt3
23 Kt × Kt	Q × Kt
24 R—B8ch.	K—B2
25 Kt—Kt5ch.	

45.—A g a i n, compare with the former drab combinations t h e following very individual ingenious play by Alekhin:

Black, Dr. Alekhin, to
45   play

Dr. Tartakower

1	Q × P
2 R—Kt1	Q × P
3 P × Kt	....

This move was not made, but it forms the principal variant of the combination.

3	QR—Q1

Before making this series of moves Black had to take into consideration, besides other minor variations, 4 P × P, R × Q; 5 B × R, P–K7 ! (so as to reply to 6 Pawn Queens with Pawn Queens), 6 R–K3, Q–Q7 with advantage. Again 4 Q–Kt3, Q × B; 5 R × KP, Q–Kt5; 6 P × P, R–Q7; 7 R–Kt3, Q–Q5ch. followed by 8 ...., R–Kt1 and Black has a fair position. Finally, 4 Q–K4, QR–K1 (not KR–K1 on account of 5 P × P to be followed by Pawns Queens); 5 Q–Q3, R–Q1 and draws.

A combination must be sound. An unsound combination is no combination at all. It is merely an attempt, an error, a failure, a nonentity.

But a combination must not only be correct, it must satisfy other conditions that we shall now discuss. Therefore, besides the art of discovering and creating combinations there is also an art or science of *criticism* of combinations.

Of several combinations simultaneously existent you have to choose, in the position, the one yielding the greatest advantage; of several Mates you have to select the simplest one because that Mate is least open to error, because unfortunately *humanum est errare*.

True, one cannot demonstrate that this is simpler than that; one can decide such a question by intuition only. Here the science of combination c o m e s into contact with the science of the beautiful with which we shall deal in another chapter. But let us state it at once, that only an inferior taste could prefer that which is unnecessarily complicated to that which is simple. The healthy mind chooses of two equally suitable moves the one that is more straight forward and less sophisticated.

It is then the function of the critic to give recognition to and to bring into prominence that which is valuable, to correct that which is well meant but weak, to speak with a loud voice against what is pretentious and a sham.

46

Black, Steinitz, to play

Bird

46.—Steinitz played here
1 ...., P—Q5, and his biographer (L. Bachman, *Schachmeister S t e i n i t z*, first volume, page 167) remarks concerning t h i s move :—

" Steinitz conducts this difficult ending to victory with admirable correctness and a nice judgment of position. A game equally remarkable for the excellent attack of the victor and the obstinate defence of the loser." Nothing of all that is true. If Bird had played rightly he would easily have drawn. After

1	....	P—Q5
2	Kt—Q5ch.	K—K4
3	Kt × B	P × BP

He should now not have played 4 K—K3? but

4	Kt—Q7ch.	K—Q3
	Best.	
5	Kt × BP	P × Kt
6	K—K2	....

Whereupon 6 ...., P–B5 would actually lose, while 6 ...., P × P would just manage to draw. Thus 6 ...., P–B5 ? 7 K–Q1, K–K4; 8 K–B2, K–B5; 9 K × P, K × P; 10 P–R4, etc. If 8 ...., K–Q5; 9 P–B4, K–K5; 10 K × P, K × P; 11 P–R4, P × P; 12 P–Kt5, K–K4; 13 K × P and wins. Best is 6 ...., P × P; 7 P × P, K–K4; 8 K–Q3, K–B5; 9 K × P, P–Kt4; 10 K–Q4, K × P; 11 K–B5, K × P; 12 K × P and draws.

It is no exaggeration to say that the literature of Chess abounds with faults of the above description.

Schlechter played
1 P × KP

To be sure, if as actually occurred in the game, 1 ...., R × R; 2 P × Kt disarranges the whole King's side. But if the Black Knight gets desperado and commits suicide in a fashion becoming a warrior with

1 ....   Kt × P

what then? Black would have won.

47

Salwe

White, Schlechter, to play

47.—In this position, at St. Petersburg, 1909, Schlechter made a combination that was awarded the brilliancy prize. But the combination is not correct.

48

Steinitz

White, Tschigorin, to play

48.—Here Tschigorin made the sacrifice 1 Kt × BP and won in a few moves. With *one* voice the Chess press—newspapers, magazines, books, applauded. Nobody criticised. In fact, the combination was a half-sublime, half-ludicrous error. To win the game 1 P–R5 was amply sufficient. Say 1 .... B × RP; 2 R ×

P, Q–Q1; 3 Kt–KKt5, but
to elucidate this is certainly
unnecessary, since Black
virtually fights with a Rook
minus and cannot bring it
into play before White has
inflicted m o r t a l damage.
The sacrifice 1 Kt × BP, on
the contrary, immediately
lets out that Rook and imperils the issue of the game
concerning w h i c h there
should have been no doubt.
Let us examine the combination!

1 Kt × BP   K × Kt
2 P—K6ch.   K × P
3 Kt—K5   ....

Now Steinitz should have
posted the Queen on K1
with the intent of sacrificing
it to break the attack; he
should not have left square
KB2 unguarded, viz., 3
........., Q–K1; 4 R–K1,
K–B3; 5 P–Kt4, P–KR4;
6 P × Kt, Kt × P; 7 Kt–Kt4
ch., P × Kt; 8 R × Q, QR ×
R; or 6 B × Ktch., Q × B; 7
P × Kt, QR–K1; 8 Kt–Kt4
ch., P × Kt; 9 R × Q, R ×
R; 10 Q × P, R–R3. Thus
Black could hold out a long
time and the final issue, on
account of the strength of
the Black Queen's side
Pawns, would be doubtful.

Even the most lenient
critic would have to say
that Tschigorin fought with

a corpse, gave him a new
spell of life and then killed
him again.

49
Black, Janowski, to play

Lasker

49.—Black played here
1 ...., Q–K5? The sequence was 2 O–O, B–B3;
3 R × B, P × R; 4 B–B3,
Q–K4; 5 Kt × Pch. and
won. That Black played
badly is true: he should
have played 1...... Q × Rch.
But this sacrifice does not
lead to a forced win, its
issue is problematical; yet
for many years one met
throughout Chess literature
the assertion that this combination would have led to
a win. Nobody, indeed,
doubted it. I smiled. I
showed the right play; but
what could I say with my
feeble voice to drown the
thunder? The analysis
given in the Chess literature ran 1 ...., Q ×
Rch.; 2 Kt × Q, B–B3;

3 O–O, B–Ktch., followed by 4 ...., B ×
Kt. But the law of combination is to ponder *all* possibilities. Why 3 O–O? Is
nothing else possible, not
3 Q–B1, not 3 QKt–Kt5 ? At
last the analysis was rendered correctly in Dr. Tarrasch's *Die Moderne
Schachpartie*. The move 3
Q–B1 would not suffice because after 3 .... B × Kt;
4 P–Kt5, the threat could
very well be parried by 4
.... Kt–K4 and Black
then would win. The correct
move is 3 QKt–Kt5. Then
Black has nothing better
than 3 ...., B × Kt, for
after 3 ...., Kt × Kt,
the Check 4 Q–B1 would
be painful, for 4 ....,
K–Kt1 would lead to
" Philidor's legacy," 5 Q–
B4ch. and Mates in a few
moves. Hence 3 ...., B
× Kt; 4 Kt × B, Kt × Kt;
5 K–B2; and the position is
about even though still full
of problems.

As evident from the history of this combination,
the Chess student should
not trust an analysis merely
because he sees it in print.
He must examine, he must
do his own thinking and by
conscientious work he must
form his own judgment.

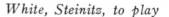

Lasker 50

White, Steinitz, to play

50.—Shall White here
play 1 P–Q5? L. Bachmann, the biographer of
Steinitz, cites a long analysis which starts out with the
judgment "decidedly better
(than 1 P–K4, as played by
Steinitz) would have been
1 P–Q5." Oh no! Decidedly
worse! Black defends as
follows

1 P—Q5 ?	Q—K4
2 Kt—B4	Kt—K2
3 K—R2	....

The reply to 3 Kt–K6
would be 3 .... R–K1.
White looks in vain for
moves to continue his
attack, because his QP is
pinned and his KP is weak.
If 3 Q–Q4, Q × Q; 4 P × Q,
P × P; 5 Kt × P, Kt–B4
with an advantage sufficient
to win.

3	P × P
4 Kt × P	Kt—B4

The points of view above
indicated are bases for the

understanding and criticism of a combination; they are the elements which the creative faculty needs for healthy development.

A few examples are here given in illustration. It is noteworthy that they are not invented positions, but arise from the struggle of two brains passionately antagonistic to each other and gifted with all the required talent for mastership, battling for the ideals in Chess.

They will be examined and criticised from the points of view we have already enumerated.

51
Black, Molina, to play.

Capablanca

51.—The White Queen is in a commanding position and must be driven off. The attack by 1 .... P—K4 is refuted (Capablanca, *My Chess Career*) by 2 Kt—K6 dis.ch., K—B3; 3 P—B4! The right move is

| 1 .... | P—B4 |
| 2 Q—Kt3 | .... |

The Q is still menacing. Black played, too passively,

| 2 .... | K—R3. Better is |

| 2 .... | P—B5 |

After 3 Q—Kt4, P—K4 could fearlessly be played; hence

| 3 P × P | Kt—B4 |
| 4 Q—Kt4 | Kt—KR3 |

For White now to play for a win would be very hazardous. If for example 5 Q—R4, Q—Q7 and the attack has passed to Black.

Capablanca's book has many excellent qualities, but his analysis of the above combination and his judgment thereon are not accurate.

Silvestre   52

White, Caldas Vianna, to play

52.—White is in difficulties. A continuation of the attack against the King by Checks or threats of Mate is not on the board. An exchange of Queens is offered and his Queen has no escape. If the Knight did not block the Rook Q–Q5 ch would at once terminate the game, but there it stands and cannot be removed at once, for the Check with the Knight would open to the Black King a safe square simply by capture of the Knight. One understands the mood in which White resolved to play.

1 Kt—Q6   ....

Now the correct and good play was 1 .... Q × Q; 2 Kt × Q, B × P; 3 Kt × R, B × R; 4 R–K5, B–Kt5. Probably Black played hastily

1 ....   P × Pch

and now the situation for Black has become perilous.

2 K—R1   ....

Now the exchange of Queens will leave White with a better Ending, 2 .... Q × Q; 3 Kt × Q, P–B7; 4 Kt × B, R–Q8; 5 R (B5)–B1, whereby Mate is threatened and thus White wins. Black, recognizing that the Ending would be lost, tries to hold the position by obstinate defence.

2 ....   P—KR3
3 Q—Q5 ch   K—R2
4 Q—K4   K—Kt1
5 Q—K6 ch   K—R2
6 R—B6 !   ....

which menaces 7 R × Pch.

6 ....   KR—B1
7 Q—B5 ch   K—Kt1
8 R × R ch   R × R
9 Q × R ch

The Queen cannot be captured because of 10 R–K8 Mate and Black resigns.

53

Snosko—Borowski

White, Dr. Bernstein, to play

53.—The Black King has an insecure position, but if 1 Q × P ch, K–B1, the King will establish itself on K2 under the protection of his centre Pawns.   White, in possession of heavy pieces with which to harass the King and because Black's two Rooks for the moment are unprotected and hampered by the Kt at Q2, embarks upon the following sacrifice :

1 Kt × P   P × Kt
2 Q × KP ch   K—R1

The King is driven into the corner because the Queen otherwise would Check and simultaneously attack one of the unprotected Rooks.

3 Q—K7   Q—Kt1
4 R × P ch   Q × R
5 Q × R ch   Kt—B1
6 Q × Kt ch and wins.

54

v. Bardeleben

White, Steinitz, to play

54.—The Black King is exposed, the KKtP a possible target, the Black Queen unprotected, the Knight in the line dominated by White. However, no temporizing would do, because Black threatens exchanges. If White evades them with 1 QR–Q1, so R–B3, forcing retreats; hence, this is the moment to seek the combination. *Hic Rhodus, hic salta!*

The beginning of the attack is indicated. There is a move threatening Mate in two and putting the Black Queen in jeopardy at the same time, unquestionably a powerful move.

1 Q—Kt4   P—KKt3
2 Kt—Kt5 ch   K—K1

So far, so good. Now let us investigate the functions. Of course, Black's Rooks are desperately anxious to be getting into action. The King has to guard the Queen, the Queen has to guard the KR. These two pieces besides have to guard the Knight. Are they not overburdened? Let us see!

3 R × Kt ch   ....

Indeed they are. If the King captures, it becomes immediately a target for 4 R–K1 ch and, being hampered by its function, is soon driven into a desperate position as follows: 3 .... K × R ; 4 R–K1 ch, K–Q3 (or 4 ...., K–Q1 ; 5 Kt–K6ch. and wins the Queen); 5 Q–Kt4 ch, K–B2 (or R–B4 ; 6 R–K6 ch) ; 6 Kt–K6 ch, K–Kt1 ; 7 Q–B4 ch and wins. In this emergency Black bethinks himself to threaten a Mate with his Rook.

3 ....   K—B1
4 R—B7 ch   K—Kt1
5 R—Kt7 ch   ....

The Rook is immune because Black cannot suffer his Queen to be captured with Check.

5	K—R1
6 R × Pch.	K—Kt1
7 R—Kt7 ch	K—R1
8 Q—R4 ch	....

and White Mates in eight more moves.

8	K × R
9 Q—R7 ch	K—B1
10 Q—R8 ch	K—K2
11 Q—Kt7 ch	K—K1
12 Q—Kt8 ch	K—K2
13 Q—B7 ch	K—Q1

or K–Q3; 14 Q × BP ch.

14 Q—B8 ch	Q—K1
15 Kt—B7 ch	K—Q2
16 Q—Q6 Mate	

55

Black, Tschigorin, to play

Schiffers

55.—The White King stands immobile and strongly under the pressure of two Rooks and two Bishops. The situation calls for an investigation of all direct attacks employing the most forceful moves that

Black has at his command. Well, let us try them.

1	R—R8 ch
2 Kt × R	B—R7 ch
3 K × B	R—R1 ch
4 K—Kt3	

(or 4 K–Kt1, R × Kt Mate)

4	Kt—B4 ch
5 K—B4	R—R5
	Mate

Truly, the combination succeeds. And it was easy as it was based only on one motif and containing only two variants (not counting the useless interposing of the White Bishop). It is surprising that this forced Mate should have escaped Tschigorin.

Harmonist   56

White, Schiffers, to play

56.—The Black KBP is thrice attacked and thrice guarded. The Black KR has also the function of guarding the last rank. To drive him away from the protection of the BP would expose the King greatly, since it would then only be guarded by Black's two most valuable pieces, King and Queen.

1 R—K8   R × R
2 B × P ch   K—R1

Otherwise, if 2 ...., K—B1, the King would be driven into the open by 3 Kt × Pch.

3 B × R   Kt—K7 ch

That is all very well, but the Black King is immobile and under pressure.

4 K—R1   Kt × R
5 Kt—B7 ch   K—Kt1
6 Kt—R6 ch   K—B1
7 Q—Kt8 ch   K—K2
8 B × Kt   P × B
9 Q × P ch   K—Q1
10 Q—-B8 ch   K—Q2

Now the King is an obstruction and therefore left where it is. White uses this moment for bringing up his reserves.

11 Kt—K4   Q—Q1
12 Q—Q6 ch   K—K1
13 Kt—B6 ch   Resigns

57   *Dr. G. Flues*

White, Nimzowitsch, to play

57.—Can White play 1 P × Kt? To be sure, if 1 ...., B × P; 2 Kt × B, R × Q; 3 KR × R, P × Kt; 4 P–B5, R—Kt1; 5 QR–Kt1 and Mate follows. But the situation is complicated by counter-attack. How can 1 ...., R–R3 be met? The threatened mate would force White to play 2 B–R5 and 3 R–K1 unless the Bishop can get to B3 in time and the blocking of KR be got out of the way. At least one of these aims must be attained with a Check or else the defence will be insufficient. These are the main considerations whence the following play is evolved :

1 P × Kt   R—R3

Now not 2 P × B ch, R × P ; 3 B–R5, R × B ; 4 R–K1, Q × RP ch ; 5 K–B1, Q–R8 ch ; 6 K–K2, Q–K5 ch ; etc.

2 P × P ch   K—Kt1

or 2 ...., K × P ; 3 B–B3ch. with an easy defence.

3 Kt—B6 ch   K × P
4 Kt × R ch   K—B1
5 Q × B ch   K × Q
6 KR—Q1ch. K moves

7 B—B3 and wins by superiority of material force.

58

Black, Mieses, to play

58.—The White Queen must guard the Check Q–K6 which would lead to a Mate in two. Hence

1 ....   R—Kt6
2 Q × R   B—R5
and wins

59

Black, W. Cohn, to play

Przepiorka

59.—The position of the White King is weak. The RP is guarded only by the King, the KtP by that RP, the square KKt2 belongs to Black, KB2 is defended only by the King. The

White Queen guards nothing essential, obviously it should stand on Q4. The moment is precious and White must not be given time to play Q–Q4 or R–Q2, which would drive off the Black force or strengthen the weak points.

1 ....   R × RP
2 K × R   R—B3

White resigns for the Queen cannot guard KKt3 nor KR6 and the threatened disaster can no more be warded off.

60

Forgacs

which threatens powerfully 2 Kt–Q6ch. If 1 .... K × R ; 2 Kt—Kt5 Mates.

White, v. Freymann, to play

60.—The QP guards Black against B–B4. which would be a catastrophe. It also has to guard the point K5. That is too much.

1 Kt—K4   ....

which threatens powerfully 2 Kt–Q6ch. If 1 .... K × R ; 2 Kt—Kt5 Mates.

1	....	P × Kt
2	B—B4	K—Kt1
3	R × Kt dis.ch	K—R2
4	R × KtP	Kt—B3
5	Q—B5	Resigns

61

62

Black, Davidson, to play

Em. Lasker

White, Rubinstein, to play

61.—B l a c k   obviously threatens R × Kt. White defends by counter-attack and wins.

1 R—B1 .... R × Kt

Better would have been 1 ...., K–Kt1; 2 R–B5, Q–B5; 3 P–Q5, R × Kt; 4 Q–B1, R–K5.

2 R × B ch .... P × R
3 Q—B1 ! .... R × P

Also after 3 .... R–K4; 4 Q × P ch, K–Kt1; P × R, Q × P; 6 R–B1 White has an excellent position.

4 P × R .... R—Q2
5 Q × P ch .... K—Q1

6 R—B4 and won the Ending.

Dr. Esser

62.—The Black King attacks the weak spot. The White KtP has to guard the RP, the BP has to guard both KP and KtP, the KP has to stop P–K6, which would lead to the win of the KtP and the RP. Therefore, P–B5 is suggested.

But when should this be done? Now, because if Black allows White time to play K–B1 he would improve his position, not impair it.

1 .... P—B5
2 KtP × P

or 2 KP × P, P–K6; 3 P × P; K × KP and afterward by K–B6 win all the other Pawns.

2 .... K—Kt5
3 K—K2

When will be the right moment to capture the helpless RP? After White's King has left its favourable position where he supports the advance P—B3, which would yield him a Passed Pawn.

3   ………   P—R4
4 K—B1

If 4 P—B3 ch, P × P ch ; 5 K—B2 Black has still a move in reserve, P—Kt3, and thus holds his BP.

4   ………   K × P
5 K—Kt2   K—Kt5
6 K—R2   K—B6
7 K—Kt1   P—R5
8 K—B1   P—R6

and wins all White's Pawns in exchange for his RP.

63   *Blackburne*

White, Mackenzie, to play and win

63.—To sum up the functions and intentions as clearly indicated by the position. The White King must block the KRP, the Rook on B1 must stop the KP and guard the first rank. It is exposed to B—R6 which at the same time would threaten Mate.

The Rook on Q4 has to attack the KBP and to attack the Black King, eventually to pin the Bishop. It is noteworthy that the Black King has no way to get into action because the White Pawns hinder it and the White Rook menaces it.

White will ward off the threat of B—R6 by an inactive piece. Not 1 R—KR4?, P—K7 ; 2 R—K1, R—Q1 ! but

1 P—Kt4   ………

Now Black is obliged to concentrate his effort on getting that obstruction out of the way.

1   ………   P—K7
2 R—K1   R—R5
3 R—KB4   ………

If now 3 ……… B × P ; 4 R—B8 ch, B—B1 ; 5 R × BP, and Black has no attack left.

3   ………   R × P
4 R × R   ………

not 4 R × BP ??, R—Kt8ch.

4   ………   B × R
5 K × P   B—B4
6 K—Kt3   B—K5
7 R—KR1

It is hard to defend the Black King.

7   ………   K—B1
8 P—B6   P × P
9 QP × P   K—Q1
10 K—B4   B—Q4
11 K—K5   B × RP
12 K—B6   B—Kt1

13	R—R8	P Queens
14	R × B ch	Q—K1
15	R × Q ch	K × R
16	K—K6	K—Q1
17	K—B7 and wins	

Had Black played 2 ...., R—Kt1 White would have answered 3 K × P, B × P; 4 K–Kt3 and with the King in action White would have been quite safe.

Again, if

7	....	P—R3
8	P—Kt6	P × P
9	P × P	K—B1
10	K—B4	B × P
11	K—K5	B × P
12	K—Q6	

Finally

7	....	P—R3
8	P—Kt6	K—B1

Black thus keeps the point Q3 guarded.

9	R—R8 ch	K—Q2
10	P × P	K × P
11	P—Q6 ch	K—B3
12	R—R1	

and wins at his ease.

64

Black, Em. Lasker, to play

Dr. Tartakower

64.—The White BP has the function of guarding K5 and thus preventing Kt–K4.

1	....	P—Kt4

If now 2 P × P, Kt–K4; 3 B–B5, R–Q8; or if 3 KR–B1, R–Q7.

2	Q—R2	P × P
3	R—K2	Q—Kt3
4	Q—B2	K—R2
5	Q—B3	R—KKt1
6	K—R1	Q—R4
7	R—Q2	P × P

with an easy win.

65

Black, Spielmann, to play

Rubinstein

65.—The threat R–B8 ch is guarded by Rook and Bishop. The double guard is needed because also the Black Rooks are doubled. The very same pieces guard the KP. This suggests the question whether B × P would be effective. The move threatens mate and therefore indirectly guards the Queen. The formidably posted Bishop would have to be captured and the way to R—B8 ch opened. The question is only whether the sacrifice would drive the White King into such difficulties as would be considered by Black sufficient compensation for the sacrificed material. If 2 B × B, R–B8 ch; 3 R × R, R × R ch; 4 K–Kt2, R–Kt8 ch; 5 K–B3, Q–R4 ch; 6 K –K3, Q × P the White KtP will fall and Black will surely have compensation. But there is another variation, 2 R × B which appears more promising. This line of play was actually adopted. Its course was as follows :

1	B × P
2 R × B	R—B8 ch
3 B × R	R × B ch
4 K—Kt2	Q—B7 ch
5 K—R3	R—KR8
6 R—B3	Q × RPch
7 K—Kt4	Q—R4 ch
8 K—B4	Q—R3 ch
9 K—Kt4	P--KKt4

The King is made immobile. White had to play R × P and is lost after eight moves.

The " Zugzwang " and the Stalemate

There are combinations not subject to the foregoing motifs which play an equally prominent part in all contests of Life. They none the less are combinations, in that they are brought about by the faculty of the mind to combine various concepts and of thinking logically and towards a logical purpose. But they differ from the combinations studied above inasmuch as they are not emanations of the power of the pieces but rather of the subtleties of reasoning. They have something mathematical, something of scholastic finesse. They never speak with the voice of thunder, they reflect the despair of a proud and heroic heart battling against titanic forces. Their triumph is the triumph of a tricky lawyer who has discerned a loophole in the wording of a law. Man has erred in framing the law— the moral and social intent of Law is defeated by an ambiguity of language, by the inappropriateness of an arbitrary expression — the logical mind gains an advantage over the heroic mind and exalts.

Of this nature are combinations based on the motifs of *Zugzwang* and stalemate.   According to the rules of play, one cannot waive the right of moving.   You may waive rights in Life, but not in play. The right to move may become very irksome—you have attained an excellent, an unimprovable position; you want to stay there, but the wording of the rule forces you to make some change.   Your position is such that any change is undesirable, yet you must consent to it. Thereby your position becomes inferior, you lose ground, you lose the game.

The obligation to move, which is the same as the right to move, has no name in English.   It is usually called by the German name of *Zugzwang*.   There is nothing that exactly corresponds to it in real Life.

It is very much the same with the Stalemate.   Possibly the idea of sanctuary, where a criminal would find protection as long as he clung to it, has a remote likeness to the idea of Stalemate.   All in all, combinations based upon these motifs, though subtle and sharp, require no boldness, no will-power, but merely ingenuity.

1

1.—T h i s   Elementary Ending   illustrates   both motifs   in   their   simplest form.   If Black is to move, White wins by *Zugzwang*. 1 .... K–Q1 ; 2 P–Q7 Black cannot be drivn off by force, but he must move. 2 .... K–B2, 3 K–K7, and now force wins.   If White to move, the *Zugzwang* is obviated by the Stalemate. 1 P–Q7 ch, K–Q1 ; 2 K–Q6, Stalemate.

2

Black to play and draw

2.—This is the final stage of a study by Troitzki. With 1 .... K—B8 Black keeps the QP mobile, and

if 2 Q × P Black is Stalemated. With this joke
Black snaps his fingers at
the White Queen made
powerless by the wording
of a rule.

The *Zugzwang* occurs
almost exclusively in endings where few forces are
left on the board, mostly in
endings of King and Pawns
against King and Pawns.
The Pawns, not being able
to repeat moves, are usually
blocked and then it is the
King which has to bear the
burden of the *Zugzwang*.
In the struggle of the Kings
under the *Zugzwang*, geometrical conditions play an
important part, such as the
O p p o s i t i o n   and   the
"triangle." Sometimes
also the mathematical idea
of correspondence or function is implied.

These endings are there-
fore no trial of combative
energy, but of mathematical
reasoning, of the faculty for
calculation.

3

White to play and win

3.—Here both *Zugzwang*
and Stalemate are the leading motifs. The Black
King must play neither to
K1 nor K2 because of P—
B6. Its field is restricted to
B3, Q1 and B1. White can
defend his BP from Q5, Q4,
B4. The mobility of White
is greater than that of Black
and in the play for *Zugzwang* he has therefore the
advantage. He utilizes the
"triangle" Q4, Q5, K5 for
the purpose of losing a
move.

1	K—K5'	K—B3
2	K—Q4	K—Q2

If 2 .... K—Kt4 ; 3 K—
Q5 and White soon attacks
the KtP or pushes P—B6
and wins.

3   K—Q5   ....

Now White has lost a
move and Black under the
pressure of *Zugzwang* and
unable to play K–K2 must
give way.

3	....	K—B1
4	K—K6	K—Q1
5	K—Q6	K—B1
6	K—K7	K—Kt1
7	K—Q7	K—R1

Now not 8 K–B7 on ac-
count of Stalemate, but

8   P—B6   P × P

9 K—B7 and Queens his
Pawn.

The idea of the "tri-
angle" is here made mani-
fest. The King, dominat-

ing a " triangle," can make three moves to return to his original post; the King, not so favoured, uses for the same purpose two or four or six, in short, an even, never an odd, number of moves. Thus the King in the " triangle " can always lose a move and place the opponent under *Zugzwang*.

4   *By Weenink*

White to play and win

4.—The White KtP is exposed, yet the White King desires to march to QKt5 in order to win the Pawn there. Hence, White must force the exchange of his weak Pawn for the strong BP.

| 1 | K—K4 | K—Kt5 |

But now Black has the Opposition. If 2 K–K5, K–Kt4, White can make no headway. Consequently, White must somehow contrive to lose a move.

| 2 | K—Q5 | K—R4 |

or 2 .... K–Kt6; 3 K–K5, K—Kt5; 4 K—B6, etc. Or again, 2 .... K–B4; 3 K–Q4, K–Kt5; 4 K–K4, and the end is attained.

| 3 | K—B6 ! | .... |

Now 3 .... K—Kt3 would hold the Opposition, but that is useless because of 4 K × P, whereupon the White King would have time enough to return for the capture of the BP.

3	....	K—Kt4
4	K—B5	K—R5
5	K—Q4	K—Kt5
6	K—K4	K—Kt4
7	K—K5	K—Kt5
8	K—B6	K—Kt6
9	K—B5	

The exchange of Pawns now being forced, White wins without trouble.

5

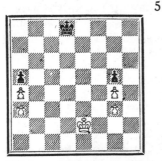

White to play and win
Black to play and draw

5.—Here the central squares correspond to each other as follows. Whenever the White King stands on B4 the Black King must be on QB3 so as to avert both K–Kt5 and K–Q5. Whenever the White King comes to K4, the Black King must counter by K–K3 in order to defend both his Pawns. To the point Q4 corresponds Q3. After having established the correspondence thus far, we may easily continue it further. If the White King enters upon the Q3 ready to go to either B4, Q4, or K4, the Black King must be ready to go to QB3, Q3 or K3 and therefore occupy Q2. Analogously in correspondence are the points QB3 and QB2, K3 and K2, QB2 and QB1, Q2 and Q1, K2 and K1. Consequently, White, having the move, wins by 1 K–Q2, and Black having the move Draws by 1 ...., K–K1. The mode of winning is here indicated: 1 K–Q2, K–B1; 2 K–K3, since K2 is inaccessible to Black. 2 .... K–Q2; 3 K–Q3, K–Q3; 4 K–Q4 and has the Opposition and thus forces the fifth row and wins. If, however, Black to move, he plays 1 ...., K–K1 and wherever White may move, Black enters the corresponding square; and since this rule can be followed forever, White is forever unable to enter the fifth row.

Muurlink   6

White, Schelfhout, to play White to win

6.—In the diagonal from KR1 to QR8 the White Bishop has three squares of mobility, whereas the Black Bishop guarding the QBP has only two squares at its disposal. White has to lose a move, for if Black to move, he loses either the KRP or the QBP with immediately fatal results, as is readily seen. To lose the move is a simple matter as it was in the case of the "triangle."

1 B—R1   B—Q2
2 B—Kt2   B—K1

or 2 .... K–Kt3; 3 B–B3 wins the RP and forces an entrance for the White King.

3 B—B3   B—Q2

With 3 .... B–B2, the valuable BP is lost. 4 B × BP, B × P; 5 B–K8, B–Kt6; 6 P–B6, B × P; 7 P–B7.

4	B × RP	B—B1
5	B—K8	B—Kt2
6	B—Q7	K—Kt3
7	K—Kt3	K—B3
8	K—B3	K—Kt3
9	K—K3	K—B3
10	K—Q4	B—R1
11	B—B8	....

Zugzwang has hampered Black all along and now *Zugzwang* forces him to resign.

7

By Em. Lasker after an idea of v. Gottschall

White to play and draw

7.—The Black Queen is pinned. Can White force Stalemate or keep the Queen pinned indefinitely? That is the idea of a study bv von Gottschall which, if I remember rightly, had the following form : *White*— King on QKt1, Queen on QB2, Pawn on KR4; *Black*—King on KR2, Queen on KKt3, Pawns on QB6, KKt2, KR4 and the solution 1 K–R1. In my modified form 1 K–R1

would not work because of 1 ...., P–R3 and White in *Zugzwang* must abandon the pin. The solution is

1	K—R3	P—R3
2	Q—Kt1	

and White maintains the pin. Of course, if 2 ...., K–R3; 3 Q–B1ch., K–R2; 4 Q–B2.

By Troitzki   8

White to play and win

8. The motif of *Zugzwang* is here finely executed. First the Black King is impeded in its mobility then the Bishop, and finally a catastrophe is brought about.

1	K—R6	K—R1
2	Kt—R4	....

If now 2 .... B–Kt1 ; 3 Kt–Kt6 Mates. The Black Bishop is thus forced to remain on its exposed post.

2	....	K—Kt1

Now the Knight can improve its position without losing its hold upon the precious square KKt6.

3 Kt—B3   K—R1
4 Kt—K5   K—Kt1
5 Kt—B6   K—R1
6 Kt—K7, the catas-
trophe.

The Promotion of the Pawn

Far more natural than the motif of *Zugzwang* or Stalemate, is that of the promotion of a Passed Pawn on reaching the 8th rank. The Pawn has succeeded to the extreme of its possibilities until at its death it is rewarded with a new life—thus a Buddhist might put it—or, as we Westerners say, it is promoted to higher rank on account of the efficiency it has shown.

The promotion of the Pawn is the final stage of a slow process which runs through three phases.

1. The first phase consists in obtaining a " Passed " Pawn by getting the opposing Pawn out of the way by capture or by forcing it to capture a piece or a Pawn.

2. The second phase consists in the advance of the Pawn in spite of the resistance of the enemy.

3. The last phase is the conquest of the square of promotion either by advancing or by capturing on the last rank.

9

Black to play, White wins

9.—White threatens 1 R —R8 guarding the Pawn by geometrical motif. Black is helpless, since the King, for fear of Check, cannot enter the third rank.

10

Black, S. Bergh, to play

Dr. Lindehn

10.—

1	Q—B8 ch
2 Q × Q	P—K7 ch
3 Kt—B2	P × Q=Qch.

and wins

11   *Harrwitz*

White, Dufresne, to play

11.—White wins by means of his Passed Pawn, which is able to advance to the seventh rank with discovered check and therefore virtually is already on the seventh rank.

1 Q—K8   K—R2
2 P—B7   and wins

12   *Dr. Tarrasch*

White, Maroczy, to play

12.--The game proceeded 1 K—B6, R—B8 ch; 2 K—Kt6, R—B5! threatening

R–R5; 3 R × P, R × Pch.; 4 K–B5, R–QR5 Draws. White could have won as follows:

1 R × P   K × R
2 K—R6   K—Kt6
3 P—Kt5   K—B5
4 P—Kt6   K—K4
5 P—Kt7   R—QKt8
6 K—R7   K—Q3
7 P—Kt8=QchR × Q
8 K × R   K—B3
9 P—R6 wins.

13
Black, Dimer, to play and win

Hallgarten

13.—The White King or Rook has the function of guarding the BP. The White Rook must stay on the QKt file to stop Black's KtP. The combination consists of over burdening the King as well as Rook and so getting the BP out of the way.

1 ....   P—R4ch.
2 K × P

The Pawn unless captured, would become dangerous.

2 ....   P—R4

If the King returns, 3 ...., R–Q5ch., and 4 ...., R–QKt5 obstructs the White Rook and Queens the Pawn.

3 P—R3   R—K7

White is in *Zugzwang*. The Rook cannot move without losing the BP, the King cannot go to R6 because of the Checkmate by R–R7, it cannot return on account of Rook Checking on fifth row, as, for instance,

4 K—Kt4   R—K5 ch
5 K moves   R–QKt5

and Queens the Pawn and wins.

14

From Chess Player's Chronicle

Black to play, White wins

14.—In spite of the simplicity of the position a variety of motifs comes here into play. Firstly, the Passed Pawn. Black being unable to stop it on his first rank (1 .... R–R1 ; 2 R–R8 wins at once) must stop it from the Kt's file. Unfortunately, the King is on that file, so that only *one* square is open to the Black Rook on that line, KKt3.

1 ....   R—R3 ch

Now White cannot win by 2 K–B7, R–KKt3, nor by 2 K–K7, R–R2ch. because the White King cannot escape the Checks of the Rook. But where does White move? Remember that after Black will have played R—KKt3 neither the White Rook nor the Pawn can move and that Black is in a similar predicament. Therefore White utilizes *Zugzwang*.

2 K—Q5   R—KKt3
3 K—K5   K—Kt5

Forced by *Zugzwang*. Now the Black King and Pawn are sufficiently distant from each other to enable White to make use of the geometrical motif.

4 R—R1   K—B6
5 R—B1 ch   K—K6
6 R—B7

soon to be followed by K–
B5, K–B6, and then White
wins easily.

15

Leonid Kubbel

White to play and win

Leonid Kubbel   16

White to play and win

15.—The Black Pawn
cannot gain its square of
promotion, but White can
keep the Bishop from both-
ering the White Pawn. To
that end the Bishop must
be kept from the diagonal
dominating KR8 within the
two moves that the Pawn
needs for Queening. Naturally, Kt–K2 is not so strong
as Kt–K6, where the
Knight threatens two
Checks.

1 Kt—K6   ....

If 1 ...., B–K8 or
B–R5; 2 Kt–B5ch., King
moves; 3 Kt–K4 success-
fully shuts the Bishop out.
And if 1 ...., B–Kt6; 2
Kt–Q4ch., King moves; 3
Kt–B3 is similarly effective.

16.—H e r e the Passed
Pawns play the capital part.
The BP is menacing, the
K n i g h t can stop it
but only by the aid
of a Check which speeds
the Knight on.   T h e n
t h e Black King will
hurry to support and the
White King is far from
action. This the setting of
the drama. How very bal-
anced the situation is
becomes evident from the
analysis of the tempting 1
Kt–K5.   The reply is 1
........., K–Kt4; 2 Kt × P,
K–B5; 3 P–K4, P–R4; 4
K–Kt2, P–R5; 5 K–B2,
P–R6; 6 K–Q2, P–R7; 7
Kt × P, K–Q5 and Draws.
The right line of play is:

1 Kt—Q6   P—B7
2 Kt—B4 ch   K—Kt4
3 Kt—Q2

Since now 4 K–Kt3 is
threatened, which would
keep off the Black King,

Black must get his King into action at once.

3	....	P Queens
4	Kt × Q	K—B5
5	K—Kt2	K—Q6
6	K—B1	K—K7

This is a bitter necessity, since by K–Q1, and K1 and B2, etc., White would otherwise build up a firm position.

7 P—K4   K × Kt

If now the White Pawn marches, the Black Pawn does so likewise, gets to R7, and there according to a well - known elementary Ending the P, supported by its King, makes a Draw against the Queen by Stalemate. But White makes use of the great distance between the Black King and Pawn by menacing that Pawn first and thus approaching with his King.

| 8 | K—Q2 | P—R4 |
| 9 | K—K̃3 | K—Kt7 |

or else the Black Pawn would be stopped.

10	P—K5	P—R5
11	P—K6	P—R6
12	P—K7	P—R7
13	P Queens	P Queens

Now the White King is near enough to carry through a victorious attack.

14	Q—Kt6 ch	K—R6
15	Q—R5 ch	K—Kt7
16	Q—Kt4 ch	K—R7
17	K—B2 and wins.	

17

Black, Dr. Tarrasch, to play

Tschigorin

17.—

1 ....   P—R7

The Passed Pawn, supported by the Rooks is sufficient compensation for the loss of the Queen.

2 R × Q ch   ....

Has the Queen not been paid for too dearly with the Rook?   But if 2 Kt–Kt5, Black replies 2 ...., K–K2. If then 3 Q–R7, K–Q3, now the White Queen is hampered by the necessity of guarding the Mate in two threatened by the Black Rooks.   The Black King is made comparatively safe and the Passed Pawn becomes a terrible weapon.

2	....	P × R
3	R—Q1	R—Kt8
4	Q—B1	R(B7)—QKt7
5	Kt—Q2	....

The square QKt1 must be guarded, since 5 .... R × R; followed by 6 ...., R–Kt8 is the threat.

5	R × R
6 Q × R	R × Kt
7 Q—QB1	R × P
8 K—Kt2	....

To give a series of Checks would be useless, since Black can play so that the series terminates.

8	R—QB6
9 Q—QR1	R—B7 ch
10 K—B3	P—Q6
11 Q—Q1	R—QKt7
12 Q—R4	P—Q7

Now the QP Queens, followed by R—Kt8, is the threat, and White resigns.

18

Black, Marshall, to play and win

Thomas

18.—The motif here is the formidable effect of the Black Rook on the eighth involving simultaneous attack on King, Bishop, Knight, the weakness of White's QKt2 and the force of the Passed Pawn.

1	B—Kt4 ch
2 K—Kt1	P × P

If now 3 Kt-B2; R—QB1 or 3 Kt-Q3; R—R8.

3 B—Q2	R—R8
4 P—B3	R—Kt8
5 K—B2	R × P
6 K—Kt3	P—Kt6
7 P—B4	R × B
8 R × R	B—Kt5
9 R—Q1	B × Kt ch
10 R × B	B—Q6
	and wins

By R. Reti   **19**

White to play and draw

19.—Most remarkably White can here utilize the nearly helpless BP to aid his King in winning two important moves.

1 K—Kt7	P—R5
2 K—B6	....

Now 3 K—K6 threatens to give life to the White Pawn.

2	K—Kt6
3 K—K5	....

and threatens again by K-Q6 to give life to the White Pawn.

3 ....   K × P
4 K—B4 Draws.

20

An old method of breaking through

White to play and win

20.—The White array of Pawns is able to obtain by force a Passed Pawn in breaking through the opposing array.

1 P—Kt6   BP × P
2 P—R6   P × RP
3 P—B6

Of course, if 1 ....
RP × P; 2 P–B6, P × BP; 3 P–R6.

21   *Em. Lasker.*

White, Dr. Tarrasch, to play

21.—Here Dr. Tarrasch could have won by making a combination the motif of of which is to break through with his Pawns. He tried it but missed the right continuation.

1 P—Kt5   ....

I moved here 1 ...., R–KB2, whereupon 2 R–R3 would have won, but White answered 2 KtP × P and the game ended in a Draw.

1 ....   BP × P
2 P—B6   R—KB2
3 B—Q4   R—Q2
4 R—K3 !   ....

If now 4 .... R × B; 5 P–B7, R–Q1; 6 R × B. R–KB1; 7 R–K7 ch, K × P; 8 K–Kt4, K–B3; 9 K × P, K –Q3; 10 K–B6 wins.

4 ....   B—B4 (or
                   Variation A)
5 R—K7   R × R
6 P × R   B—Q2
7 K—B3   K—B3
8 K—K4   K—Q3
9 B—B5 ch   K—B3
10 K—K5 and wins
Variation A.
4 ....   B—B3
5 R—K7   R × R
6 P × R   K—B1
7 K—Kt4   K—Q2
8 B—B6   K—K1
9 K × P   K—B2
10 K—B4   K—K1
11 K—K5   K—Q2
12 B—Kt5   B—Kt2
13 K—B6   B—Q4

or 13 ...., K–K1 ; 14 K
–K6.

14 P—Kt7   B × P
15 K—B7 and wins

22   *Janowski*

White, Em. Lasker, to play

22.—The task for White
is evidently to obtain a
Passed Pawn on the King's
side. Black cannot attempt
to counter-balance this by
obtaining a Passed Pawn on
the Queen's side on account
of his Doubled Pawn, un-
less he achieves that end by
bringing up his pieces to
make an attack against the
White Queen's side Pawns.

White has to begin the
attack with an apparently
paradoxical move. The
ordinary method of pro-
cedure would be to advance
first of all the Pawn that has
no vis-à-vis. The KP is
half passed; if it can get
the KBP out of the way it
will have reached the goal
of becoming a Passed
Pawn. But the natural
move 1 P–K5 would be bad
for the Bishop, the Bishop
would be shut out of action
by its own Pawns. The
move P–K5 may follow
later on, since the Bishop
can give it support.

1 P—B5   P—KB3

Dr. Tarrasch (*Die Mod-
erne Schachpartie*) blames
this move for all the trouble
that ensues, and he may be
right in so far as the move
is made by Black too readily
but he is certainly wrong in
thinking that Black may do
without this move. True,
Black can fight for the
square K4 with his pieces
alone, viz., 1 .... Kt–B3 ;
2 B–B4, R–K2 ; 3 R–K3,
KR–K1 ; 4 P–Kt4. White
will threaten to force P–K5
by R(Q1)–K1 and thereby
cause Black to play Kt–K4
ch, B × Kt, R × B, K–B4.
In the long run Black will
be unable to guard the point
K4 without P–KB3 which
permits the attack P–Kt5.

2 P—Kt4   R—K2
3 B—B4   KR—K1
4 R—K3   Kt—B3
5 P—Kt5   ....

After 5 P × P ; 6 B × KtP
White will be able at length
to conquer the square K5

5 ....   Kt—R4
6 P—KR4   Kt—B5
7 R—K2   R—-B2
8 R—KKt1   K—Q2
9 P—R5   Kt—Q3
10 P—R6   ....

If now 10 ...., P ×
RP; 11 P × BP obtaining
two formidable P a s s e d
Pawns.

10	BP × P
11 R × P	P—Kt3
12 P × P	P × P
13 R × KtP	KR—B1
14 R—Kt7	R × R

15 P × R and won easily.

These instances will
suffice as a beginning. It
would be easy enough to increase their number. But it
is not the multitude of examples that is instructive,
for the multitude is confusing; it is the *method* which
carries value as instruction,
and the method has been
sufficiently illustrated above
to be thoroughly intelligible. The reader must now
work by himself so that he
may acquire the ability to
apply the method however
the circumstances may vary
in detail.

On Made-Up Combinations and on Combinations Arising in the Course of a hard-fought Game.

To construct positions
according to the motifs discussed above and thus to
invent surprising combinations is as easy as telling a
fairy tale. The reader may
do so for practice, but is
earnestly advised to do only
a little of it. A method
commonly followed with
this end in view is to construct the final position
which has some very sur-
prising feature and then to
lead up to it by a forced
move and again to lead up
to that position and so, always going backward a
move to arrive at a
position where the funda-
mental idea is fairly hidden.
Thus many combinations
have been composed from
time immemorial. Again,
you may take up a combination that arose in actual play
get rid of non-essentials
and thus refine it. This
method is superior. But
there are masters in the art
of composing combinations
who follow their own
methods and who, perhaps,
work with no method rely-
ing only upon their fertility
of invention. Of this art
and its strong æsthetic impression, more in another
chapter. For the moment
may it suffice to say that
artistic combinations, the
solution of which is often
concealed as deeply as
human wit can hide itself,
have been published in immense numbers and have
given pleasure to millions.
But for all that, it is only
the hard-fought game which
produces the profoundest
and most precious ideas,

just as Nature, not the artist, creates the most wonderful works, just so again as the precious metal is not discovered in the retort of the alchemist but in Nature's own recesses : in the mountains and in the rivers.

Not too completely, therefore, must the adept of Chess give himself over to the charms of constructed combinations. R a t h e r should he strive to trace and to master the combination in actual over-the-board play. But to this end, beside a knowledge of the motifs entering into a combination, he will have need also of another method of investigation, and this other method appears to be foreign to combination at first sight, even antagonistic to it. Like most first impressions this is deceptive. Before proceeding to explain this other method of investigation, which is done in the following chapters, let us unmask the reason for this false impression. With such a multitude of resources at his command, many of them of a spectacular nature, the learner is at first disappointed to find that manœuvres of this kind are not always occurring. He loves to believe that truth is beautiful and the beautiful true. For no other cause than lack of experience he fails to recognise the truth and consequently the beauty of the efforts of the Chess master. But if he courageously follows our counsel—that he should serve his apprenticeship with the live contest he will assuredly become awakened to a beauty that he had not known before and the charm of which will fail him no more.

FOURTH BOOK

POSITION PLAY

Whereas by combination values are transformed, they are proved and confirmed by "position play." Thus, position play is antagonistic to combination, as becomes evident when a "combinative player" meets with his counterpart, the "position player." The two often are wholly different in make-up and constitution. The combinative player an adventurer, speculator, gambler, the position-player believing in rigid dogma, happy only in a firm position, afraid of all dangers, parsimonious with all he holds, even with the minute values; the former perhaps careless of detail and large visioned, the latter penny wise and pound foolish. The combinative player calls the position-player Philistine, pedant, woodshifter; the position-player replies with invectives such as romancer, dreamer, presumptuous idealist. One meets with pronounced types of the two kinds and they poke fun at one another. Thus the following story is told of an on-looker at a game. He was a combinative-player. Suddenly he interrupted the players: "I see a magnificent combination, a sacrifice of the Queen," he excitedly called to him who was to move. "If vour opponent then takes the Pawn, he is Mated, and if he goes out of Check, he is Mated in two." "Well," replied the player, "but the principal question is: what am I to do if he captures the Queen?" "That is the only variation," replied the combination player "which I have not yet looked into."

However obviously the majority of Chess-players may be divided into two big classes of combination- and position-players, in the Chess-master this antagonism is transformed into a harmony. In him combination play is *completed* by position play. By combination the master aims to show up and to defeat the *false* values, the *true* values shall guide him in his position play, which in turn shall bring those values to honour. The master is like a man in a learned dispute who knows sophistry but does not make use of it, except for the purpose of exposing the sly subtleties of an artful opponent who disputes a true, sound, vigorous thesis with m e r e trickery.

The Plan

The thought which gives life a combination, is called the *idea*, the thought behind position play is called the *plan*. The idea has a point which surprises, which changes at one blow the state of affairs; the plan has breadth and depth which are imposing and which, by slow, methodical building, give a structure to the position.

The methods followed in the analysis of a given position by combination and by the creation of plans are differentiated by the direction of the underlying thought. The combination-player thinks forward: he starts from the given position and tries the forceful moves in his mind; the position-player thinks backward: he conceives a position to be arrived at and works toward that position of which he is more conscious than the one on the board. He sees successive stages of the position aimed at and he visualises the stage in a reverse order. If one position, according to his plan, is to follow another he sees the one that is to follow first and he deduces, as it were, the anterior position from it.

In looking for a combination the given position is the essential thing, in the conceiving of plans the intended position is the root of my thinking. When following the former process I seek to find out whether among the positions that I can derive from the present position by a succession of forceful moves I may not be able to detect one desirable to me and to envisage it; with the latter process I hope to be able to attain to a position that I have in mind and try to find out whether ways leading up to that conceived position may not start from the given position. Can I, by method, by systematic procedure, start my antagonist on the way to the position I aim at? This is the question uppermost in the mind of the position-player, and this is the essence of plan making.

When looking at the results of analysis, it is true, I cannot determine by logical deduction through which particular process of thought the result has been arrived at. But to this end, though logic fails me, psychology will aid me. A spirit with a large and roomy brain who without error could keep in mind millions of variations would have no need of planning. Frail, weak man can clearly keep in mind only half a dozen variations since he has but little time to spare for Chess. And if he by chance had more time for it and in addition had genius for the game, to see through hundreds of variations would turn his brain. His reason was not made to be a substitute for a printed table. His mind has a marvellous faculty which enables him to conceive deep and far-sighted plans without being subject to the necessity of examining every possibility. From the psychology of frail man I can decide whether this move belongs to a combination; that one to a plan.

There are simple positions by the analysis of which one can practise combining and planning at the same time. One can understand such positions either way, and to do this is pleasurable. But let it be said at once that the method of planning has not been made for what is simple but only for what is complicated, immense, infinite. True, complication is merely relative; to a mathematician, for instance, the complex movements of the planets round the sun are very much simpler than the sequence of prime numbers. For all that, every spirit, however great or small, in combat with what to him is complicated has need of this admirable faculty of conceiving plans with which Nature has provided him.

For the Chess-player the importance of planning is sufficiently manifest and is now-a-days acknowledged. So says Nimzowitch (*My System*, 1929, page 33)— "Settle on your objective is the rule. . . . Aimlessly to drift from one to another, this will expose you to a strategical disgrace."

The plan shall provide for long and manifold series of moves and conduce to a desirable end. In this the plan is different from a combination. Some combinations of artificial positions are long and complicated it is true, but they can be registered in a few lines or, at the utmost, in several pages, in a contest of two well matched masters the net of variations would fill volumes, they multiply indefinitely and the Chess-player, to grasp the immense number of possibilities, would have need of Ariadne's thread, namely, of a plan.

Examples

1   L. Paulsen

White, Metger, to play and win

1.—Let us contemplate this position without seeking for a combination. Black's ideal is to have his King on QR1 or on Kt2 after his Pawn has been got rid of. He sees his King in the corner, sure that the opponent cannot dislodge it. Alternatively he sees the Bishop on R7, the White Pawn on QKt6, his King on QKt2, moving to R1 and back to Kt2 and meanwhile the White King at bay lest it Stalemate. He tries to bring one of these positions about, resisting every drift that would tend in another direction.

White sees the Black King kept from QR1. A move of the KtP, he thinks, must be countered by P–R6. He aims at manoeuvering his King so as to drive the opposing King off by *Zugzwang*.

Out of this web of plans the following play logically results :

1 K—Q4   ....

The KtP must not be allowed to advance Checking, since the reply to that advance is to be P–R6.

1 ....   K—B3
2 B—Kt6   K—Q3

Of course, if 2 ...., K–Kt4; 3 K–Q5 and conquers QKt7.

3 K—B4   K—B3
4 K—Kt4   K—Q3
5 K—Kt5   K—Q2
6 B—Kt1   K—B2
7 B—R2 ch   K moves
8 K—Kt6 and wins.

2.—A somewhat more complicated example follows :

2

White to play

White conceives the plan of forcing the Black King away from the square K4 and thus of dominating the important points Q4 and Q5 with King and Rook.

1 R—KR8   ....

Black resists. He wants to get his King to K5 or K6.

1	....	B—B4
2	R—R4 ch	B—Kt5
3	K—Kt2	....

White forces the Black King by *Zugzwang*.

3	....	K—Kt4
4	K—Kt3	B—B4
5	R—R8	B—Kt3
6	R—KB8	B—K5
7	R—K8	....

The Black King is now driven off his fourth rank.

7	....	K—B3
8	K—B4	B—Kt7
9	R—QR8	K—B2

Here White is unable to take the Opposition owing to its King on B5 being exposed to Check by the Bishop.

10 K—K5   ....

White dominates the important points. He has achieved what he set out to do. His plan now includes the capture of the P with the Rook in a position where the single Pawn would win, that is when Black's King has been driven away from the immediate vicinity of Q7.

10	....	B—K5
11	R—R7 ch	K—K1
12	K—K6	K—Q1
13	K—Q6	K—B1
14	R—R8 ch	K—Kt2
15	R—Kt8	B—B6
16	R—Kt3	B—K5
17	R—QB3	B—Kt7
18	R—B5	....

Now the King has been forced away from the vicinity of Q7 and R × P follows decisively.

The above is not the only plan that would win. The White King might have marched to QB3, the Black King driven from the vicinity of the White P, the White King then proceeds to B5, the Rook to K5 and if need be the Black King is driven away from Q2 as above.

Philidor   3

White to play.

3.—White's plan must be to separate the Black King from the Pawn and also, if possible, to lead his King to attack the Pawn. Now the King may be driven to his K3 and then by a Check at K8 to Q4 where the King will obstruct the Rook. Then *Zugzwang* may be utilized by placing the Queen on QB8 and Black gets into difficulties. Or the Rook may be on its QB4, the Queen on K8, the King on Q4. Can Black resist? Can he turn the game to a different issue?

1 Q—R7 ch   K—K3

Or 1 .... K—Q1 ; 2 Q—B7, K–B1 ; 3 Q–QR7. The Rook has to guard the square K2, where the Queen would be powerful; hence 3 .... K–Q1 ; 4 Q–Kt8ch, K–Q2 ; 5 Q–Kt7 ch, K–Q1 ; 6 Q–B6, K–K2 ; 7 Q–B7 ch, K–K3 ; 8 Q–Q8.

2 Q—B7   R—B4
3 Q—Q8   R—K4
4 Q—K8 ch   K—Q4
5 Q—QB8   R—K5 ch

There is no help for it. If the King moves, Q–B6 follows. To move the Rook away from King would permit fatal simultaneous attacks.

6 K—B5   R—K4 ch
7 K—B6   ....

The fifth rank has been forced by the King, but not yet the King's file.

7 ....   R—K5

Now to force the Rook from the K's file.

8 Q—Kt7 ch   K—Q5
9 Q—Kt4 ch   K—Q4
10 Q—Q2 ch   K—B3
11 Q—B2 ch   K—Q4
12 Q—Q3 ch   R—Q5

At last! Now the King to the vicinity of the Pawn.

13 Q—Kt5 ch   K—K5
14 K—K6   K—K6
15 Q—Kt6   K—Q6
16 Q—Kt3 ch   K—K5
17 Q—B3   R—Q6
18 Q—K1 ch   K—B6

The Black King and Rook are separated. Now to keep them so and let *Zugzwang* do its work.

19 K—Q7   R—Q5
20 K—B6   R—Q6
21 K—Kt5   P—Q4
22 K—B5   K—B5
23 Q—K2, and the struggle is over.

When we consider the amount of room required by the Queen for the execution of the plan, we see that Black would not lose if the Pawn had been on Black's second row, nor if it had stood on the Kt's file. Of course, a Pawn on the seventh rank would be so

threatening as to make a
sure draw. If the Pawn is
on the border, wholly different motifs present them-
selves.   Obviously,   the
resources of the defence
would thereby be further
limited.

4   *Spielmann*

White, Forgacs, to play.

4.—White plans to get the
Pawns which obstruct his
pieces out of the way and to
enter the Black camp with
his heavy artillery.

1 P—B4   B—Q2
2 P—B5   P × P
3 B × P   ....

If 3 ...., P × B, 4 R–
K1ch.; and if the King
moves, 5 R × P; if the
Bishop interposes, 5 P–Q5.
The plan is realised. Now
follows a brief struggle.

3 ....   R—Kt5
4 R—K1 ch   B—K3
If 4 ...., K–Q1 ; 5 R
× P wins.

5 Q—R1   K—Q3
6 R—R7   Q—Kt1
The Queen has to keep
the Bishop protected, else
R × B ch.

7 B—Kt3   R—K5
8 R × P   R—QB1
9 Q—B1   R—B3
10 R × R   Resigns

5

E. Cohn

White, Forgacs, to play.

5.—White plans to bring
superior forces to bear
against the Black King
and to throttle the resistance
of the few Black pieces
which could be collected in
that narrow quarter. Black
plans to make an advance in
the centre, but he needs
much time for the preparations necessary to put such
a plan with so little developed force into execution.

1 Q—Kt4   P—QKt3
2 Q—R5   B—Kt2
3 R—K4   B—Kt5
4 R—Kt4   ....

The march of the Rook to the King's side, a difficult enterprise, has been accomplished.

4 .... B × Kt

One enemy less.

5 P × B   K—R1
6 Kt—Kt5   R—K2
7 Kt—K4   R—Q1
8 R—Q3   P—QB4
9 Kt—B6   ....

White threatens Q × P ch.

9 ....   Kt—Kt3
10 R—R3   ....

6   Salwe

White, Dr. Perlis, to play.

6.—White, who on the Queen's side is hopelessly inferior, resolves to abandon his Queen's side to its fate and to concentrate all his efforts upon the King's side. Therefore, he lets even the KP go and advances his BP so as to narrow down the space available to Black.

1 P—B5   R—B3

Black must block the Pawn which would otherwise advance impetuously with new threats at each move.

2 QR—K1   K—R1
3 P—Kt4   B—Q2
4 Kt—Kt6 ch   Kt × Kt
5 P × Kt   R × P
6 R—B7   Q—Kt3 ch
7 K—R1   R—Kt2
8 Q × P   R—KKt1
9 QR—KB1   Q—Kt4
10 QR—B2   Q—B4
11 R × R   Resigns

7

Black, Spielmann, to play

Vidmar

7.—Black, having a Passed Pawn on the Queen's side which will occupy at least one of the White pieces, plans to attack on the King's side with superior force and to keep a remote Pawn there on a weak, unprotected spot, so as to have a target for his attack.

1 ....   B—R6

Thus selecting as a target the White RP which must not be allowed to march to safety.

2	B—R3	P—KKt4
3	B—Kt4	K—Kt3
4	P—B4	K—R4
5	B—R3	K—Kt5
6	B—Q6	B—Kt7
7	K—B6	B—B8
8	K—Kt7	

By the pressure on the RP Black has driven White from the centre. Thence he can threaten attacks on either wing.

8 ....   K—B4

If 9 K × P; B × P and wins with his two Passed Pawns of which one will cost the Bishop while the other Queens.

9	P—B5	P—R6
10	P—B6	P—R7
11	P—Kt4 ch	K—K5
12	B—K5	P × P
13	B—R1	P—B4
14	K × P	P—B5
15	K—Kt6	K—Q6
16	K × P	P—B6
17	Resigns.	

Lewis   8

White, MacDonnell, to play

8.—White, who has a Pawn plus on the King's side whereas by the pin of the Rook Black is hampered in mobility and action, plans to maintain the pin while his King's side Pawns advance. Thus the game proceeds.

1 P—B4   ....

to make difficult the liberation of the Rook by 1 ...., P—Q4; 2 ...., ..., K–Q3.

1 ....   P—B3
2 P—KKt4?   ....

Too soon! First P–QKt4 was indicated.

2 ....   P—Q4?

Black does not grasp the opportunity. First .... 2 P—QR4, then (eventually after the interlude 3 P–QR3, P–R5); 4 .... P–Kt3 and at last P–Q4.

3 P–B5   ....

That maintains the pin indefinitely.

3 ....   P—Kt3
4 P—Kt4   P—Q5
5 R—K5   P × P
6 P × P   P—KR3

Useless to advance the QP which White would stop with his inactive piece, the King.

7 K—B2   R—K2
8 K—K2 wins the QP

and the game easily.

9   *Capablanca*

White, Marshall, to play

9.—In his *Die Moderne Schachpartie*, p. 207, Dr. Tarrasch very pertinently makes the following comment which interests us not only for its bearing on this particular position but for its logical context: " Now the players have to conceive a plan, the natural plan, the plan manifestly indicated by the position. For White this plan was to advance his King's side Pawns by P–K4, P–B4 and to make them count and, if possible, to evolve a King's side attack therefrom. But Marshall . . . fails to grasp this plan, though it is the only suitable one, and therefore his play appears to be guided by no recognisable plan and his opponent thereby gets the advantage."

The game proceeded as follows :

1 KR—B1   QR—Kt1
2 Q—K4   Q—B2
3 R—B3   ....

Before now for tactical reasons, White should have taken the open file.

3 ....   P—QKt4

" Capablanca on his part conceives the appropriate plan, namely, to make his majority of Pawns on the Queen's side tell, and conducts the plan to its logical conclusion." (Dr. Tarrasch)

4 P—QR3   P—B5
5 B—B3   KR—Q1

" Capablanca demonstrates to his opponent all his omissions." (Dr. Tarrasch.)

6	R—Q1	R × R ch.
7	B × R	R—Q1
8	B—B3	P—Kt3
9	Q—B6	Q—K4
10	Q—K4	Q × Q
11	B × Q	R—Q8 ch
12	K—Kt2	P—QR4
13	R—B2	P—Kt5
14	P × P	P × P
15	B—B3	R—Kt8
16	B—K2	P—Kt6
17	R—Q2	R—QB8
18	B—Q1	P—B6
19	P × P	P—Kt7
20	R × P	R × B
21	R—B2	B—B4
22	R—Kt2	R—QB8
23	R—Kt3	B—K5 ch
24	K—R3	R—B7
25	P—KB4	P—R4
26	P—Kt4	P × P ch
27	K × P	R × P

and White soon resigned.

10

Black, Capablanca, to play

Nimzowitsch

10.—Concerning this position Capablanca writes in *My Chess Career*, p. 143: "Evidently White's plan is to consolidate his position and finally win with the extra Pawn. He fails, however, to take the best measures against Black's plan which consists in placing his Rooks in the open lines, bringing his Knight round to QB5, if possible, and through the combined pressure of the Bishop, the two Rooks and Knight, and the Queen if necessary against the QKt and QRP, to regain his material, keeping the upper hand at the same time. The plan in this case is masked by the direct attack against the KP."

1	....	Q—K3
2	P—B3	Kt—Q2
3	B—Q2	Kt—K4
4	Q—K2	Kt—B5
5	QR—Kt1	R—R1

"The real attack begins. Black is bound to regain the Pawn without thereby losing ground. If White now plays 6 P–QKt3, then 6 ...., Kt × B; 7 Q × Kt, R–R6; and the QRP must go. White however, having nothing better, should have adopted this line."

6	P—QR4	Kt × B
7	Q × Kt	Q—B5
8	KR—Q1	KR—Kt1
9	Q—K3	R—Kt5
10	Q—Kt5	B—Q5 ch
11	K—R1	QR—Kt1

The rest of the game requires no comment. White threatened by B × Kt, tried the sacrifice of the exchange and lost.

11

Black, Capablanca, to play

Dr. Kaufmann and Fähndrich

11.—From Capablanca's *My Chess Career*, p. 130, we cite

1 ....   R—Kt3

" The beginning of a very elaborate plan, the first object is to force the advance of one of White's Queen's side Pawns, so that the White Rooks cannot be free to manoeuvre and attack Black's Queen's side Pawns."

2 P—Kt3 ....

In citing above Capablanca's and Dr. Tarrasch's r e m a r k s, o u r main object, of course, i s to show in what manner great masters plan and how they judge plans. Here,

as a matter of detail, I should have liked to know Capablanca's opinion of 2 R–Kt3, which obviously would have given the game a different turn. Capablanca attaches no comment to the above move. Suppose the reply to have been 2 ...., R × R; 3 RP × R, P–QR4, whereby Black would keep the Doubled Pawn under restraint.

2	R—QB1
3 Kt—Q4	R—KB3
4 R—B4	K—Kt3

" Forcing the BP to advance, which is part of Black's plan. If R–B2 the BP will soon advance and the Black Rook go to QB6."

5 P—B3	K—Kt4
6 Kt—K2	R—R3

" The plan is maturing . . ."

7 P—R4 ch	K—B3
8 P—R4	P—Kt4 !
9 P × P	R—R8 ch
10 R—B1	....

" If 10 K–B2, K–K4 followed by R–R7 threatening R × Kt and K × R."

10	R × R ch
11 K × R	K—K4
12 Kt—Q4	P—B5
13 R—R3	R—KKt1
14 K—K1	R—Kt8ch.
15 K—K2	R—Kt7ch.
16 K—B1	R—Kt7
17 K—K1	P—KR4

" Now the King must move to Q1 and after forcing the exchange of the Knight for the Bishop the Passed Pawn cannot be stopped."

18	K—Q1	B—B4
19	Kt × B	K × Kt
20	P—B4	....

" If 20 R–Q3, K–K5; 21 R–Q4ch., K–K6; 22 R × QP, P–B6; 23 R–K5ch., K-B5; 24 R–K7, P–B7; 25 R–B7ch., K–K6; and White must finally give up his Rook for the BP."

20	....	K—K5
21	R—QB3	P—B6
22	K—K1	P—Q5
	Resigns.	

12

Black, Capablanca, to play

Janowski

12.—From Capablanca's *My Chess Career*, p. 172.

1	....	B—Q2 !

" Black's plan consists in advancing the QKtP in due time and posting the Knight at QB5. White will then be compelled to take it off, and Black will retake with QKtP, undoubling his Pawns and increasing the pressure against White's QRP and QKtP....."

2	B—K2	....

2 " B–Kt5 is better since it would hinder Black's plan."

2	....	P—K3
3	O—O	B—Q3
4	KR—B1	K—K2
5	B—B3	KR—QB1
6	P—QR3	Kt—R4
7	Kt—Q2	P—B4

" To delay the advance of White's KP."

8	P—KKt3	P—QKt4
9	P—B3	Kt—B5

" Black's first plan is completed. . . Now for two or three moves Black will devote his time to improving the general strategic position of his pieces before evolving a new plan . . ."

10	B × Kt	KtP × B
11	P—K4	K—B2
12	P—K5	B—K2
13	P—B4	P—QKt4

"Black has already established his position . . . It is, therefore, time to evolve a plan of attack, which in this case will be to fix as many White pieces as possible on the Queen's side by threatening P–Kt5, then somewhat to break up the King's side through P–Kt4 and then through the greater mobility of the Rooks to occupy the KKt file."

14	K—B2	R—R5
15	K—K3	KR—QR1
16	QR—Kt1	P—R3
17	Kt—B3	P—Kt4
18	Kt—K1	R—KKt1
19	K—B3	P × P
20	P × P	QR—R1
21	Kt—Kt2	R—Kt5
22	R—Kt1	QR—KKt1
23	B—K1	P—Kt5 !
24	P × P	B—QR5
25	R—QR1	....

"This makes matters easy for Black. He should have played R—QB1."

25	....	B—B7
26	B—Kt3	B—K5 ch
27	K—B2	P—R4
28	R—R7	B × Kt
29	R × B	P—R5

and Black won in eight more moves.

The History of Planning in Chess

The human mind can evolve plans in multitude. Of the basic reasons Hamlet says, they are as cheap as blackberries. But plans that prove themselves are as scarce as reasons that hold good. It was at least a thousand years before the Chess fraternity had learned anything about planning. Would it be rash to conclude that *homo sapiens* is by no means so wise as he considers himself?

Planning in Chess started on its career with the theory of the Ending—King and Rook v. King. That Ending follows a definite plan as, no doubt, was soon discovered. But then, proud of this achievement, the human Chess intellect took it easy for a long while. In the fourteenth century a game was played in Barcelona that by some chance has survived. Its record has been kept in the archives of the city. It clearly shows the poverty of the planning of that generation. They conceived plans of a kind, of course, but they never held to them; soon they conceived another and again another; they played with plans as children do with sand castles.

The modern history of the art of planning began at the time of the Renaissance in Italy. The Italian masters of that period conceived a fertile and sound plan : to get the pieces rapidly into play, to leave the Pawns out of consideration and to institute a sudden and vehement attack against the King. The counter-play on its part did not fail in evolving an antagonistic plan : to develop the pieces and to post them at safe points, to accept the sacrifices and to exchange the threatening pieces of the opponent, and to win by superiority in material force. The masters of the attack invented the brilliant combinations which began by cramping the King and proceeded to sacrifices in order to gain time and space for a direct assault on the King. The masters of the defence invented the systematic exchange of pieces which decreases the vigour of the hostile onslaught and at last breaks it. The masters of the fierce attack discovered the Gambits, those of the defence the Giuoco Piano, the Fianchetti Openings, and the Sicilian Defence.

The Chess history of those days has left us few books and documents to judge by. But however considerable may have been the progress of Chess in those days, that progress certainly was made in the art of combining only. In the evolution of planning the next step forward was made by Philidor, a French musical composer of the eighteenth century who fled before the disorders of the Revolution to Holland and to England and there made his living by playing Chess and writing on the scientific aspects of the game. He made a wonderful name for himself, such as Euclid did in Geometry. His idea of planning is clearly implied in his well-known proposition that the Pawns are the soul of Chess. The masters of combination must have thought such an assertion heretical if not ridiculous. Probably his contemporaries considered his thesis a clever but ill-founded paradox. Nothing shows that they understood it. He was admired, but, as far as comprehending souls were concerned, wholly isolated. We can clearly see what his saying implies. It is this : the Pawn, being much more stationary than the pieces, is an element of the structure of the position; the way the array of Pawns is placed determines the character of a position and hence also the plan appropriate to it. This is true *ceteris paribus*, i.e., if the pieces fairly balance each other. At the time of the Italian masters such a balance practically never was realized. Thus, their experience would not have led them to believe the Pawns of any considerable importance. P h i l i d o r showed the value of the Pawn in slow manœuvring for the purpose of opening lines desired open and of obstructing lines dominated by the enemy. And again he showed how to assault a firm position by advancing an array of Pawns against it, the pieces following on their heels. He showed it more in his games than by word or writing, but his contemporaries understood neither.

They appreciated, however, Philidor's analysis of simple Endings. This analysis, artistic and profound, has become classical.

2.—Once, however, the White King gets on the sixth row undisturbed, Black loses, as shown in the following diagram.

2

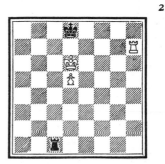

Black to move, White wins

1	....	K—K1
2	R—R8 ch	K—B2
3	K—Q7	R—B7
4	P—Q6	R—B8
5	K—Q8	R—B7
6	P—Q7	R—B8
7	R—R4	

This is the decisive move. If Black replies with 7 ...., R—B8, White wins by 8 R—B4 and 9 K—B7. Otherwise, the game proceeds as follows.

7	....	R—B7
8	R—B4 ch	K—Kt2
9	K—K7	R—K7ch
10	K—Q6	R—Q7 ch
11	K—K6	R—K7 ch
12	K—Q5	R—Q7 ch
13	R—Q4 and wins.	

1

1.—Black, with or without the move, Draws. If 1 ...., R–B3; 2 P–Q6, R–B8, and the White King cannot be guarded against the Checks of the Rook.

3

White to move and win

3.—In this position it is noteworthy that the White King and Bishop are excellently placed and that consequently the White Rook is enabled to threaten Mate from either side. Of course, White will not allow Black to disturb the position of the White King, hence the first move is a Check to tie up the Rook.

| 1 R—B8 ch | R—Q1 |
| 2 R—B7 | .... |

threatening R–KR7.

| 2 .... | R—Q7 |

The following point in Philidor's analysis is deep. The Black Rook is made to leave the seventh row and forced on to the sixth rank. With the Rook there the Bishop and King will be able to exert a stronger pressure upon it than if it stood further distant.

3 R—QR7	R—Q8
4 R—KKt7	R—KB8
5 Б—Kt3 !	....

The Bishop guards K1 and thus prevents Check; it also prevents the Rook from returning to the seventh rank.

| 5 .... | R—B6 |

With the Rook on the sixth row comes an interlude. The Bishop returns without losing any time.

| 6 B—Q6 | R—K6 ch |
| 7 B—K5 | R—B6 |

Again another episode; the White Rook, without losing a move, goes to KKt4.

8 R—K7 ch	K—B1
9 R—QR7	K–Kt1
10 R—Kt7ch.	K—B1
11 R—Kt4	K—K1

and now all is prepared for the winning coup.

| 12 B—B4 | .... |

The Bishop dominates K3 and thus prevents the saving Check; it also obstructs the Rook; all is at an end.

This lovely main-play is completed by two fine variations.

5	K—B1
6 R—Kt4	K—K1
7 R—QB4	R—Q8

or 7 .... K–B1; 8 B–K5, K–Kt1; 9 R–KR4.

8	B—R4	K—B1
9	B—B6	R—K8 ch
10	B—K5	K—Kt1
11	R—KR4	

In the third variation the circumstance of the Chess-board's having only eight, and not nine, lines is made use of to catch the Black Rook, the Black King being unable to fly to an (imaginary) ninth line.

4	....	K—B1
5	R—KR7	R—KKt8
6	R—B7	K—Kt1
7	R—B8 ch	K—R2
8	R—R8 ch	....

If the Chess-board extended further, Black could save himself and the ending would be a Draw. As it is, the Rook is lost.

It is difficult to understand the above Ending from the viewpoint of combination: to understand it from the viewpoint of planning seems decidedly easier. We discover the same circumstance in Philidor's games. In the following game, one of three played simultaneously blindfold, he let his Pawns make the assault. A combination player would be hopelessly lost in the maze of variations, whereas his plan guides Philidor surely and lucidly to victory.

White—Count Brühl.
Black—Philidor.

1	P—K4	P—K4
2	B—B4	P—QB3
3	Q—K2	P—Q3
4	P—QB3	P—KB4

White should have developed more rapidly, in order to be able to open the lines for his pieces with advantage.

5	P—Q3	Kt—B3
6	P × P	B × P
7	P—Q4	P—K5
8	B—KKt5	P—Q4
9	B—Kt3	B—Q3
10	Kt—Q2	QKt—Q2
11	P—KR3	P—KR3
12	B—K3	Q—K2
13	P—KB4	P—KR4

Philidor fears a phalanx of Pawns such as White threatened to form by P–Kt4.

14	P—B4	P—R3
15	P × P	P × P
16	Q—B2	O—O
17	Kt—K2	P—QKt4 !

The Black Q Knight intends to take up a menacing position on QB5 and if captured there thus strengthen the central Pawn formation.

18	O—O	Kt—Kt3
19	Kt—Kt3	P—Kt3
20	QR—B1	Kt—B5
21	Kt × B	P × Kt
22	Q—Kt3 ch	Q—Kt2
23	Q × Q ch	K × Q
24	B × Kt	KtP × B
25	P—KKt3	QR—Kt1

Now Black heaps pressure on the QKtP.

26 P—Kt3   B—R6
27 R—QB2   P × P
28 P × P   QR—B1

The Rooks want to enter the hostile camp.

29 R × R   R × R
30 R—R1   B—Kt5
31 R × P   R—B6
32 K—B2   R—Q6
33 R—R2   B × Kt
34 R × B   R × KtP
35 R—B2   P—R5

Now the BP becomes a target.

36 R—B7 ch   K—Kt3
37 P × P   Kt—R4
38 R—Q7   Kt × P
39 B × Kt   R—B6 ch
40 K—Kt2   R × B

Black has united Passed Pawns, the White Pawns are weak; the issue is not in doubt.

41 R × P   R—B6
42 R—Q8   R—Q6
43 P—Q5   P—B5
44 P—Q6   R—Q7 ch
45 K—B1   K—B2!
46 P—R5   P—K6
47 P—R6   P—B6

and Black, threatening Mate, drives the King off and Queens his Pawns.

Philidor wrote a book, *L'Analyse*, in which he analyzed particularly the Openings. In applying his principles to the ancient problem of the Openings he naturally aroused criticism and antagonism. The system of Philidor, slowly and deliberately to form columns of Pawns, however magnificent as a strategy in a large variety of positions, is certainly not adapted to the Opening stage and it certainly did not suit the temperament or the intelligence of La Bourdonnais, a compatriot of Philidor's who succeeded him on the throne of Chess. And thus La Bourdonnais, in vanquishing, as it were, the Philidor system became the father of the soundest plan known to the history of Chess: to combat every developed unit of the enemy in the centre with a force at least equal to it and to follow the enemy, after having thrown him back in the centre, with a well-supported advance post in the heart of his position. La Bourdonnais, it is true, never expressed this plan in words; but he did not write Chess, he played it, and his moves express his intentions.

As instance and proof, let us look at the following game:

White—De la Bourdonnais.
Black—Mac Donnell.

1	P—Q4	P—Q4
2	P—QB4	P × P
3	P—K3	P—K4
4	B × P	P × P
5	P × P	Kt—KB3
6	Kt—QB3	B—K2
7	Kt—B3	O—O
8	B—K3	P—B3
9	P—KR3	....

Very serviceable as preventing Knight and Bishop from attacking White via KKt5.

9	....	QKt—Q2
10	B—Kt3	Kt—Kt3
11	O—O	KKt—Q4

White has the supremacy in the centre.

12	P—QR4	P—QR4
13	Kt—K5	....

An advance post harassing the enemy.

13	....	B—K3
14	B—B2	....

White chooses as a target the Black King's side.

14	....	P—KB4

This blocks the White Bishop but strengthens the White KKt.

15	Q—K2	P—B5

Black leaves the White KB a free diagonal which is serious.

16	B—Q2	Q—K1
17	QR—K1	B—B2
18	Q—K4	....

White has now completed preparations.

18	....	P—Kt3
19	B × P	Kt × B
20	Q × Kt	B—B5
21	Q—R6	B × R
22	B × P	P × B
23	Kt × KtP	Kt—B1

Better if Black had given up the Queen by B—B3, though the struggle would still have been in White's favour.

24	Q—R8 ch	K—B2
25	Q—R7 ch	K—B3
26	Kt—B4	....

wherewith Kt–K4 threatens Mate.

26	....	B—Q6
27	R—K6 ch	K—Kt4
28	Q—R6 ch	K—B4
29	R—K5 Mate.	

La Bourdonnais played many hard match games with Mac Donnell. He was an extraordinary genius. The plan of the above game is adaptable to many positions. However the adversary chose to march h i s troops, intrepidly La Bourdonnais followed him and fought for the centre of the board with courage and imagination.

La Bourdonnais died young in London, and the goddess of Chess, Caissa, very much g r i e v e d, mourned for him and forgot to inspire the masters with her sunny look. A dreary time then came over the Chess world. The masters played a dry style, without enthusiasm, without imagination, without force, and the Chess fraternity was full of the wrangles of the mediocrities. It is true, the goddess soon repaired her omission. She flirted—Goddess! pardon me this vulgar expression, but the coarse human language does not know the shades of meaning such as undoubtedly you would be able to express by means of Chess pieces—she flirted, I beg to say, with the English historian Staunton and prevailed upon him to organize in 1851 an international chess tournament in London, during the great International Exposition of that year. And then—fickle Goddess—she gave her love to a young mathematician, the German Anderssen, and inspired him to superb combinations. And then—Oh the weakness of her—she spied with her great sunny eye in far distant Louisiana a boy, highly talented; she forgot all about Anderssen, guided the steps of the young American, fell in love with him, introduced him to the world and said triumphantly: "Here is the young P a u l M o r p h y,

stronger and greater than master ever was." And the world listened and applauded and cried "Hurrah for Paul Morphy, the King of Chess!"

In Paul Morphy the spirit of La Bourdonnais had arisen anew, only more vigorous, firmer, prouder. He never formed columns of Pawns for the purpose of assaulting a firm position as Philidor had taught, he always fought in the centre, only a few Pawns in front, and if he needed the lines open, he sacrificed even these few advanced posts. Should the adversary make use of Philidor's maxims, Morphy's pieces occupied the gaps in the oncoming mass of Pawns and opened up an attack, so as to leave the enemy no time for slow, methodical manœuvring. Paul Morphy fought; on good days and on bad days, he loved the contest, the hard, sharp, just struggle, which despises petted favourites and breeds heroes.

But then the Civil War broke out in the United States and broke the heart and the mind of Morphy.

When Paul Morphy, despairing of Life, renounced Chess, Caissa fell into deep mourning and into dreary thoughts. To the masters who had come to ask her for a smile she listened absent-mindedly, as a mother would to her children after her favourite had died. Therefore, the games of the masters of that period are planless; the great models of the past are known, and the masters try to follow them and to equal them, but they do not succeed. The masters give themselves over to reflection. One of them reflects a long time and intensely on Paul Morphy, and gratefully Caissa encourages him; and the greatest landmark in the history of Chess is reached: William Steinitz announces the principles of strategy, the result of inspired thought and imagination.

Principles, though dwelling in the realm of thought, are rooted in Life. There are so many thoughts which have no roots and these are more glittering and more seducive than the sound ones. Therefore, in order to distinguish between the true and the false principles, Steinitz had to dig deep to lay bare the roots of the art possessed by Morphy. And when Steinitz after hard work had bared these roots, he said to the world: Here is the idea of Chess which has given vitality to the game since its invention in the centuries long past. Listen to me and do not judge rashly, for it is something great, and it overpowers me.

The world did not listen but mocked at him. How should this insignificant-looking person have discovered anything great? He can play Chess—but what of that—he has practised it. But should a player be a teacher for serious ends? In a University classroom you do not find children playing marbles.

So the world spoke and acted accordingly, but the world was entirely mistaken. The world would have benefited if it had given Steinitz a chance. He was a thinker worthy of a seat in the halls of a University. A player, as the world believed he was, he was *not*; his studious temperament made that impossible; and thus he was conquered by a player and in the end little valued by the world, he died. And I who vanquished him must see to it that his great achievement, his theories should find justice, and I must avenge the wrongs he suffered.

The Theory of Steinitz

Steinitz's investigation starts from the principle that a plan must have a reason. That everything must have a reason, a cause, humanity has known for a long time, and g r e a t thinkers have written concerning it; for instance, Plato, Aristotle and Leibnitz. And Aristotle's " prima causa," now called the First Cause, has made world history; and many large volumes have been written concerning the principle of causality, a very celebrated one by Schopenhauer " on the fourfold root of the principle of sufficient reason," but in all this extended literature you will find little or nothing on the reason of a plan. The basic reason of a plan is not the cause of a change such as the lighting of a match is the cause of a flame that had not been there before; nor is this reason a logical reason for knowledge, since a plan is not knowledge; nor is this reason a motive for action, because our enquiry is not concerned with some person's plans or actions, but with our desire to know why a given plan is successful in such a position and unsuccessful in another. The

reason for a plan is a *raison d'être*; a reason for existence, a *ratio essendi* and in a very particular sense, and before Steinitz nobody had recognized it.

Steinitz felt that a plan, being a prescription or a rule for successful action on the Chess-board, could *not* be based on the reason ascribed to it during his time, namely, the genius of the player, the creative fancy of a master, but another reason—a reason residing not in the persons or minds of the players but in the positon of the board; yet not to be conceived as being a combination the solution of which depends upon the necessary consequences of moves, but as something wholly different, namely, a *valuation*. He fe l t this, and this consciousness led him to formulate his theory.

Whereas the existence of a cause is *a priori* certain, the reason for a plan has no such certainty. If only players had an intellect vast enough they could do without any plan by relying solely on their power of c o m b i n a t i o n, since they would be able to see through the net of millions of variations with mathematical exactitude. For mere man with his limited mental powers this method would not work. That another method suitable to a normal human mind should exist is not *a priori* certain, but is a discovery just as was the dynamo.

The reason for a plan's having no existence *a priori*, is that its existence is merely *asserted*, and to make such an assertion requires the boldness of genius. For this assertion implies that the position on the board must show a sign, a characteristic moment, which tells us what plan to follow and thus relieve us of the necessity of searching through an immense mass of variations. It is not enough, of course, to assert the existence of such signs; they have to be pointed out and proven true. Such marks, evidently, would be for the painfully seeking Chess-master what the "Philosopher's stone" promised to be to the alchemists. These alchemists had p a s s i o n a t e l y searched for that stone many centuries, had consistently failed to find it and had become objects of derision. Steinitz had the colossal boldness to believe in such a stone, available, it is true, not for science, but for the Chess-master.

Steinitz demonstrated his assertion by the analysis of an enormous number of games played by masters. The analytical work of Steinitz extends over thirty years and is very valuable. In the *Field*, in the *Tribune*, in his publication, *International Chess Magazine* and in his book *Modern Chess Instructor*, one may find his penetrating and profound analysis.

The world did not comprehend how much Steinitz had given it; even Chess players did not comprehend it. And yet his thought was revolutionary, because, of course, it is not limited to the Chess-board—the royal game, after all, is of slight importance—but extends to every activity directed towards meaning and purpose. Surely, Chess, being a very conventional game, that had undergone many changes, child, to a large extent, of chance, is no exception to a thousand and one other games that have been or could be invented. What is true of Chess must hold by analogy for other games. And games being, at least in intent, modelled on Life—simplified, to be sure, but still resembling it in essentials—there must be some analogy between them. Every activity, then, directed by rules and having a meaning and purpose, such as, for instance, a dispute between persons taking different sides of a question and applying logical rules in their argument, every such activity, without exception, has to follow the very same fundamental principle which Steinitz discovered as governing the game of Chess. And if this principle can simplify our search for combinations, though their number be millions, it must have the power also of guiding our search for suitable and efficient action.

This fundamental and universal principle may be briefly expressed as follows : the basis of a masterly plan is always a valuation.

To value, to valuate, to judge, to estimate a thing does not pretend to exact knowledge. But knowledge by estimate, by judgment, by valuation, though not exact, according to the principle of Steinitz, is still an efficient guide for the master. And such a master is no exceptional person ; you yourself might become a master if you cared to. But even if a player is not wholly a master, he may obtain almost equal advantage by observing the principle. Thus he may confidently follow his own esti-

mates. In a given position you value the Rook as being superior to a Knight and Pawn ? Believe it, act on it, play to win !

What now is the reason for my valuation ? Valuations again ! . . True, in each instance the reason is simpler, more sure, more trustworthy than its consequence, but the reason of a valuation is always itself yet another valuation. Finally, all my valuations originate from my experiences : my first losses and wins which gave me pain or joy ; my first draws that called forth in me a variety of sentiments ; my first analysis, which was crude and faulty. From then on I valued and continued to value ; and with practice I became capable of more exact valuations. And from this rough material is generated, by continued trial and intelligent criticism, the series of valuations by which the master arrives at his conclusions.

How novel, how surprising, how opposed to every sentiment of his time the conceptions of Steinitz must have been becomes manifest when in play over the games of the greatest match won by him, the one against Zukertort. Zukertort relied on combinations, and in that field he was a discoverer, a creative genius. For all that, in the majority of the games of the match, though he had lost none of his faculty, he was unable to make use of it, the positions yielding no response to his passinonate search for combinations. Steinitz seemed to have the mysterious capacity for divining combinations long before they were realizable on the board, to encourage combinations favourable to himself and to forestall those which were unfavourable. Thus Zukertort, the great discoverer, searched in vain, whereas Steinitz, rather a poor hand at combinations, was able to foresee them. Zukertort could not understand how Steinitz was able to prevent combinations nor how he could win by such a method, since up to that time—this seemed to Zukertort indisputable — games, fairly won, had been won by fine combinations. Zukertort tried for four years to solve this riddle, but he never approached its solution by even one step, and he lost the mastery that he possessed into the bargain. He died a comparatively young man.

And thus it is not to be wondered at that the Chess-world did not understand Steinitz, neither his manner of play nor his written word which treated of his " Modern School." Nor did any patron of Chess, in sympathy with his genius and divining his greatness, ever come forward to his support.

It is almost obvious that our age is suffering from a delusion as to the nature of genius. It is in our blood to think that in the struggle of two evenly matched adversaries, ruse, deception, wit or paradox decide the issue; that what is common, or expected should carry off the victory seems to us impossible. For instance, we acclaim no scientific theory unless it is startling; we believe in no philosophy based on common sense; what we acclaim, what we believe, is mysterious and unintelligible. Such are we to-day. The magical power to vanquish one who is as strong as the victor can be vested only in the spirit, and the spirit is creative, dazzling: this feeling is very deeply rooted in us. But in truth the spirit, even though it be creative, is by no means dazzling, witty, paradoxical; and Chess may do its little share in spreading this truth.

Let us consider this same

question from another point of view. The impression generally prevails that what is strong must also be beautiful. To make a deep æsthetic impression seems to humanity to be an attribute of all genuine power. That Odysseus fools the giant Polyphemus is proof of the power of mind over matter. The Greeks of the time of Homer could not have endured the thought of Polyphemus Checkmating Odysseus, and in our hearts we would not believe the defeat of Odysseus possible. But in reality, in the circumstances depicted by Homer, it would have been a thousand to one on Polyphemus winning his game against Odysseus easily and safely. The spirit is creative for all that and sometimes dazzling and surprising and antithetic, but the wit of the spirit is profound and subtle, not artificial and laborious as is the common wit of man.

Now let us turn back to Steinitz and demonstrate his revolutionary achievement from his history and from his writings.

The Youth of Steinitz.

Steinitz lived his youth in an age on which two great personalities, Anderssen and Morphy, had left a

profound impression. At that time everybody thought that victory in Chess was gained by ingenuity alone. Often had the Chess-world seen Anderssen produce an unexpected combination as if by magic, and Morphy equally undertake a successful attack. Thereby the Chess-world had come to believe that these combinations, these formidable attacks had been created out of nothing by sudden, inexplicable intuitions. Steinitz, unquestionably, harboured the same belief for many years. The style he displayed in his youth makes this fact manifest. He usually played Gambits and had often to torture himself with very bad positions on that account, obviously under the illusion that such situations were the necessary accompaniment of an attack and that one was obliged to attack in order to wait and to hope for the sudden and inexplicable inspiration, no matter how great the cost. In this style he continued to play for a number of years, not differing in this respect from any of his contemporaries.

The style with which Steinitz began his career was strange and narrow, but it was the style predominating in his time. To place one's King in safety, to prepare an attack by slow degrees, to decline a proffered sacrifice were tactics not well understood and even less esteemed. The play was wholly dominated by the feverish desire to make a rush against the hostile King and to this end furiously to assail the obstructions, regardless of the sacrifices required. An instance out of many is the following game played by Steinitz, 1859, against the strongest Viennese master.

White: C. Hampe.
Black: W. Steinitz.

1	P—K4	P—K4
2	Kt—QB3	Kt—KB3
3	P—B4	

The KP is an obstruction —it has to be got out of the centre; hence it is assailed from the wing.

3	....	P—Q4
4	P × QP	Kt × P

Of course 4 ...., P × P would have been simpler but the Queen must get an outlet at once, and there is that promising looking check on R5.

5 P × P

Not 5 Kt × Kt, Q × Kt; 6 P × P. Oh, dear, no! That would have been considered dull.

5	....	Kt × Kt
6	KtP × Kt	Q—R5ch.
7	K—K2	

White could not resist the temptation to win a pawn— a matter of honour—though the King have to wander.

7	....	B—Kt5ch
8	Kt—B3	Kt—B3
9	P—Q4	O—O—O
10	B—Q2	B × Ktch.
11	P × B	

If 11 K × B, R × P would most certainly have followed.

11	....	Kt × P
12	P × Kt	

The idea 12 Q—K1 was repressed; such a move would have been considered shameful.

12	....	B—B4
13	Q—K1	Q—B5ch.
14	K—Q1	Q × P
15	R—QKt1	Q × KBPch.
16	Q—K2	R × Bch.

Embarrass de richesse.

17	K × R	R—Q1ch.
18	K—B1	B—R6ch.
19	R—Kt2	Q—B6
20	B—R3ch.	

Hope springs eternal, etc.

20	....	K—Kt1
21	Q—Kt5	Q—Q7ch.
22	K—Kt1	Q—Q8ch.
23	R × Q	R × R mate.

At that time Steinitz's age was twenty-three years and it was natural and also beneficial that he learned from his environment and shared its prejudices.

T h r e e   years   later Steinitz is in London.   In the Tournament he meets the   forty-four   year   old Anderssen.

White: Anderssen.
Black: W. Steinitz.

1	P—K4	P—K4
2	Kt—KB3	Kt—QB3
3	B—Kt5	

The   n a t u r a l   master chooses a solid opening.

3	....	Kt—B3
4	O—O	Kt × P
5	P—Q4	B—K2
6	P—Q5	

The attack starts on its way.

6	....	Kt—Kt1

Better the counter-thrust Kt–Q3 to be followed up by P–K5 etc.

7	Kt × P	O—O
8	R—K1	Kt—KB3
9	Kt—QB3	P—Q3
10	Kt—B3	P—B3
11	B—R4	B—Kt5
12	Q—K2	B × Kt
13	P × B	

One   of   the   Kings   is exposed!

13	....	R—K1
14	B—KKt5	P—Kt4
15	B × Kt	P × B

Now the other one also!

16	P × P	P × B
17	P—B7	Q—Q2

White has been able to make a pretty pointed combination. Black should not have rushed out with the QB pursuing an illusory attack against the K, but should have played P–QR3 to threaten P–QKt4 and thus to free his cramped position.

18	P × Kt=Q	QR × Q
19	Kt—Q5	K—B1
20	Q—K3	K—Kt2

Now White could have won with ease by 21 K–R1 and occupying the KKt file —all would have been over —but there is a piece to be captured and no enemy combination in sight—but is there one?

21	Kt × B	R—Kt4

There is!!   Black threatens R–K4.

22	Kt—B5ch.	

A bad move of violence. With 22 P–KB4, K–B1; 23 P–B4, R × P; 24 P–KB5 or 23 ...., R–KR4; 24 Q–KB3, R–R6; 25 Q–Kt2, White could have retained his advantage but Steinitz's last move excited his adversary.

22	....	R × Kt

Now the Rook cannot be captured because of R–Kt4ch., followed by Q–R6.

23	Q—Q3	KR—K4
24	K—R1	R—B5
25	R—Kt1ch.	R—Kt4
26	R—Kt3	Q—B4?

Why Black should have proposed to e x c h a n g e Queens here is explicable only from the supposition that he looked out for some violent, some forcing move. The natural move was Q–B3.

27 Q × Q

N o w White has obviously the best of it, all of the Black Pawns being weak. Moreover, Steinitz did not defend patiently and thus failed to make use of the slender opportunities he had. White won the Ending with ease.

In London Steinitz acquired a knowledge of the Close Openings: French, Sicilian, QP, the Centre-C o u n t e r, e t c. The School of Gambits in Vienna had taught him games of t h e following type.

White: W. Steinitz.
Black: Green.

1	P—K4	P—K4
2	P—KB4	P × P
3	Kt—KB3	P—KKt4
4	P—KR4	P—Kt5
5	Kt—K5	Kt–-KB3
6	B—B4	P—Q4
7	P × P	B—Q3
8	P—Q4	Q—K2
9	O—O	Kt—R4
10	R--K1	O—O
11	Kt—Kt6	Q—B3
12	Kt × R	K × Kt
13	P—B3	Q × P

Now after only 13 moves the White King entrenched behind one solitary Pawn faces a whole army.

14	Kt—Q2	P—B6
15	Kt × P	P × Kt
16	B—R6ch.	Kt—Kt2
17	B × Ktch.	K × B
18	Q × P	B--KKt5
19	Q—K3	B—Kt6

In the heat of the fight Black entirely forgets to get his QKt out, though he would then win in a canter. The eyes of the contestants seem fatally attracted by the opposing King.

20	B—K2	Q—R7ch.
21	K—B1	Q—R8ch.
22	Q—Kt1	Q × Qch.
23	K × Q	

White breathes again.

23	....	B × R
24	B × B	B—Kt6
25	B—B8	Kt—R3

A blunder. T h e QRP should have moved, White would then have had no more than two Pawns for the piece.

26	B × P	R--QKt1
27	B × Kt	R × P
28	B--B4	

Black has still a strong position and should attempt R–QB7 but gave the game up as drawn, presumably because the continuation would have been " dull." Had he chosen a solid opening, Steinitz would have annihilated such opponents. Compare with the above his fine game against Mongredien.

White: W. Steinitz.
Black: Mongredien.

1 P—K4	P—Q4
2 P × P	Q × P

Fortunately, White can now attack without jeopardising his King.

3 Kt—QB3	Q—Q1
4 P—Q4	P—K3
5 Kt—B3	Kt—KB3
6 B—Q3	B—K2
7 O—O	O—O
8 B—K3	P—QKt3
9 Kt—K5	B—Kt2
10 P—B4	QKt—Q2
11 Q—K2	Kt—Q4
12 Kt × Kt	P × Kt
13 R—B3	P—KB4
14 R—R3	P—Kt3
15 P—KKt4	

This is vigorous and enterprising play.

15	P × P
16 R × P	

And this also! Thus do combinations arise.

16	Kt × Kt
17 BP × Kt	K × R
18 Q × P	R—KKt1
19 Q—R5ch.	K—Kt2
20 Q—R6ch.	K—B2
21 Q—R7ch.	K—K3
22 Q—R3ch.	K—B2
23 R—B1ch.	K—K1
24 Q—K6	R—Kt2
25 B—Kt5	Q—Q2

26 B × Pch.	R × B
27 Q × Rch.	K—Q1
28 R—B8ch.	Q—K1
29 Q × Q Mate.	

The Evolution of the Theory of Steinitz.

The aggressive and inventive style of the Steinitz who had been raised in the German School of combination pleased the English amateurs, for they were able to learn a great deal from him just as, conversely, Steinitz did from their more solid play. From the imaginative, heroic temper of Anderssen's combinative style, the large-visioned, systematic position-play of the English school a synthesis arose in the mind of Steinitz, which was destined to make history.

I fancy that one day he reflected how it could have come about that the magician Morphy beat the magician Anderssen. That there should be *one* magician is quite natural, but it is really absurd to think that there should be two magicians fighting each other. That a magacian wins is obvious, but how can a magician lose? Also, how could a magician not lose if two magicians fight For winning and losing at the same time is a logical contradiction which no witchery can explain. Therefore, I fancy, Steinitz, by slow degrees, was led to believe that Chess, after all, must be subject to a reason of its own not to be affected by invention, intuition, inspiration, genius, or any thing else of the kind.

Reason, however, by force of its meaning and power, cannot be subject to mere chance. Consequently, if Steinitz continually took pains to discover combinations, the success or the failure of his diligent search could not be explained by him as due to chance or good or bad luck or any other such term. Hence, he concluded that some characteristic, a quality of the given position must exist that to a discerning eye would indicate the success or the failure of the search before it was actually undertaken. And this characteristic, if explicable by reason, of what could it possibly consist if not an advantage or a disadvantage The winning player had Chess reason on his side provided the win was forced : this seemed a logical conclusion from the premises. Chess reason gave therefore the win to him who held the advan-

tage. And an advantage, if reasonable, what could that be except the thing that was generally termed so : greater material force, greater mobility, greater effect against the King—in short, things that Chess experience had already settled and defined.

Surely, Steinitz's heart beat when for the first time the thought came to him that the master should not look for winning combinations, unless he believed, unless he could prove to himself that he held an advantage. That meant making no attempt at winning in the beginning of the game. And since Steinitz lived in a milieu where to play to win right from the start was considered the only honourable course to take, this thought must at first have had a timid reception in his mind and a hard time establishing itself.

But an important thought is not to be intimidated for long. It must have led him to analyze fine combinations commonly ascribed to some form of supernatural ability, and, having become critical, he must have noticed that they were always founded upon an advantage in mobility and efficiency of the pieces. Thus the fine combination that

Boden made against Mac-Donnell in 1869, will hardly have surprised him.

Black, Boden, to play

Mac Donnell

1	....	Q × Kt
2	P × Q	B—R6ch.
3	K—Kt1	R—K3
4	Q—B2	R × P
5	B × R	Kt × B

and soon mates.

Steinitz, in looking at the position, would certainly have anticipated the existence of some such forcible conclusion, because Black has a Rook more in action than White, and, whereas, some combination winning for Black might conceivably exist, none winning for White could possibly have been expected.

After having come to this point, he had not yet found a new method of play, but had only made some c o n f u s e d notions plain and had disposed of a s u p e r s t i t i o n.

His thought became at once fertile when he insisted on knowing wherein an advantage could consist, and hazarded that the answer was not only in a single important advantage but also in a multitude of insignificant advantages. For instance, if my Bishop has four squares to move to, the hostile Bishop only three squares, I hold, *ceteris paribus*, an advantage, which, it is true, is minute, but by accumulation of such minute advantages at last a big plus is collected.

The big plus arising by accumulation is discharged in a combination. This fact is upheld by experience. Why this should be so cannot be deduced by mere reasoning, but in Chess one may state the law : no combination without a considerable plus, no considerable plus without a combination. This accumulated advantage brings about a tension and this tension, discharging itself like an electric current, produces the conditions for a combination. One cannot deduce that logically, but the fact is far from astonishing. In L i f e a tension within Society always leads to a revolutionary political act, a great tension in the sentiments conduces to a re-valuation of established values, and it cannot sur-prise us if in Chess a ten-sion brings about a combin-ation. But, whether sur-prising or not, the fact had to be discovered, and, as soon as it was discovered, it illuminated that which was obscure and was fertile in suggestions.

For if a great advantage is the necessary and suffi-cient condition for the exis-tence of a combination, this longed for but seldom attained goal, the laborious search for it can be method-ically made and thereby facilitated. With such a method one possesses a magic wand that is efficient indeed. Steinitz saw this clearly. Therefore, h i s maxim : In the beginning of the game ignore the search for combinations, abstain from violent moves, aim for small advantages, accumulate them, and only after having attained these ends search for the com-bination—and then with all the power of will and in-tellect, because then the combination must exist, however deeply hidden.

That this maxim should have at once reformed the style of Steinitz so as to make it clean and vigorous, the world in which and with which Steinitz lived

did not permit. His gener-ation did not comprehend, did not even suspect his trend of thought. The people among whom he lived were willing to re-ward nonsense and humbug if dressed up magnificently. Alas, truth appears seldom in fine garb.

Another circumstance, a weakness of Steinitz, handi-capped his style. He was obstinate. Naturally, he wanted to follow his maxim and to beat those who did not follow it; but thereby, though he was not aware of it, his Chess style became provocative. He provoked his antagonists into play-ing to win, by giving them an excuse or at least a p r e t e x t for doing so. To this end he made the most extraordinary, most unusual moves. Then, as a punishment for their presumption, he would beat them. That by his new methods he manifested his desire not to play to win from the start was entirely lost on his opponents, be-cause their experience had taught them to expect just the contrary. This whole process was subconscious with Steinitz, and no logi-cal necessity brought it about, but it was the o u t c o m e of Steinitz's psychology.

I heard in London, that a London master, Mr. Potter, who loved unusual and strange moves, had influenced Steinitz greatly. The two were friends, and Steinitz somehow began to copy Potter's style. However that may have been, I can well believe that a strange style would rise, almost of necessity, at a time so romantic, so superstitious as that time was. Potter probably saw through the emptiness and the presumption of the style then dominating and with his style of play he seemed to call out to his contemporaries: " You want to beat me right from the start by force of your greater genius? Look! I make ridiculous moves, and yet you cannot beat me. Become, I pray you, more modest and more reasonable."

When Steinitz, in 1866, won a match against Anderssen, the germs of his theory were already discernible in his play. This is one of the games of that match—the thirteenth :—

White : Anderssen.
Black : Steinitz.

1	P—K4	P—K4
2	Kt—KB3	Kt—QB3
3	B—Kt5	Kt—B3
4	P—Q3	P—Q3
5	B × Ktch.	....

White here without necessity abandons a small advantage : the pinning of a Knight by a mobile Bishop. By the exchange Black's QR and QB gain in mobility, presenting Black with another small advantage.

5	....	P × B
6	P—KR3	

Loss of time incurred in order to prevent B–Kt5. Anderssen seems to have considered the Knight stronger than the Bishop, a valuation for which no motive can be adduced. The Pawn move weakens the phalanx of the White King's side Pawns as will be explained shortly. Perhaps this game was the historical event which caused Steinitz to conceive his theory of the phalanx.

6	....	P—Kt3

Preparation for an assault by a mass of Pawns as taught by Philidor. For this purpose it is essential to maintain many obstructions in the centre. The Bishop which aids the centre from Kt2 is there well placed.

7	Kt—B3	B—KKt2
8	O—O	O—O
9	B—Kt5	P—KR3
10	B—K3	P—B4

To prevent P—Q4 which would open the centre and give White a fighting chance.

11 R—Kt1

White has certainly no advantage on any part of the board, yet he resolves upon an attack. That was the style of the time. Anderssen should have tried to anticipate Black's attack and to take up a firm position, to retire the somewhat exposed Knight B3 to KR2 and possibly to KB1 and to await developments. His play otherwise was in the centre, say by Kt-K2, P—QB3 and, after preparation, P-Q4, not with the intent of attacking but of gaining some mobility. Black disregards White's attack and proceeds with his own.

11	Kt—K1
12 P—QKt4	P × P
13 R × P	P—QB4
14 R—R4	....

White is hypnotized by the idea of attack, so he selects a random target, the QRP. Of course, R-Kt1 was in every way superior.

| 14 .... | B—Q2 |
| 15 R—R3 | P—B4 |

The phalanx marches.

| 16 Q—Kt1 | K—R1 |
| 17 Q—Kt7 | P—QR4 |

The attack was easily met.

| 18 R—Kt1 | P—R5 |

There are no more targets in sight. White's troops are wholly disarranged.

| 19 Q—Q5 | Q—B1 |
| 20 R—Kt6 | R—R2 |

Now Black is opening the attack in earnest. He threatens P × P followed by B × P

21 K—R2	P—KB5
22 B—Q2	P—Kt4
23 Q—B4	Q—Q1
24 R—Kt1	Kt—B3
25 K—Kt1	Kt—R2

The KtP having been protected, the phalanx can set itself again into motion.

26 K—B1	P—R4
27 Kt—Kt1	P—Kt5
28 P × P	P × P
29 P—B3	Q—R5
30 Kt—Q1	Kt—Kt4

The pieces post themselves behind the phalanx menacingly. Soon the lines will be opened, which will allow the major pieces to approach the White King.

| 31 B—K1 | Q—R7 |
| 32 P—Q4 | .... |

Desperation! The Rook on R3 shall be thrown into the fight even at the expense of an important Pawn. But it is too late. Black is not to be deterred by a trifle like this.

32	P × BP
33 P × KBP	Kt—R6
34 B—B2	Kt × Kt

Black has won a piece.

35 P × BP	Q—R6ch.
36 K—K1	Kt × Pch.
37 R × Kt	Q × R

and Black won easily.

The Lasting Advantages

One recognizes in the above game a trend in the style of Steinitz towards Philidor and away from La Bourdonnais. The theory of Steinitz approached that of Philidor as soon as he examined the minute advantages that *endure*.

T h e small advantages arising from the superior position of pieces are hard to maintain; often the disadvantage of lack of mobility or of an exposed position is repaired in *one* move. Small disadvantages appertaining to the position of Pawns, however, are difficult to repair and have a tendency to last. Manifestly, Pawns having to lean upon the support of pieces are less desirable than those that require aid of Pawns only, and mobile Pawns can make a better fight than blocked Pawns. Now consider two neighbouring P a w n s. The strongest position, according to the above, is the *phalanx*,

the weakest position the *Doubled* Pawn

a medium value the *backward* Pawn

Here the White Pawn on the left-hand side is backward, the other one is blocked. T h e backward Pawn can advance only if supported by pieces or as a sacrifice.

Another medium value two *isolated* Pawns

The two Pawns are distant from each other and, if attacked by pieces, can save themselves only by the aid of pieces or by flight.

Particularly weak, t h e *blocked isolated* Pawn

Before the isolated Pawn is a hostile man which deprives the Pawn of its mobility.

Steinitz added to the rules of Philidor : A phalanx must advance so as to be able to resume the shape of the phalanx again until its advance is no more needed.

And this corollary to the plan of La Bourdonnais : As a place for an advance post the square in front of a hostile backward Pawn, the " *hole* " in the array of Pawns, is most suitable, for from that post an officer can most effectively obstruct and harass the enemy, while it is at the same time safe from attack by Pawns.

Black has on B4 a backward Pawn, White has a Passed KP which hampers the Black King. These advantages suffice to produce a winning combination.

1 Kt—B1   B—Kt5
2 Kt—Q3   B—B6
3 Kt—B4ch.   K—K2

4 Kt × P ch. and wins by his pawns.

If Black had played 3 ...., K–Q2, White would have won equally with 4 P–K6ch., K–K2; 5 Kt × P ch., P × Kt; 6 P–B6.

Black, Steinitz, to play

Bird

Here Steinitz himself violates his theory. In an off-hand game, played in 1866 at Simpson's Divan in London, the above position arose. B l a c k is cramped and should Castle and soon advance P–Q3, to liberate his pieces. And after 1 ...., O–O; 2 P–

White, Zukertort, to play

QKt4, Kt–K3; 3 Q–K4; he had 3 ...., P–KB4. Instead of Castling, which is defensive, Steinitz played 1 ...., P–QKt3, which has an aggressive intent, although an advantage for Black cannot be detected. Therefore, Black is justly punished.

1	....	P—QKt3
2	P—B5	Kt—Kt6
3	Q—K4	Kt × R
4	P–B6	B—B4ch.
5	K—R1	R—QKt1
6	P—K6	....

and Black has no efficient defence.

Steinitz's Maxims for Practical Play.

Steinitz, possessed by the above ideas, strove to transform small advantages that rapidly disappear into small advantages that endure, and thus to accumulate them. Such lasting advantages were to him isolation of a hostile Pawn, majority of Pawns on the Queen's side far away from the hostile King, weakening of the phalanx of hostile Pawns, especially in the vicinity of the hostile King, a securely placed advance post, the domination of open lines. To this end he cultivated p l a y in the centre, the play of pieces and Pawns, leaving the King, at least to begin with, out of the reckoning, thus following in the steps of Morphy and La Bourdonnais. He cultivated also the assault by a chain of Pawns on the Queen's side which has the effect of cramping the opponent and of threatening him, thus going beyond Philidor who directed s u c h attacks mainly against the King.

In defence, conversely, Steinitz carefully avoided creating lasting weaknesses of the above type unless forced to do so by his opponent.

Examples of His Play.

White : Steinitz.
Black : Sellmann.

(Played in 1885 at Baltimore.)

1	P.—K4	P—K3
2	P—Q4	P—Q4
3	Kt—QB3	Kt—KB3
4	P—K5	KKt—Q2
5	P—B4	P—QB4
6	P × P	B × P
7	Kt—B3	P—QR3
8	B—Q3	Kt—QB3
9	Q—K2	Kt—Kt5
10	B—Q2	P—QKt4
11	Kt—Q1	Kt × Bch.
12	P × Kt	Q—Kt3
13	P—QKt4	....

to win space on the Queen's side and to w r e s t the diagonal held by Bishop and Queen from Black. It is noteworthy, too, that the point QB5 now becomes strong, and in addition QB4 remains guarded against an entrance of hostile pieces by the QP.

| 13 .... | B—K2 |
| 14 P—QR3 | P—B4 |

This blocks the Pawns on the King's side, but Black deprives himself of an opportunity thereby, namely, of opening lines on that side by P—B3.

15 R—QB1	B—Kt2
16 B—K3	Q—Q1
17 Kt—Q4	Kt—B1
18 O—O	P—KR4

Black released his KR with this move besides preventing P—Kt4 which would set the King's side in motion. But such is not White's plan. He wants to effect an entrance on the Queen's side where he holds all the trumps.

| 19 Kt—QB3 | .... |

This Knight makes five moves to occupy a strong point. A great deal might happen in five moves; it is a long time.

19	K—B2
20 Kt—Kt1	P—Kt3
21 Kt—Q2	Kt—Q2
22 QKt—Kt3	R—QB1
23 Kt—R5	....

At last!

23	B—R1
24 R × R	Q × R
25 R—B1	Q—QKt1
26 Q—QB2	B—Q1
27 QKt—B6	Q—Kt2
28 Kt × B	R × Kt
29 Q—B7	....

All Black squares on the Queen's side are dominated by White.

| 29 .... | Q—Kt1 |
| 30 B—B2 | .... |

And also on the King's side Black has very weak points on black squares.

30	Q—Kt3
31 Kt—B3	Q × Q
32 R × Q	K—K1
33 Kt—Kt5	Kt—B1
34 B—B5	Kt—Q2
35 B—Q6	....

Any of the few moves at Black's disposal mean heavy material loss, he has no possible counter-attack and so resigns.

White: Zukertort.
Black: Steinitz.

(The Thirteenth Game of the Match).

1 P—Q4	P—Q4
2 P—QB4	P—K3
3 Kt—QB3	Kt—KB3
4 B—B4	P—B4
5 P—K3	P × QP
6 KP × P	P × P

White has an isolated Pawn but the freer game.

7	B × P	Kt—B3
8	Kt—B3	B—K2
9	O—O	O—O
10	R—K1	B—Q2
11	Q—K2	Q—R4
12	Kt—QKt5	P—QR3
13	B—B7	P—QKt3
14	Kt—B3	KR—B1
15	B—B4	P—QKt4

The Black Queen has parried the assault and now Black assumes the initiative by pushing the Queen's side Pawns, so as to gain space for his pieces.

| 16 | B—QKt3 | Q—Kt3 |
| 17 | KR—Q1 | Kt—QR4 |

An advance post on QB5 is to be established !

| 18 | B—B2 | Kt—B5 |
| 19 | B—Q3 | Kt—Q3 |

Why the advance post so soon retires is not clear, unless it is so that the Knight may take up a waiting position where it keeps its eye on two strong posts, QB5 and KB4.

20	Kt—K5	B—K1
21	B—Kt5	Q—Q1
22	Q—B3	R—R2
23	Q—R3	P—R3
24	B—K3	QR—B2

Black is well developed, he has the superiority in the centre and is aggressive on the Queen's side.

| 25 | P—Q5 | .... |

To get rid of the isolated Pawn. Black gives for the central Pawn the side Pawn and thereby gains further superiority in the centre.

25	....	P—Kt5
26	Kt—K2	Kt × P
27	B × QRP	R—R1
28	B—Q3	B—KB3
29	B—Q4	Kt—Kt4
30	Kt—KB3	Kt × B
31	KKt × Kt	R—R4

The QRP is helpless, the White Knight on Q4 pinned, the Black pieces have a great deal of space : the result of the attack by the Black Queen's side Pawns is excellent.

32	Q—B3	B—QR5
33	R—K1	Kt—K2
34	Q—K4	P—Kt3
35	P—QKt3	B—K1
36	B—B4	Kt—B4

The White Knight cannot be defended. If 37 QR–Q1, R–Q2

| 37 | Kt × P | .... |

a desperate sacrifice.

37	....	P × Kt
38	B × Pch.	K—Kt2
39	QR—Q1	Q—K2

Herewith Black loses a move, which in the defence is a matter of importance. He should at once attack the Queen with 39 ...., Q–R1. If 40 Q × P, Kt–R5 and Black, who has a firm hold on the QRP also, would assume the offensive against the King. That was the logical conclusion, but Steinitz failed here and afterwards failed again,

when the Queen on K2
came under the fire of the
White Rook and at last lost
the game. It is useless to
record the remaining moves
of the game; they would
tell nothing, whereas up to
the present point the idea of
an attack by Pawns advancing on the Queen's side is
well exemplified.

White : Steinitz.
Black : Zukertort.
(The Sixth Game of the
Match).

1	P—K4	P—K4
2	Kt—KB3	Kt—QB3
3	B—Kt5	Kt—B3
4	O—O	Kt×P
5	R—K1	Kt—Q3
6	Kt×P	Kt×Kt
7	R×Ktch.	B—K2
8	Kt—B3	O—O
9	B—Q3	B—B3

Here 9 ...., Kt—K1
was a possibility; because
10 Q–R5 could be met by
10 ...., P–KKt3; 11
Q–R6, Kt–Kt2; and 10
Kt–Q5 by 10 ...., B–
B4, after which Black
attains development by advancing the QP.

10 R—K3   P—KKt3

Steinitz in his notes to
the game declares Black's
move to be a challenge to
his theory not to move
Pawns on the King's side
when under attack, unless
there is no alternative.
Well, here R–K1 was an

alternative for the threat
11 B×Pch., K×B; 12 Q–
R5ch., K–Kt1; 13 R–R3
was thereby parried.

11	P—QKt3	R—K1
12	Q—B3	B—Kt4

Black should not
abandon the important
diagonal, but he believes
he sees an attack that har-
asses the White QP.

13 R×Rch.   ....

Was this exchange
forced? Had White moved
13 B—Kt2, possessing
himself of the diagonal
bearing down upon KR8,
with the Knight threaten-
ing to enter, via Q5 or K4,
the "hole" B6 would
surely have been a suffi-
cient equivalent for the
sacrifice of the exchange. A
matter of valuation, of
course, but methinks, to
raise the question is to
answer it. Let us give an
instance: 13 ...., B×R;
14 BP×B. Now 15 Kt–Q5
menaces. If 14 ...., P–
QB3; 15 R–KB1 which
threatens 16 Kt–K4; 15
........, Q–K2; 16 B–R3
and Wins. Or 14 ....,
R–K3; 15 R–KB1 threat-
ning 16 B–B4. But
let us suppose that
Steinitz and Zukertort had
seen a hidden parry to this
terrible attack, why was the
above possibility not mentioned, either in their notes

or in those written by other critics of that match? It seems that notes to games are often negligently written, with a negligence that in some cases is downright immoral. Steinitz, one may be quite sure, at the time he wrote his notes, must have been exceedingly excited and too fatigued to give consideration to the question, else he would quite certainly have investigated it thoroughly.

13 ....   Kt × R
14 B—Kt2   P—QB3 !

An excellent move which Schallopp in his book on the match most unjustly criticised. According to Bachmann, Schallopp says of White's 14th move: "White herewith abandons his QP. By capturing it Black would have exposed himself to strong attack but at last would have 'brought his superiority to bear.'" His demonstration: 14 ...., B × P; 15 Kt–K4, B–Kt4; 16 Kt × B, Q × Kt; 17 R–K1, Kt–Kt2; 18 R–K7 (the Rook is here en prise). Probably what he intended to write was 18 B –B6 and 19 R–K7. However this " analysis " was intended, it is shocking. What happens if 16 B–B4? After 16 ...., P—Q4; 17 Kt × B, Q × Kt; 18 B × P, Black may resign.

And Steinitz indicated another attack starting with 15 B–B4 which also wins. Thus negligently did Schallopp, a pupil of Anderssen, report a match for the world's championship, the historian of which he aspired to be and in which another pupil of Anderssen's, Zukertort, was a contestant. And not a soul has arisen until now to draw attention to this scandal.

15 Kt—K4   B—K2

Black has strengthened his position by going on the defensive.

16 Q—K3   ....

to force P–B3 and to send the KRP against the KtP effectively.

16 ....   P—Q4
17 Q—Q4   P—B3
18 Kt—Kt3   B—K3
19 R—K1   Kt—Kt2
20 P—KR4   Q—Q2
21 P—R5   B—B2
22 P × P   B × P !

If 22 ...., P × P; 23 Q–KR4 with force. Black has defended with care.

23 Q—K3   K—B2
24 Q—B4   R—K1
25 R—K3   ....

From the fourteenth move until this moment Black, on the defence, has played very good Chess. Now White has no immediate threats and Black, to give a direction to his game, has to follow his own i n i t i a t i v e: he has to o r i g i n a t e a plan. But that is exactly what Zukertort did not understand. Steinitz with whom he contested had furnished the intellectual armament needed for planning, but Zukertort did not comprehend his antagonist and was entirely lost when confronted by such a task. His right plan was to keep his attention riveted on his weak points KB4, QB4 and KB3, a n d consistently work for a Draw by exchanging dangerous pieces. His initiative lay in building a phalanx by P–QB4 to be used, if needed, to blockade a Bishop.

This plan was certainly a difficult one to execute, but Zukertort did not even try to conceive this or any other plan and failed, and was bound to fail, since the theory of Steinitz carried no message to him.

25 ....   Kt—K3 ?

Leaves the points KB4 and KR4 but feebly protected.

26 Q—KKt4   Kt—B1
27 Kt—B5   B—B4
28 Kt—R6ch.   K—Kt2

and after a few repetitions of moves with which

Steinitz wanted to gain time for deliberation :—

35 B × B   ....

with t h i s combination Steinitz wins a Pawn :

35 ....   Q × Q
36 Kt × Q   R × R
37 BP × R   K × B
38 Kt × P

and Steinitz won the Ending with his Pawn plus. For our purpose the Ending is of no interest and so we conclude at this point.

White : Zukertort.
Black : Steinitz.

(The Seventh Game of the Match).

1 P—Q4   P—Q4
2 P—QB4   P—K3
3 Kt—QB3   Kt—KB3
4 P—K3   P—B4
5 Kt—B3   Kt—B3
6 P—QR3   P × BP
7 B × P   P × P
8 P × P   B—K2
9 O—O   O—O
10 B—K3   B—Q2
11 Q—Q3   ....

The Queen is better placed on the King's file, but White wants to exert pressure on Black's KRP.

11 ....   R—B1
12 QR—B1   Q—R4
13 B—R2   KR—Q1
14 KR—K1   ....

The KR seems better posted on Q1; however, for comprehending the play of

Steinitz and Zukertort this question is of little account.

| 14 | .... | B—K1 |
| 15 | B—Kt1 | P—KKt3 |

Zukertort has forced a weakening of the Black King's side but, as his succeeding moves indicate, he does not understand the real significance of it.

| 16 | Q—K2 | B—B1 |
| 17 | KR—Q1 | B—Kt2 |

Black immediately guards his weak points.

| 18 | B—R2 | Kt—K2 |
| 19 | Q—Q2 | .... |

Here the Queen within range of the Black KR is less favourably posted than it was. Zukertort has already lost the thread. He threatens a joke, in Kt–Q5, but the threat has force for an instant only.

| 19 | .... | Q—R3 |
| 20 | B—Kt5 | Kt—B4 |

A difficult p o s i t i o n. White should now defend by 21 Q–K1 in order to try for P–Q5. But Zukertort, not understanding t h e theory of minute advantages, gets impatient and uses violent tactics.

| 21 | P—KKt4 | .... |

Now White of his own will has weakened the square KB3 and his whole King's side and Black retorts by rapidly opening lines for attack.

21	....	Kt × QP
22	Kt × Kt	P—K4
23	Kt—Q5	R × R
24	Q × R	P × Kt
25	R × P	Kt × Kt
26	R × Kt	R × R
27	B × R	Q—K7

Black attacks the two KtP's simultaneously and has shown up the fallacy of White's quasi-attack.

| 28 | P—R3 | P—KR3 |

Here Steinitz does not make the best of it. Steinitz did not play Endings sufficiently well, firstly, because he had no need of this somewhat mechanical art—he w o n without it; secondly, because his rich imagination did not care for mere calculation. The correct continuation was 28 ...., B × P; 29 Q–B5, Q–Q8ch.; 30 K–R2, B–K4 ch.; 31 K–Kt2, Q × Bch.; 32 Q × Q, B–B3; and wins methodically by means of his Pawn plus.

| 29 | B—QB4 | .... |

Zukertort does not comprehend his good luck. He should have played 29 B–K3, whence he attacked the point KR6, the QRP and made the King secure.

29	....	Q—B6
30	Q—K3	Q—Q8ch.
31	K—R2	B—QB3
32	B—K7	B—K4ch.
33	P—B4	B × Pch.

33 ......, P–KKt4 would have won still more rapidly.

34 Q × B   Q—R8ch.
35 K—Kt3   Q—Kt8ch.
Resigns.

White : Zukertort.
Black : Steinitz.

(The Ninth Game of the Match).

1 P—Q4	P—Q4
2 P—QB4	P—K3
3 Kt—QB3	Kt—KB3
4 Kt—B3	P × P
5 P—K3	P—B4
6 B × P	P × P
7 P × P	B—K2
8 O—O	O—O

Hitherto White has developed. Zukertort treats that part of the game in a masterly fashion. Steinitz does not aim for mere development, even at this early stage of the game— he follows a plan : he wants to isolate the QP so as to have a target handy. Such a strategy has its drawbacks, since it permits the opponent to obtain a free development. Possibly one might say without exaggeration that in the opening the plan should be rapid development and nothing else—at any rate, very little else.

9 Q—K2   ....

Zukertort seeks combinations. He ought to conceive a plan — say 9 B—KKt5, gaining strength on the QB file and trying to accumulate pressure on the Black KRP—modifying his plan as Black is seen to conceive one of his own. But accumulation of minute advantages is not Zukertort's style.

9	QKt—Q2
10 B—Kt3	Kt—Kt3
11 B—KB4	QKt—Q4
12 B—Kt3	....

It is hard to see any purpose, a logical sequence in Zukertort's moves. He simply puts his pieces on squares where they enjoy mobility and hopes for complications in which to exercise his talent for combination.

12	Q—R4
13 QR—B1	B—Q2
14 Kt—K5	KR—Q1

Black has now completed his development and aims at the QP whereas White has no target.

15 Q—B3	B—K1
16 KR—K1	QR—B1
17 B—KR4	....

A semblance of a plan at last, by B × KKt White wants to drive the QKt from its commanding post.

17	Kt × Kt
18 P × Kt	Q—B2
19 Q—Q3	....

This is mere dilly-dallying. The natural move, now that the QB has accomplished its object, was 19 B–Kt3, B–Q3; 20 P–B4. Make the centre pawns do something.

19	Kt—Q4
20 B × B	Q × B
21 B × Kt	....

giving away a mobile Bishop for a Knight that had no wish to escape the exchange.

| 21 .... | R × B |
| 22 P—QB4 | .... |

Now there is little purpose in this, since the Pawns have no minor pieces to harass.

| 22 .... | KR—Q1 |
| 23 R—K3 | .... |

But White wanted to make a combination against the King. He has not enough material force to attack that stronghold. He should have played KR–Q1 and simply defended his phalanx.

23	Q—Q3
24 R—Q1	P—B3
25 R—R3	P—KR3
26 Kt—Kt4	Q—B5

Black wants to prevent sacrifices which would force him to change the logical course of the game.

| 27 Kt—K3 | .... |

The attack has fizzled out. The counter-attack begins, since the White KR is misplaced.

| 27 .... | B—R5 |

To force the Rook from the first rank.

28 R—B3	Q—Q3
29 R--Q2	B—B3
30 R—Kt3	P—B4

The White troop is in disorder and must fly, and should fly; for instance, 31 Kt–Q1. But Zukertort seeks combinations.

| 31 R--Kt6 | B—K5 |
| 32 Q—Kt3 | .... |

Threatening P–B5.

| 32 .... | K—R2 ! |

All right! Now make a combination !

33 P—B5	R × P
34 R × P	R—B8ch.
35 Kt—Q1	Q—B5
36 Q--Kt2	R—Kt8
37 Q—B3	R—QB1
38 R × B	Q × KR

Resigns.

If Zukertort has a plan in mind, he is a match for Steinitz, possibly even his peer. Compare with the above games the one that follows. Every move of Zukertort's pointed towards a vigorous co-operation of the pieces united to attack the King—at first against its initial position, then against the Castled King.

The forceful concentration of pieces against the King is the old Italian plan; Zukertort found it ready made, and in the tactics of mere execution he was a g r e a t master.. Steinitz, however, discovered sound and successful plans *over the board.*

White : Zukertort.
Black : Steinitz.

(The Fifth Game of the Match).

1	P—Q4	P—Q4
2	P—QB4	P—QB3
3	Kt—QB3	Kt—B3
4	P—K3	B—B4
5	P × P	P × P

In his notes Steinitz indicates 5 ...., Kt × P, as the stronger move.

6	Q—Kt3	B—B1

Nowadays this variation is continued with the offer of a Pawn 6 .... Q–Kt3; 7 Kt × P, Kt × Kt; 8 Q × Kt, P—K3. Black, however, hardly gets sufficient attack.

7	Kt—B3	Kt—B3
8	Kt—K5	P—K3
9	B—Kt5	Q—B2
10	B—Q2	B—Q3
11	P—B4	O—O
12	R—QB1	....

The pressure on the Black QKt is strong. The threat is now 13 B × Kt, P × B; 14 Kt–Kt5, Q–Kt1; 15 Kt × B, Q × Kt; 16 B–Kt4.

12	....	B × Kt

relieves the pressure but opens a line for the White Rooks.

13	BP × B	Kt—K1
14	O—O	P—B3
15	B—Q3 !	....

Prevents 15 ...., P × P, since 16 B × Pch. would be the answer.

15	....	R—B2
16	Q—B2	....

This weakens the King's side. If 16 .... P-KKt3; 17 B × P. If 16 .... P–KR3; 17 B–Kt6.

16	....	P—B4

Now White prepares to open the B line by P–KKt4 and prepares it thoroughly. Such play is straight forward and strong.

17	Kt—K2	B—Q2
18	R—B2	R—QB1
19	B—B3	Q—Kt3
20	Q—Q2	Kt—K2
21	QR—B1	B—Kt4
22	B—Kt1	Q—R3
23	P—KKt4	P—KKt3
24	P—KR3	R—B2
25	R—K1	Kt—Kt2
26	Kt—B4	Kt—B1
27	P × P	KtP × P

If 27 ...., Kt × P; 28 P–K4, P × P; 29 B × P and the QP advances to weaken the position of the obstructive Knight. Then the decision comes about in the centre. Now it falls on the KKt file.

28	R—Kt2	K—R1
29	K—R2	Q—B3
30	QR–Kt1	Kt—K2
31	Q—KB2	Q—K1

A blunder, but the Black position, weak on all Black squares and battered on the KKt file, was untenable.

| 32 | R × Kt | Resigns. |

Thus, an intelligent plan makes heroes of us, and absence of plan cowards and dullards.

Steinitz Advances his Theory beyond the Needs of Practical Chess and thus Enters the Domain of Science and Philosophy

The practical maxims of Steinitz : the accumulation of small advantages, their change into lasting advantages, his teaching concerning weak P a w n s and points, his counsels referring to attack and defence— in short, everything that has been touched upon thus far, constitute a system sufficient to explain the play of Steinitz and to make master-players. But Steinitz went far beyond this point. He was a profound thinker, he had a passion for thought, he felt and saw its power and he was not minded to stop at maxims of merely practical value.

Hence, he attacked problems far surpassing in importance and in breadth the tasks set for the master who confines himself to his game. To what end? There seems to be in man a mysterious power to foresee the needs of the future and to sacrifice himself to them. In the animal world we see this power at work— sacrifice in the interests of the Future is there the common rule; in the life of the thinker, we may assume, the course of Nature is no different. C e r t a i n l y, Steinitz derived from his p r o f o u n d investigations nothing b u t disappointment. Nobody understood even his practical maxims, far less his more extended researches. He simply followed his conscience, which commanded him to go on. Thus he spoke of the " balance of position." A wonderful conception, but beyond practical Chess. A true, genuine balance does not exist in our game, noble and most human though it is. A true balance exists in the infinite domain of Life and it has a logical existence in philosophy, but one must not demand it of Chess which after all is finite and therefore has its limits.

For the practical needs of Chess the concept " compensation " suffices. If the advantages held by my opponent are compensated for by my advantages, the position is balanced. Then no attack, the intent of which is to win—so argues Steinitz—must be undertaken. The idea of balance is enough to convince us that *balanced positions with best play on either side must lead again and again to balanced positions.* Only after the balance of the positions has been disturbed, so that one player holds an uncompensated advantage, may this player attack with intent to win. And here Steinitz elevates himself to the level of a genuine philosopher in demanding that that player *must* attack with intent to win or else be punished by b e i n g deprived of his advantage.

T h i s "must" connotes an ethical power. To obey the command is hard and irksome. Not to obey— well he who obeys may become an artist, if he does not he will never do so. He who obeys will often fail and lose; he who does not obey will often enough win by the mistakes of his opponent, and will run no risk. For all that, he only will grow to be an artist who obeys the command. An artist is one who is observed by the world gladly

and attentively and without regrets; a man who has personality, who can mould plastic things into varied shapes so that they express essential truths and realities, bringing joy and edification to a multitude. Would you become one of this type? Then you must obey the ethical command of your struggle, in Chess or elsewhere—at school, in the garden, in dispute, in negotiation or wherever you may contend. That is a fundamental l a w in the world and Steinitz felt it, and in a mysterious way had understood that it operated also on the Chessboard.

Principle of Attack

In C h e s s the ethical command means: Search for the combination which brings home your advantage. Believe in the existence of that combination and seek to discover it. And if you have searched in vain a hundred times, continue. Possibly the advantage that you think you hold is only an illusion; your valuations may be at fault: prove them and improve them. But, first of all, search diligently; work, for such work is rewarded.

Steinitz desires to aid the searcher. He orders the

attack, but he also gives advice as to how this order can be successfully carried out. He asks which direction the attack has to take, and he answers: the target for the attack has to be a *weakness* in the hostile position. He therefore compares the position of your opponent to a chain of many links and yourself, the assailant, to one who wants to break the chain. He advises you to look for the point where the connection is weakest and against that to direct your efforts. Of course, if the chain offers the same resistance in every link, one cannot see a motive for selecting by chance one of these points but the chain is never equally strong in all of its links, and the master c h o o s e s after conscientious consideration, the point of least resistance as the target for his efforts.

One has no need to follow this rule in Chess accurately—from a practical point of view one is not punished therefor; and if one tries to obey the rule, one will hardly be the better for it as far as winning games at Chess is concerned —this rule goes far beyond Chess. Chess is too limited for such a rule. The rule is founded on the old and celebrated i d e a of the *"linea minoris resistentiæ."* The stroke of lightning, the train drawn by the locomotive, a defeated army all pursue the line of least resistance. On the Chessboard there are no lines, only points; hence Steinitz speaks of weak points. The most successful, the most effective combination a s well as the widest-visioned and deepest plan of attack— thus his idea—proceed, as if by a miracle, in the direction of the weak points, for the same Reason which governs the world governs also the Chess-board

Examples of the Principle of Attack

The brief games which had been terminated by s u r p r i s i n g l y sudden attacks, of which countless examples are to be found, had generally been concluded by attack upon the KBP, the weakest point in the initial position. To give one instance out of the multitude,

White :
Capt. MacKenzie.
Black : Amateur.
1 P–K4, P–K4; 2 B–B4, Kt–KB3; 3 P–Q4, P–B3; 4 P×P, Kt×P; 5 Kt–K2, Kt×P; 6 O–O, Kt×Q; 7 B×Pch., K–K2; 8 B–Kt5 Mates.

As in the short games, so in the longer games the points KB2 and KB7 were equally the objects of combinations at least during the initial stages of the contest. To judge by these instances, the weak point of the initial position seems to attract the combination. And in the further course of an extended game the same fact is discernible as soon as it is viewed in the light thrown upon it by the theory of Steinitz, viz., Attack the weakest points in the enemy camp.

Black, Marshall, to play

1

Salwe

1.—Black is a Pawn minus, but he has on Q6 a strong advance post and the lines for his pieces are open. He has the advantage. An obvious weakness in the position of the White King, is that it stands immobile, guarded on the diagonal only by an undefended weak Pawn, and in

front by a Pawn easily attacked by P–R5. Marshall looks for the combination directed against this weakness and discerns it.

1	....	B—B3
2	Q—B4ch.	K—R1
3	Kt—K4	QR—K1

The Rook wants to command the seventh rank.

4	Kt × B	....

not 4 Kt–Q6 ? Q–K3 !

4	....	R × Kt
5	B—B1	KR—K3
6	B—R3	

A little better was 6 R–Q1, Kt—K8; 7 P–QR4, R–K7; 8 R–Kt2, but Black commands the seventh row and the White position remains very weak.

6	....	R—K7
7	QR—Q1	Kt—K8
8	B × P	

Unthinking despair !

8	....	Kt—B7ch
9	K—Kt2	Kt—Kt5ch

and Mates in a few moves.

Dr. Tartakower. 2

White, Capablanca, to play

2.—White has a protec-
ted Passed Pawn and his
Rook cuts the Black King
off; hence, White is bound
to attack.   The hostile
weaknesses are the King
on the border and the
Black KBP. But how to
get at them? White him-
self is in distress.   Never
mind, search! Capablanca
evolves the following combination:

| 1 K—Kt3 | R × Pch. |
| 2 K—R4 | R—B6 |

Black would have done
better by 2 ...., R–B8,
but also then the KBP falls
as follows: 3 R–Q7, R–
R8ch.; 4 K–Kt3, P–B3; 5
R–Q6.

3 P—Kt6	R × Pch.
4 K—Kt5	R—K5
5 K—B6	....

This march of the King
has cost two Pawns, a great
deal in an Ending, but the
compensation is an immediate attack on the hostile
weaknesses, the King and
the KBP. If now 5 ....,
K–K1; 6 P–Kt7 is decisive.

| 5 .... | K—Kt1 |
| 6 R—Kt7ch. | .... |

So as to drive the King
into a position which en-
ables the KtP to advance
with Check.

6	K—R1
7 R × P	R—K1
8 K × P	R—K5
9 K—B6	R—B5ch.
10 K—K5	R—Kt5
11 P—Kt7ch.	K—Kt1

After the exchange of
Rooks B l a c k would of
course be lost.

| 12 R × P | R—Kt8 |
| 13 K × P | |

and Black shortly resigned.

Anderssen   3

White, Morphy, to play

3.—Look at the aggrega-
tion of weak points. The
Black King and KB stand
on an open line, a target for
the Rook. The point KB3
is guarded only by the
same KB, is overpower-
ingly assailed by Bishop
and Q u e e n and P;
h e n c e, this point is a
s a f e p l a c e for an
effective a d v a n c e post.
Also, the Black KRP and
the square KR3 are weak.
Black can support the position by R—B2 and by the

Queen in the vicinity of KB. The QB is in the way and its development costs a move. This sums up the weaknesses. Now look at the attack as executed by Morphy who had, of these theories at least, no *abstract* knowledge.

1 R—B3   B— Kt4

If .... Q–B1 ; 2 R–R3, but for all that to abandon a Pawn was the most promising way out of Black's distress.

2 R—Kt3   R—B2
3 B—B6   ....

threatening Q—R6. Black is pinned. If, for instance, 3 ...., K–R1 ; 4 Q-R6, Q–KB1 ; 5 Kt × B, P × Kt ; the White reserve force, the King, decides the issue by attacking the advanced QKtP while the Black pieces are held fast. 6 R × B, R × R ; 7 K–B2, etc.

3 ....   P—B5

A sacrifice intended to open the way to the QB for defence of KRP and for blocking the Kt file.

4 Kt × B   P × Kt
5 Q × P   Q—KB1
6 Q—R6   K—R1
7 R × B   R × R

8 K—B2 and Black soon resigned.

Dr. Bernstein 4

White, Teichmann, to play

4.—White conceives the plan of attacking by way of KB6 which is manifestly weak.

1 Kt —Q5   R—R2

If 1 ...., Q–R4 ; 2 B–K1 and thence to B3.

2 B—R4   B—Q5ch.
3 K—R1   K—Kt2
4 B—B2   ....

forcing the exchange of Bishops and gaining its diagonal for the White Queen.

4 ....   B × B
5 R × B   Q—R4
6 Q—K2   ....

The command of the diagonal is now assured.

6 ....   P—KB3
7 Q—Kt2   R—KB1
8 P—Kt4   ....

threatening Kt × KBP followed by P–Kt5.

8 ....   P—R3
9 P—R4   P—Kt4
10 P—B4   ....

forcing the passage for the KtP and at last gaining the post aimed at.

10	....	P × RP
11	Kt × KBP	R—B2
12	P—Kt5	B—B3
13	R—Kt1	Q—R6
14	P × Pch.	K × P
15	R—R2	B × Pch
16	Kt × B	Q—B6ch.
17	Q—Kt2	Q × Qch.
18	R(R2) × Q	R × BP
19	R—Kt6ch.	K—R2
20	Kt—B6ch.	Resigns.

5

Black, Riga, to play

Berlin

5.—Black has a Pawn plus, his QP holds the Rook to its exposed post guarded by the White Queen only. It is attacked by the hostile Queen and is liable to further attack by a Rook on K8. Also, the White King has no safe retreat. White certainly has a menace on the Queen's side which threatens to become formidable in

two moves (P—Kt6—Kt7); hence, Black has no time to lose.

| 1 | .... | R—K5 |

Now 2 P–Kt6 is defeated by 2 ...., R–K8ch.; 3 K–Kt2, R × R; 4 P–Kt7, R–Kt8ch.; 5 K–R3, R–KKt1; 6 P–R7, P Queens; 7 either P Queens, Q–Kt7 ch. and Mates shortly.

| 2 | K—Kt2 | R—K8 |
| 3 | R(R3)—R1 | .... |

Now the greatest weakness is the Rook on Queen square which has to block the formidable QP. But Black has to pay attention always to White's terrible counter-thrust, P–Kt6

| 3 | .... | Q—Kt7 |

If 4 Q × QBP, R–Q1, threatening 5 ...., Q × R; 5 Q–QKt6, R(Q1)–K1 whereupon the White King becomes the target.

4	Q—B2	Q × R
5	R × Q	R × R
6	Q × QP	P × P
7	Q—Q5	R(R8) × P
8	Q × KtP	R—R7ch.
9	K—R3	R(R7)—R4

Black has now a safe superiority and wins methodically by first safeguarding his King by P–R3 and K–R2 and then doubling his Rooks on the

seventh row against the
RP. The BP is easily
protected, but not so the
weak White Pawn. Berlin
made another seven moves
and then resigned.

Morphy.

7

E. Cohn

6

White, Duras, to play

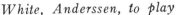

White, Anderssen, to play

6.—The Black King,
open to attack by the
Queen and the two Rooks is
defended only by a Knight
and two separated Pawns.
The protection is weak, the
attack should aim at the
King. The weak obstruc-
tion is torn away by sacrifice.

1 R × P ch.	K × R
2 Q—K7 ch.	K—Kt3
3 R—Kt8 ch.	K—B4

The geometrical motif is
here operative; therefore.
the following further sacrifice to deprive the Black
Queen of its support:

4 R × Kt ch. and s o o n
wins the Queen.

7.—Anderssen, who in
s e e k i n g combinations
merely follows his instincts,
does not guide himself by
the form and nature of
weaknesses and therefore
does not discover the
strongest line of play. Obviously, the KR file is a
Black weakness, also, the
second and the third ranks.
On the other hand, the
position of the White Kt,
Queen and KR in the same
diagonal would invite Q–
Kt4, if only the R on Kt3
were away, for the Knight
on B4 is insecurely
posted, the QP is weak.
Therefore, *not* 1 R–R3 as
indicated by a well-known
book on Morphy, but first
evaluation of the Knight on
B4.

1 B—K5	B × B
2 P × B	Kt × P
3 Kt—Q6	QR—B1
4 R—R3	R— Kt2

After 4 ...., K–Q1
White would occupy the Q
and QB files.

5 R—R5   ....

and White wins easily by
systematic attack on the
weak Black Pawns. Instead
of this winning line of play,
White chose a much weaker
procedure, failed again and
again and at last lost the
game.

8   *Schlechter*

*White, Dr. Tarrasch, to
play*

8.—White, with perfect
judgment, wanted to bring
his superiority of Pawns on
the King's side to bear.
The weakness of Black is
the KtP assailable by both P
–B5 and P–R5. The Black
RP has to protect it, the
Black King again is pro-
tected by the RP. Which
then is the right mode of
attack? Certainly 1 P–R4 is
indicated, to be followed

up, after due preparation—
White has any amount of
time for preparation, since
Black has no counter-
threats—by P—R5.

But White had a wholly
different plan. He made an
advance, not against the immobile and therefore per-
manent weakness, but
against a very mobile and
therefore wholly illusory
weakness, the B.

1 P—Kt4   ....

and now, all at once, as by
a miracle, Black has a
hidden defence. White's
BP is weakened thereby.
Black replied correctly

1 ....   R—KB1
2 P—Kt5   B—Kt2

White hastily went on
3 K—Kt3   ....

in order to prepare P-R4-
R5. He should have
played R–B2, thus keep-
ing at least a trifling advantage. Now, as punishment,
as it were, for the illogical
execution of his attack,
White could have been
forced to consent to a Draw
by
3 ....   R × P

for if 4 K × R, B–K4ch.;
5 K–B3, Q × Pch.; 6 K–
B2, Q–R7ch.; etc. But
Schlechter did not make
this combination and lost.

Principle of Defence

As the reverse side of his theory of attack Steinitz enunciated a principle of defence. He who is at a disadvantage must be willing to defend himself, he must be willing to make a *concession*. But his guiding star must be the *principle of economy*. Hence, he must seek to make the least concession that just suffices, not an ounce more, not the dot of an " i " too much. That comprises, as it were, the ethical command given to a defender.

Steinitz also points the way to the defender who asks himself *how* to achieve this end. He advises: improve the worst weakness voluntarily. The ideal of a position for defence is that it have no *linea minoris resistentiæ*, that all of its l i n e s of resistance be equally strong, that the chain contain only joints of equal strength. But this ideal can never be attained. Approach it, as far as you are able! That is the test of how you do your duty as a defender. Thus, in this manner you serve your cause well, even if you lose the game. This train of thought is manifestly a logical conclusion from the principle of attack. The effort which the aggressor has to make varies inversely as the degree of the weakness, the defender accordingly forces the assailant to make the greatest possible effort when the attack will exact only a minimum toll. In other words, as the *stability of a position is gauged by its least stable point, attempt to achieve at every point the same degree of stability*.

Examples of the Principle of Defence

9

Black, Anderssen, to play

Morphy

9. — Anderssen played here 1 ...., P–QR4; the answer was 1 Q–K7 and the B l a c k BP fell, the QKtP remained weak, and White soon won. A reasonable move would be 1 ...., P–QKt3, which does away with the threat of the White QR and therefore mobilizes t h e Black Bishop and indirectly the Black QR. If then 2

R–K7, Q–Q3; or if 2 B–B4, R–Q2. The game would continue and Black, though always under pressure—say 2 Kt × BP, B–B3; 3 Kt–R6 dbl. ch. K–R1; 4 B × B, P × Kt—would do his best to defend the inferior position and follow the ethics of defence. If he then lost, he might have spoken in the words of a famous loser :— "All is lost save honour."

The move 1 ...., P–QR4 which loses quickly is contrary to the teachings of Steinitz. The move is aggressive, although Black obviously has an inferior force in action. It leaves the QKtP almost helpless, it coerces the White Queen to i n c r e a s e its effect, it squanders the scanty means of defence.

10   *Golmayo*

White, Steinitz, to play

10.--The White King is exposed, but White has a Pawn plus. What should

White's strategy be?   To strengthen the worst weaknesses, QB2 and KKt2 and remove the blockade of the QP, the function of which is to protect the valuable K P.   Unquestionably, therefore, t h e defensive move is here indicated 1 Kt–K1.

Black, aspiring to prevent the advance of the QP, played 1 ...., Kt–QKt5. If now 2 P–Q3, Kt × BP; Steinitz replied 2 P–QR3, KR–K1 ; 3 P × Kt, Kt × P; but White now had the saving Check 4 Q–B5 and won the game handsomely.

11

Black, Tschigorin, to play.

Steinitz.

11.—In the second game of his first match with Steinitz, Tschigorin in the above position could have played 1 ...., Kt—R5. According to the opinion of the spectators, he ought then to have won. But Tschigorin has the worst of the game; their opinion was in contradiction to the theory of Steinitz and based on insufficient analysis. They had considered only the variation 2 P×B, whereupon 2 ...., Kt–Kt7ch. would have actually won, since 2 K–K2 is bad because of Q×Pch., and 2 K–B1 on account of Kt×Pch. They also perceived Black's threat 2 ...... Kt–B6ch. But Steinitz would have had an excellent defence by 2 K–B1 depriving the Knight of the square Kt7. Against 2 ...., Q–Kt4ch. White would reply simply 3 Q–K2 and against 2 ...., Kt–B6; 3 P×B, in each case with an easy win for White. Tschigorin, undoubtedly, saw this combination and selected another move, though with no better result in the end.

Gavilan and Steinitz

12

White
Ponce and Tschigorin.
to play

12.—Black threatens 1 ...., P–Kt5; 2 B–K2, P–Kt6; 3 P×P, R×KtP, winning immediately.

The right defence was 1 K–R1 which does away with the greatest weakness. Steinitz comments thereon as follows: 1 ...., P–Kt5; 2 B–K2, B×P; and now the important 3 P–Kt3. True, Black then can make a violent attack with 3 ...., Q–KR3 but White would not reply with the disastrous 4 P×R nor with the purely defensive 4 Q–Q3. He had then the counter-attack 4 Q–Q5 which secures a Draw.

White played 1 P–KR3. It was a plain invitation to 1 ...., P–Kt5 of which Black promptly availed himself. For after 2 B×P the sequence is 2 R(Kt1)×B; 3 P×R, R×BP and annihilation follows. Therefore, 2 P×P, P–KR4! This makes an inactive piece most active. Manifestly because of 3 ...., R×B White must not open the Kt line. White continued 3 P–Kt5, R×KtP; 4 K–R2, R–R5ch.; 5 K–Kt1, Q–B5; 6 R–K1, R×Pch. and Mates in two moves.

The move chosen by White 1 P–KR3 was open to grave suspicion because the RP has the function of guarding the R square as a retreat for the King. To let the opponent inveigle such a Pawn forward into a fight was bad policy. The general rule of Steinitz is here confirmed, and one may unhesitatingly say that it has few exceptions, in fact only where particular circumstances necessitate other tactics, whereas the rule, under the condition of *ceteris paribus* is always valid.

13   *Black, Steinitz, to play*

Tschigorin

13.—It is Steinitz's 14th move of the third game of his match against Tschigorin. Steinitz is pressed hard, since his adversary has the only open line and the KB cannot escape exchange for the Knight — disadvantages that are not compensated for. Shall he play 1 .... P–QR3? But that would be a concession. It would forever weaken the square

QKt3 a little. This concession does not appear necessary to Steinitz, though not to make it requires a laborious manœuvre of defence against the advanced White Knight. No —thinks Steinitz—rather suffer the assault; at the very last the White QKt, though threatening, is exposed.

1   ....   Kt—Q1

in order to deploy its activity on the central square K3. True, the Knight is there not quite stable.

2 P—B4   ....

But now 2 .... P–QR3 is unavoidable? No, Black can still do without that move.

2   ....   Kt—K3
3 P—KR3   ....

Invitation to exchange the Bishop. If it is not accepted, the Knight on K3 will be still more exposed. But so many lines being open, the Bishops are strong and mobile. The Knight on K3 is not afraid. It can fight

3   ....   B—R4
4 P—B5   ....

Since Bishop or Knight must guard QBP, the White Pawn is safe.

4   ....   B—K2
5 Q—Q5   ....

The QKtP and the Knight on K3 are assailed and the same Knight has to protect QB2. M a n y a player would now lose his presence of mind.

5 .... Q—B3

The position is still maintained.

6 B—QB4 ....

Again t h e Knight is threatened and it must not recede. And the way out of the difficulties by 6 ...., Q × Q is blocked, on account of the sequence 7 P × Q, Kt × P; 8 Kt × BP, R–QKt1; 9 B × Kt, B × B; 10 Kt–K6 winning. Is 6 ...., B–B2 satisfactory? White replies 7 Q × Q, P × Q; 8 B × Kt, P × Kt; 9 B × B, R × B; 10 R–Q7 and wins at least a Pawn.— Steinitz ponders. What now? Are my principles here at fault? Let me see once more. The points K3, QB3, QKt4 are decisive. Ah, the salvation! No, my principles are not erroneous.

6. .... B—K1

It is apparent that the Knight on K3 is no more in danger than the White Knight on Kt5. Still the phalanx of the Black Pawns is in perfect order and the furor of White's attack has passed its climax.

7. P—QR4 ....

Fatigued by the hard r e s i s tance encountered, White makes an error. He should play for safety with 7 P–QKt4.

7 .... Kt × P?

But Steinitz also is fatigued and perhaps too certain of victory. The correct move was 7 ...., P–QR3, now entirely justified since White had weakened his Queen's side ·by his attack. Since the White Knight must not recede— otherwise the QBP will fall — exchanges must follow. 8 Q × Q, B × Q; 9 B × Kt, P × Kt; 10 P × P, B × KP, and Black would have got out of this scrimmage with advantage. Tschigorin profited from the mistake of Steinitz by 8 B × Kt, B × B; 9 Q × Q, B × Q; 10 Kt × BP etc. to the extent as above shown. Steinitz defended the lost position until the 83rd move and then surrendered.

The Declining Years of Steinitz.

The demonstration and evaluation of the above principles was a task which gave Steinitz enough to do during a long life rich in labour. To announce an established principle, as a historian does, is a simple thing, but to discover a new principle, to give it a structure and to make it heard and felt by unresponsive contemporaries requires a diligent and virile man. Besides, the first discoverer of a great thought is more intimate with it than any one of his adherents and pupils. The pupil learns only what can be said and written, the discoverer has the thought in his very blood; the former acquires the thought through his mind and understanding, to the latter it is part of his being.

That Steinitz at the age of fifty-nine years was defeated by me and later also by others is due to no defect in his theory. His theory is and forever remains the classical expression of the idea of Chess. But in his play over the board no man rises beyond the height attained by his own time. In the creative years of a man's youth he will try hard to rise to the top; as soon as he has arrived there, he will rest on his laurels, for the Future, which calls the discoverer, has no interest in the passing glories to be won in over-the-board play. A very old and profound truth proclaims that Nature does nothing in vain. The laws

of Hammurabi are still alive, the philosophy of Plato still exerts its influence — the struggles of Hammurabi, the cares and deeds of Plato are forgotten. The practice of Life is of account for one generation only. Had Nature endowed Plato with a talent for practical matters, say agriculture or the local politics of Athens, the philosopher in him would have been a loser to just that extent. And so it was with Steinitz. His talent for over-the-board play was not considerable. Blackburne and Zukertort in that respect were easily superior to him although he beat them decisively because he was a profound thinker and his adversaries were not.

When Chess - masters arose who were trained for systematic thinking, who therefore understood at least the abstract portions of Steinitz's theory and who besides had natural talent for over-the-board play, Steinitz was confronted with a task that in his old age he could not perform. Had Steinitz lived in our period of improved Chess technique he would have played better Chess than he did and fought also to-day with honour. For he had all the qualities of a great fighter : force, discernment, conscientiousness, undaunted courage. But his claim on posterity is that he was a great discoverer.

Criticism of and Additions to Steinitz's Theory.

I now come to the gaps which Steinitz left in his theory for the problem to be solved was not pointed out to him until too late in his life, if at all.

Steinitz, after his advice to both the attacking and defending parties, does not speak of the strategy that a player should follow who feels that he is neither the attacker nor the defender. What plan has the player to follow in a balanced position ? Of course, none with the immediate intention of winning, none which embodies the fear of losing, none that would n o t develop the pieces—these answers to the query may be anticipated, but they are not decisive. I should say that besides all of the above he must play—and this is the essential point—to maintain the *co-operation* of his pieces.

In Steinitz's writings the concept of co-operation is not made clear. There was a reason for this. Firstly, because in the games of his contemporaries he hardly ever saw a balanced position; secondly, because the grand simplicity of his theory would have been impaired by this extension of his fundamental concepts. His very basis, the principle of accumulation of advantages, would have had to be broadened. Let us consider t h i s question attentively; it is of importance to the position-player who has to prepare for attacks and defences long before they become actual.

The idea of the accumulation of small advantages is based on the conception that an advantage is the equivalent of a weight. If y o u accumulate small weights, their mass grows consistently and the sum total may finally be large. For instance, two or more weights make a certain sum; if you replace that sum total of weights by a single weight equal to it in mass, the value of the sum remains the same.

But evidently it is not quite so in Chess. For instance, two Pawns have a very different value according to their mutual position—this is even one of the basic considerations of Steinitz—we cannot substitute for one of the Pawns another equal in value to it and leave the value of the sum of the two original Pawns unchanged. This value, at least, cannot be compared to a sum of weights.

The simplification effected by Steinitz is ingenious and very practical, but this must not blind us to the fact that it is a short cut to truth which does not quite reach it. It is an inner but not a bull's-eye.

The alternative to this conception of weight is that of a co-operation—say, a group value. Thus, two or more advantages will form a group and there will be interaction between its members.

Hence there is co-operation and interaction between any two Chess values, and *this interaction has a certain typical character* which always manifests itself whenever two values come into co-operation. That must be so, or co-operation would not be subject to reason and Chess would be a game of chance.

The result of co-operation, in attacking positions is to strengthen each element of the group; in positions of defence, to protect each other; in positions of balance, to complement each other. Let us, as an instance, consider two Pawns. For the attack they are better separated so that both may attack the same point, thus doubling their aggressive action. They complement each other best in the phalanx, each Pawn guarding the square where a hostile piece would block his neighbour; in this position their co-operation is at its climax. In defence they are driven into a position where one of them protects the other—one of them sacrifices himself to save the other and for the common good, provided, of course, the enemy has taken pains to enforce such a sacrifice. That Pawn will be saved which is first attacked, unless there should happen to be a tangible difference in the value of the two Pawns.

It is not very different with pieces.

Two Bishops always complement each other, the action of one never doubles nor obstructs that of the other. Their co-operative value is perceptible to such a degree that two Bishops are commonly preferred to two Knights or to Bishop and Knight. Two Knights which stand alongside each other or are in other ways posted so that they divide their effectiveness equally on a multitude of important points, complement each other better than two Knights protecting each other; the latter attitude is one of defence enforced by perils threatening one or other of them. A Bishop and a Pawn complement each other when the Pawn is not of the same colour as the Bishop, they take up a position of defence when Bishop and Pawn attack the same object. And thus the idea originally exhibited in the phalanx recurs in a multitude of ways which it would seem almost impossible to enumerate in detail.

Of course, one may be forced to give up the position of strongest co-operation, for instance, in following a plan of attack requiring the doubling of pressure on certain important points. According to the ideas of Steinitz, one should make concessions in s u c h emergencies; b u t again according to the same principle, one should be parsimonious with such concessions. The stronger co-operation in the above sense is always a position of greater mobility than the weaker co-operation would allow. Or, to use another term, say flexibility, or adaptability or elasticity. The main idea of this co-operation is to in-

crease the range of possible plans to follow, without specifying too early which road you would prefer to travel. By co-operation you aim to keep the position plastic, alive; by lack of co-operation you take the life out of your position, and to infuse it with new life you will need outside aid.

Examples of Co-operation.

As with all examples concerning values, the examples here are restricted to the material in question. In practice positions are in general very much more complex; the rules discussed here are *ceteris paribus* valid there. This is as it should be. Consequently we are able to explain the complex by the simple.

Black to play 1

1.—Knight and Bishop do not complement each other here, they double their effectiveness unnecessarily. The Knight is wanted on KKt3 so as to form with the Bishop a phalanx, to keep out the Black King. At present, White is in peril.

1	Q—Kt2
2 K—K3	Q—B3
3 Kt—Kt3	Q—Kt7

Black has lessened the co-operation between the White King and his pieces. The Black King may now approach and get White into difficulties.

Black to play

2

2.—Black cannot win, since he is unable to advance either of his Pawns. For instance, 1 ...., K–Q5; 2 K–Kt2, K–K6; 3 K–B1, K–K5; 4 B–R5, K–Q4; 5 K–Kt2, K–B4; 6 K–R3. The Bishop on R4 is wholly inactive, the Pawns have deprived it of all useful work. The Bishop is dead, the position rigid.

3

White to play

3.—What a difference between this and the preceding position! The Black Bishop and Pawns complement each other, they work in harmony. Black wins with ease. Say 1 K–Q1, B–Kt5ch.; 2 K–B1, P–Q6. White loses by *Zugzwang*.

Black to play

4

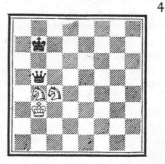

4.—White prevents the approach of the Black King and therefore Draws.

Black to play

5

5.—The Knights are in difficulties. Black drives the White King away and Stalemates it, then one of the Knights must move and both are lost, viz., 1 ...., Q–B2ch.; 2 K–Kt2, Q–QB5; 3 K–R3, K–B6; 4 K–R4, Q–B4, and White faces the catastrophe.

The Principle of Justice.

Not willing to increase the number of above examples beyond proportion, I now attempt to describe in words the principle upon which a l l co-operation hinges. But it is difficult to express Chess ideas in words, because the spoken language has sprung from a social intercourse which is devoted to tasks entirely different from the incidental tasks undertaken here. The language is pregnant with Life, and how should our poor little game, even in the smallest detail, bear comparison to infinite Life ?

Yet, since we have to speak in words, our task must be accomplished as best we can. Leave this task undone ? But it has value. You learn no art by anxiously restricting yourselves to it ; you have to seek its association, and its logical connections a n d analogies with the rest of things. Otherwise, you will learn no more than the craft, the technique of your art and never attain to a full comprehension or easy mastery of it.

If one thinks of the co-operation of Chess pieces one is led to think, by analogy, of social co-operation : friendship, a life of many in unison, enmity, contest, of antagonistic parties. A Chess piece is supported by some comrades, it antagonizes some enemies, and thus it has tasks and functions to fulfil. How shall the Chess-p l a y e r determine the functions of his various pieces and to what extent shall he support them ?

The reply of the Chess-master is, that the pieces ought to be supported according to their usefulness, according to their *value*.

Well understood, this value changes according to the degree of activity exhibited by the piece. If a piece has succeeded in drawing upon itself a great deal of the enemy's fire, it has gained just that much in value, in importance, in utility, and so far it deserves more support than its average value would justify—at least the support which threatens a counter-attack. On the other hand, if a piece is not sufficiently active, it has to be given a chance to do its share of the work, whether to relieve other pieces or to undertake new tasks. Certainly, the master will not assign to it work already done; it has to complement the work of others; by no means double it. In return for the labour which a piece is required to do for the common cause, it enjoys safety and support, and the more valuable the piece, the greater the task assigned to it and the greater the obligation to safeguard it.

What is the equivalent to this practical rule of the Chess-master, who measures thereby the work to be done by his Queen and Rooks and minor officers and Pawns and even by the King, in the infinite game of social intercourse? Surely a social principle.

But whereas the game of Chess is rather well understood by half a dozen masters and fairly comprehended by a few dozen lesser masters and—say—a thousand amateurs, our social intercourse is, alas! not conducted by masters, not even by near-masters, not even by any comparable in skill and insight to those thousand amateurs. Let us not be conceited about our statesmanship. Is it necessary to whisper that our life is directed by mediocre people, with the exception of a few men of talent and very rare men of genius? But no, we are not so ill-advised, as has been stated frankly by many good men. Unfortunately, the men who lead us, though not egotistical, are not uninterested. The attitude of a man of science, guided by his passion for truth and knowledge, is beyond them. Some particular interests, party or national interests at the very least, which certainly are not the clean-cut interests of humanity or of the Future, have a share in determining our politicians and our politics. That will change, since everything in the long run changes for the better. In the meanwhile, a word is needed to distinguish the peculiar attitude of the Chess master who, in dealing with his pieces of wood, is not led astray by any outside interests. The word I refer to is, alas! soiled by our history, and its significance is thereby covered up as is the sparkle of a diamond that has fallen into the dust. With this reservation let us use the word *justice*.

Principle o f justice! Thou art a power effective in history in spite of all that has been done to thee by the army of liars, that want to hurt thee, yet have to play the hypocrite, for the people instinctively love thee. Hypocrisy is tribute paid to thee by t h i n e enemies. It is a tacit admission that the true statesman would at all risks uphold thee.

On the Chess-board lies and hypocrisy do not survive long. The creative combination lays bare the presumption of a lie; the merciless fact, culminating in a checkmate, contradicts the hypocrite. Our little Chess is one of the sanctuaries, where this principle of justice has occasionally had to hide to gain sustenance and a respite, after the army of mediocrities had driven it from the marketplace. And many a man, struck by injustice as, say,

Socrates and Shakespeare were struck, has found justice realised on the Chessboard and has thereby recovered his courage and his vitality to continue to play the game of Life. Later generations, not so narrowminded as ours, will recognise and appreciate this merit of our noble game.

But let us return to our task. Though we have to look at it occasionally from a wide perspective, we must not lose sight of it. Principles have to extend from the heaven of ideals to the soil of our daily work.

Examples.

Since the more valuable piece has to enjoy the greater safety, the less valuable pieces must advance and draw the attack upon themselves; of course, not advance to be mere spectators. A good instance is Rook and Passed Pawn; the Pawn in front, the Rook, supporting it from behind. The Passed Pawn thus forces the opponent to pay attention to it. A weak Pawn, however, must, if possible, be protected by the Rook sideways so as to leave the Rook free for counter-attack. The Rook would rather abandon the Pawn than be tied to its defence.

White to play and win.

1.—The strongest force is in the RP, because the hostile King is too far away. Much weaker is the QBP which the White King can stop at his convenience. Hence 1 P–R4, R–R1 ; 2 R–R1, R–R4. The Pawn would advance further, unless stopped at once. 3, K–B1, K–B2 ; 4 K–K2, K–K3 ; 5 K–Q3, K–Q4 ; 6 K–B3, K–B4. Now the KBP has to speak 7 P–B4, K–Kt3 ; 8 K–Q4, R–KB4 ; 9 K–K4, R–B1 ; 10 P–R5ch., K–R3 ; 11 P–B5. The co-operation of King and Pawn *versus* Rook is perfect here. White wins quite easily.

Another example of great frequency is Knight and Pawn. A very bad co-operation is Knight in front of the Pawn which makes the Pawn immobile and is of no help to the Knight. The Knight behind the Pawn is aggressive, since the effectiveness of the Pawn is doubled : the Pawn guarding the Knight is defensive, t h e Knight guarding the Pawn is still more so, the Knight obliquely one square behind the Pawn is the position of the phalanx as well as two squares sideways from the Pawn. In the latter position the Pawn protects the Knight from the attack of its worst enemy, the hostile Pawn. The farther away the Knight from the Pawn, the less co-operation.

Generalising the latter consideration, we may state that a Knight gains in value, when the points of importance are near each other ; for instance, those which a Passed Pawn has to traverse. If these points of importance are distant from each other, the Knight has lesser co-operative value. The presence of obstruction, on the other hand, decreases its value not at all while it impairs the usefulness of Bishop, Rook and Queen.

The co-operation of King and Pawn is important, since a Pawn is nearly always in the company of the King. For defence the King stands best exactly behind the Pawn, which thus protects the King against attacks of Queen,

Rook and Knight. If the King accompanies a Passed Pawn it stands best obliquely in front of the Pawn. To stand obliquely behind the Pawn indicates that the King is flying to seek safety elsewhere.

These considerations, of course, could be multiplied, but no multiplication of them would exhaust them. They are directions for arriving at evaluations of co-operative values, they show a certain method at work; the results will not be given completely; this would be both impossible and undesirable.

My Pupils.

I want to train pupils to think for themselves and exercise just criticism. I will not teach them mere formulæ, mere generalities, but will instil into them lasting principles that will grow and blossom; which are alive, and vital. They must be ready and willing to put their conceptions, laws and valuations to the proof, again and again, diligently and cheerfully, from a sheer joy of the law and from veneration of the fact.

Antagonism of Pieces.

As the total value of several pieces is not found equal to the sum of the values of the pieces taken separately, since a value of co-operation has also to be considered, just so antagonistic pieces, that compensate each other in value, leave still a surplus on the one side or the other according to the circumstances of their antagonism. This resultant is always to be considered, wherever the antagonism of two pieces persists, no matter to what extent these pieces may differ in absolute value.

The fundamental principle by which to judge the resultant of this antagonism is again the principle of justice, coupled, of course, with the reservation implied in the phrase *ceteris paribus*.

Consider the very frequent case of piece against Pawn. Obviously, the principle of justice requires that the piece be the aggressor. It should drive the Pawn into blockade or capture it. In the blockade a stationary state is arrived at, where the Pawn is helpless but for aid rendered it. If the reserve force of the opponent at any moment attains superiority against the square where the Pawn is blocked, the Pawn falls a prey. If aid comes in superiority, the blocking piece is driven off. (Compare the investigations of Nimzowitsch, *Die Blockade*.) If the stationary state is not brought about, the antagonism of piece *versus* Pawn has not been permitted to run its logical course, for instance, by aid arriving to support the Pawn or by an urgent need that calls the piece away.

Other very frequent instances are the contest of Bishop *versus* a Bishop of the same colour, of Rook *versus* Rook, of Queen *versus* Queen. These pieces will aim at performing important tasks, will collide in these aims and assail each other. This direct attack is the critical point. If either player can assail the other and force an exchange, the pieces are exactly balanced, otherwise not. That player has the advantage who can assail important points without his opponent's daring to offer an exchange.

2

White to play and win

2.—1 B–B3, B–Q3; 2 K–K3, K–B2; 3 K–K4, K–K3; 4 P–QKt4, B–B2, to keep the QKtP off Kt6 5 P–Kt5. But Black runs short of moves. 5 ...., K–B3; 6 P–Kt4, K–K3; 7 P–Kt5, P–Kt3; 8 B–Kt2, Black is in *Zugzwang*. If 8 ...., B–Q1; 9 B × P, B × P; 10 P–Kt6 and the Pawn Queens. White has the advantages, firstly, that Black cannot propose an exchange; secondly, of being able to block the KP; these suffice to force a win.

3.—The same antagonism is illustrated by the following example:

3

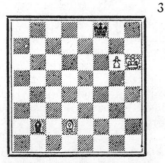

White to play and win.

The important points are obviously KKt7 and KKt8, which have to be gained so as to force the Pawn ahead. The Black Bishop will be forced off by the threat of exchange. Hence 1 K–R7, B–Q5; 2 B–R6ch., K–K1;

3 B–Kt7, B–B4; 4 B–Kt2, B–B1; 5 B–R3 and wins.

Distance.

A defect in co-operation is often indicated by the great distance between the points which the pieces occupy—often, not always. In the last resort, the spirit dominates, not the material. But, considering t h e simple geometry of the Chess - board and t h e laws of motion of the pieces, d i s t a n c e is a first, though inexact, measure of the degree of co-operation of the pieces. Two pieces of the same party near each other almost always have functions that complement each other, an effectiveness intensifying each other. Two antagonistic pieces near each other nearly always are parties to a hot conflict. If, on the other hand, the distance of two pieces, for instance of two Knights, is very great, a co-operation or a conflict between them is possible only in the future, unless they co-operate or contend with each other indirectly, for instance, the one sacrificing itself so that the other one may gain time, or the one making an attack so as to hamper the other one.

A few examples : The Bishop on QKt2 and the Rook on the KKt file co-operate on KKt7. With them great distance is not necessarily an indication of lack of co-operation. But even with them, co-operation is much closer, when they approach each other, for instance, if the Bishop is on K5 or B6, the Rook on Kt5 or Kt6. The means of defence for the opponent by obstruction, by flight of the attacked pawn or piece, by counter-attack, have then so much less variety, the attack on other neighbouring points is also correspondingly stronger. If a Knight stood on QKt2, another on KKt3, their co-operation would extend only to the middle of the board, for instance, on Q3 and K4, and for many purposes they would have to approach each other. Co-operation between the KRP and the QRP is almost impossible and can only be attained when one is threatening whereas the other is threatened, e.g., when both are passed pawns. There is, however, a great surprise for us in the co-operation of two distant Pawns, such as the QRP and KKtP, as seen in the following Ending :

4

White to play and win.

4.—1 P—R5   ....

White first seizes his R's 5th square and then has only to pass the square R7 to win. Black hurries to get possession.

1 ....   B–R3
2 P–Kt5ch.   ....

The configuration happens to be such that the KtP can force the Bishop into obstructions.

2 ....   B × P
3 K—K4   B—R5
4 K—B3 and wins.

We are surprised, because ordinarily, as soon as one wing attacks, the other one is assailed and has to be put into a state of defence.

5.—We are not at all surprised to see pieces near each other in undisturbed co-operation as in the following Ending :

5

Whether with or without the move White wins. The Rook cannot sacrifice itself for both of the Pawns. The White King will support the advance of the Pawns on White squares, the Bishop on Black squares. For instance, 1 P–K6ch., K–K1 ; 2 P–B6, R–KB8 ; 3 K–K4, to come to the support of the advance to B7.   3 ...., K – B 1 ; 4 B–K5, K–K1 ; 5 B–B4, K–B1 ; 6 K–B5, K–K1 ; 7 K–Kt5, R–Kt8ch. ; 8 K–R6, R–KB8 ; 9 B–Kt5, R–K8 ; 10 K–Kt7 and wins.

The Value of Points.

It is wholly in harmony with the Steinitz theory that the computation of the value of co-operation takes stock of the value of the points : the weak points, the strong points, the important points, the less essential points. Particularly are the weak and strong points of account. The effect of these is decisive; all else is of secondary importance.

Examples

White: Rubinstein.
Black: Salwe.

1	P—Q4	P—Q4
2	P—QB4	P—K3
3	Kt—QB3	P—QB4
4	P×QP	P×QP
5	Kt—B3	Kt—QB3
6	P—KKt3	Kt—B3
7	B—Kt2	....

Already this mode of developing the Bishop is determined by the weakness of Black on Q5.

7	....	P×P
8	KKt×P	Q—Kt3
9	Kt×Kt	P×Kt
10	O—O	B—K2
11	Kt—R4	....

W h i t e concentrates against QB5 and QB6.

11	....	Q—Kt4
12	B—K3	O—O
13	R—B1	B—KKt5

B l a c k should rather strengthen QB3 by B–Q2.

14	P–B3	B—K3
15	B—B5	KR—K1
16	R—KB2	Kt—Q2
17	B×B	R×B
18	Q—Q4	KR—K1
19	B—B1	KR—QB1
20	P—K3	Q—Kt2
21	Kt—B5	Kt×Kt
22	R×Kt	....

Now B5 is gained and the Pawn at B3 fixed; that Pawn therefore becomes the target.

22	....	R—-B2
23	KR—B2	Q—Kt3
24	P—QKt4	....

White threatens P–Kt5. Black has no time for 24 .... B–Q2. The sequence is 25 P–Kt5, QR–B1; 26 Q–B3 and Black cannot liberate himself. Again, if 24 ...., B–Q2; 25 P–Kt5, KR–B1; 26 P×P, B×P; 27 Q–B3.

24	....	P-.QR3
25	R–R5	R–Kt1
26	P–QR3	R- -R2

Black cannot guard all of his weak spots.

27	R×BP	Q×KR
28	Q×R	R—R1
29	Q—B5	Q—Kt2
30	K—B2	....

The intent is to guard his own weaknesses, particularly on the second and third ranks.

30	....	P—R4
31	B—K2	P—Kt3
32	Q—Q6	....

The QB file is important because open.

32	....	Q—B1
33	R—B5	Q—Kt2
34	P—KR4	P—R4

A desperate attempt at a counter-attack.

35	R—B7	Q—Kt1
36	P—Kt5	P—R5
37	P—Kt6	R—R4
38	P—Kt7	resigns.

This game illustrates how much greater weight the effect of the pieces on weaknesses has in comparison to their effect on other points.

White : Duras.
Black : Rubinstein.

1	P—K4	P—K4
2	Kt—KB3	Kt—QB3
3	B—Kt5	P—QR3
4	B—R4	Kt—B3
5	P—Q3	P—Q3
6	P—B4	....

This advance is testimony that White overrates his position. True, Black is prevented from P—Q4 but White has weakened his Q3 and Q4. Moreover, a move is spent, an opportunity for development is lost, a serious matter at such an early stage of the Opening.

| 6 | .... | P—KKt3 |

Preparing to aim at White's Q4.

7	P—Q4	P × P
8	Kt × P	B—Q2
9	Kt × Kt	B × Kt
10	O—O	B—Kt2
11	Kt—B3	O—O
12	P—B3	Kt—Q2
13	B—K3	Kt—K4
14	B—Kt3	P—Kt3

The White QBP obstructs the KB; hence, it is made immobile.

| 15 | P—B4 | Kt—Q2 |

The Knight has been driven back, but White's K4 is now the target.

16	B—Q4	Kt—B4
17	B × B	K × B
18	B—B2	P—QR4

Kt and RP co-operate well. The Kt is safe on an advanced and threatening post.

| 19 | Q—Kt4 | .... |

White does not examine the weaknesses, or he would have played 19 Q–Q4ch. to exchange Queens. If he desired to avoid the Ending, 19 P–B5 was the move. The Black Knight already has a fine post; it would therefore not matter to allow another on K5, and White would have been the gainer by opening the KB file for his Rooks.

| 19 | .... | Kt × P |

Black will dominate the KB line though he must in compensation rid White of a weak spot.

20	Kt × Kt	P—B4
21	Q—B3	P × Kt
22	B × P	B × B
23	Q × B	Q—B3

In Rubinstein's play the aim against the weaknesses is very apparent. As the weaknesses vary, he varies his plans accordingly.

24 R—B2   QR—K1
25 Q—Q5   Q—B4

Black gains the open line to dominate it a long time.

26 R—Q1   R–K5
27 P—KKt3   KR—K1
28 K--Kt2   P—R4

White's QB4 and KB4 are targets, also Q4 and K4 are weak points, the Black KRP wants to advance further.

29 P—Kt3   R—K6

Preparation for P—QR5 which rends the White Pawns.

30 R—Q4   K—B3

In order to have the King handy for entering the White camp.

31 P—KR3 ?   ....

Again White does not consider what and where are his weaknesses. The basis of his defence are the Rooks Pawns; to guard them well he should retreat QR–Q2. Against 31 .... Q–Kt5 he had then 32 R–B3, and in any case, though at a disadvantage, he would have made a better fight.

31 ....   P—KR5
32 Q × Qch.   P × Q
33 P × P   R—Kt1ch
34 K—B1   ....

The KRP is indefensible.

34 ....   R × RP
35 K—K2   R—K1ch.
36 K—Q2   R × RP

and Black won by material superiority.

A g a i n it is manifest that Rubinstein's play, by b e i n g mainly directed against the weaknesses of the opponent, attains to a high degree of force.

Attack and Defence in Balanced Positions.

Balanced positions are not without means of attack or defence, only, in contra-distinction to unbalanced positions, the defence has to make no greater concessions than counter-attack can regain. In balanced positions, therefore, de-fence and counter-attack are so adjusted that with best play on either side the bal-ance is again established.

In such positions attacks may be ferocious, defences subtle, combinations deep but at the end, when com-parative tranquility reigns again, neither side can claim to have achieved an advantage.

An attack in a balanced position bears some likeness to a thunderstorm. The clouds hovering over a peaceful landscape carry here positive, there negative electricity, and suddenly, after they have approached each other sufficiently, there are discharges, from cloud to cloud or from cloud to earth. The landscape is frightened, a terrific turmoil is let loose; after a little while the clouds break, the turmoil ceases, the sun shines again and the landscape laughs merrily like a child. So in a balanced position, White has here an advantage, Black there, the tension grows until the weapons clash, and there is the drama of action. That lasts a while, the master is frightened, since the slightest mistake may seal his doom; he fights courageously, he does his duty; then suddenly the disadvantages on either side have disappeared, the position has rid itself of its tension and, the moves becoming of slight menace, the master breathes easily and is glad to have been equal to his task.

The direction of attack and defence is also circumscribed by the rules of Steinitz in balanced position. The events may not have quite the force, the action not quite the tension as in positions where one side has the superiority and has to bring it to bear against the efforts of a well-conducted defence eager to assume counter-attack. For all that, the connoisseur, observing how the master keeps the finely drawn line of balance enjoys the situation profoundly. He who does not comprehend the language of the moves that maintain the balance is unable to read the signs which predict the advent of great events; he who knows that language understands also the logic by which such events are brought about.

The task of following the principles of Steinitz in balanced positions is no easy one. In a position where I hold the advantage, I do the hitting, my opponent may have to be patient and submissive and may have to lose in the end nevertheless. I am hammer, he anvil, and the gallery applauds. But in balanced positions I am hammer in one part of the board and anvil in another; the gallery may not understand, but this is a harder test. Each move where I obtain an advantage, is paid for by a disadvantage. This play of give and take is most appealing when the master gives material force to obtain positional advantage. He then makes a " sacrifice for position." Such positions show the character of the player. It takes courage to shoulder the responsibility of such momentous decisions. The master must then be the scales to weigh advantage and disadvantage; and he knows no certainty, for this is no combination, it is his judgment which decides for good and for evil. Then it is your duty to act according to your belief. Not so easy as it looks. You think that you should embark on a venture hazardous but promising? but you fear blindly, unreasonably, the unknown possibilities and the certainty of having to apply yourself vigorously. You should act nevertheless. You may see a ruse, deeply hidden, which, you feel sure, your opponent will not see through and that would save you all the trouble. You see the weak spot of your deception, do not try the trick, keep your self-respect, keep your style clean. Do not bank upon your opponent making a mistake.

One may err, but one must not deceive oneself. He who bravely follows his judgment may lose but even his loss profits him, provided he seeks to discover the reasons for it; and he grows to be a master, an artist. But he who no longer ventures to back his opinion loses the quality of a fighter and approaches his fall.

Examples of Sacrifices for Position

White—La Bourdonnais.
Black—McDonnell.

1	P—Q4	P—Q4
2	P—QB4	P × P
3	P—K4	P—K4
4	P—Q5	P—KB4
5	Kt—QB3	Kt—KB3
6	B × P	B—B4
7	Kt—B3	Q—K2

Not 7 .... P × P; 8 Kt—KKt5. Now 8 ...., B × Pch. is threatened.

8 B—Kt5	....

A mistake. He should have Castled.

8.	B × P ch
9 K—B1	....

Better to capture since he would regain the Pawn, viz., 9 K × B, Q—B4 ch; 10 K–K1, Q × B; 11 Kt × P, Q–R3. Black has an advantage, White fighting chances, for instance, with 12 R–KB1.

9	B—Kt3
10 Q—K2	P—B5
11 R—Q1	B—Kt5
12 P—Q6	P × P
13 Kt—Q5	....

In this situation Black has the choice of suffering the attack or of beating back every attempt to attack him by giving up his Queen. His judgment inclines towards the latter alternative and, being a brave man, he follows it.

He probably saw several menaces such as 13 ...., Q–Q1; 14 Kt×BP, P×Kt; 15 P–K5 or 13 ...., Q–B1; 14 B–Kt5ch. and Black is prevented from Castling. On the other hand he weighed the chances after Kt×Kt. For his Q he gets two pieces, two valuable pawns and an outpost position for his Kt at K6. So he made his decision. He did not make a combination, for he could not have calculated the maze of variations for it was too involved. He judged and valued and acted.

13 ....   Kt×Kt
14 B×Q   Kt—K6 ch

White might now have tried 15 Q×Kt followed by B×P, but his judgment, though perhaps at fault, advised him to see the attack through.

15 K—K1   K×B
16 Q—Q3   R—Q1
17 R—Q2   Kt—B3
18 P—QKt3   ....

But here White errs. To develop his force he should offer a sacrifice by 18 R–B1, so as to rid himself of the oppressive Knight on K6. If then 18 .... QR–B1; 19 B–Kt3 or 18 .... B–QR4; 19 R–B2. The Pawn move only weakens his position. La Bourdonnais had not recognized this clearly. The theory of Steinitz, explaining these points, was not evolved until fifty years later.

18 ....   B—QR4
19 P—QR3   QR—B1

With sure instinct McDonnell aims at White's vulnerable spot. If now 20 P–Kt4, Black is master of the QB file. The sequence is 20 ...., Kt×P; 21 P×Kt, B×P; 22 B–R2, B×Kt; 23 P×B, R–B7.

20 R—Kt1   ....

In his dire need White visualises an attack on the seventh rank which, however, has no force.

20 ....   P—QKt4
21 B×P   B×Kt
22 P×B   Kt—Q5
23 B—B4   Kt×P ch
24 K—B2   Kt×QR
25 R×P ch   K—B3
26 R—B7 ch   K—Kt3
27 R—Kt7   QKt×B
28 P×Kt   R×P

and Black won.

White—Pillsbury.
Black—Em. Lasker.

1 P—K4	P—K3
2 P—Q4	P—Q4
3 Kt—QB3	Kt—KB3
4 P—K5	KKt—Q2
5 P—B4	P—QB4
6 P × P	Kt—QB3
7 P—QR3	Kt × BP
8 P—QKt4	Kt—Q2

This retreat is incomprehensible to me now. Of course, 8 ...., P—Q5 was indicated. If then 9 QKt–K2, P–Q6; 10 Kt–Kt3, Q–Q5 and B l a c k has the initiative.

9 B—Q3	P—QR4

Proof of nervous impatience.

10 P—Kt5	QKt—Kt1
11 Kt—B3	Kt—B4
12 B—K3	QKt—Q2
13 O—O	P—KKt3

Black herewith perpetuates his weakness on the King's side, but he has only a choice of evils, having lost too much time.

14 Kt—K2	B—K2

Now 14 ...., B–Kt2 would have made the better fight.

15 Q—K1	Kt—Kt3
16 KKt—Q4	B—Q2
17 Q—B2	QKt—R5

Black plays to attack the QKtP and prevents P–QR4, but he should conceive less ambitious plans.

17 ...., Q—B2 would have been right.

18 QR—Kt1	P—R4

Otherwise White could open the KB line by P–Kt4 and P–B5.

19 P—Kt6 !	....

This Pawn is a veritable wedge. It is sufficiently supported and opens the square QKt5 to the White pieces.

19	Kt × B
20 P × Kt	B × P

Black wants to set White a task. The situation merits attention. Black has a Pawn plus, an immediate danger is not apparent. If White does not threaten, Black fortifies his position by B–Kt5. White must not wait, but where is Black's m o s t vulnerable spot? The answer is evidently that the Black King is badly placed. B u t the way to it is strewn with impediments. Removing these impediments m a y cost much but, according to Pillsbury's judgment, the high price is not too high; hence the sacrifices for position which reveal Black's hidden weakness with most becoming justice.

21 P—B5	KtP × P
22 Kt—B4	....

menacing Q–Kt3–Kt7.

22	P—R5
23 R—R1	B—K2
24 R × Kt	B × R

The Bishop is diverted from K3.

| 25 KKt × KP | P × Kt |
| 26 Kt × KP | .... |

Now Q × BP is threatened in addition to other more obvious threats, for instance, 26 ...., Q–B1; 27 Q × BP, Q–B3, and now stronger than 28 R–B1, which also would win 28 B–Kt5. Black played 26 ...., B–Q2 and lost, as in such a position he ought to.

The Principle of Proportion.

The principles of attack, defence, and balance give directions f o r planning. They tell us when and how we should strive for a positive aim, or resist changes, or prepare ourselves for the coming crisis. That is a great deal, a very great deal. One may say that *he who has not Steinitz's theory in his grasp does not understand how to conceive sound plans, either on the Chess-board or elsewhere.*

Certainly, he will sometimes be able to hit upon a sound plan, not like the swallow that in midst of its flight catches its prey with ease, but like a poodle which clumsily jumps after a fly.

T h e theory as above presented does not, however, embrace all of the fundamental principles of a contest. To put them together with sufficient explanations so that they will be lucid is rather a formidable task. My first attempt was made in 1906 in my book *Struggle,* and another and more successful one in my system of philosophy, *Das Begreifen der Welt (Comprehension of the World)* 1913, *Die Philosophie des Unvollendbar (The Philosophy of the Unattainable)* 1918, both books at present only in a German edition. This philosophy—pardon, reader, this is my conviction which is not entirely vain — t h i s philosophy will some day be known and esteemed by man. The presages therefor are plain even now. But my philosophy is young, only fourteen years of age. My second work was written during the years of the World W a r, through which, as if by miracle, I lived in quiet, though starving. That book has therefore an age of only seven years. Philosophical systems can very well bear an age of a few thousand years; in the first century of their life they are small babies. One must not, therefore, wonder that man does not seem to know much of a theory of "struggle," and still less should one draw from this fact the conclusion that probably it is of little importance. W h a t ripens soon, fades soon. To good and weighty theories public recognition comes late. *The theory of struggle, divined by men like Machiavelli, N a p o l e o n, Klausewitz, moulded by Steinitz in accurate detail for the Chess-board, longingly desired by some philosophers, established by myself in universal validity, therefore philosophically, will some day regulate the life of m a n.* I do not in the least hesitate to say so. The theory of struggle is the only theory that is pragmatic. It, therefore, joins the virtues of a theory, definition and finiteness; to the virtues of historical things: reality and infinity.

In order to round off the theory of Steinitz as above outlined, I should like to mention one more principle. Steinitz has felt it but not formulated it. It is, that the aim of an attack must be proportionate to the advantage upon which the plan for the attack is based. The attack wants to change the basic advantage which is fluent and unstable into a permanent advantage. The principle of proportion tells us that to the greater basic advantage should correspond the more ambitious plan. In the same way, of course, the defender should apportion his concession.

The game of Chess has not been designed to serve as paradigm for very subtle questions and it happens not to express the above principle as well as it might. So far as the end of the game is concerned, it knows only three values: win, loss, draw, and this number is insufficient to allow of an accurate estimate to be made of the advantages leading up to the issues. Other games, which have a larger variety of results, for instance, Whist or still better, the Japanese game of Go, have also a varied scale of values. And Life with its infinity of values gives, of course, a much more comprehensive idea of proportion than any game. For all that, Chess is not entirely devoid of instances in which the principle of proportion may be demonstrated in a clear light.

A well-known example is that of "playing to win" which Dr. T a r r a s c h pointedly h a s renamed "playing to lose." That always happens when the player overrates his advantage or for other reasons seeks to derive from a minute advantage a great return such as a forced win.

Another example concerns the way in which conclusions are drawn from examples. You must not draw too general a conclusion from too few examples. Unfortunately, this error is made far and wide. In politics and in our social life rash judgments, out of all proportion to the scarcity of facts to prove them, are passed most readily. To uphold a prejudice men will go to any lengths. This game would be laughable were it not so serious. In Chess fortunately we may laugh good humouredly at most of these attempts. Yet we have to do our duty and see to it that no lasting harm is done to the game. Hence, a few words on how i n d u c t i v e conclusions should be drawn in Chess.

A rule or law or stratagem pertaining to Chess does not come down from heaven but must have connections and analogies in Life; it must therefore be *natural*. For instance, the rules of development telling us to get the pieces out in the quickest manner compatible with safety reminds us of the setbacks that an inactive man suffers, and it appeals to us at once. After having discovered what presumably is such a rule, we must associate it with Chess as closely as possible. But not with purposely thought-out positions : with natural positions, which could, nay even assuredly would, crop up in well-contested games. If the rule applies under such conditions, we hold a rough diamond. Then we have to cut it, so as to bring out its lustre, by trying to change the rule a little this way and a little that way. If the rule can be thus twisted about and yet seem to apply, it is a bad sign. The right rule, right in wording and content, cannot be changed in the slightest manner without losing some of its point or application.

This method is not followed, nowadays, either in the act of discovery or in that of criticism. The so-called "hyper - modern" school almost lives by *not* following it, but by erecting magnificent structures out of flimsy material. For all

that, this school has its
good points. It has quick-
ened our imagination, it has
taught us to suspect mechanical Chess, it has insisted
on the high value of the
central Pawns, it has
warned against their premature advance. But these
accomplishments were due
to a most diligent research
of highly gifted young men
who during the last dozen
years have played many
hard games—thousands of
them, with passionate devo-
tion. Nor are these rules
new; but they had never
been so tested before nor
applied within a range so
wide as they have by these
youths. The purely logical
gain of the hyper-modern
school cannot be viewed
with too much suspicion.
Its inductions, generalisa-
tions, constructions, even
its definitions, are made
with an insouciance that is
enviable as a mood but un-
business-like.

Examples of the Principle of Proportion.

White: Te Kolste.
Black: Torre.

1	P—K4	P—K3
2	P—Q4	P—Q4
3	Kt—QB3	Kt—KB3
4	B—Kt5	B—Kt5
5	Kt—K2	P×P
6	P—QR3	B—K2

7	B×Kt	P×B
8	Kt×P	P—Kt3
9	KKt—B3	B—Kt2
10	Q—B3	....

Though check with the
Kt is now threatened,
White's intention is not
aggressive but merely the
protection of the KKtP.

10	....	P—B3
11	O—O—O	P—KB4
12	Kt—Kt3	Kt—Q2
13	B—B4	....

But here White begins to
be aggressive and thereby
he puts himself in the
wrong for his aim is not
even remotely warranted by
his advantage. Again he
should strive to safeguard
his KKtP by 13 Kt R5, to
be followed by R—Kt1,
and afterwards possibly by
P—R3 and P—KKt4 with
some little pressure on the
centre and on the KRP,
proportionate to his advantage in mobility. As he
plays White begins to slide
first very slowly; afterwards
more quickly.

13	....	Q—B2
14	KR—K1	Kt—B3
15	Q—K2	O—O—O

Black has defended con-
scientiously. If White now
continues 16 Kt×P, Q–B5
ch.; 17 Kt–K3, R×P; 18
B–R6 he can still obtain
equality. But here is the
parting of the ways:

16	B×Pch.	....

White fancies that he holds an advantage and attempts to win. The punishment is immediate.

16	P × B
17 Q × Pch.	R—Q2
18 Kt × P	B—Q1
19 Kt—K4	Kt × Kt
20 R × Kt	K—Kt1
21 P—KKt3	B—B1
22 Q—R6	R—B2
23 Kt—K3	R × P

and White resigned after four more moves.

In the following game both opponents overrate their position and Reti is thereby caused to commit a downright blunder.

White: Reti.
Black: Colle.

1 P—KKt3	P—Q4
2 B—Kt2	P—QB3
3 P—QB4	P × P
4 Kt—QR3	B—K3
5 Q—B2	P---KKt3
6 Kt × P	B—Kt2
7 Kt—B3	Kt—Q2
8 O—O	Kt—Kt3
9 Kt × Kt	P × Kt
10 P—Q3	P—R3
11 B—Q2	Q—B1
12 B—B3	Kt—B3

White has a fair position. He might now continue with 13 KR–K1, safeguard by P–QR3, contend for central points such as Q4; in brief aim for small gains. But he now conceives the ambitious plan of gaining a decisive advantage on QKt6. He succeeds, but in justice his opponent obtains counter action on the other wing.

13 Kt—Q2	B—R6

True, this is careless. Why not 13 ...., P–QKt4 to start with?

14 Kt—B4	R—R3
15 P—R4	P—R4
16 Q—Q2	P—R5

But now Black wants to annihilate his opponent outright. With 16 ...., B × B; 17 K × B the Queen was free, then 17 ...., P–R5; 18 Q–K3, Q–Q1, and Black has a favourable position.

17 Q—K3	K—B1
18 Kt × P	R × Kt
19 Q × R	P × P
20 BP × P	B × B
21 K × B	Q—R6ch.
22 K—B2	Kt—Kt5ch.
23 K—K1	B × Bch.
24 P × B	Kt × P
25 R—KKt1	Q—K3

Impossible to find a safe retreat for the White King and therefore as long as the Queens stay on the board Black has a good fighting chance.

The normal, patient, suitable continuation for White would have been 26 R–Kt2, Kt–B6ch.; 27 K–B2, Kt–K4; and perhaps 28 Q–Q4, R–R6 with a difficult game for either party. But White judges that he has a big advantage, looks for a winning combination and too easily persuades himself that he has discovered it.

26 Q—Q8ch.   K—Kt2
27 Q—Q4ch.   K—Kt1
28 K—Q2??   ....

At least 28 Q-K4 should now have been played, although 28 ...., Q-Kt6 would have been a disagreeable retort.

28 ....   Kt—B6ch.

White resigns, because the Black Rook comes down to its seventh rank.

As an instance of the kind of induction above objected to, I cite some notes of Reti concerning the game he played against Te Kolste at Baden-Baden, 1925. Reti had Black. The game started. 1 P–K4, Kt–KB3; 2 P–K5, Kt–Q4; 3 Kt–QB3, Kt×Kt; 4 QP×Kt. In Kagan's *Neuesten Schachnachrichten* Reti calls this move a "*Positionsfehler*," a positional error. That is at least debatable. But what he then says runs contrary to all proportion. "The game will show how by modern Chess technique a minute but clear positional advantage incurred in the Opening can be easily converted into a win." Into a win? No, this proportion is not

the right one. Into initiative, into a promising game; such an assertion would have to be conceded, but no more, unless the opponent errs again. Reti's plan in the above game was to make use of White's doubled Pawn by getting the superiority of Pawns on the King's side. First rate! He succeeded in this too. But for all that he was very far from having a winning game. The combination by which he wanted to force the win leaves White with no disadvantage whatever. For this combination see the following diagram.

Te Kolste here made the mistake of offering the exchange of Rooks, which loses, because the White QRP is backward and

White to play.

Black gets a Passed Pawn. Reti remarks, that the right move 1 P—QR3 would have lost equally, but his analysis contains an oversight. 1 ...., P×P;

2   P–QKt4,   P–R7;   3
R–R3,   P–Q4.   Reti
makes White here play
4   P × Pch., whereupon
the QKtP is untenable, but
it was easy to see that 4 R–
R6ch., King moves; 5 R ×
RP, P × P; 6 R–B2 would
make White secure and
eliminate all advantage.
And this combination
should be the culminating
point of a strategy resulting
from White's fourth move
and bringing about an inex-
orable win! I admit that
after 1 P–QR3, K–B4! 2
P–QR4 Black still exerts
slight pressure; to say
aught beyond that would be
an exaggeration.

Wide-visioned strategical
plans must not have so frail
a basis. On a motif such as
was indicated by Reti, one
cannot build the plan of a
whole well-contested game;
it is too meagre, too thin,
too puny for such an end.
Reti's explanations, wherever they are concerned
with an analysis which
covers a few moves are correct and praiseworthy. As
yet nobody has been able to
do much more than that except to conceive plans as
the game proceeded. The
reader of Reti's remarks is
led to think that an altogether new and profound
strategy has recently arisen
and is probably tempted to

cast very deep strategical
plans of the same order. He
is in danger of losing his
s o u n d judgment, and
neither he nor Chess is well
served thereby.

An Enquiry into the Logical Origin and the Domain of Application of Steinitz's Theory.

A f t e r having gone
through these various ex-
amples and verifications one
cannot help but admit that
the rules of Steinitz are confirmed by well played
games. Are these rules
then the result of an
analysis Steinitz made of
thousands of master games;
conversely, has the men-
tality of Steinitz called these
rules into being with the
intention of reconciling his
experience and his obser-
vation with them as far as
possible? D i d Steinitz
start his investigation as
an analyst or as a thinker,
from the material of games
or from his imagination
which moulded principles?
We need to be clear on this
point.

To attack this problem it
is sufficient to concentrate
our attention upon any one
of Steinitz's principles. Let
us consider the simple proposition, that in a faultless
game he wins who has con-
tinued to hold the advan-
tage. Let us assert outright

and bluntly, but briefly and clearly, that the superior force always wins. Can such an opinion be deduced from analysis or observation? Or is its origin elsewhere?

T h e experience that Chess-players gather every day is certainly very far from suggestive of such an opinion. The ordinary experience is rather that he who has a slight disadvantage plays more attentively, inventively and more boldly than his antagonist who either takes it easy or aspires after too much; thus a slight disadvantage is very frequently seen to convert itself into a good, solid advantage. A budding Chessmaster, during his period of growth, would be hugely surprised if he were confronted by our assertion. He would not be interested in it. He would call it metaphysics, but not Chess. His experience is that he wins, when a happy thought strikes him, and that he is in bad disposition or has ill luck, when no such thought occurs to him. True, he has had experiences of superior force when a boy. In wrestling and boxing the superior force was brought home to him. But Chess would appear to him as being of a different order of things. That Mental power wins in Chess would be the firmest of his impressions.

But we reply that we speak of the force of the pieces, the force of their cooperation. He would probably be somewhat stunned by this suggestion and keep his peace. But he would be right in asking, whether such a thing as that really and truly exists. In mathematical books one is likely to find two vectors (a, b) called forces with a demonstration of Newton's parallelogram of forces attached thereto. Mathematically, the assertion will be true, though a couple of vectors is a logical thing and not a reality like muscular power. Is it, perhaps, no different in Chess?

Well, it is almost a miracle, but it is not so in Chess. As already shown, Steinitz did not grasp his conceptions out of empty space, but formed them according to vivid impressions which suggested analogies, and he oftentimes put them to the test. He was very far from creating new concepts as mathematicians do who discover such ideas as prime number or ellipse or congruence and on them string their propositions. He thought as the poet thinks who searches for an expression that will pregnantly picture his sentiments and impressions.

Thus understood, the proposition of Steinitz, as is apparent, far from stating an experience, is rather of the nature of a demand. He *postulates* his proposition, though in Life it is not always fulfilled, and in Chess not so very often, even in the games of masters, if the truth be told, by no means always. Not that this postulate originated with Steinitz. Mankind has framed it, the poet who continually gives expression to it is only its mouthpiece. The small army of Greeks vanquishes the enormous number of Persians; history repeats a thousandfold the victory of the smaller number; we explain that superior morale and strategy had conferred this force upon the outnumbered army. Before we ever investigate we are resolved to uphold the proposition that superior force wins, provided, of course, that every kind of force, physical, moral, mental, etc., is reckoned with. And nothing whatever will make us deviate from this resolve. This proposition, surely, does not originate with experience, but we strive with

might and main to explain our experience, no matter how it turns out, in its terms. This feeling is the home of poetical justice, as of many fine things to which we aspire but which Life often denies us. The same feeling, undoubtedly, dominated Steinitz when he maintained his proposition. What he searched for in long years was not the proposition, in which he believed from the start, but the interpretation that the proposition needed to comply with experience. And in this endeavour he met with full success.

His method was *fertile*, Chess lent itself to make it so; hence, his deed was ingenious, a memorial both for the investigator and his object. Hitherto, in all history, this method had remained sterile, of value, no doubt, to the historian who looks back upon events, but of no use to the statesman who wants to predict them. Hitherto, we knew only *after* the deed how the higher morality or culture or will-power or strategy had to be valued, and the use of such knowledge is small. In Chess we know in advance. Steinitz has shown the way. The teaching of Steinitz demands from us an accurate valuation. The game of Chess itself is severe in this respect and will immediately depose the master who is unable or unwilling to satisfy that postulate.

There is another point in which the theory of Steinitz is ahead of any theory at present in use for pragmatic ends. It is based on the assumption of faultless play, and this assumption can be realised in Chess at least to a high degree of approximation, and the theory can thus be subjected to severe tests. But how could we in pragmatic affairs hope at present to verify such an assumption? In Life we are all duffers. Error and mistake are our daily bread. In Chess we can test the players and do so test them, and have a pretty accurate idea of their strength. If we should attempt to introduce into business or statesmanship or engineering or science any such accuracy of measurement, not only should we have a difficult problem to solve, but there would be bloodshed. And the efficient people would in all likelihood be persecuted and think twice before they made evident their superiority.

An illustration of the process in Chess will illuminate what has been said. A master has made a sacrifice and has won the game. Has the lesser number of pieces beaten the greater by some kind of witchery? Many think so. They opine that the genius of the master was the charm. The investigator who proceeds methodically denies that; he asserts that also in this case the superior force has been victorious, the mentality of the players remaining out of the reckoning. Now the critic enters and demands a precise demonstration. "Here in the Opening," the critic says to the investigator "A Pawn was sacrificed and afterwards the game was won. According to your view the sacrifice was compensated for by position. But please weigh the compensation, for in Chess words are air; in our game the analysis, conducted to the point where the final result can be clearly gauged, is admitted as the only proof." Thereupon the investigator examines the records of many positions and replies: "All right, I will specify that compensation. Three to four moves advance in development suffice to compensate for the loss of an important Pawn.   This rule can be put on trial by reviewing a hundred games of masters and has been confirmed." Wherever in Chess apparently the weaker force is victorious, a compensation can be detected, and *this compensation can be accurately circumscribed in terms of a general rule.* In other domains of human activity we have as yet no such method.   Perhaps the future will some day bring about a change for the better.

The above statements are valid for the contests of masters.   Games, starting from the initial position where slight mistakes, if any, are made, run such a course. Artificial positions, c o m p o s e d, constructed, thought out by a man sitting in his study, are necessarily exempt from the above rules and valuations. One must bear in mind this contrast or else one will be unable to comprehend the real meaning of Steinitz's theory. The contrast is the same as that between theory and practice, between logic and metaphysics, between thought and reality, between h u m a n wit and nature.   The contest of masters produces situations different from the construc-

tions of him who wants to make a combination by spinning the thread of his own thoughts. To the latter activity, which is not a duel between unyielding antagonists, the teachings of Steinitz do not apply.

It is easy to invent positions so peculiar, so strange, involved, artificial, I might even say crazy, that one could n o t possibly apply to them the theory of Steinitz.   That theory is not meant for them. *For any position which can be brought about by the play of masters the theory holds good, not for the unnatural products of a fanciful brain.* If an unnatural position is examined with a view to determining how it could have come about by play from previous positions, one readily sees that there is something akin to insanity in it.   Such a situation cannot be produced by the play of reasonable minds. As an example to test the theory, it thereby ceases to have any weight. In a position that has a history arising out of a contest, the method of Steinitz is always practicable and in this sense the superior force always wins at Chess.

But here I must stop a moment, for I have been guilty of an exaggeration.

The theory of Steinitz is always valid when intelligently applied to contests occurring in Life, in reality. In this sense I maintain the validity of the rule, though, of course, with philosophic reasons. In the last resort this is a matter of belief and therefore appertains to philosophy. If you want to follow and to probe this train of thought, you may read my two books on philosophy. But there are many games, particularly mathematical games, to which during centuries of investigation an immense body of literature has been devoted and which yet have no origin in the struggles of Life. These games have a theory that vastly differs from that of Steinitz. The game of Chess, it is true, has real struggle as an ancestor, but in the course of its long history the original intent was forgotten, rules were added which w e r e logical, formal, precise, but not true to life. And therefore the theory of Steinitz, even in master games, is not absolutely true.

Therewith the proof that the theory of Steinitz originated in his mentality is confirmed anew. I can imagine how Steinitz had to struggle and to search before he was able to apply his ideas to tournament and match practice. The witchery of creative fancy, the inexplicableness of disposition or indisposition for hard play, the elusiveness of his object resisted his efforts. In addition, the lack of understanding, the ill-will of a time too narrow-minded, too avaricious, weighed down on him. His struggle was hard. We all lose in the end, that is the intention, and the brave man is not afraid of it; but there is a measure and a limit to human endurance. For Steinitz the struggle was too hard, and his nature abandoned t h e effort, when his intellect at last refused the ungrateful service.

But the cause which he served lives.

That Chess follows the principles of Steinitz only in some points is no fault of his theory which would indeed deteriorate if it tried to embrace all possibilities. The fault lies in the rules with which, in course of time, the game has been burdened. The a i m of Chess is to reconstruct, in the terms of a game, the war of a few thousand years ago, but it contains arbitrary rules made after. the original idea had been forgotten. Castling and the valuation of Stalemate as a draw are instances. To this extent the theory of Steinitz loses its efficiency; for instance, every Stalemate is in contradiction to it. The theory of Steinitz is valid for reality, not for rules spun out of bloodless abstractions. That constitutes its limitation as well as its greatness.

FIFTH BOOK.

THE ÆSTHETIC EFFECT IN CHESS.

The æsthetic effect of a Chess game becomes manifest to the spectator provided he follows the events of the game, as they unroll themselves, w i t h interest and comprehension. The players might be indifferent to him, yet the spectator may derive pleasure from the game to the point of delight, or else he may find it dull, or even object to it to the point of disgust. He has a whole scale of sentiments ready to respond to the play of the pieces. The players may exist or not, they may be abstract persons such as White and Black—that matters not a bit—the spectator responds to the call, to the charm of the Chess contest.

It is this scale of sentiments that I should like to name the *æsthetic valuation*. T h e spectator is highly pleased with a move and calls it " brilliant " or " beautiful." He likes the look of a position and praises it as natural, alive, suggestive. Another position is cramped, improbable to him. All of these and many similar terms refer to an æsthetic valuation.

The æsthetic valuation, obviously, depends upon the personality of the spectator. An old Latin adage says " *De gustibus non est disputandum.*" This is as true in Chess as anywhere else. But it is noteworthy that we have assumed the spectator to be not only interested but also comprehending. We may know nothing, to start with, of his æsthetic valuations, but we may assume that we know a great deal concerning his comprehension. That is the Archimedian point where we might apply our lever. And again, the game appeals to a great many, to a multitude. Positions, many centuries old, have been handed down to us because of their strong æsthetic effect. One man may be exceptional; a multitude of men conversing with each other brings forth a public opinion which is likely not to be so. If " the spectator " is a mul-

261

titude, we might be able to specify his valuations.

In this hope then we may propose the problem of shedding light on æsthetic valuations in Chess.

Chess, of course, is no exceptional case. Æsthetic valuations evoked in Chess are likely to be met in other fields of endeavour. To what category must we assign Chess so as to account for its æsthetic effect? Manifestly, the class of *achievements*. It is the achievement of the pieces on the Chess-board, nothing else, that grips the interest of the spectator and carries him along and excites him. Unless t h e spectator observes a n achievement which seems to him out of the common, his interest will slumber. Only when a move discloses a task to be solved which seems difficult if not impossible, or when, for some reason, the spectator expects such a move or series of moves, the æsthetic valuation begins. The achievement may be manifold; the giving of a Mate, or its prevention, or the desperate fight of a minority which causes the superior force to doubt its victory, are among t h e many instances. It is always the achievement of

the pieces which comprehended by the spectator, causes his excitement. And this excitement runs its course, as the game proceeds, and at length culminates in an æsthetic valuation. The interest of the spectator is fired by an achievement that appeals to him and rivets his attention.

The achievements speak to the spectator in a language of their own. The player need not speak in words, the move announces an intention and a meaning. True, the spectator must not be deaf and dumb to this language, else he perceives nothing or misunderstands. But the spectator by no means need be a master. The master can create, the sympathetic spectator, not gifted with the genius of discovery, comprehends. H e h a s imagination to follow the drama of the game with interest, and he has intellect to understand what each move aims at and accomplishes.

For the æsthetic effect the language of the move and nothing else is of any account whatever. What the move says, expresses, discloses, announces—that it is that excites and stirs the spectator. The spectator enjoys not a game of Chess, but history, drama; that a Chess- board is its stage, and Chess pieces its actors, matters not. If the drama of a Chess game be presented by human actors on the stage of a theatre, its æsthetic effect would not be a particle different—provided onlv, as stated above as a condition, the spectator has interest and comprehension·

True, the human language which has a long and wonderful history, the language o f pantomime, that of the human anatomy and of the human emotions, is a thousand times more eloquent than the language of the Chess pieces. Yet it is a fact that Chess games and Chess positions have a hold upon many, a hold strong enough to make them burst into applause and to cause these games and positions to be preserved in books and to be fondly remembered. And as a matter of pure theory we may conceive of a spectator so conversant with Chess that to him the language of the move is very rich. What we want to establish beyond a doubt is the thesis that this language alone matters, as long as the æsthetic effect alone is considered. Of other effects we do not treat. For this effect the medium is of importance only in so far as it must have a history and therefore be able to make itself understood, to be eloquent, to be heard by a multitude of understanding minds.

But if this is true, it follows that for the purpose of grasping the meaning of æsthetic effects and its laws we may make use of analogy. Thus we may gather observations and experiences in many fields and may apply them to each field individually and so multiply their capacity for teaching us what we desire to know.

Let us now conceive of the simple case of a recital. We are told a story. David, no larger nor stronger than any one of us, vanquishes the challenging giant by means of a sling. If David approached his enemy, the giant would use his exceeding power and his terrible weapons, the brutal force would consume its adversary as a dragon would a lamb. But the brutal force does not get its way, it is subdued by the force of the spirit. When mind overcomes matter, we are charmed.

In Chess the brutal force is composed of the number,

strength, and mobility of the pieces and the difficulty of the task set. If this brutal force is bested by the few in number, the slight in strength, in moves which indicate rather weakness than force, which announce rather defeat than triumph, by the power of the spirit, by an idea which, seemingly absurd, yet is truth itself, we are delighted.

By P. Morphy.

White to play and Mate in two moves.

Here a task is set, a difficult one. If White had only to solve the problem of how to win this Ending, difficulties enough, so it seems, would await him. He would have to guard his P and to gain the Black KtP by methodical attack. But the above task demands that we Checkmate in two moves. White's second move has to be a Mate. The task is

like an overpowering opponent. And now its solution. No demonstration of force like giving of a Check or capturing an enemy : the strongest piece offers itself as a sacrifice : 1 R—R6. And yet, it is true, this almost absurd move and this alone solves the problem.

The ideal of our Chess ancestors was the following game which they named The Immortal Game.

White—Anderssen.
Black—Kieseritzki.

1	P—K4	P—K4
2	P—KB4	P × P
3	B—B4	P—QKt4
4	B × P	Q—R5ch.
5	K—B1	Kt—KB3
6	Kt—KB3	Q—R3
7	Kt—B3	Kt—R4
8	Kt—KR4	P—QB3
9	Kt—B5	Q—Kt4
10	R—KKt1	P × B
11	P—KKt4	Kt—KB3
12	P—KR4	Q—Kt3
13	P—R5	Q—Kt4
14	P—Q3	B—B4
15	Q—B3	Kt—Kt1
16	B × P	Q—B3
17	Kt—Q5	Q × P

(See diagram next page)

18	B—Q6 !	Q × Rch.
19	K—K2	B × R
20	P—K5 ! !	Kt—QR3
21	Kt × Pch.	K—Q1
22	Q—B6ch	Kt × Q
23	B—K7 Mate.	

*Position after Black's
seventeenth move.*

The end of the game is undoubtedly splendid. The Checkmate represents a m a x i m u m achievement; three minor officers, unaided, execute the incredible Mate in the face of the whole hostile army. The Opening of the game, however, offends our feelings, although our ancestors were not sensitive on that score.

Let us return now to our story of David and Goliath. Imagine that we added the explanation, that the whole matter had been a game to arouse the spirit of the army : Goliath had really been a fake. The effect would be that the sympathy of the listener would go to the deluded army and completely turn away from David.

We feel the same way, whenever an achievement claims our attention. There must be reality to it. The task must be real; its consummation too. Otherwise we turn aside or, in the most favourable case, we think it comic and laugh.

A real task, that means a real danger. Not an unnecessary task. In a city well supplied with water I should feel very little interest in an effort to discover an Artesian spring; in the desert such a search would captivate all my attention. The task must be necessary, and its achievement in just the fashion it is done must be necessary also, or else the æsthetic impression is less or may dwindle entirely or may turn into displeasure.

The ideal would be that the task is of vital importance and the achievement can be consummated in *one manner only, so that the very slightest change or variation of action or of circumstances would nullify the effort.* If this ideal cannot be attained, and it can never be fully attained, it m u s t be striven for, because *to the extent that we approach the ideal we achieve depth of æsthetic impression.*

But the æsthetic impression is, after all, an impression made on our feelings. The spectator must *feel,* not know, that the ideal has been aimed at. True, his sympathy is with him who struggles against stupendous difficulties, as we poor mortals, whose powers are very limited, struggle against odds and miraculously overcome t h e m. Nevertheless, the spectator does not desire to make an extended investigation; he wants to comprehend in a flash.

It is therefore easy to betray, to bluff, the spectator. Should this be done playfully, t h e spectator himself, after discovery, will smile. But if done in earnest, the bluff often offends deeply and the vengeance of the spectator is terrible. A master, who kept on playing quasi-brilliant games would lose his following.

These considerations are valid in every case, where a search, a task, a contest excites interest. For instance, the composition of a Checkmate in two moves is for the public that has solved such problems and has learnt to value them, as real a task as a good match between t w o ambitious players. The problemist will try to solve them; the spectator who watches a game of masters will try to foresee the next move;

hence, they comprehend the nature of the task and of its achievement and in time acquire an instinctive judgment for it. They reach the point of being connoisseurs. It would be very hard to bluff them. Of course, they would understand the comic effect of p l a y f u l infringements. There is such a thing as buffoonery in Chess, and it has a meritorious function. But for all that, the æsthetic effect of a Chess task on the connoisseur has nothing whatever to do with its comic effect and is measured solely in terms of the ideal.

When this ideal is approached as far as possible within the given limitations, we may speak of a *consummate* achievement. A Checkmate, in which every piece on the board participates to the limit of its capacity and has to do so in order to achieve the end, is an example. For consummate achievements the principle of economy holds: t h e purpose is attained by the least possible means. It is very remarkable that the guiding principle of defence recurs here.

That to the spectator, particularly to the connoisseur, the Chess pieces are beings which act and feel and speak, is wholly justified. To our remote ancestors everything was alive and gifted with secret powers· This was one of man's very early religions, and it persists in the æsthetic impression. The musician listening to good music, becomes a poet and may weave fanciful stories into it. The Chess player, animated by the sight of fine Chess, begins to envisage heroic deeds by the pieces. Both dream fairy-tales in which all things are alive and speak and feel. They are caught in a gracious illusion. The fairy - tale progresses as the Chesspieces in their positions and movements fulfil their parts in the drama.

I do not know to what extent these considerations may claim originality. The literature on æsthetic questions is surprisingly large, though, it seems, distressingly inefficient. The æsthetics of Chess, happily, is an exception. In other fields, for instance, in Art, hardly any theory, hardly a point of any theory, has been acknowledged; the contentions are wide and furious, and some of the fanciful constructions of the thinkers border on insanity. There is an abundance of theoretical investigation also in the art of composing Chess problems. A great many views have been advanced and a number of "schools" have been founded. This is probably as it should be. But to me it seems that to say more than has been said would be very venturesome. In fact these considerations would need to be elucidated, explained, safeguarded, worked out in greater detail. Shall I proceed to do so now? Everything has its time. I work, I like to work, and I understand its function but I am also a firm believer in the words of the Bible which says: "Sufficient unto the day is the evil thereof."

Examples.

1.—In the following position the two Bishops hold a witty conversation.

I

By Comte de Villeneuf.

White to play and win.

The principal actors are obviously the two Rooks' Pawns. With 1 P–R7 White does not win, because the Bishop on R7 has a nice reply in store for that clumsy move. 1 ...., B–K4; 2 K×B, P–R7; 3 P Queens, P Queens ch. and Black wins.

The right method is:—

| 1 Kt—Kt4 | K×Kt |
| 2 P—R7 | B—K4 |

This Bishop smiles.

3 K×B	**P—R7**
4 B—K1ch.	K—Kt6
5 B—B3	....

This Bishop laughs heart- iiy.

5	K×B
6 P Queens	P Queens
7 K—Q5ch. and wins.	

2.—The following posi- tion is highly humorous:

2

By an unknown composer.

White to play.   In how many moves will White be checkmated?

The question, to begin with, is contrary to the usual seriousness of Chess. And the position is funny. Black has on the board the whole box of pieces; not one is missing; but with all their tremendous power they seem to be beating the air. White, on the other hand, is quite feeble. His King is saved only by the ridiculous Black Knight on Kt2 which could not have had any possible business there.

His Rook is mobile but must presently hide. His Bishop has no earthly chance of escape, his P slouches in the corner and talks to the Bishop concerning what he happens to see. Only the two White Knights are in good trim. But they, chivalrous fellows though they are, know their weakness. Two light cav- alrymen against a whole army. True, the Black King, a little fat, ringing the bell for his servants, has by some inadvertence only a few small pages at hand. Well, he thinks, that will soon be remedied. The two impudent boys, the White Knights, will have to get a sound spank- ing.

The White K n i g h t s speak: "A pretty mess. *We* have to do the fighting.

It is a joke. Well, we must do our bit. Will you start Checking?" "No, you'd better." "Well then, here goes."

1 Kt—Kt4ch. ....
"Check! Mr. King."
1 ....   K—K2

"Be careful," the King says to the Knight, "that one of my servants does not lay his hands on you, you good-for-nothing."

2 Kt—B5ch. ....
"Did you speak to me, Mr. King,"
2 ....   K—Q2

"Insolent fellow."

3 Kt—K5ch.   K—B1
Home at last.

4 Kt—K7ch. ....
To the Bishop on Q1 :—
"Keep watch on our Castle in the corner, or you will hurt yourself." The Bishop only stares at the Knight.

4 ....   K—Kt1
5 Kt—Q7ch.   K—R2
"Oh!"

"Terrible, this narrow lane. But also that helps some, the boys won't be able to follow here." The White Knights think he will get away. Over such rough ground no horse can go.

6 Kt—B8ch.

"Hullo, here I plunge."

6 ....   K—R3
7 Kt—Kt8ch. ....

I must mind my horse doesn't stumble here.

7 ....   K—Kt4

"Ah! here I have room."
The White King: "Do not come too near me, Your Majesty; whenever feet are to be trod upon I like to take the initiative."

8 Kt—R7ch. ....

That was some jump!

8 ....   K—Kt5
9 Kt—R6ch. ....

"That's better than yours."

9 ....   K—B6
10 Kt—Kt5ch. ....

"Open country, at last."

10 ....   K—Q6
11 Kt—Kt4ch. ....

"This is fine."

11 ....   K—K7
12 Kt—B3ch.   K—B7

"Quickly away from the horrible K8."

13 Kt—Q3ch.   K—Kt6
14 Kt—K4ch.   K—Kt5
15 Kt—K5ch.   K—B4
16 Kt—Kt3ch.   K—B3
17 Kt—Kt4ch. ....

"Shall we run it all over again, Mr. King "

3.—Here follows a consummate achievement by two Knights from a very ancient Persian document.

3

White to play and win.

The seriousness of the contest is believable. Each side is attacking a Knight, but much more to the point Black threatens mate on the move to which White has no defence but counter-attack. The t w o Black Knights seem to frustrate any such plan. A fine idea, however, f o r c e s these helpers of their King to help their enemies.

1 R—R7ch.   K—Kt1
2 Kt—B6ch.   K—B1
3 P—K7ch.   Kt × P
4 R—B7ch.   Kt × R
5 Kt—K6 Mate.

This Mate is remarkable for its economy; there is no duplication of action. From a modern point of view the two Black Rooks and the Black Pawn would be judged unnecessary encumbrances, but in the olden days they were useful as providing a setting suggestive of a hard fight.

By S. Loyd.   4

White to play and Mate in three moves.

4.—Another consummate achievement.

The motif of the problem is "catching the Bishop." In spite of its mobility which extends over five squares, the Bishop is caught and thereby t h e Mate effected·

1 Q—KB1   ....

No other move would do. For instance 1 Kt–K6, P R4; 2 Q–B2, P–Kt3; 3 Q × P and takes four moves to Mate. Similarly 1 Kt–Kt6ch., P × Kt; 2 Q × P, B –B3 !

The threat is 2 Q–QKt1, menacing Mate, 2 ...... P–Kt3; 3 Q × B Mate. Black can meet the threat by moving 1 ...., P–Kt6 threatening Check, but then 2 Kt–Kt6ch., P × Kt ; 3 Q–R3 mate. Hence, the Bishop must move. If 1 ...., B–Kt7 ; 2 Q–QKt1 ; if 1 .... B–B6 or Q5 ; 2 Q–Q3 and if 1 .... B–K4 or B3 ; 2 Q–B5. One of the great masterpieces of composition.

5   *Dufresne.*

White, Anderssen, to play.

5.—This is the position where Anderssen made the combination on account of which the game was named "evergreen."

White can win with 1 B–K4 because his a t t a c k is irresistible, whereas Black's counter-attack is then frustrated. For instance, 1 B–K4, P–Q4 ; 2 B × QP, Q × B ; 3 QR–Q1 and wins. Or 1 ...., Q–R6 ; 2 P–Kt3, R × Pch. ; 3 P × R, Q × Pch. ; 4 K–R1, B × P ; 5 R–K2 wins. Or again 1 ...., R–Kt5 ; 2 Q–B2 with a winning position.

Anderssen, h o w e v e r, made the move

1 QR—Q1   ....

This is the greatly admired introduction t o astounding sacrifices. *The Lärobok i Schach,* published only a few years ago, extols the move highly. Yet it cannot sustain criticism.

But let us first view the continuation, as it actually took place.

1 ....   Q × Kt

This reply is evident to the many. From this point the combination is perfect.

2 R × Ktch.   Kt × R

or 2 ...., K–Q1 ; 3 R × P ch., K–B1 ; 4 R–Q8ch. and wins.

3 Q × Pch.   K × Q
4 B—B5ch.   K—B3
5 B—Q7 Mate.

The Mate is nearly pure, except that the square Q6 is doubly barred.

The move 1 QR–Q1, which has such a brilliant point, is, as we have seen, not necessary for the purpose of winning. The question remains whether it is, at least, sufficient to that end, for to be necessary and sufficient is the criterion by which we gauge any and every achievement that aspires to the ideal before us.

The practical game, bound rigidly to its practical purpose, can seldom approach that ideal. We have, therefore, to make allowances. But a brilliant combination bewitches men to such an extent that they willingly believe falsehoods and are blinded to the truth. Then criticism, which in the long run comes as irresistibly as death, has to voice its unbiassed judgment.

The sufficiency of Anderssen's move has hitherto not been established, although many writers have many times diligently investigated it. The move

1 ....   R—Kt5

causes difficulties. The Black King thereby gains an outlet on KKt1. If then 2 R × Ktch., Kt × R; 3 Q × Pch., K × Q; 4 B—B5ch., K–K1; and the King escapes. If the Queen moves, R × Pch. initiates counterattack, if 2 B—K4, P–Q4.

Hence, the æsthetic value of Anderssen's move has as yet not been demonstrated. On the other hand, it is understandable that the move roused to enthusiasm the immediate spectators and many others who were not critically inclined and who felt that the move was necessary, though surprising, and sufficient though most perilous.

White—Mason.
Black—Winawer.

1	P—K4	P—K4
2	Kt—KB3	Kt—QB3
3	B—B4	B—B4
4	P—Q3	P—Q3
5	B—K3	B—Kt3
6	QKt—Q2	P—KR3
7	Kt—B1	Kt—B3
8	P—KR3	Kt—K2
9	Kt—Kt3	P—B3
10	B—Kt3	B × B
11	P × B	Q—Kt3
12	Q—Q2	P—QR4
13	P—B3	P—R5
14	B—Q1	B—K3
15	O—O	Q—B2
16	Kt—R4	P—QKt4

More necessary was 16 .... Kt–Q2. Besides, the Black Pawn position is unstable, since a counterthrust such as P–B4 may at some future time disarrange it.

17	B—B2	P—B4
18	QKt—B5	B × Kt
19	Kt × B	Kt × Kt
20	R × Kt	Kt—Q2
21	QR—KB1	P—B3
22	B—Q1	P—R6
23	B—R5ch.	K—K2
24	P—QKt3	KR—KB1
25	KR—B3	Kt—Kt3
26	R—Kt3	K—Q1
27	B—Kt4	Q—K2
28	B—K2	K—B2
29	P—Q4	....

Now the thrust against the weakened army of Black Pawns sets in forcefully.

29	P—B5
30 R—Kt1	P—Kt4
31 KtP × P	KtP × P
32 R—QKt4	Q—K3
33 P—Q5	Q—B1
34 B × P	Kt—R5
35 B—Kt5	Kt—B4
36 Q—K2	P—B4
37 P × P	P—K5
38 B—B6	R—QKt1
39 Q—R5	R—B3
40 R × KtP	....

A charming conception.

40	P × R
41 Q—R7ch.	Kt—Q2
42 B × Kt	Q—Kt1
43 R—Kt7ch.	K × R
44 B—B8ch.	K—R1
45 Q × Q	R × P
46 Q—Q8	Resigns.

White—Pillsbury.
Black—Em. Lasker.

1 P—Q4	P—Q4
2 P—QB4	P—K3
3 Kt—QB3	Kt—KB3
4 Kt—B3	P—B4
5 B—Kt5	P × QP
6 Q × P	Kt—B3

This offers White the opportunity of 7 B × Kt, P × B; 8 Q—R4, P × P; 9 R –Q1, B—Q2; 10 P—K3, P– B4. Black has no disadvantage thereby, since the Doubled Pawn is compensated for by the two strong Bishops and good development, for instance,

11 Q–Kt3, P–KR4; 12 B × P, P–R5; 13 Q–B4, R– KKt1; 14 Kt–K5, Kt × Kt; 15 Q × Kt, P–R3; 16 O– O, R–B1. If Black chooses he can evade these complications by 6 ...., B–K2.

7 Q—R4	B—K2
8 O—O—O	Q—R4
9 P—K3	B—Q2
10 K—Kt1	P—KR3

Thus either the Bishop must be exchanged or the White Queen stay where it is.

11 P × P	P × P
12 Kt—Q4	O—O
13 B × Kt	B × B
14 Q—R5	Kt × Kt
15 P × Kt	B—K3
16 P—B4	....

Threatening 17 P–B5. Black replies with a combination.

16	QR—B1
17 P—B5	R × Kt
18 P × B	R—QR6

This was the point

19 P × Pch.	....

Or 19 P–K7, R–K1; 20 P × R, Q–Kt3ch.; 21 K–B2 (if 21 K–R1, Black would soon win by 21 ...., B × Pch.; 22 R × B, Q × Rch.: 23 K–Kt1, R × P) R–B1 ch.; 22 K–Q2, B × QP and White has no defence.

19	R × P
20 P × R	Q—Kt3ch.
21 B—Kt5 !	

Against other moves the attack becomes overwhelming.

| 21 .... | Q × Bch. |
| 22 K—R1 | R—B2 |

Fifteen moves an hour were prescribed and I had consumed n e a r l y two hours. Thus I had to make these moves in a hurry. 22 ...., Q–B5 was the logical continuation. It would have made it impossible for White to guard his second rank.

| 23 R—Q2 | .... |

Now White can breathe again.

23	R—B5
24 KR—Q1	R—B6
25 Q—B5	Q—B5
26 K—Kt2	....

A mistake. 26 K–Kt1 was indicated.

26	R × P
27 Q—K6ch.	K—R2
28 K × R	....

If 28 K–Kt1, B × P; 29 Q–B5ch., P–Kt3; 30 Q–Q7 ch., B–Kt2 wins.

28	Q—B6ch.
29 K—R4	P—Kt4ch.
30 K × P	Q—B5ch.
31 K—R5	B—Q1ch·

and Mates next move.

White—Zukertort.
Black—Blackburne.

1 P—QB4	P—K3
2 P—K3	Kt—KB3
3 Kt—KB3	P—QKt3
4 B—K2	B—Kt2
5 O—O	P—Q4
6 P—Q4	B—Q3
7 Kt—B3	O—O
8 P—QKt3	QKt—Q2
9 B—Kt2	....

This Bishop is here undeveloped, since the White QP cannot be easily got out of the way.

9	Q—K2
10 Kt—QKt5	Kt—K5
11 Kt × B	P × Kt
12 Kt—Q2	QKt—B3
13 P—B3	Kt × Kt
14 Q × Kt	P × P

This facilitates White's task, since its accords his QB a chance of greater mobility.

| 15 B × P | .... |

If 15 P × P Black would have attacked this Pawn in force.

| 15 .... | P—Q4 |

Whilst this immobilises White's QB it equally immobilises his own.

16 B—Q3	KR—B1
17 QR—K1	R—B2
18 P—K4	QR—QB1
19 P—K5	Kt—K1
20 P—B4	P—Kt3
21 R—K3	P—B4

Black strives to obtain for his King a stable position. The square KB1 is exposed to the White QB; also the KRP is weak.

22 P × P e.p.   Kt × P

But now the weak KP is pinned. The Queen should have captured.

23 P—B5   ....

The commencement of a very great and admirable combination (Steinitz).

23 ....   Kt—K5
24 B × Kt   P × B
25 P × KtP !   R—B7
26 P × Pch.   K—R1
27 P—Q5ch.   P—K4
28 Q—Kt4

Magnificent and decisive (Steinitz).

28 ....   QR—B4

If 28 .... Q × Q White Mates in seven moves : 29 B × Pch., K × P; 30 R—R3 ch., K–Kt3; 31 R–B6ch., K–Kt4; 32 R–Kt3ch., K–R4; 33 R–B5ch., K–R3; 34 B–B4ch., etc.

29 R—B8ch.   ....

" The preceding moves and the one just made form one of the finest combinations, perhaps the most beautiful that has ever been made over the board. We do not know how to express our admiration at the grand style in which Zukertort played this game."— (Steinitz).

29 ....   K × P
30 Q × Pch.   K—Kt2
31 B × Pch.   K × R
32 B—Kt7ch.   Resigns.

White—Reti.
Black—Bogoljubow.

1 Kt—KB3   Kt—KB3
2 P—B4   P—K3
3 P—KKt3   P—Q4
4 B—Kt2   B—Q3
5 O—O   O—O
6 P—Kt3   R—K1
7 B—Kt2   QKt—Q2

Both masters develop according to correct principles, Black could not play 7 ...., P–K4 on account of 8 P–B5.

8 P—Q4   P—B3
9 QKt—Q2   Kt—K5
10 Kt × Kt   P × Kt
11 Kt—K5   P—KB4
12 P—B3   ....

White's plan is to get the Pawns quickly out of the way, since his Bishops are more effiectively p l a c e d than Black's.

12 ....   P × P
13 B × P   Q—B2
14 Kt × Kt   B × Kt
15 P—K4   P—K4

Otherwise, as Alekhin indicates, the KP advances and eventually W h i t e opens the game by P–Q5 or P—KKt4.

16 P—B5   B—KB1
17 Q—B2   P × QP
18 P × P   QR—Q1

White has carried out his plan. The lines are open and he has a start in development. Now a charming combination ensues.

19 B—R5	R—K4
20 B × P	R × KBP
21 R × R	B × R
22 Q × B	R × B
23 R—KB1	R—Q1

Or 23 ...., Q–K2; 24 B–B7ch., K–R1; 25 B–Q5, Q-B3; 26 Q–B8 and wins.

| 24 B—B7ch. | K—R1 |
| 25 B—K8 | Resigns. |

White—Rubinstein.
Black—Teichmann.

1 P—Q4	P—Q4
2 P—QB4	P—K3
3 Kt—QB3	Kt—KB3
4 B—Kt5	QKt—Q2
5 P—K3	B—K2
6 Kt—B3	O—O
7 Q—B2	P—QKt3

The regular move is 7 ...., P–B4.

8 P × P	P × P
9 B—Q3	B—Kt2
10 O—O—O	P—B4
11 P—KR4	P—B5

Therewith Black closes his own lines; with R—K1, to be followed by Kt–B1, and Kt–K5. Black would probably have had better chances.

12 B—B5	R—K1
13 B × KKt	Kt × B
14 P—KKt4	B—Q3
15 P—Kt5	Kt—K5
16 P—R5	Q—K2

Schlechter here indicated the better defence; 16 ...., Kt × KtP; 17 Kt × Kt, Q × Kt; 18 B × Pch., K–R1; 19 QR–Kt1, Q–R3.

17 QR—Kt1   P—QR3

Position after Black's seventeenth move.

18 B × Pch.   ....

If Teichmann had foreseen the ultimate consequences of this sacrifice, he would have played 17 ...., P–KKt3. But the sacrifice took him by surprise. The point of the sacrifice becomes clear four moves later.

18 ....   K × B
19 P—Kt6ch.   K—Kt1

Not 19 ...., P × P because of 20 Kt × Kt, P × Kt; 21 Kt–Kt5ch., etc.

20 Kt × Kt   P × Kt

The Queen must not take on account of P × Pch.

21 P—R6 !   ....

This was the idea. If
21 ...., P × Kt ; 22 P × P
ch., K × P ; 23 Q–Kt6ch.,
followed by 24 P × P.

21	P—B3
22 P × P	P × Kt
23 R—R8ch.	K × P
24 R—R7ch.	K—Kt1
25 Q—B5	P—B6

Black can do nothing. If
Queen moves, Q–R5 or Q
× P(B6) soon makes an end
of it.

| 26 R × Q | Resigns. |

The following game was
played to analyse the Opening of a match-game which
Bogoljubow had essayed
against Spielmann in 1919
at Stockholm.

White—Bogoljubow.
Black—Amateur.

1 P—K4	P—K3
2 P—Q4	P—Q4
3 Kt—QB3	Kt—KB3
4 B—Kt5	B—K2
5 P—K5	KKt—Q2
6 P—KR4	B × B

To accept this sacrifice is
now considered inadvis-
able. At the time this
Opening was the object of
many analytical researches.

7 P × B	Q × P
8 Kt—R3	Q—K2
9 Kt—B4	P—QR3
10 Q—Kt4	P—KKt3
11 B—Q3	P—QB4
12 Q—Kt3	....

which threatens a sacrifice
on Q5.

| 12 .... | Kt—Kt3 |

Hence the Knight must
occupy an unfavourable
post.

| 13 P × P | Q × P |
| 14 O—O—O | Q—B1 |

To guard against a sac-
rifice on Kt6.

*Position after Black's
fourteenth move.*

| 15 B—K4 | .... |

A move of rare beauty !
The sacrifice at Q5 is again
threatened.

15	P × B
16 QKt × P	QKt—Q2
17 Q—QB3	Q—K2
18 Kt—B6ch.	....

If 18 ...., K–Q1 ; 19
Q–R5 ; or 18 ...., K–B1 ;
19 Kt × Pch., K–Kt2 ; 20
Kt–Rch., and Mates soon.

18	Kt × Kt
19 P × Kt	Q—B1
20 Q—B7	Kt—Q2
21 Kt—Q5	P × Kt
22 KR—K1ch.	Kt—K4
23 R × Ktch.	B—K3

Now Black threatens Q–
R3ch. and Castling.

24 K—Kt1	R—Q1
25 QR × P	R × R
26 R × R	Resigns.

1 *Hromadka.*

White, List, to play and win.

1.—Here is a very fine study arising out of an actual game. White must Queen one of his Pawns, and it seems almost immaterial which of the two he should advance first. But, in fact, he can win in one way only. 1 P–Kt7 would not win. After having seen the difficulties that White has to encounter even if he selects the best method of play, one will readily appreciate the difference between the two Pawn moves.

1 P—R7	B × P
2 P—Kt7	P—Kt6
3 P—Kt8=Q	P—Kt7

Now some very beautiful play with the Queen follows which wins because the Bishop at present does not protect the Pawn.

4 Q–QKt3	B—Q5

If 4 .... K–B8; 5 Q–B3ch., K–Kt8; 6 Q–B4, B–Kt8; 7 K–Kt6, K–R8; 8 Q–R4ch., K–Kt8; 9 K–B5 and wins by bringing the King into action. If White after 4 .... B–Q5 would equally try to win by 5 K–Kt3, he would gain nothing, since Black replies 5 ...., B–R1, when Pawn and Bishop would be equally out of peril.

5 Q—R2 ....

threatening Q—Kt1.

5 .... K—B7

6 Q–R4ch. and wins, as readily seen.

By Troitzki. 2

2.—The solution is not difficult, since White obviously must act at once. It is, however, elegant.

1 R—K6ch.	R × R
2 Q—R6ch.	K—Q4
3 Q—B4ch.	K—Q3

If 3 ...., K–K4; 4 Q
–B3ch. wins the Queen.

4 Q—B5ch.   K—Q2
5 Q–R7ch. and wins the
Queen.

3   *By Troitzki·*

White to play and draw.

3.—The task is very defi-
nite. Manifestly, Black will
Queen and it is just as
manifest that White can-
not prevent it. How can
White make the most of the
move?

The Knight must try to
get to KKt3 or K3. It may
go via R5—but that is out
of connection with Black
King—or via B5, where a
Check on K3 would be
possible. How can the
Knight get to B5, whilst
the Black King remains in
its present position exposed
to a Check on the same K3?
It seems impossible.

But, no, it is not, as the
solution shows

1 R—Q5   P Queens

If 1 ...., K × R, then 2
Kt–B5. Draws, of course.

2 R—Q4ch!   K × R
3 Kt—B5ch.   ....

and, strange to say, with
his slender force White
succeeds in winning the
Queen. Truly, a maximum
effect, a consummate
achievement of a l o n e
Knight.

By Troitzki.   4

White to play and draw.

4.—The idea is witty.
The White Pawn that can
Queen has no value except
it can Queen and Check at
the same time· Black can
always avoid exposing his
King to a Check, but, of
course, the Black King,
though exceedingly mobile,
is hampered by its func-
tion. In making use of this
circumstance, the lone
Knight succeeds in draw-
ing by Perpetual Check
against a very mobile
King, a unique feat in the
annals of Chess.

1 Kt—B2ch.   K—Kt6
2 P—B7   P—R7
3 Kt—K4ch.   ....

the Black King now fears a Check by either P—B8 = Queen or P × Kt = Queen.

3 ....   K—B6
4 Kt—Q2ch.   K—K6
5 Kt—B4ch.   K—K5
6 Kt—Q2ch.   K—K4
7 Kt—B4ch.   ....

It is useless, the Black King cannot escape the Checks of that Knight

5   *By Ratner.*

White to play and win.

5.—This study makes an excellent impression. The achievements of the White pieces are beyond every expectation. The White army is composed only of heroes. The economy of the pieces here functioning is very pleasing. N o n e of the White pieces have weight, nor do they present the chance of increased value as a Pawn does; yet there is a way, a very definite, a unique, a narrowly circumscribed one that leads to the goal.

The solution is also difficult, for Black wins one of the White Knights. The White Bishop must move, the Black King gives a Discovered Check and the Black Bishop attacks the two Knights, one of which will be lost, but Black must play so as not to permit either of the Knights to escape by means of a Check. Black can do this, no matter how White may move.

It is incredible, but true, White succeeds, in extracting the utmost from the position and makes with his puny army, a successful attack against the King.

1 B—K2   ....

This move is the only one to win. If B–B1, the White King, in keeping clear of the Bishop, would be drawn too far away. And if B–Q3, the Bishop would get into the field of action of the Black King, as will be shown shortly.

1 ....   K—Kt2ch.

1 ...., K–R4ch. would not do, because if 2 K–Kt2, B–Q5; 3 Kt–Kt3ch.

2 K—Kt2   ....

Again the only move to win. If K–B1 or to R1 the

KtP would later on march to Kt5 and become formidable and if K–R2, the B checks when capturing the Kt.

| 2 .... | B—Q5 |
| 3 Kt—Kt3 | .... |

Of course, the only move to win. It drives the Black King into difficulties. Even so, the way to win is still hidden.

| 3 .... | B × Kt |
| 4 Kt—R5ch. | .... |

The Black King is now s i n g u l a r l y embarrassed. Neither Kt3 nor R2 nor Kt1 are open to the King for fear of losing the Bishop. B u t were the White Bishop now on Q3, the Black K i n g could march to Kt3 and regain the piece, viz., 5 Kt–B4ch., K–B4; 6 Kt × B, K–Q5. The Black King cannot go to B1, either because of 5 B–Kt4ch., winning t h e Bishop with the Knight. Hence, the White Bishop could not be played to B1 in the first move. Every move is definitely provided for.

4	K—R1
5 Kt—B6	B moves
6 B—R6	....

Now the White King threatens to m a r c h via White Squares to QB8 and support B–Kt7ch. If Black could get his KtP to Kt5,

all would be well, but if 6 P–Kt4; 7 K–B3, the King stops the Pawn just in time. The end is now in sight.

6	P—Kt4
7 K—B3	B moves
8 K—Kt4	B moves
9 K—B5	B moves
10 K—K6	P—Kt5
11 K—Q7	P—Kt6
12 K—B8	P—Kt7
13 B Mates.	

The above composition comes near to the ideal. Even the slightest change in the circumstances would invalidate the solution. And the economy is extreme.

By Leonid Kubbel. 6

White to play and win.

6.—The idea of the author was, to express the geometrical motif of Queen against Queen in the only two possible ways that is on a rank or file and on a diagonal. Of course, he built up his position in a way that might occur in practical play, so that, in consequence, the position has an easy natural appearance. And, of course, since a consummate achievement of the pieces involved is striven for, he makes use of the least material that will suffice for the task.

The idea of d o u b l e attack is made use of with every move.

> 1 Kt—K2   K × Kt

If 1 ...., K–B7; 2 P Queens, P Queens; 3 Q–Kt6ch. K × Kt; 4 B–Kt5ch. K–Q7; 5 Q–Q4ch., K–B7; 6 B–R4ch., K–Kt8; 7 Q–Q3 ch., K–R8; 8 Q–B3ch., K–R7; 9 B–Kt3ch., K–Kt8; 10 Q–B2ch., K–R8; 11 Q–R7 mates. Also, in this variation the geometrical motif is made use of for the purpose of driving the King into the Mating position.

> 2 B–Q1ch.   ....

If 2 ...., K × B; 3 P Queens, P Queens; 4 Q–Kt1ch., the geometrical motif on the rank.

> 2 ....   K—B7
> 3 B—B3   K × B
> 4 P Queens P Queens

5 Q–Kt7ch., the geometrical motif on the diagonal.

By Leonid Kubbel.   7

White to play and draw.

7.—The intention is to produce Stalemate. T h e White pieces are used to their fullest capacity. First of all, the Knight must force the Black King to capture it.

> 1 Kt—B3ch.   ....

Now 1 ...., K–B8 cannot be played because of 2 Kt–K2ch., followed by 3 Kt–Kt3. Again 1 ...., K–R8 is unplayable on account of 2 R–R8ch., followed by 3 Kt–Q1ch.

> 1 ....   K—B7
> 2 Kt—Q1   ....

The Pawn cannot Queen for fear of 3 Kt–K3ch.

> 2 ....   K × Kt
> 3 K—R8   ....

Black is now unable to move the Bishop, since that would leave the road free for 4 R–KB8. If the Pawn Queens, 4 R–Kt1 Draws.

> 3 ....   K—K8
> 4 R–Kt2 and Draws.

The economy of the complex achievements of the White pieces is of a high order.

By Henri Rinck.

8   *By Henri Rinck.*

White to play and win.

8.—The Passed Pawn is supported by the Bishop, and opposed by the Rook. The latter is badly obstructed by its KBP.

The Bishop is able, in making use of various motifs, to block the KKt file.

  1 B—K3   ....

Direct attack on the square Kt1.

  1 ....   R—B6
  2 B—Kt5   ....

After 2 ...., P × B obstruction by the Black Pawn, if 2 ...., R–KKt6; 3 B–R4 pinning. The Pawn cannot be stopped.

The composition is clean, economical, precise.

White to play and win.

9.—The win of the Queen by Rook and Knight which succeed in harassing the Queen is here represented in a variety of ways.

  1 R—R8   ....

Attack on the Queen to deprive it of its mobility. The Rook is guarded by the threat of a fork.

  1 ....   Q—Kt4

Of the 17 squares originally open to the Queen no less than 16 are barred by direct attack or the threat of a fork.

  2 Kt—B5ch.   K—B3
  3 R—R6ch.   K—K4

Continued threats of forking K and Q force the King to this spot.

  4 R—K6ch.   K—B5

or 4 ....,K–Q4; 5 P–B4ch.

  5 R–K4ch. and wins the Queen next move.

A variegated, fragrant bouquet.

SIXTH BOOK.

EXAMPLES AND MODELS.

White—I. Berger.
Black—P. Gaspary
(Athens)

1 P—K4   P—K4
2 Kt—KB3   Kt—QB3
3 B—Kt5   Kt—B3
4 P—Q3   Kt—K2

If 5 Kt × P, P–B3; 6 Kt–B4, Kt–Kt3; the White pieces get into difficulties.

5 B—QB4   P—B3
6 Kt—B3   Kt—Kt3

White here should have proceeded with P–KR4, which disarranges the Black position again.

7 Kt—KKt5

But also this retains an advantage in development.

7 ....   P—Q4
8 P × P   P × P ?

Black ought to have driven the Knight away by 8 ...., P–KR3. The Knight would have gone to K4 with a good game for White; nevertheless, that was Black's best chance.

9 Kt × QP !   Kt × Kt
10 Q—B3   B—K3

Now the diagonal QR5 to K1 has no defence.

11 Kt × B   P × Kt
12 B–Kt5ch.   K—K2
13 B–Kt5ch.   Kt—B3
14 Q × Pch.   K—Q3
15 B—Q2   P—QR4

If 15 ...., P–K5; 16 P–Q4, P–K4; 17 Q–B6ch., K–K2; 18 B–Kt4ch., followed by B–B4ch. If 15 .... Kt–Q2, White Mates in five moves, and if 15 ...., Kt–Q4; 16 P–QB4. (This note is taken from I. Berger's book, *Probleme, Studien, Partien.*)

16 P—QB4   Resigns.

White—Dr. Tarrasch.
Black—Pillsbury.

(Played at Monte Carlo, 1903).

1 P—K4   P—Q4
2 P × P   Q × P
3 Kt—QB3   Q—Q1
4 P—Q4   Kt—KB3
5 B—K3   P—B3
6 B—Q3   B—Kt5
7 KKt—K2   P—K3
8 Q—Q2   B—Q3

Black has not played the Opening to the best advantage, and his last move is weak. White threatened to cut off the retreat of the

QB by Kt–Kt3; hence, B–R4 was here the reply.

9 Kt—Kt3   Q—B2
10 P—KR3   B × Kt

This should lose. The lesser evil was B—R4.

11 P × QB   ....

The R file being open, P–Kt5–Kt6 is threatening.

11 ....   Kt × P

with the courage of despair.

12 P × B   Q × Pch.
13 B—B2   Q × P
14 B—K4   Q × Bch.
15 Q × Q   Kt × Q
16 K × Kt   P—KKt3

Position after Black's sixteenth move.

Black, in his three Pawns plus, has a material equivalent for the White Bishop, but White has an enormous start in development. Therefore, White had to attack. Where? On the Queen's side, where White is clearly superior;

by no means on the King's side, where the Black Pawns have it all their own way. The target for the attack, as Dr. Tarrasch justly states in his book, *Die Moderne Schachpartie,* is QB6. After 17 P–Kt4 White threatened immediately P–Kt5. If 17 ...., P–QR3; 18 P–R4, whereupon P–Kt5 cannot be prevented, the Black Queen side pawns are sure to be weakened and the supremacy of the White pieces decides the fight long before the Black Pawns can get into action.

White adopted this plan only after losing much valuable time; he lost his superiority in development, and the game was eventually drawn. The further course of the game does not seem to be of sufficient interest.

White—Burn.
Black—Snosko Borowski
(Played at Ostend, 1906).

1 P—Q4   P—Q4
2 P—QB4   P—K3
3 Kt—QB3   P—QB4
4 P × QP   KP × P
5 Kt—B3   Kt—QB3
6 B—Kt5   B—K2
7 B × B   KKt × B
8 P—K3   ....

In reply to 8 P × P Black plays best 8 .... P–Q5;

9 Kt–K4, O—O; 10 P–K3,
Q–Q4.   Then possibly 11
Kt–Kt3, P × P; 12 Q × Q,
Kt × Q,   13   B–B4   or   11
........., B–Kt5; 12 B–K2,
whereupon neither side has
alarmingly weak spots.

8 ....   P × P
9 Kt × P   Q—Kt3

Black menaces the KKt
and the QKtP. If White
feels he must avoid the isolation of his QP, he loses a
move. Black having only a
minimum of weaknesses,
White would be unable to
compensate this loss of time
by an attack. Hence, the
best move seems clearly
indicated here : 10 Q–Q2.
If then 10 ....,Kt × Kt;
11 P × Kt, O—O; 12 B–K2,
B–K3; 13 O–O, White has
some initiative, for instance, by Kt–R4–B5 or by
taking the K file.

10 Kt—Kt3   ....

Now the start in develop-
ment belongs to Black who
therefore seizes the initiative.

10 ....   B—K3
11 B—Q3   O—O
12 O—O   KR—Q1
13 Kt–R4   ....

Movements for attack un-
backed by superiority. This
is the wrong plan. Instead,
White should look for
safety and stability by, say,
Kt–K2

13 ....   Q—B2
14 R—B1   Q—K4
15 Q—K2   QR—B1
16 P—B4   ....

Attack at all costs !

16 ....   Q—B3
17 P—B5   B—Q2
18 QKt—B5   P—QKt3
19 Kt × B   R × Kt

Now the " logic " of the
attack   becomes   evident.
The Pawn at B5 had to ob-
struct the hostile Bishop,
now what is the position ?
It actually obstructs its own
Bishop.   If Governments
behaved   like   that,   the
people would get into a
pretty mess.

20 P—Kt4   ....

Doing the work of pro-
tection twice and certainly
overdoing it; the Pawn at
B5 is safe enough. The
move would be strong if
the aggressive intent, P–
Kt5, could be realised, but
on black points Black holds
the sway.

20 ....   QR—Q1
21 K—R1   R—Q3
22 R—KKt1   Q—Kt4
23 QR—B1   P—Q5

To open the centre and to
get on to the seventh or
eighth row, whereby the
White King would be im-
perilled.

24 P—K4	Kt—K4
25 R—Kt3	KKt—B3
26 Kt—Q2	………

permitting Black a further gain of space. True, if the game continues systematically, White is without hope. In such situations it is best to accelerate the coming of the crisis; the sooner it comes, the better. Neither the position nor the nerves can stand the strain.

26 ………	Kt × B
27 R × Kt	Kt—K4
28 R—KKt3	P—Q6
29 Q—Kt2	R—QB3
30 Kt—B3	Kt × Kt
31 Q × Kt	R—B8
32 KR—Kt1	R × R
33 R × R	Q—Q7

If now 34 Q–Kt2, Q–QB7 and the Passed Pawn marches.

34 R—QKt1	Q—K7
35 Q—Kt2	Q—K6
36 R—Q1	P—Q7
37 P—KR3	Q—K8ch.
38 Q—Kt1	Q—K7
39 P—K5	R—Q6

Resigns.

This g a m e was not played by the old master with the strength native to his style, but is highly instructive by the conclusive manner in which the errors committed were shown up.

White—Janowski.
Black—Em. Lasker.

(Played in the Match of 1909).

1 P—K4	P—K4
2 Kt—KB3	Kt—QB3
3 Kt—B3	Kt—B3
4 B—Kt5	B—Kt5
5 O—O	O—O
6 P—Q3	P—Q3
7 B—Kt5	B × Kt
8 P × B	Kt—K2
9 B—QB4	Kt—Kt3
10 Kt—R4	Kt—B5 !

White has not treated the Opening with sufficient precision. His 9th move almost amounts to the loss of a move, instead of which the Kt should at once have gone to R4, in order to open the way for P–KB4.

11 B × QKt	………

11 Q–Q2 does not do because of 11 ………, Kt × KP. But 11 B–Kt3 seems feasible, since thus the advance of the Black QP is deprived of some of its force. It also would parry the threat 11 ………, P–KR3 by 12 B × QKt, P × B; 13 Kt–Kt6 which would be no longer a real menace.

11 ………	P × B
12 Kt—B3	B—Kt5

Not so strong is the move B–K3 recommended by Dr. Tarrasch. White counters by 13 B–Kt3, P–Q4; 14 Kt

–Q4, and White has a fair game, because he gets the K's file.   On the other hand, the move played pinning the White Knight ties up White.

13 P—KR3   ....

An error, which weakens the King's side very much. White should defend by 13 Q–Q2, in order to occupy the KKt file after 13 .... B × Kt; 14 P × B, Kt–R4; 15 K–R1.   From now on Black has the advantage.

13	B—R4
14 R—Kt1	P—QKt3
15 Q—Q2	....

If instead 15 P–Kt4, P × P e.p.; 16 P × P, P–Q4! 17 P × P, Kt × P; 18 Q–Q2, P–KB3 soon to be followed by B–B2 and Black has the best of it both for Middle and End-game.

15	B × Kt
16 P × B	Kt—R4
17 K—R2	Q—B3
18 R—Kt1	QR—K1
19 P—Q4	K—R1
20 R—QKt5	Q—R3
21 QR—Kt5	P—KB3
22 QR—Kt4	P—Kt3 !

Stronger than 22 ...., P–KB4, whereupon White on the open lines would get counter-action. Black's advantage consists in White's inability of his own accord, to open lines; Black's task is therefore to select the most favourable time and opportunity for forcing the lines open.

| 23 B—Q3 | R—K2 |
| 24 P—B4 | .... |

This gives Black the desired opportunity to conduct his Knight to a central square.   Sooner or later Black would have been able to achieve that end by advancing, when in perfect readiness, P–KKt4 a n d thus setting the Knight free.

| 24 .... | Kt—Kt2 |

If now the BP is captured, the Knight via K3 wins the QP, and then White would be hopeless, since all black squares would be firmly in the hand of Black.

| 25 P—B3 | Kt—K3 |

The threat is Kt–Kt4, whence B6 and R6 are assailed.

26 B—B1	P—KB4
27 QR—Kt2	R—B3
28 B—Q3	P—KKt4

At this point the threat is 29 ...., Q × Pch.

| 29 R—KR1 | P—Kt5 |
| 30 B—K2 | Kt—Kt4 |

The final break up of White.

| 31 BP × P | P—B6 |
| 32 R—Kt3 | P × B |

Resigns.

White—Schlechter.
Black—Suchting.

(Played a t Karlsbad, 1911).

1	P—Q4	P—Q4
2	P—QB4	P—QB3
3	Kt—KB3	Kt—B3
4	Kt—B3	Q—Kt3

In the Queen's Gambit the QKtP is somewhat weak. Guarded only by the QB it prevents, as long as the Bishop has to fulfil this function, the development of the QR. It is easily menaced, when the QBP has moved, by Q–Kt3. He who makes this move first has a certain start. But Black has hardly good ground to lay hold on this advantage, since to further his own development, not to hinder W h i t e ' s development, should be his first aim.

5	Q—B2	....

Developing and at the same time guards the KtP, threatens P × P and prevents B–B4.

5	....	B—Kt5
6	P—B5	....

Abandons the pressure on Black's Q4 and gets little in return. Moreover, the White QP is now burdened with the defence of the BP and is hard put to it to watch the Black KP which will strive to attack it. The proper move was 6 P–K3.

6	....	Q—B2
7	Kt—K5	QKt—Q2
8	Kt × B	....

Thereby Black gets the superiority on his K4. White might still have fought for this point by 8 B–B4. If then 8 .... Kt–R4 ? 9 P–KKt3, P–KKt4 ? 10 Kt × Kt, P × B ; 11 Kt–K5 with various compensations. Probably it would have been the best course for Black to reply to 8 B–B4 by Kt × Kt; 9 B × Kt, Q–B1 followed by 10 ...., Kt–Q2 so as to prepare P–K4.

8	....	Kt × Kt
9	Q—B5	P—KR4 !

Directed against B–B4, which would now be answered by P–K4

10	P—K4	....

To profit by the absence of the Black KKt from B3.

10	....	P—KKt3

Strengthening the intended advance of the KP by driving the White Queen to its KB4; economy of time.

11	Q—B4	P—K4
12	P × KP	B × P
13	P—K6	QKt—K4
14	P × Pch.	K—Q2 ?

A pity ! On Q2 the King is not safe, whereas on B1 it is well guarded. T h e game is thus thrown out of its logical path.

15 P × P   ....

Now, since P–Q5 was no more to be apprehended, White might have played 15 B–K3. The move made is too bold.

15 ....   KKt × BP
16 P × Pch.   P × P
17 Q—QR4   Kt × P?

Incomprehensible! Black should most certainly seize the Rook and return with the Knight, so as to keep the QR from the Queen's file.

18 B—K2   Kt × R
19 B—KB4   B—Q3

The Black King finds safety nowhere. That the gain of the exchange is no equivalent therefor is evident.

20 R—Q1   ....

Not Castles, because the King has to watch the square B2.

20 ....   K—K2
21 R × B   Kt × R
22 Kt—K4   QR—Q1
23 Q—Q4   ....

There are many threats. Black must seek counter-attack since mere defence will not suffice.

23 ....   Q—R4ch.
24 P—Kt4   Q—KB4

Q–Q4 loses on account of B–Kt5ch.

The Queen wants to prevent the Knight from moving. If 25 Kt × Kt, Q–Kt8 ch., leads to a draw or the pinning of the White KB and thus lessens the perils of the King, viz., 26 B–Q1, KR–B1, and White has not sufficient material for a Mating attack and is in all likelihood forced to concede a draw.

25 B × Ktch.   R × B
26 Q × Rch.   K—B2
27 B—B4ch.   K—Kt2
28 Q—Q4ch.   K—R2
29 Q × Pch.   ....

Redoubtable though it seems 29 Kt–B6ch. was not sufficiently strong. T h e consequence would be 29 ...., K–R3; 30 Kt–Kt4 ch., P × Kt; 31 Q × Rch., K–Kt4 and Black obtains a counter attack, thus obtaining a draw.

29 ....   K—R3
30 Q—K3ch.   P—Kt4
31 P—KR4   R—K1
32 B—Q3   K—Kt2
33 K—Q2   ....

Now Kt–Q6 is threatened.

33 ....   Q—B5
34 P × P   Q × Qch.
35 K × Q   Kt—Kt6
36 K—Q4   Kt × Kt
37 B × Kt   R—QR1
38 B × P   ....

This Pawn would not have run away. First of all B—Kt1 should have been played.

38	R × P
39 P—Kt5	K—Kt3
40 P—Kt6	K × P

Black here overlooks a chance to obtain a Stalemate. 40 ...., P—R5 ; 41 P–Kt7, R—Kt7 ; 42 K—B5, R × QKtP ; 43 B × R, P–R6. Now 44 P × P leads eventually to stalemate on KR1, otherwise the two Knights' Pawns are lost.

41 P—Kt7	R—Kt7
42 K—B5	R—B7ch.
43 K—Kt6	R—Kt7ch.
44 B–Kt5	Resigns.

White—Capablanca.
Black—Marshall.

(The Sixth Game of the Match.)

1 P—K4	P—K4
2 Kt—KB3	Kt—QB3
3 B—Kt5	P—Q3
4 P—B3	B—Kt5
5 P—Q3	B—K2
6 QKt—Q2	Kt—B3
7 O—O	O—O
8 R—K1	P—KR3

Black had here the choice between two plans : P QR3 and advance of the QKtP and QP or quietude on the Queen's side and in the centre, but attack on B6 by Kt–R2–Kt4. The first plan has prospects, the second one also has merits, principally that no weaknesses are created thereby.

9 Kt—B1	Kt—R2
10 Kt—K3	B—R4
11 P—KKt4	....

Almost forced, although KB4 remains weak. On the other hand, the Knight gets a firm hold on KB5.

11	B—Kt3
12 Kt—B5	P—KR4 ?

Black wanders from the straight road. He should continue with 12 ...., Kt –Kt4. For instance, 13 K–Kt2, Kt × Kt ; 14 Q × Kt, B–Kt4 ; 15 R–R1, B × B ; 16 QR × B, Kt–K2 ; 17 P–KR4, P–KB3. Black has counter-play in the centre. White's attack would be difficult, since it is based on P–Kt5 which would open the KB line for Black.

13 P–KR3	P × P ? ?

This exchange opens the R line for the benefit of White. Henceforth, Black has a hard task.

14 P × P	B–Kt4
15 Kt × B	Kt × Kt
16 K–Kt2	P–Q4

Better 16 ...., P–B3 followed by Kt–K3 and K–B2 and occupation of the KR line. Black could not have executed the whole of this programme, but he would at least have maintained his Knight on K3.

17 Q—K2	R—K1
18 R—R1	R—K3

This is no place for the Rook but for the Knight. From this point the Black position is untenable. Naturally White plays to attack; he does not trouble to gain material force by B × KKt and P × P because he is sure to win by the development of his heavy artillery if only he maintains a sound position.

19 Q—K3   P—B3
20 B—R4   Kt—K2
21 B—Kt3   P—B3

The Bishop on Kt3 holds the Black pieces to the support of their QP and keeps occupied therefore much more than its own equivalent.

22 Q—Kt3   P—R4
23 P—R4   Kt—B2
24 B—K3   P—Kt3

To parry B–B5, but all this is only a makeshift.

25 R—R4   K—B1
26 QR—R1   Kt—Kt1
27 Q—B3   ....

Menaces Q5 and forces the exchange of the Bishop, whereby the KKt line is opened.

27 ....   B × Kt
28 KtP × B   R—Q3
29 Q—R5   R—R2

Now follows the final assault. The White heavy pieces approach the enemy.

30 Q—Kt6   KKt—R3
A weak dam !

31 R × Kt   P × R
32 B × Pch.   K—K2

If 32 ...., Kt × B ; 33 R × Kt, the Rook penetrates to R8 and all is over. The effect of the Queen which stands so near to the Black King is terrible.

33 Q—Kt7ch.   K—K1
34 Q × Ktch.   K—Q2
35 Q—R7ch.   Q—K2
36 B—B8   Q × Q
37 R × Qch.   K—K1
38 R × R   Resigns.

From a game played at Debreczin, 1925.

Dr. Seitz.

White, Dr. Tartakower, to play.

White is at a disadvantage. He has three weak points : QKt3, QR4, KB5. To defend them is out of the question, since the Black King has penetrated into the White camp. But one must do one's duty. Therefore, Tartakower reviews the situation, looking out for counter-attack. Matters are bad. The sole target for the White Bishop is KB7, for the White King is KR6, but the road to KR6 runs over KKt4, KR5, both of which points are barred by the Black Bishop. It is a matter of mere counting; in no more than three moves the KtP and QRP must fall and in no more than eight moves a threatening Black Queen will stand on QR8.

But Tartakower, an old fighter, a fighter in good and bad situations, a fighter of inviolate honour, of passion, and also one with a remarkable ingenuity discovers a way to escape the break-down.

1	B × P	B × P
2	B × B	K × B
3	K—Kt4	K × P
4	K—R5	K—Kt4
5	K × P	P—R5
6	K—Kt7	P—R6
7	P—R5	P—R7
8	P—R6	P Queens
9	P—R7	....

Black cannot win, because he has no chance to approach with his King before White Queens his Pawn.

From a tournament in Argentine, 1925.

G. Boneo.

White, Coria, to play.

Black has, it seems, an overwhelming position. He threatens to win at once by R–Kt1. His Pawns form a p h a l a n x, he has two Bishops against Bishop and Knight. The White central Pawn is weak, also the QKtP. Only one cause for reflection: the Black King is very susceptible to attacks on his first or second row, because his Pawns have gone forth to attack.

White profits by this opportunity skilfully.

| 1 | B—B4 | .... |

If now 1 ...., R–Kt1; 2 B × Pch., K–Kt2; 3 Q × R, Q × Q; 4 B × R, and the Rooks are powerful.

| 1 | .... | R(R7)—R2 |
| 2 | B × Pch. | K—Kt2 |

Black wants to win a move, by keeping the Queen assailed. If at once

2 ...., P × B; 3 Q × P ch., K–Kt2; 4 Kt × P, B–K1; 5 Q × Q, R × Q; 6 R × R, B × R; 7 Kt–B4; White has still fight left in him. Black should nevertheless have played just that way, because he would have kept the advantage.

| 3 B × P | .... |

Unfortunately for Black, the Queen has no intention of flying.

| 3 .... | R × Q |
| 4 B × R | .... |

If now 4 ...., P–K5, White counters by 5 P–B6.

| 4 .... | R–Kt1 |
| 5 P–B6 | .... |

B l a c k cannot play 5 ...., R × B, because White simply recaptures and the Pawn can no longer be stopped.

| 5 .... | P–K5 |
| 6 P–B7 and wins. | |

The mistake made by Black on his second move cost him the game which otherwise would have led to an Ending rather in his favour.

White—Dus Chotimirski.
Black—Capablanca.

(Played at St. Petersburg (Leningrad), 1914).

1 P—Q4	P—Q4
2 Kt—KB3	Kt—KB3
3 B—B4	P—B4
4 P—B3	....

Capablanca in his *Magazine* remarked here that if White wanted to make this move he should have done so before developing the QB. He adds no further comment and his opinion seems to be that by means of 3 P–B3 Black's P–B4 would have been prevented, since it would have cost a Pawn.

4	Q—Kt3
5 Q—B2	P × P
6 P × P	Kt—B3
7 Kt—B3	B—Q2

If 7 ...., Kt × P; 8 Kt × Kt, Q × Kt; 9 P–K3 with a stinging attack.

8 P—K3	R—B1
9 R—B1	P—K3
10 B—K2	B—K2
11 O—O	O—O
12 Q—Kt1	....

B l a c k threatened 12 ...., Kt–K5; 13 Kt × Kt, Kt × P. True also 12 Kt–Q2 would have parried the threat.

| 12 .... | Q—R4 |

" After reflecting half an hour I resolved upon this move. I thought it necessary to keep my Queen upon the Queen's side and at the same time to prevent a White Knight from gaining the post on QB5, as long as the White QB dominated the open diagonal.'' (Capablanca).

13 Kt—Q2   P—QR3
14 Kt—Kt3   ....

This is too soon. First 14 P—QR3 to hold QKt4, then White had a fair position, having two plans at his disposal—both auspicious. Firstly Kt–Kt3–B5, secondly Q–R2, P–QKt4 and occupation of QB5 by a Knight.

14 ....   Q—Kt5

Very skilfully Capablanca makes use of the slight chances offered him to impede the opponent's attempt at occupying QB5.

Position after Black's fourteenth move.

15 Kt—B5   ....

A miscalculation, as Black soon demonstrates. If 15 B–Q1—says Capablanca — the sequence would have been 15 ...., Kt–QR4; 16 P–QR3, Q–Kt3; 17 Kt–B5? B × Kt; 18 P × B, R × P; 19 P–QKt4, QR–B1; 20 P × Kt, Q × Q; and Black, regaining his piece, has a decisive advantage. The right plan would have been, it seems, to secure the QB by 15 P–KR3, then to press a little against the King's side with B–Q3 and for the rest to await the dispositions of Black.

15 ....   Kt × P
16 P × Kt   B × Kt
17 P—QR3   Q × QP

The rest is silence.

White—Bogoljubow.
Black—Romanowski.

(Played in a Match at Moscow, 1924).

1 Kt—KB3   Kt—KB3
2 P—B4   P—Q4
3 P × P   Kt × P
4 P—Q4   P—KKt3

Here B–B4, Marshall's move, is commendable. Black must make a fight for the command of the point K5.

5 P—K4   Kt—KB3
6 Kt—B3   B—Kt2
7 P—KR3   ....

When, as here, the lines are opening, the Bishops are stronger than the Knights and must be guarded against exchange.

7 ....   O—O
8 B—K3   P—B3

The Double Fianchetto would develop the QB, but would weaken the QBP too much.

9 Q—Q2   R—K1
10 B—Q3   QKt—Q2

*Position after Black's
tenth move.*

White dominates the centre, but Black wants to simplify his game by P–K4 and to regain a share of the centre. The strength of the White centre consists in the restriction it imposes on the hostile pieces; and this centre is in danger. A means of encountering the peril was 11 B–QB4, because P–K4 could then be met by 12 B × Pch., K × B; 13 P × P with terrific attack.

11 P—K5!   ....

Bogoljubow, however, justly chooses a move which meets the danger once for all and one which results from the logic of the position. Black's P–KKt3 had weakened KB3 and KR3 and invited the advance of the White KP. White accepts the challenge.

11 ....   Kt—Q4
12 Kt × Kt   P × Kt
13 O—O   P—B3

Black is willing to fight. Apparently, he has now shaken the point K4.

14 B—R6   ....

But White discovers the combination which enables him to hold on to K5. The Black Bishop cannot escape exchange, because after 14 ...., B–R1?; 15 P–K6, followed by B–QKt5 wins at least the exchange.

14 ....   P × P
15 B × B.   ....

If now 15 ...., P–K5, White wins by rushing the King's side, viz., 16 Q–R6, P × Kt (Kt–Kt5 was threatening); 17 B × P, P × B; 18 B–R8, K–B2; 19 Q–R7ch., K–K3; 20 KR–K1ch., K–Q3; 21 Q × KtPch. (now Kt–B3 would not do, on account of B × Kt) P–K3 (or 21 .... K–B2; 22 QR–B1ch., K–Kt1; 23 Q–Kt3ch., P–K4; 24 R × P); 22 Q–Kt3ch., K–K2; 23 R × Pch., K × R; 24 R–K1ch., Kt–K4; 25 Q × Ktch., K–Q2; 26 Q × Pch., K–B2; 27 Q–B5 ch., K–Q2 (27 ...., K–Kt1; 28 R × R); 28 Q–Kt5ch., winning, and if 22 ...., K–B3; 24 QR–B1 ch. etc.

| 15 .... | K × B |
| 16 P × P | .... |

*Position after White's
sixteenth move.*

The situation has changed. The central Pawns now occupy posts to which they will cling and have lost a good deal of their mobility. The centre is divided up. White, by reason of his KP, has the supremacy on Black squares. His Rooks also are more active than those of Black. The Knight is now stronger than the Bishop, since the Black squares are those that matter most.

16	Kt—B4
17 Kt—Q4	Kt—K3
18 Kt—K2	....

White declines to exchange the Black Knight except against the White Bishop.

18	R—B1
19 P—B4	Q—Kt3ch.
20 K—R2	Kt—Q5
21 Kt—B3	P—K3

Black could not help shutting in his Bishop. If 21 ...., B—K3; 22 Kt–R4, Q–B3; 23 P–QKt3 White threatens too many things at once.

| 22 QR—Q1 | Kt—B4 |
| 23 B × Kt | .... |

Now the superiority of White on the Black squares has become evident.

23	R × B
24 Kt—K2	B—Q2
25 Kt—Q4	R—B2
26 P—KR4!	....

Subtle as well as strong! White prevents 26 ...., P–Kt4 once and for all, whereas he keeps the possibility of opening the King's side in hand. He may, for instance, eventually push P–R5, exchange the Pawns and then occupy the point Kt5, say by his Knight. True, the bargain is not one-sided; the White King has been weakened. But the Black pieces will be kept busy by the White ones, so that the White King will need little protection by Pawns.

| 26 .... | QR—KB1 |

Here Black allows himself to be carried away by his spirit of offence. Defence by occupation of the QB file was s o u n d e r, though even then the superiority of White, slight as it may be, remains unshaken.

27 R—B3   K—R1
28 R—QB1   Q—Q1
29 K—Kt3 !   ....

In spite of Black's preparations for attack White does not fear to employ his King actively in the defence. White needs all his troops on the QB file, where the issue will be decided.

29 ....   Q—Kt1
30 Q—Kt4   R—Kt1

Black's plan is maturing. He wants to arrive at P–KKt4 by means of P–KR3.

31 Q—Q6   ....

B u t White, steadily working to obtain the advantage for the ending, nips Black's plan in the bud. If now 31 ...., Q × Q; 32 P × Q, R–Q1; 33 R–B7, B–K1; 34 KR–B3, R × QP; 35 R × R followed by 36 R–B7 White has the superiority both on black squares and on the seventh row and wins easily.

31 ....   Q—K1
32 R—B7   B—B1
33 R × R   Q × R
34 R—B3   Q—K1

Not R–B1 because of 35 K–R3.

35 R—B7   R—Kt2

Black defends as well as he can.

36 Kt—Kt5 !   ....

But White profits by every card, even the smallest one that he holds.

36 ....   P—QR3
37 Q—B5 !   R × R
38 Kt × R   Q—B2

If 38 ...., Q–Q1; 39 Q–Q6, Q × Q; 40 P × Q, K–Kt2; 41 Kt–R8 and wins the Bishop by Kt–Kt6. If 38 ...., Q–Kt1; 39 Q–K7, Q–Kt2; 40 Q–Q8 ch., Q–Kt1; 41 Kt–K8, again winning the Bishop.

39 Kt × QP   ....

White has won an important Pawn. The rest is mere technique.

39 ....   B—Q2
40 Kt—B6   B—B3
41 Q—Q6   P—KR4
42 K—R3   K—Kt2
43 P—KKt4   B—B6
44 P × P   P × P
45 Q—Q3   B—Kt5ch.
46 Kt × B   P × Ktch.
47 K × P   K—R3
48 Q—Q8   K—R2
49 Q—B6   Q—Kt1ch.
50 Q—Kt5   Q—QB1
51 P—R5   Q—B3
52 Q—Kt6ch.   K—R1
53 K—Kt5   Resigns.

A game which charms by its life and logic.

White—Dr. Tartakower.
Black—J. Mieses.

(Played at Baden-Baden, 1925.)

1	P—Q4	P—KB4
2	P—K4	P × P
3	Kt—QB3	Kt—KB3
4	P—KKt4	....

This move, though it weakens the White King's side, is thoroughly logical, because White wants to assail, he does not want the Black King's side to remain in peace, if he is to find safety it must be on the Queen's side.

| 4 | ...., | P—Q4 |

Of all the various moves which Black may here choose, viz.: P–K3, P–KR3, P–KKt3, P–QB4, P–Q3, the move made is certainly the most natural one.

| 5 | P—Kt5 | Kt—Kt1 |

Here B–Kt5 might have been played, as after 6 B–K2, B × B; 7 Q × B, KKt–Q2; 8 Kt × QP, Kt–QB3; 9 Q × P, P–K4; Black plays a promising Gambit, for instance, 10 P × P, Kt–B4; 11 Q–Kt2, Kt–Q5; 12 Kt–K3, B–K2, probably regaining Pawns or else 12 ...., Q–Q2 followed by Castling Queen's side with a goodly choice of attacking variations.

| 6 | P—B3 | P × P |

In this position KB4 is a strong point for Black, therefore 6 ...., B–B4 was commendable; later on White prevents that move. The consequence might be 7 P × P, P × P; 8 B–Kt2, P–K3; 9 Kt × P, Kt–QB3; 10 Kt–K2, KKt–K2; and Black has counter-attack.

| 7 | Q × P ! | .... |

B–B4 is now prevented and the attack on the KB file opened.

Position after White's seventh move.

A remarkable Gambit. It is almost impossible for Black to retain his Pawn. Rather than try he should play for counter-attack by Kt–QB3. If then 8 B–K3, P–K4. Or else 8 Q × P, P–K3 (*Bis dat, qui cito dat*).

| 7 | .... | P—K3 |

Black attempts to hold on to the Pawn.

| 8 | B—Q3 | P—KKt3 |

According to the rules of Steinitz, Kt–K2 or B–Q3 was indicated. The Pawn move weakens the wing too much.

9 KKt—K2   Q—K2

B–Kt2 is likewise of no avail. The points QB2 and K4 are weak, P–KR4–KR5 threatens also, the KP cannot be held in the long run. White has many pieces in play, Black none, at these odds everyone would like to play Gambits.

10 B—KB4   P—B3
11 B—K5   B—Kt2
12 Q—Kt3   Kt—QR3

Or 12 ...., Kt–Q2; 13 B–B6, Q–Q1; 14 R–KB1 wins.

(Dr. Tartakower in *Kagan's Neuesten Shachnachrichten*).

13 O—O   B—Q2
14 B—Q6   Q—Q1
15 Q—B4   ....

Also Q–K5 would have given a jolt. Black resigns.

White—Bogoljubow.
Black—Reti.

(Played at Baden-Baden, 1925).

1 P—K4   P—K3
2 P—Q4   P—Q4
3 Kt—QB3   Kt—KB3
4 B—Kt5   B—Kt5
5 P—K5   P—KR3
6 B—Q2   B × Kt
7 B × B   Kt—K5
8 B—Kt4   ....

Leading soon to equality. White retains more initiative by 8 B—Q3

8 ....   P—QB4
9 B × P   Kt—QB3

Somewhat complicated, though no more, if as much, is attained thereby than by the simple Kt × B followed by Q–R4ch.

10 B—R3   Q—R4ch.
11 P—B3   Kt × QBP
12 Q—Q2   ....

Position after White's twelfth move.

12 ....   Kt—R5

Black had here the choice between this move and Kt–K5, whence the Knight, after Q × Q and P–R4, would have had to fight his way back. His decision is a wise one.

13 Q × Q   Kt × Q
14 P—QKt3   Kt—Kt3
15 Kt—B3   ....

White has some advantage, because the two Black Knights are inactive. He is approximately two moves ahead. On the other hand, Black has no weak points so that the loss in time is not so perceptible.

15 ....   B—Q2
16 B—Q3   Kt—B3
17 K—Q2   P—Kt4 ?

Position after Black's seventeenth move.

Now White has that of which he stood in need, viz. a target, the KKtP. That Reti should offer a target to the White Rooks, the action of which is already concerted, whilst the Black Rooks are still separated, is difficult to comprehend. Impossible that he should value the temporary threat against Q5 as sufficient equivalent for a disadvantage sure to be lasting. Fairly strong was 17 ...... P–QR4 and Kt–B1 was also good. The only possible explanation is that Reti hereabouts followed a plan which he at once abandoned and which

therefore cannot be perceived.

Bogoljubow, on the other hand, from this point plays with winning precision and invention.

18 P—R3   Kt—B1
19 P—KKt4   ....

Marking visibly the Black KKtP as the target. Black, of course, sees the peril, but it is too late for successful defence.

19 ....   KKt—K2
20 P—R4   P × P

Forced, for if 20 ...., R–KKt1 ; 21 P × P, P × P ; 22 R–R5 and the doom of the Pawn cannot be averted.

21 R × P   O—O—O
22 QR—R1   KR—Kt1
23 R—KKt1   R—R1
24 B—Q6   Kt-–Kt3
25 B × Kt   P × B
26 QR—KR1   ....

Sooner or later the KRP had to fall. Black resolves on exchanging the White KtP, so that the Pawn plus remains a backward one.

26 ....   P—KR4
27 P × P   P × P
28 R × P   R × R

Black exchanges a Rook, so as to facilitate the use of his King for defence.

29 R × R   R—Kt1
30 K—K3   P—Kt3
31 R—R4   ....

preventing 31 ...., R–Kt5. First of all, White makes his position sound.

31 ....   R—Kt2
32 Kt—R2   ....

The Knight aims at B6. On that dominating post it shall aid in forcing the decision.

32 ....   B—K1
33 R—R8   K—Q2
34 P—B3   Kt—K2
35 B × Kt   ....

Of course! The Black Knight would have loved to have established itself on KB4, but he had no safe road to reach that point.

35 ....   K × B
36 Kt—Kt4   K—B2
37 P—R4!   B—B3
38 R—QKt8   ....

White seeks to prevent the Bishop getting to a square where it is defended without protection from King or Rook; consequently he must make the development of the Bishop on the diagonal QR3 to KB8 impossible. Otherwise, counter-attacks would be feasible.

38 ....   K—Kt3
39 Kt—B6   R—QB2
40 K—Q2   K—B2

The King does not go to B4 because White would reply R—KB8.

41 R—Kt8   P—Kt4
42 P—R5   ....

Pursuing the previously mentioned plan. White avoids the exchange which would develop the Bishop. White now seeks to play R–Kt1–QB1 or K to B3–Kt4 and enforce the exchange of Rooks. Black makes a desperate attempt to secure counter-attack.

42 ....   P—Kt5
43 R—KR8!   K—Kt3
44 R—Kt8   P—R3
45 R—Kt6   ....

This the point! 45 R × P would have been bad because 45 ...., B–Kt4 would have shut the Rook in.

45 ....   K—B4
46 R × RP   K—B5
47 R—Kt6   K × P
48 R × P   ....

and Black resigned after a few uninteresting moves.

White—Torre.
Black—Yates.

(Played at Baden-Baden, 1925).

1 P—Q4   Kt—KB3
2 Kt—KB3   P—KKt3
3 Kt—B3   P—Q4

Black cannot well leave the whole of the centre to White without a struggle.

4 B—B4   ....

But now White has the advantage on K5.

4   ....   P—B3

Probably unnecessary; therefore, loss of time.

5 P—K3   B—Kt2
6 B—Q3   O—O
7 O—O   QKt—Q2
8 R—K1   ....

White saves the move 8 P–KR3, because, if 8 ...... Kt–R4, the White QB, by 9 B–KKt5 can still evade exchange.

8   ....   P—B4
9 Q—Q2   P—QR3
10 Kt—K5   ....

Position after White's tenth move.

White tries to gain the QBP and to make play on the Q file. The incisiveness of White's play is remarkable; he has played hitherto without any weakening Pawn moves, a true disciple of the theory of Steinitz.

10   ....   Kt × Kt

That facilitates White's task. 10 .... Kt–R4 was now necessary. If 11 Kt × Kt, B × Kt; 12 Kt × P, B–QB3 or 12 P × P, Q–R4. In either case Black would have a fine game, so that only 12 B–K5 remains to be considered, whereafter 12 ...., B–QB3 was playable.

11 B × Kt   P—B5

Now correct, because pressure on Q5 evidently is useless and 12 P × P was threatened.

12 B—K2   B—B4

But that is not in line. The logical continuation was 12 ...., P–QKt4, so as to fight against the advance of the White KP with B–Kt2.

13 B—B3   P—K3
14 Q—K2!   ....

An excellent move which menaces B × Kt followed by P–KKt4 and at the same time exerts pressure on QB4.

14   ....   P—KKt4

The lesser evil would have been 14 ...., P–KR4; 15 P–KR3, P–R5.

*Position after Black's
fourteenth move.*

15 P—K4   ....

The force of this advance
which uproots the Black
QBP and at the same time
gains space for attack
against the adverse King is
manifest.

15	P × P
16 Kt × P	Kt × Kt
17 B × Kt	B × QB
18 P × B	Q—B2
19 Q—B3	....

Again an excellent move
directed against the weaknesses QKt7, KB5 and 6,
and simultaneously frees
the KR.

19	B × B
20 R × B	QR—B1
21 P—KR4	....

The culminating point of
White's plan. The Black
KKtP cannot be held. The
sequence is little more
than elementary technique.

21	Q—K2
22 P × P	K—R1
23 Q—K3	R—KKt1
24 P—B4	P—Kt4
25 R—Q1	QR—Q1
26 KR—Q4	Q—B4
27 K—B2	R—QB1
28 R—KR1	Q—K2

At the finish a mistake;
Black should have played
28 ...., R—Kt2, but
probably did not delib-
erate, having no hope
left and possibly being resigned to the approaching
end.

White Mates in five
moves by 29 R × Pch., etc.

White—Samisch.
Black—Spielmann.

(Played at Baden-Baden,
1925).

1 P—Q4	P—K3
2 Kt—KB3	P—QB4
3 P—K4	P × P
4 Kt × P	Kt—KB3
5 B—Q3	P—Q3
6 O—O	B—K2
7 Kt—Q2	O—O
8 K—R1	QKt—Q2
9 P—QB3	P—QR3

Here 9 ...., P—Q4
would have given Black a
comfortable game.

10 Q—K2   ....

White takes no pains to
impede Black's develop-
ment, as he could have
done by preventing P–Q4.
His idea is a thoroughly

practical one. Knowing Spielmann's desire to make combinations, he hopes as a result to get a favourable opportunity.

10	....	Q—B2
11	P—KB4	P—QKt3
12	QKt—B3	Kt—B4
13	B—B2	....

Position after White's thirteenth move.

Black has a fair position. He need not fear the attack White has prepared and may continue with 13 .... B–Kt2. If then 14 P–K5, KKt–K5 the Black Knights are firmly entrenched, since for P–QKt4 White needs much preparation as long as the QBP is unguarded. And 14 Kt–KKt5 is very problematical on account of 14 ...., P–R3; 15 P–K5, P×Kt; 16 P×Kt (else 16 ...., KKt–K5), B×P; 17 P× P, B–K4; 18 P–Kt6, P ×P; 19 R×Rch., R×R; 20 B×P, R–B3 or 20 P–

Kt4, Q–B2. To summarize White cannot take the position by violent assault because he is not sufficiently developed.

| 13 | .... | P K4 |

But with this move, intended to prevent P–K5 for good—(unnecessarily, since that move would not hurt) ---Black gives White two strong Bishops.

| 14 | Kt—B5 | .... |

More lucid and also stronger play would have been 14 P×P developing the QB and after that Kt–B5.

14	....	B×Kt
15	P×B	P—K5
16	Kt—Q4	P—Q4
17	B—K3	B—Q3
18	P—KKt4	....

White has a firm position, Black a weak spot on Q4. For all that the decision had not yet arrived, but Black now commits the grave error of forcing the decision with incomplete preparation and thereby imperils his own game.

| 18 | .... | Kt—Q6 |

Sacrifice of a Pawn in order to occupy the square K5 with a piece, but the compensation is insufficient

19 P—Kt5	Kt—Q2
20 B × Kt	P × B
21 Q × P	Kt—B4
22 Q—K2	KR—K1
23 R—B3	Q—K2

The Queen would probably better have taken the diagonal QB1 to KR6, one Rook the square K5, the other one on K1.

24 Q—Kt2	Q—K5
25 QR—KB1	....

Black's position looks fine, but he is a Pawn minus and threatens nothing. Nor can he invent threats; White is posted too firmly.

25	Kt—Q6
26 P—B6	B—B4
27 P × P?	....

Here P–B5 was important. Now Black has a chance.

27	B × Kt
28 P × B	QR—B1

But that is an error! Black could still have fought if he had played Q–B4. He had to prevent the White Pawns from gaining white squares. After Q–B4 White, in order to resume his attack, would have had to dislodge the Black Queen, for instance, by R–R3–R6–B6, or Q–R3 or Q–Kt4 after due preparation. In the meanwhile Black could have pursued his own attack, say by P–QR4–R5. The QB file was Black's in any case.

29 P—B5	....

That is decisive, because White has threats, Black none.

29	R—B3
30 P—Kt6	BP × P
31 P × P	K × P
32 B--R6ch.	Resigns.

The above game was not free from guilt and error, but is rich in temper and invention.

White—Alekhin.
Black—Marshall.
(Played at Baden-Baden, 1925).

1 P—Q4	P—Q4
2 P—QB4	Kt—KB3
3 P × P	Kt × P
4 P—K4	Kt—KB3
5 B—Q3	....

If 5 Kt–QB3, P–K4! forcefully. 6 P × P, Q × Q ch.; 7 K × Q, Kt–Kt5; 8 Kt–R3 with a fairly even game.

5	P—K4
6 P × P	Kt—Kt5
7 Kt—KB3	Kt—QB3
8 B—KKt5	B—K2
9 B × B	Q × B
10 Kt—B3	QKt × P
11 Kt × Kt	Q × Kt
12 P—KR3	Kt—B3
13 Q—Q2	B—Q2
14 Q—K3	B—B3
15 O—O—O	O—O

White, having repulsed the somewhat precipitate attack launched by Black, has impressed his signature on the position. In Castling Queen's side he has given a target to the adversary, but he has also prepared a forceful advance on the other wing. Since the attack on KR7 can soon be initiated White's attack seems to have the start over Black's. In any case, White has retained the initiative.

16 P—B4   Q—K3

Here Black slides into the downward groove. In the centre the Queen is in peril. 16 ...., Q–QR4 was more natural and also preferable.

17 P—K5   KR—K1

If 17 .... Kt–Q4; 18 Kt × Kt, B × Kt; 19 B × P ch., K–R1; 20 B–B5 with a manifest advantage.

18 KR—K1   QR—Q1

But now it was high time to remove the Knight to Q2. B l a c k does not willingly submit to defensive tactics but he is forced to do so because White has the better development and has Pawns to sustain the fight, whereas the Black Queen's side Pawns are for the present mere spectators.

19 P—B5   Q—K2
20 Q—Kt5   Kt—Q4
21 P—B6   Q—B1

22 B—B4   ....

Excellent! T h e Black Knight obstructs the White QR which is intended to attack the Black QR that is already indirectly threatened by the White Q. Black has no time for P–KR3 on account of P × P.

The move made is at once decisive.

22	Kt × Kt
23 R × R	R × R
24 P × P	Kt × Pch.

In order to continue with 25 ...., Q–B4ch. if the Knight be taken. Nevertheless, it was not advisable to remove the Knight from the centre at this critical moment. Better 24 .... Q–K1 to reply to the formidable 25 P–K6 with R–Q4. True, if White plays correctly, he must win, viz., 24 ...., Q–K1; 25 P × Kt, R–Q3; 26 B × Pch. or 25 .... B–Q4; 26 B–Q3, B–K3; 27 B × Pch., K × B; 28 R–K4. But, even so, Black would thus have had the chance of White committing the error 25 P–K6.

25 K—Kt1   ....

Even B × Kt would have won in spite of the pleasantry 25 ...., Q–B4ch.; 26 K–Kt1, B–K5ch.; 27 K –R1, White's formidable threats cannot all be met.

25	Q—K1
26 P—K6	B—K5ch.
27 K—R1	....

Of course !

27	P—KB4
28 P—K7ch.	R—Q4
29 Q—B6	Q—B2
30 P—K8	Resigns.
= Queen ch.	

White—Nimzowitsch.
Black—Bogoljubow.

(Played at Baden-Baden, 1925).

1 Kt—KB3	Kt—KB3
2 P—K3	P—Q3
3 P—Q4	QKt—Q2
4 QKt—Q2	....

Recently a style has come into vogue to play the Opening indifferently. Of course, one need not desperately strive for initiative, one may win while on the defensive and in counter-attack, and by lack of initiative one by no means permits the game to get out of hand, but all in all, it pays to play incisively. Here the natural move would have been 4 P–B4 and 5 Kt–B3, to hem Black in.

4	P—KKt3
5 P—KKt3	B—Kt2
6 B—Kt2	O—O
7 O—O	P—B4
8 P—Kt3	Q—B2
9 B—Kt2	R—Kt1
10 P—B4	P × P
11 P × P	....

If 11 Kt × P, P–QR3; the point QB4 remains in Black's possession.

11	P—QKt4
12 R—K1	R—K1
13 R—QB1	Q—R4

*Position after Black's
thirteenth move.*

Black has had time to
develop his game. White's
KB3 is weak. Black, how-
ever, has less space than
the first player.

14 P—QR3   P × P
15 Kt × P   Q—R4

Now White is weak on
Q5, but he has the major-
ity of Pawns on the
Queen's side. All in all, a
balanced position.

16 P—QKt4   Kt—Kt3

In reply to 16 ....,
Kt–Q4 White might have
played KKt–K5.

17 Kt × Kt   ....

Very just! Not Kt–R5
because of 17 ...... QKt–Q4.

17 ....   P × Kt
18 Kt—Q2   B—Kt5
19 Q—B2   B—R3

Black wants to force P–
B4 in order to weaken the
KKtP. Bogoljubow's play,
though careful, is vigorous.

20 P—B4   B—B4

Preparing to play P–
KKt4 which would other-
wise be parried by P-B5.

21 Kt—K4!   B—Kt2
22 Kt × Ktch   B × Kt
23 Q—Q2   B—K3

The threat was 24 B–B6
followed by P–Q5.

24 B—B6   KR—QB1
25 Q—Kt2   P—Q4
26 P—Kt5   R—Q1
27 P—QR4   R—Q1

The Middle-Game is
played finely and strongly
by both masters. Black's
plan is to counter the
attack that White has initiated on the Queen's side by
an attack on the KKtP. To
begin with, the point KR6
must be secured.

28 Q—KB2   B—B4
29 B—B3   ....

But here White falls off
perceptibly. The Bishop
bound for some time to
guard Q4, would better
have been left alone. The
logical continuation was R–
R1 and P–R5.

29 ....   B—K5
30 P—R5   P × P
31 B × RP   KR—QB1
32 B—B3   Q—R6

Now it is manifest, how
heavily the loss of time B–
B3–R5–B3 weighs. If a

Rook stood on the QR file and the Q Bishop on Kt2 White now might have strengthened the weak spot KKt3 by R–R3 and caused Black's attack to slow down.

33 R—K2 ....

If 33 Q–B1, Q–Kt5; 34 R–K3, P–Kt4 with a good game.

33	....	P—R4
34	R—Q2	K—Kt2
35	R—K1	P—R5
36	Q—B1	Q—B4
37	B—Kt2	P × P
38	P × P	R—KR1
39	R—Kt2	B × R
40	K × B	R—R3

White resigned. Black's strategy has carried the day. From the time that the White Bishop erred off to QR5 the energy of Black's attack and the logic of his play were a model.

White—Reti.
Black—Alekhin.

(Played at Baden-Baden, 1925).

1	P—KKt3	P—K4
2	Kt—KB3	P—K5
3	Kt—Q4	P—Q4
4	P—Q3	P × P
5	Q × P	....

The Pawn position would be more compact after 5 BP × P. But Reti plays for development which is furthered by getting the Queen out of the way of his Rooks.

| 5 | .... | Kt—KB3 |
| 6 | B—Kt2 | B—Kt5ch. |

The idea is to block the point QB6.

7 B—Q2 ....

But Kt–Q2 was probably better. The Black KB is already in some little danger and White is not well advised to exchange his fine QB for it.

7	....	B × Bch.
8	Kt × B	O—O
9	P—QB4	Kt—R3
10	P × P	Kt—QKt5
11	Q—B4	QKt × QP

Position after Black's eleventh move.

The development is accomplished. White has somewhat the better of it in the centre, but Black has brought his pieces more rapidly to the scene of action.

12 QKt—Kt3 ....

White espies a weakness of Black's on QB4, accentuated by the Bishop on Kt2 which retards P-QKt3.

12 ....   P—B3

Black with this move admits the weakness of his QB4.

13 O—O   R—K1
14 KR—Q1   B—Kt5
15 R—Q2   Q—B1

Black seeks compensations by exerting pressure on the King's side.

16 Kt—QB5   B—R6
17 B—B3   B—Kt5

Black is ready to consent to a Draw.

18 B—Kt2   B—R6
19 B—B3   B—Kt5
20 B—Kt2   B—R6
21 B—B3   B—Kt5
22 B—R1   ....

In relying upon the strength of his advance post on QB5, White refuses the Draw.

Position after White's twenty-second move.

Here Black could have prevented the attack by the White Queen's side Pawns, which, of course, he saw coming, by P-QR4. He resolves, however, to allow the storm to break because he senses as it were, a profound combination directed against the White King.

22 ....   P—KR4
23 P—Kt4   P—R3
24 R—QB1   P—R5
25 P—R4   P × P
26 RP × P   Q—B2
27 P—Kt5   ....

White is here too impetuous. On the one hand, he should not have aided the development of Black's QR; on the other hand, he had to drive the Black Knight on Q4 from its strong post sooner or later, and the right moment had now arrived. There was no cause for holding the KP back, it should now have its say. With 27 P–K4, Kt–Kt3; 28 Q–B3, QR–Q1; 29 KKt–Kt3 White had a favourable position, for instance, 29 ...., R × R; 30 Q × R, R–Q1; 31 Q–B4, Q–B1; 32 P–R5. If 27 .... Kt–K2, where the Knight has a better post than on Kt3, White had time for 28 P–B3, upon which 28 ...., Q × Pch., of course, would not be playable, and the B l a c k B would become embarrassed. All in all, with 27 P–K4 White had slightly the better of it and kept the initiative. But from the moment that White omitted that move Black took the initiative out of White's hands.

27 ………   RP × P
28 P × P   R—K6 !

If 29 P × R, Q × Pch. is deadly.

29 Kt—B3   ………

Still White is unwilling to simplify. 29 B–B3 was bitterly needed. Now the Knight is missing on the Queen's side.

Position after White's twenty-ninth move.

29 ………   P × P

The introduction to one of the most charming combinations known to Chess.

30 Q × P   Kt—B6
31 Q × P   ………

There is nothing else.

31 ………   Q × Q
32 Kt × Q   Kt × Pch.
33 K––R2   Kt—K5 !

To have captured the Rook would have profited nothing, but if now 34 P × R, Kt × KR and wins the exchange or a piece.

34 R—B4   ………

White is equal to the task ; play and counter-play are on the same high level. If 34 ………, Kt × R ; 35 Kt × Kt, R–Q6 ; 36 Kt–B5.

34 ………   Kt × BP !

Now the King becomes the target.

35 B—Kt2   ………

This Bishop is too valuable for defence to allow its exchange.

35 ………   B—K3
36 QR–B2   Kt—Kt5ch.
37 K—R3   Kt—K4ch.
38 K—R2   R × Kt
39 R × Kt   Kt—Kt5ch.
40 K—R3   Kt—K6ch.
41 K—R2   Kt × R
42 B × R   Kt—Q5

White resigned, because after 43 R–K3, Kt × Bch. ; 44 R × Kt, B—Q4 wins. The play in this combination was rich in invention and variety by both winner and loser.

White—Sir George
                    Thomas.
Black—Rubinstein.
(Played at Baden-Baden, 1925).

1	P—K4	P—K4
2	Kt—KB3	Kt—QB3
3	B—Kt5	P—QR3
4	B—R4	Kt—B3
5	O—O	B—K2
6	R—K1	P—QKt4
7	B—Kt3	P—Q3
8	P—B3	O—O
9	P—KR3	Kt—QR4
10	B—B2	P—B4
11	P—Q4	Q—B2
12	QKt—Q2	Kt—B3

Position after Black's twelfth move.

13	P—Q5	....

Black threatened to win a Pawn on White's Q4, but that Pawn could not have been maintained and White therefore could ignore the threat. In not doing so he shuts off the centre and puts all his weight on to the wings. But there Black has as much advantage as White — on the Queen's side even the greater one, since there he enjoys more freedom than White.

13	....	Kt—Q1
14	Kt—B1	Kt—K1

Now, according to Philidor, the Pawns in front, Knights and Bishops backing them up.

15	P—QR4	....

On the Queen's side White has nothing to look for. His chances are on the King's side. White should have omitted this move and immediately started with P-KKt4, so as to make himself strong on the KKt file.

15	....	R—Kt1

The temporary possession of the QR file avails White nothing.

16	P × P	....

Best, since otherwise the QB would have to watch his QKtP.

16	....	P × P
17	P—KKt4	P—Kt3
18	Kt—Kt3	Kt—KKt2
19	K—R1	P—B3
20	R—KKt1	Kt—B2
21	Q—B1	B—Q2
22	B—K3	R—R1

Now the counter-thrust prevents White from employing his Rooks as he would desire. Hence, he cannot execute his plan of Q–Kt2 and Kt–B5.

23 Q—Kt2   R × R
24 R × R   Q—Kt2
25 K—R2   R—R1
26 Q—B1   R—R3
27 Kt—Q2   ....

White must retreat, for Black holds the QR file and threatens to enter with his Rook or Queen into the White camp.

27 ....   Q—R1
28 R × R   Q × R
29 Kt—Kt3   Kt—Kt4

Now Black has the advantage on the King's side, because the White KKt has to stand guard on QKt3. Black brings his advantage home in a model fashion. To begin with, he forces the weakening advance of the adverse RP.

30 K—Kt2   P—R4
31 P—R4   Kt—B2
32 P × P   P × P
33 K—R2   Q—B1
34 Q—Kt2   K—B1
35 Kt—Q2   P—B4

Now the attack is opened up against the White RP in the process of which the White KP is torn away from its phalanx and the QP becomes weak.

36 P × P   B × RP

Position after Black's thirty-sixth move.

37 P—B6 !   ....

White also plays in masterly fashion. He makes the utmost use of the untenable BP and gets up an attack against the King and the RP.

37 ....   B × P
38 Q—B3   B—R5

If now 39 Kt × P? or 39 B—R6, Black replies B–Kt5.

39 B—Kt6   B × Ktch.
40 P × B   B—B4
41 B × Kt   ....

White prefers to play for an attack instead of regaining his Pawn. His judgment is perfectly right, since the End-Game resulting from 41 B × P, Kt × B ; 42 Q × Kt, owing to the strength of the KP and the weakness of the White QP, would be hugely in favour of Black.

41	K × B
42 Kt—K4	Q—Q2
43 B—R6	K—Kt3
44 B × Kt	K × B
45 P—QKt4	....

But therewith White surrenders the possibility of supporting his QP by P–Kt3 and P–B4. The right plan was to assume with 45 Kt–B2 a firm position, to play the Queen to Q2 or K3, the King to Kt2 and to threaten counter-attacks as soon as the Black Queen strays too far away from its King and QP. Against such a tenacious defence Black would still have had to overcome great difficulties.

45	P—B5
46 Kt—Q2	....

And also here 46 Kt–B2 would probably have been preferable.

46	Q—KB2
47 Q—K3	....

If 47 K–Kt2, B–Kt3, and the White QP must eventually fall.

47	Q × P
48 Q—Kt5ch.	B—Kt3
49 Q—K7ch.	K—Kt1
50 Q—Q8ch.	K—B2
51 Q—Q7ch.	K—B3
52 Q—Q8ch.	K—B4
53 Q—Q7ch.	K—B3
54 Q—Q8ch.	K—Kt2
55 Q—K7ch.	Q—B2

There was no other way; the King could otherwise find no protection.

56 Q × P	Q—B7ch.
57 K—R3	K—R3
58 Kt—Kt1	....

The game was not to be saved since 58 ...., P–K5 was threatened, but this is a blunder.

58	Q—B4ch.
59 K—Kt2	Q × Kt
60 Q—B8ch.	K—Kt4
61 Q—Q8ch.	K—Kt5
62 Q—Q7ch.	Q—B4
63 Q—Q1ch.	K—Kt4

Resigns.

White—Alekhin.
Black—Colle.

(Played at Baden-Baden, 1925).

1 P—Q4	P—Q4
2 P—QB4	Kt—QB3
3 Kt—KB3	B—Kt5
4 Q—R4	....

A novel attempt. The move here ordinarily played is P × P.

4	B × Kt
5 KP × B	....

White does not worry over the position of Pawns if he gets open lines for his Bishops. Also, the KBP, if well supported by pieces, can be of great service in an attack on the hostile array of Pawns.

5	P—K3
6 Kt—B3	B—Kt5
7 P—QR3	B × Ktch.
8 P × B	Kt—K2

The Black KB had to go to Kt5, because the KKt was destined to support the QKt from K2. Up to this point the Opening has run a logical course.

| 9 R—QKt1 | R—QKt1 |
| 10 B—Q3 | P × P |

But this is not justified. The QP should retain its post as long as possible, so as to block the White QP which in its turn obstructs the diagonal QKt2 to KKt7.

11 B × BP	O—O
12 O—O	Kt—Q4
13 Q—B2	QKt—K2
14 B—Q3	P—KR3
15 P—QB4	Kt—Kt3

Position after Black's fifteenth move.

In consequence of the censured exchange of Pawns White now has an advantage. White's strategy will be to open the lines for his Bishops, either with P–B4–B5 or by a sacrifice with P–Q5. Black cannot readily attain counter-attack, since P–QB4, his most promising line for this purpose, by opening the diagonal of the QB would endanger the King's side. Alekhin's play quickly brings the above advantages to bear and at the same time gives Black opportunities for committing errors or mistakes, wherever such opportunities can be given w i t h o u t endangering White. Thus Alekhin combines, in his style, logic and psychology.

16 R—Q1	KKt—B1
17 P—B4	P—QKt3
18 B—Kt2	P—QB3
19 Q—K2	Kt—Q3
20 Q—K5	Kt—K1
21 P—QR4	R—Kt2
22 R—K1	Kt—B3
23 QR—Q1	R—Q2

On the Q file the decision is to fall. Black has recognised this and played the Rook to the right spot.

| 24 B—B2 | P—R3 ? |

But here Black gives way. With 24 ...., Q–B2 he could assume a fairly stable position. In case the White Queen leaves its post, the Black KR moves so as to allow its King a place of refuge when needed. For instance 25 Q–K2, KR–Q1; 26 P–Q5, BP × P; 27 B × Kt, P × B; 28 Q–Kt4ch., K–B1.

25 Q—K2   Q—Kt1

At least, he should here have played R–K1.

26 P—Q5	BP × P
27 B × Kt	P × B
28 Q—Kt4ch.	K—R1
29 Q—R4	K—Kt2
30 Q—Kt4ch.	K—R1
31 Q—R4	K—Kt2
32 Q—Kt4ch.	K—R1

The repetition of moves served the end of gaining time on his clock.

33 P—KB5 !   ....

This thrust hits the weak point.

33	Kt × P
34 B × Kt	P × B
35 Q × P	....

Better than Q–R4 because after this capture of the Pawn the Black Pawns on B3 and KR3 remain very weak.

35	Q—Q1
36 P × P	R—Q3
37 Q—B4	K—R2
38 Q—K4ch.	K—R1
39 Q—K3	K—Kt2
40 Q—Q3	....

To add to the misfortune the Black QRP is now weak. The move 24 ...., P–R3 was therefore not only a lost move but it also damaged t h e aggressive power of the Queen's side Pawns.

40 ....   P—QR4

Black is helpless. The KtP is backwards, h i s King's side is disorganised and his King bereft of refuge. Alekhin w i n s methodically by making himself safe and slowly manoeuvring his opponent into a *Zugzwang*.

41 R—K3	R—Kt1
42 R—R3	Q –Q2
43 Q—K3	P—B4

This additional weakness was forced, for Black could not hide his Rook on KR1 all the time.

44 R—Kt3ch.	K—R2
45 R × R	....

The Rook is exchanged ſo p r e v e n t KR–Kt3, where White cannot exchange it without uniting the Black Pawns.

45	....	K × R
46	Q—Kt3ch.	K—R2
47	Q—Kt3	K—Kt2
48	P—R3	Q—Q1
49	Q—Kt3ch.	K—R2
50	Q—K5	Q—Q2
51	R—Q3	P—B3

Probably not necessary at this moment, but White can force it at any time by R–KKt3.

52	Q—Q4	Q—Q1
53	Q—QB4	Q—Q2
54	R—Q4	K—Kt2
55	Q—Q3	....

Now Black is in *Zugzwang*. If 55 .... K–R1; 56 Q–K3 is painful owing to the weakness of the KRP.

| 55 | .... | K—B2 |

True, 55 ...., K–R1 was still better than such a move.

| 56 | P—Kt4 | K—B1 |

For if 56 ...., P × P; 57 Q–R7ch., with deadly effect.

57	P × P	Q—K1
58	R—K4	Q—R4
59	R—KKt4	Q—B2
60	Q—K3	Q—KR2
61	R—Kt6	Resigns.

White—Bogoljubow.
Black—Mieses.

(Played at Baden-Baden, 1925).

1	P—Q4	P—KB4
2	P—KKt3	Kt—KB3
3	B—Kt2	P—K3
4	Kt—KB3	P—Q4

Herewith Black, building up the celebrated "Stonewall," fortifies the point K5, but leaves his K4 at the mercy of the opponent. Since the White KBP still endangers the Black stronghold, the scales incline a little in White's favour. Hence, it would appear suitable to advance the QP to Q3 only.

5	O—O	B—Q3
6	P—B4	P—B3
7	Kt—B3	QKt—Q2

If 7 ...., P × P? 8 Kt–Q2 !

| 8 | Q—B2 | Kt—K5 |
| 9 | K—R1 | .... |

In preparation for a manœuvre by which K5 will be much strengthened.

9	....	Q—B3
10	B—B4 !	B × B
11	P × B	Q—R3
12	P—K3	QKt—B3

Black probably senses no danger, else O—O would have been his move. Or did Black intend to lure the White Knight to his K5 and there exchange it, so as to block that point forever? The plan, though costing two moves, has its good points.

13 Kt—K5   Kt—Q2
14 R—KKt1   Kt × Kt
15 QP × Kt   Kt × Kt

To Castle would have been more cautious. Or did Black wish to avoid B × Kt followed by P–QB5, whereupon the Knight would establish itself on Q4? But Black could probably stand the pressure of the Knight without being much harmed.

Position after Black's fifteenth move.

16 P × Kt   ....

White now shows his hand. He wants to assail the Queen's side. The sacrifice of the QBP is one in appearance only, since the Pawn would soon be regained.

16 ....   B—Q2
17 QR—Q1   P—QKt4

In order to force the exchange of Pawns, to recapture with BP and to occupy the QB file with strong pressure on QB6.

18 Q—Kt2!   ....

If 18 ...., KtP × P; 19 Q–Kt7, pinning the Black pieces to their posts.

18 ....   O—O
19 Q—R3   ....

If now 19 ...., KtP × P; 20 R–Kt1 with the intention of 21 R–Kt7.

19 ....   KR—Q1
20 P × KtP   P × P
21 Q—R6   ....

The Bishop shall not be permitted to go to B3, the QRP shall be held back, and besides, the clumsy threat 22 B × P has to be provided for.

21 ....   Q—R4

(See diagram next page)

It is a pity that Black did not play 21 ...., K—R1, whereupon the logical variation would have ensued, viz.: 22 P–QR4, KR–QKt1; 23 R–Kt1 or 22 .... P × P; 23 P–B4 or 22 ...., QR–B1; 23 P × P, R × P; 24 Q × RP to the advantage of White.

*Position after Black's
twenty-first move.*

22 B × P

With a sudden change of plan White assails the hostile position like a streak of lightning.

22	P × B
23 R × Pch.	K × R
24 Q—B6ch.	K—Kt1
25 R—Kt1ch.	Q—Kt5
26 R × Qch.	P × R
27 P—B5	KR—QB1

If the Rook stays on Q1, the threat P–K7 is a trump later on, for instance 27 ...., QR–B1; 28 P–K6. B–K1? 29 P–K7; or 28 .... B–B3; 29 Q–Kt5 ch., K–R1; 30 P–B6, R–KKt1; 31 Q–K5.

28 P—K6	B—B3
29 Q—B7ch.	K—R1
30 P—B6	R—KKt1
31 Q—B7	QR—QB1
32 Q—K5	P—Q5ch.
33 K—Kt1	B—Q4
34 P—B7ch.	R—Kt2
35 Q × B	Resigns.

This game is a bouquet of varied, nicely shaded, æsthetic impressions, a monument of honour to both contestants.

White—Bogoljubow.
Black—Reti.

(Played at Breslau, 1925)

1 P—K4	P—K3
2 P—Q4	P—Q4
3 Kt—QB3	Kt—KB3
4 B—Kt5	B—Kt5
5 P—K5	P—KR3
6 B—Q2	B × Kt
7 P × B	Kt—K5
8 Q—Kt4	....

*Position after White's
eighth move.*

The position has at this early stage assumed shape. White wants to assail the King's side, Black the Queen's side.

The Black KKtP requires protection either by P–KKt3, which deprives the KBP of its future, or by K–B1; the King's side is thereby weakened in any event. The weakening effect of P–KKt3 seems greater than the concessions that K–B1 makes, because with the Pawn on KKt3 White would have a target for sacrificing combinations. With P–KR4, followed by development of the KR via R3, he could evaluate that weakness. It is true that an attack on the KKtP is staged in any case. After 8 ...., K–B1; 9 P–KR4, the threat B–Q3 followed by R–R3 is already present. A parry would be Kt–QB3–K2–B4 and by no means the only one. All in all, K–B1 is certainly worth a determined trial.

8	P—KKt3
9 B—Q3	Kt × B
10 K × Kt	P—QB4
11 P—KR4	....

Momentarily, the sacrifice B × P fails because of R–Kt1. But may the White Bishop be allowed to stand on Q3 until R–R3 has been played? Black, it is true, can play Q–K2, to give powerful support to the King. That, it would appear, would also be the best way of augmenting the pressure on the White QP.

11 ....   P—B5

But Black decides to make an end to that threat

once for all. Only he casts obstacles into the path of his own attack thereby.

12 B—K2   P—KR4

Should Black block the KRP or permit P–R5? A difficult question. Much is to be said pro and con for either alternative. For the move P–KR4 it may be argued that, though weakening the black squares on the King's side it allows Black some time, the immediate threats being lessened. Against it may be argued that the permanent weakness is worse than the temporary peril. Thus: 12 ...., Q–K2; 13 P–R5, P–KKt4; 14 P–B4, P × P; 15 Q × BP, Kt–Q2; 16 Kt–R3, P–Kt4; 17 Kt–B2, P–R4; 18 Kt–Kt4, Q–B1 (or P–Kt5). Still the Black position holds together and a counter-attack is in preparation. After the move actually made the White attack, retarded only a little while, attains such force that the counter-attack appears weak in comparison.

13 Q—B4	Kt—B3
14 Kt—B3	Q—K2
15 Kt—Kt5	P—Kt4
16 P—R3	....

This move is problematical. If it was necessary,

t h e question remains
whether the moment for
making it had arrived. In
any case, at some time or
another the square QKt4
has to be guarded against
the inroad of the Black
Queen.

16 ....   P—R4
17 P—Kt4   R—QR2

Black must not play P ×
P, since White, by pushing
P–R5 soon after, would
obtain command of the KR
file. As it is, White has
only the KKt file at his disposal, and that is blocked
by the White Knight.

18 P × P   P × P
19 R—R3   ....

This Rook serves both
attack and defence; it
strengthens the squares
QB3 and QR3.

19 ....   P—Kt5
20 R—B3   P × Pch.

Probably Black is forced
to this. Normally, the formation R–Kt2, Kt–R2–Kt4
would be preferable, but
Black cannot allow White,
whose position is so com-
manding, to obtain the
command of the QR file
also. This then, it would
appear, is the idea which
prompted the problemati-
cal move 16 P–R3.

21 R × P   R—Kt2
22 R—KKt1   Kt—R2
23 KR—KKt3   B—Q2 ?

That is a pity. Black
had the moral courage to
meet the attack that he, of
course, saw coming. He
has set a counter-attack in
motion; Kt–Kt4 was mani-
fest, and now this move
which obstructs both King
and Rook ! After 23 ....
Kt–Kt4 White would have
had to moderate the pace of
his attack and to defend,
say by 24 R–Kt1. Then, it
seems, 25 P–R4 would be
threatening, h e n c e, 24
........., P–R5. Then, to
safeguard the King, prob-
ably 25 B–Q1, aiming also
at QR4. Black would re-
main endangered, but there
would be counter-play and
tension. After the ill-
considered move of the text,
his position falls like a
house of cards.

24 B × RP   ....

If 24 ...., R × B; 25
Kt × BP; and the King
cannot get away from the
terrible White R o o k s.
Black played

24 ....   P—B6ch.
25 K—K3   ....

and then resigned. A game
which solves some ques-
tions only to suggest many

other riddles. The play of White is testimony of supreme mastery.

White—Romanowski.
Black—E. Rabinovitch.

(Played in the Russian National Tourney, 1925).

1	P—K4	P—K3
2	P—Q4	P—Q4
3	Kt—QB3	B—Kt5
4	P—K5	....

If now 4 ...., P—QB4; 5 P—QR3, B—R4?; 6 P–QKt4, P × KtP; 7 Kt–Kt5 Black gets into difficulties. After 5 ...., P × P; 6 P × B, P × Kt; 7 P × P, Q–B2. Black wins a Pawn, but White has rapid development in return. He continues with 8 Kt–B3 and is prepared to attack after Q × BPch.; 9 B–Q2, Q–B2; 10 B–Q3. And, finally, after 5 .... B × Ktch.; 6 P × B, P–B5; White, who immediately takes the initiative by Q–Kt4, has the advantage.

4	....	P—KB3

Therefore Black at once seizes the bull by the horns.

5	Kt—B3	P—QB4
6	B—Kt5ch.	K—B1

Bold but logical. Black does not want to exchange the QB, which has to support the KP. Moreover, he considers the White KB in danger. Already P–B5 threatens to gain that Bishop.

7	P × QBP	Q—R4
8	B—K2	P × P
9	O—O	....

Position after White's ninth move.

The position is interesting. White has manifold threats, and Black would probably do better to capture the Knight, than to guard the KP. True, White could try to open the game, to begin with, by P–QB4, and to assail the King. The struggle would be a hard one.

9	....	Kt—QB3

White now gets his opening in a different manner.

10	Kt × QP	P × Kt
11	P—B3	B × P(B4)
12	P—QKt4	Kt × P
13	P × Kt	B × P
14	R—Kt1	B—KB4

Black forces White to give up the exchange and White gladly allows this. But Black has a difficult task no matter how he may proceed. His central Pawns are under fire and one of them must fall, except after P–K5, whereupon White would post his Knight strongly on Q4.

15	R × B	Q × R
16	Q × P	Kt—K2
17	Q × KP	Q—K5
18	Q—Kt2	....

In such an open position, the Black King imperilled, with Queens on the board, the exchange cannot be of much account. The Black King needs three moves to achieve safety: P–KR3, K –Kt1–R2. In the meantime, White has targets to aim at: the Queen, the Knight and the QKtP for instance. White has a good development also, and his position contains no weaknesses. The sacrifices that White has made are justified by his position judgment.

18	....	R—B1
19	B—KR6	R—KKt1
20	Q—B6ch.	K—K1
21	B—Kt5ch.	R—B3

Black capitulates; the pressure exerted by the White pieces was too strong.

22	B × P	B—Q2
23	B × R	Q × B
24	R—K1	Q—B4
25	B—R6	K—Q1
26	B—B8	Resigns.

White's play demonstrates a high degree of ingenuity, vigour of invention, bold and sharp judgment.

Black—W. H. Watts to play.

White—J. H. Morrison.

1	.........,	Q—R4

Unpins the B, attacks the QRP, aims at K8—good work for one move.

2	Q—B4	B—KKt4!

2 .... R–Q5 was also strong.

The Kt has the function of guarding K1, the White R that of protecting the B.

3	P—QKt4	....

Setting imagination against imagination. But the patient R–R1 was sounder.

3 ....   B × R

Black plays energetically and resourcefully.

4 P × Q   R × Bch.
5 Kt—Kt1   B—B5 !
6 P—Kt3   R—K8
7 Q—B3   B—Q7 !
8 Q—Kt3   B × Pch.
9 P—B3   R—Kt8
10 Q—R3   B—Kt5
11 Q—K3   B—QB4
Resigns.

R. Bau.

White, E. Nebermann, plays and wins.

Black is threatening Q—Kt5 with terrible effect. But White had foreseen the threat as well as the possibility of effectual parry. An exceeding precision was required.   1   R—Q8ch. would not win because of 1 ...., K—B2; 2 R × KR, R—B8ch.; 3 K—B2, Q × P ch., and Black would win.

1 Q—R8ch.   K—B2 !
2 Q × R   Q—Kt5 !
3 R—Q7ch.   ....

3 Kt–Q8ch., K—Kt3 is worse than useless. Here White had to make accurate combination. Not the Black Queen is lost, as it might appear, but the Black Rook.

3 ....   Q × R

If 3 ...., K—K3; 4 R–Q6ch., K—B2; 5 Kt–Q8ch., K–Kt3; 6 R × Pch., P × R; 7 Q–Kt8ch. and wins easily.

4 P—K6ch.   K × P

That White should still win looks improbable, yet he just manages to do so.

5 Q—Kt8ch.   ....

If 5 ...., K–B4; 6 Q × Pch., gains the Rook. The retreat to K2 is of no use because the KtP is captured. White wins.

White—Torre.
Black—Grünfeld.

(Played at Marienbad, 1925).

1 P—Q4   P—Q4
2 Kt—KB3   P—QB3
3 B—B4   Kt—B3
4 P—K3   Q—Kt3
5 B—Q3   ....

White sacrifices the KtP because he wins thereby three moves (Q to Kt3 to Kt7 and back to Kt3) where the Black Queen even then is exposed.

5 ....   Q × KtP
6 QKt—Q2   Q—Kt3

Black did right in accepting the sacrifice since White has taken an important diagonal with his KB and, unless the KtP is captured, would be able to institute an attack by means of the rejected Pawn against the Black QBP.

7 O—O   P—K3
8 P—K4   P × P

If 8 ...., B—K2, White continues with P–B4, in order to open the lines, not P–K5, which furthers White's ends only after Black has Castled.

9 Kt × P   Kt × Kt
10 B × KKt   Kt—Q2
11 Q—K2   ....

White unites the Rooks and, as yet, in no way commits himself as to how he intends to use them.

11 ....   Kt—B3
12 B–Q3   B—K2

Position after Black's twelfth move.

The position is fairly balanced. Black has advantage in material, White in position.

13 B—K5   ....

Herewith White hampers the Knight as long as the KKtP is unguarded and by attacking the protection of the KRP increases his pressure on that point.

13 ....   O—O

But here Black goes astray. First Q–Q1 since the Queen is exposed. Castling could wait, because it indicates to White the direction in which he has to mass his pieces.

14 Kt—Kt5   ....

This forces a weakening of Black's phalanx of Pawns.

14 ....   P—Kt3

The lesser evil was 14 ......
P–KR3; 15 Kt–K4, Kt ×
Kt; 16 Q × Kt, P–KB4.
The KP remained back-
wards, but the King was
safe.

15 P–KR4?   ....

Grünfeld himself, in the
Alfiere di Re, indicates the
following subtle combina-
tion 15 Q–B3, Q–Q1; 16
Q–R3, P–KR4 (if Kt–R4:
16 Kt × RP, R–K1; 17 P–
Kt4); 17 P–Kt4, K–Kt2
(after Kt × P; 18 Q × P); 18
P × P, R–R1. Here he goes
no further, but Black seems
lost after 19 P–R6ch. At
least, the Pawn on R6
would gravely hamper
Black.

15 ....   Q—Q1

The White RP is no
grave threat. If 16 P–R5,
Black dare now reply Kt ×
P, because 17 Kt × RP, R–
K1 leaves the White
Knight endangered. White
must therefore collect new
forces or discover new
weaknesses.

16 QR—Kt1   ....

Mobilizes the Rook
against the QKtP as well
as against the King via
Kt3. But 16 KR–Q1 was
more pressing. The QP is
endangered.

16 ....   Kt—Q2

Black drives back
White's advanced pieces.

17 B—KB4   B—B3
18 KR—Q1   ....

And now P–QB3 was
necessary.

18 ....   Kt—Kt3
19 P—B4   ....

To prevent Kt–Q4, but
the move is over-bold.
What harm would have
come to Black if he played
19 ...., Q × P? After 20
B–K3, Q–K4; White
would have had no equivalent for the two Pawns.

19 ....   B—Q2

Black does not judge
right. He probably thought
that a peaceful continuation
would best preserve his advantage, but this is not so.

20 R—Kt3   R—B1
21 B—K4   ....

White has discovered
Black's weak spot: the
QKtP. That point plays a
part in all the following
combinations. Now P–B5
is threatened.

21 ....   P—KR3
22 Kt—B3   B—Kt2
23 B—Q6   P—KB4
24 B—B2   ....

At last the danger of P–
B5 is allayed, since the
Black Knight from Q4
would threaten to gain the
exchange.

24	....	R—KB2
25	Kt—K5	B × Kt
26	B × B	K—R2
27	R—Kt3	Q—K2

If Black captures RP,
White soon plays R–KR3
and the Black KRP is very
weak.

| 28 | R–Kt1 | P—B4 |

Again the QKtP was in
peril.

| 29 | B—Q3 | B—B3 |

This Bishop belongs at
B1 to support both QKtP
and KP. Torre shows that
the B on B3 is unstable.
Grünfeld proposes 29
........., R–KKt1 instead
and is certainly right. But
he is wrong in believing
that thereby he would have
had the advantage. If 29
........., R–KKt1; 30 P–
R5, P–Kt4; 31 Q–K3. This
forces 31 ...., R–QB1;
32 P–B4 or 31 .... P ×
P; 32 B × P. Now 32 ....
B–B3; 33 R–K1 would
weaken the KP too much.
Hence, White regains a
Pawn whenever he feels disposed to do so and keeps
the upper hand.

Position after Black's twenty-ninth move.

| 30 P—Q5 | .... |

The KP has the function
of guarding the KBP.

This, fundamentally, is
the idea of the combination.

| 30 .... | P × P |

This is suicide. In any
case 30 .... B–Q2 was
obligatory. If then 31 P–
R5, P–Kt4; 32 P × P and
33 R–K3 it would still
have been a fight, whereas
now it becomes a slaughter.

| 31 R × P | R—KKt1 |

After 31 ...., K × R;
32 Q–Kt4ch., K–R2; 33 B
× Pch., R × B; 34 Q × Rch.
K–Kt1; 35 Q–Kt6ch., K–
B1 White wins by 36 B–
Q6.

| 32 | R × R | K × R |
| 33 | B × P | R × B |

After 33 ...., Kt × P ;
34 Q–Kt4ch., K–B1 ; 35 B–
B4,   Q–B3 ; 36 R–K1,
White threatens 37 R–K6.

34 Q–Kt4ch.   R—Kt4
35 P × R   Q × B
36 P × Pch.   K—R2

With correct play on the
part of White, Black is irre-
trievably lost because his
King cannot find safety.

37 R—Kt3   B—Q2
38 Q—R4   Q—K8ch.
39 K—R2   Q—K5
40 Q—B6   Q—Kt3
41 Q—K7ch.   K—R1

or 41 ...., K × P ; 42 R–
KB3.

42 Q—B8ch.   K—R2
43 Q—K7ch.   K—R1
44 R—K3   Q × RPch.
45 K—Kt1   ....

The Rook guards QB1
by obstruction.

45 ....   Q—Kt2
46 Q—Q8ch.   Q—Kt1
47 Q—B6ch.   Q—Kt2
48 Q—B4   B—Kt5
49 R—KKt3   Kt × P
50 R × B and won with
ease.

White—Rubinstein.
Black—Chwojuik.
Played at Lodz, 1927.

1 P—Q4   Kt—KB3
2 P—QB4   ....

White immediately con-
structs a phalanx, in order
to be able to reply to P–
B4 with P–Q5 or—at will
—with a developing move.

2 ....   P—K3

3 Kt—QB3   ....

This holds the balance on
the point K4

3 ....   B—Kt5
4 Q—B2   ....

The merit of this move is
that the point K4 is kept
under observation and that
in case the QKt is captured
the Q may recapture. A
double pawn would lower
the mobility of the position
of pawns and thus make it
more difficult for White to
drive an advantage home.
On the other hand, a valuable opportunity for development is thereby sacri-
ficed, so that 4 Kt–B3
would after all be slightly
preferable. Another possibility 4 B–Kt5, P–KR3; 5
B × Kt, Q × B; 6 Kt–B3,
whereby White permits
two B's to Black but ob-
tains the superiority in the
centre and in development.

4 ....   P—QKt3

An attempt to get pos-
session of the point K5, but
the development of the
QKt, commenced by 4
........., P–Q3, was perhaps

the more pressing business. Also 4 ...., P–B4 is strong here. The objection to it is 5 P×P, which allows White to place a Rook on the Q file and to restrain the Black QP which is thus kept back for a while.

5 P—K4 ....

The P fights immediately.

5 ....   B×Ktch.
6 P×B   ....

White has the doubled Pawn and, in compensation therefor, much space and good development. The advantage is probably White's. Black would probably have done better with 5 ...., Kt–B3; 6 Kt –B3, P–Q3; 7 B–Q3, P–K4 or 6 P–K5, Kt–KKt1; 7 Kt –B3, P–Q3.

6 ....   P—Q3
7 P—B4   ....

White fights for possession of the point K5.

7 ....   B—Kt2
8 P—K5   Kt—K5

An insecure post for the Kt, hence KKt–Q2 was superior. White would then have continued with Kt– K2–Kt3 and taken command of the point K4.

9 Kt—B3   P—KB4

To support the KKt, but it opens the lines for the intervention of B's and R's.

10 P×P ep.   Kt×KBP
11 Kt—Kt5   Q—K2
12 B—Q3   QKt—Q2
13 O—O   O—O—O
14 R—K1   ....

The K pawn cannot be kept on K3, for instance 14 .... Kt–B1; 15 Kt×KP, Kt×Kt; 16 R×Kt. But to keep the lines closed as far as possible, the sacrifice of the P might have been advisable.

14 ....   P—K4
15 B—B5   K—Kt1
16 B—QR3   ....

A hard problem set to Black! If 16 ...., P–B4; 17 Kt–K6, whereupon White may open the lines against the Black K by 18 BP×P, P×KP; 19 P× KP.

16 ....   P—Kt3

This threat is ineffectual.

17 QP×P   P×B
18 P×P   ....

The game cannot be saved. If 18 ...., Q–Kt2; 19 P×Pch., K×P; 20 Kt–K6 ch. Black resigned after a few more moves.

The twenty-first game of the match for the Championship of the World.

White   Capablanca.
Black—Alekhin.

1 P—Q4	P—Q4
2 P—QB4	P—K3
3 Kt—QB3	Kt—KB3
4 B—Kt5	QKt—Q2
5 P—K3	B—K2
6 Kt—B3	O—O
7 R—B1	P—QR3

Black intends P×P followed by P–QKt4. If 8 P–B5? Kt–K5 would transfer the initiative to Black. White might safely proceed with 8 P×P, P×P; 9 B–Q3.

8 P—QR3   ....

But White prefers to allow Black the advance on the Q side which yields White compensating advantages in the centre.

8 ....   P—R3

Black is strong enough on the K side to permit himself this weakening advance. He thereby posts the RP, that was easily assailable by B–Q3, on a secure point.

9 B—R4	P×P
10 B×P	P—QKt4
11 B—K2	....

The idea of this retreat is to oppose his B on B3 to the Black QB, but B—R2 made the B more immediately effective.

11 ....   B—Kt2

Black permits P–QKt4 which, though assailable by P–QR4, would on the whole be advantageous to White. The more direct procedure was 11 .... P–B4.

12 O—O	P—B4
13 P×P	Kt×P
14 Kt—Q4	R—QB1
15 P—QKt4	....

Now his advance has little effect. 15 B–B3 was suggested, so as to weaken the point QB6.

15	QKt—Q2
16 B—Kt3	....

White is rather passive.

16 ....   Kt—Kt3

The Kt aims at QB5.

17 Q—Kt3	KKt—Q4
18 B—B3	R—B5

preparing for Q–R1 and KR–B1.

19 Kt—K4   Q—B1

If 19 .... Q–R1, 20 Kt–Q6.

20 R×R	Kt×R
21 R—B1	Q—R1
22 Kt—B3	....

Again rather passive. White should have played 22 Kt–QB5. If then 22

........., B × Kt; 23 P × B, R–B1; 24 B–K2, he could still have made an aggressive fight.

22	R—B1
23 Kt × Kt	B × Kt
24 B × B	Q × B

White is now wholly on the defensive. The White B has no points of aggression, the Black B has many.

25 P—QR4 ....

White wants to weaken the Black QKtP, but his plan presupposes that the White Kt is stable, whereas that Kt is unstable. The effect of the move is therefore to weaken the White QKtP and to leave the Black QKtP strong. This would have been made sufficiently manifest by 25 ...., P–K4; 26 Kt–B5, B–B1. The better plan was 25 P–B3.

25 .... B—B3

Still stronger than the above purely positional continuation.

26 Kt—B3 ....

White should first of all exhange the P's. After 26 P × P, B × Kt; 27 P × B, P × P; 28 R–Q1, Kt–Kt3; 29 Q × Q, Kt × Q; 30 B–Q6, R–B5; 31 P–R3, a patient defence might still have led to a draw.

Position after White's twentysixth move.

26 .... B—Kt7 !

Black wants to push P–K4 without obstructing his B. White cannot reply 27 R–Q1 on account of Kt × P which would allow Black a P plus and a winning ending. But this is not the finesse of the move.

The extraordinary depth of it is revealed by the combination 27 R–Kt1, Kt–R6 ! The tension between the White QRP and the Black QKtP and the omission of P–KR3, which puts on the White R the burden of guarding the mate threatened by Black's R or Q, give Alekhin the opportunity for an exceedingly pretty sacrifice. The sequence would be 28 Q × B, Kt × R; 29 Q × Kt, Q–Kt6; 30 Q–KB1, P × P; 31 P–R3, P–R6; 32 B–K5, P–B3; 33 B–R1, Q–B5. By his masterly synthesis of combinative and positional play Black has obtained an advantage that suffices to force the win.

27	R—K1	R—Q1
28	P × P	P × P
29	P—R3	P—K4

The White Kt is now driven from the centre and White loses his hold on it.

30	R—Kt1	P—K5
31	Kt—Q4	....

Desperation or miscalculation, but the game was gone because the command of the Q file and the strong position of the Black Kt and the forced retreat of the Kt to the side are a too heavy handicap.

31	....	B × Kt
32	R—Q1	Kt × P

Resigns.

From the last game of the match between Dr. Alekhin and Capablanca.

Black, Capablanca, to play.

White, Alekhin.

The question refers only to the next move of Black. White threatens Q—R5 which would simultaneously attack the QRP and the KP.

1 .... B–Kt4 is not playable on account of 2 Kt–R4, B–Q2; 3 Q–R5, Kt–R5; 4 Q × Kt, or 3 ...., Kt × P; 4 Kt × Kt, Q × Kt; 5 Q × Pch., P–B3; 6 Q–K7ch.

1 ...., KR–K1 permits 2 Q–R5, Kt–R5; 3 R × R, R × R; 4 Q × RP, Kt × KtP; 5 Q × P, Q × P; 6 B × P.

1 ...., B–B3 leads to 2 Kt–R4, Kt × P; 3 KKt–B5 ch., P × Kt; 4 Kt × Pch., K–B3; 5 Q × Pch., K × Kt; 6 P–Kt4 mate.

The move Capablanca made, 1 ...., B–K3, loses a pawn by 2 B × B, Q × B; 3 Q–R5. The right move is 1 ...., Kt–R5. If then 2 Q–R5, P–QKt4. Black has a fair position since it is not easy to guard the White QKtP. 3 Q × RP, Kt × KtP, 4 Q–K3 would produce an even game, and 4 R–Kt1, R–QR1; 5 Q–B7, Kt–Q6 would be favourable to Black.

Even after Black's best move, 1 ...., Kt–R5, White has the choice between various continuations that exert pressure on Black, for instance 2 P–Kt4, P–QKt4; 3 R × R, R × R; 4 R–B1 with manifold threats, but by 4 ...... R × Rch.; 5 Q × R, Kt–K1, Black could parry them.

The fourth game of the match.

White—Dr. Euwe.
Black—Bogoljubow.

1 P—Q4	Kt—KB3
2 P—QB4	P—Q4

This is venturesome, because Black opens the lines at a moment when his development is backwards.

3 P × P	Q × P
4 Kt—QB3	Q—QR4
5 Kt—B3	Kt—B3
6 P—K3	....

But here 6 B–Q2 was preferable, because after 6 ...., P–K4; 7 P–K4, White would threaten 8 Kt–Q5.

6	P—K4

Now Black is able to hold the balance in the centre.

7 P—Q5	....

There was no need for this. 7 B–Kt5, B–QKt5; 8 B–Q2 was preferable.

7	Kt—QKt5
8 B—Kt5ch.	P—B3
9 Q—R4	....

In a critical position the saving move. It would have been bad play to capture the P, because by recapturing with P Black would develop his B via R3.

9	Q × Q
10 B × Q	P—QKt4
11 B—Kt3	Kt—Q6ch.

Black now resolutely assails the K.

12 K—K2	P—K5
13 Kt—Kt5	P—Kt5
14 QKt × P	B—R3

Position after Black's fourteenth move.

A position full of tension.

15 K—B3	P × P

Black could have had a safe advantage by 15 .... Kt × QP, but he aims at decisive attack against the K.

16 B—R4ch.	....

White does not take full advantage of his chances.

He should have set boldness against boldness. 16 Kt × Ktch., P × Kt; 17 Kt × BP, R–KKt1; 18 B × P, R–B1. At this juncture 19 Kt–Q6 ch., would have been too hazardous, but 19 P–K4 would have consolidated the position somewhat, for instance 19 ...., R–B7, 20 B–K3, R–Kt2; 21 B–Kt3. To judge the numerous possibilities of this position would be dogmatism, but the difficulties would have been on either side of the board, whereas the line of play chosen by White leaves all the burden on himself.

16	....	K—K2
17	Kt—Q2	P—R3
18	Kt—R3	P—Kt4
19	P—Kt4	P—R4
20	Kt × P	P × Pch.
21	K—Kt2	B—R3
22	P—B4	P × P e.p.ch.
23	QKt × P	B × Kt

This is the simplest way of winning, but Black has the "embarras de richesse."

24	Kt × B	Kt—K5
25	Kt × Kt	P × Kt
26	R—B1	QR—Kt1ch.
27	K—R1	R—R6
28	B—Q2	QR—KR1

and after a dozen moves White resigned. A game replete with imagination.

———

These examples and models will suffice, if the reader will read attentively, probe deliberately and probe again and apply what he has read, until at last it becomes his property. Practice is varied, let, what is kept in mind, be wholesome, clean, slight and, before all, systematic.

FINAL REFLECTIONS
ON EDUCATION IN CHESS.

Education in Chess goes on in a most haphazard fashion. Most Chess players slowly climb to a certain rather low level and stay there. Of players to whom a master can give odds of a Queen there are millions; players of greater skill number probably no more than a quarter of a million. If we reckon the number of Rook players as a hundred and fifty thousand, of Knight players as fifty thousand, of Pawn and two-move players as forty thousand, of pawn and move players as nine thousand, and the number of those to whom no master can allow odds, as one thousand, we are possibly not very far wrong. Now let us consider the efforts made to attain this result: a literature of many thousand volumes, hundreds, maybe thousands, of Chess columns in widely read newspapers and magazines, lectures, tournaments, tournament books, courses of instruction, matches in the clubs and between clubs and cities and countries, by correspondence, by telegraph and telephone, thousands of coffee - houses, where spectators, amid lively gossip, look on, make notes, analyze — truly an imposing expenditure.

One should not take these facts too easily. Certainly, in spite of its capacities, Chess is only a game and not to be classed with business, science, technology, not to speak of religion, philosophy or the arts. No one desires to see players devote to Chess such time as they need for serious purposes. The waste of time in Chess would not matter, were it not a symptom of a sickness that has befallen our culture.

We have learnt how to organise manufacturing plants, but our general education, our mental work, our economy of ideals are not better than our education in Chess.

I will here not wail. I will only illuminate a connection, even though rapidly. Chess, from its very inception, has had coherence with Life.

Let us assume that a master who follows a good method, say, the method of this book, strives to educate a young man ignorant of Chess to the level of one who, if conceded any odds, would surely come out the winner. How much time would the teacher need for this achievement? I think that I am correct in making the following calculation:

Rules of Play and Exercises	5 hrs.
Elementary Endings	5 hrs.
Some Openings ...	10 hrs.
Combination	20 hrs.
Position Play... ...	40 hrs.
Play and Analysis	120 hrs.

Even if the young man has no talent at all, by following the above course he would advance to the class specified. Compare with this possibility, the reality. In fact, there are a quarter of a million Chess amateurs who devote to Chess at least two hundred hours ever year and of these only a thousand, after a lifetime of study, attain the end. Without losing myself in calculations, I believe I am safe in voicing the opinion that our efforts in Chess attain only a hundredth of one per cent. of their rightful result.

Our education, in all domains of endeavour, is frightfully wasteful of time and values. In Mathematics and in Physics the results arrived at are still worse than in Chess. Is there a tendency to keep the bulk of the people stupid? For governments of an autocratic type the foolishness of the multitude has always been an asset. Possibly, also the mediocre who happen to be in authority follow the same policy. This motif, it is true, is not predominating in Chess. The bad state of education in Chess is due entirely to our backwardness.

Education in Chess has to be an education in independent thinking and judging. Chess must not be memorized, simply because it is not important enough. If you load your memory, you should know why. Memory is too valuable to be stocked with trifles. Of my fifty-seven years I have applied at least thirty to forgetting most of what I had learned or read, and since I succeeded in this I have acquired a certain ease and cheer which I should never again like to be without. If need be, I can increase my skill in Chess, if need be I can do that of which I have no idea at present. I have stored little in my memory, but I can apply that little, and it is of good use in many and varied emergencies. I keep it in order, but resist every attempt to increase its dead weight.

You should keep in mind no names, nor numbers, nor isolated incidents, not even results, but only *methods*. The method is plastic. It is applicable in every situation. The result, the isolated incident, is rigid, because bound to wholly individual conditions. The method produces numerous results; a few of these will remain in our memory, and as long as they remain few, they are useful to illustrate and to keep alive the *rules* which order a thousand results. Such useful results must be renewed from time to time just as fresh food has to be supplied to a living organism to keep it strong and healthy. But results useful in this manner have a living connection with rules, and these again are discovered by applying a live method: the whole of this organisation must have life. more than that—a *harmonious life*.

This harmonious life stems from life; life is generated only by life. He who wants to educate himself in Chess must evade what is dead in Chess — artificial theories, supported by few instances and unheld by an excess of human wit; the habit of playing with inferior opponents; the custom of avoiding difficult tasks; the weakness of uncritically taking over variations or rules discovered by others; the vanity which is self-sufficient; the incapacity for admitting mistakes; in brief, everything that leads to a standstill or to anarchy.

Acquisition of harmonious education is comparable to the production and the elevation of an organism harmoniously built. The one is fed by blood, the other one by the spirit; but Life, equally mysterious, creative, powerful, flows through either. This comparison is no mere rhetorical imagery; it is a *programme*.

True, this programme, valid for all education, is in no way restricted to Chess; only a second postulate added to the above singles out Chess among all other things to be taught. It is this: to lead the pupil along the paths of the theory of Steinitz.

This theory has a history which the pupil should strive to understand because it lifts the veil a little from the mystery of human character; this theory has a meaning w h i c h became manifest after a hard contest with competing theories and won authority through a celebrated world's championship match; this theory has connections with profound problems; this theory asks the pupil to think for himself and to construct his own table of values and to keep it constantly, vigilantly, in order; this theory demands of him boldness and caution and force and economy and thus becomes to him a model for actions outside of Chess.

The road to this education requires good teachers —masters of Chess who at the same time are geniuses of teaching. But it pays to go along this road for it leads to a country of men who judge independently, act boldly and aspire after noble ideals.

How should these teachers follow their avocation? In introducing young men into the game in the right manner by lectures, good books, by live play with their pupils, by assisting at matches of the pupils and making notes and comments on the good and weak points of the games played; in short, by thus facilitating the thinking of their pupil without doing violence to it. The ways in which a good teacher may do efficient work are manifold and varied.

The Chess world has the task of breeding such teachers and, as soon as this is accomplished, to support them in their efforts. Thus the Chess-world would ease the hard life of the Chessmasters who must make a profession of Chess provided they want to do their best for Chess. But who wants to stop half-way? Who would want these Chess-masters who have the capacity for excellent teaching in them to become mediocre in Chess only in order to make them mediocre in some other profession? The function of a Chess-master, who would be principally a Chessteacher, is useful and pleasing. It is to the individual credit of Chess that in other domains of human activity, at least up to the present, teachers of the above type are not even possible.

On the Future of the Theory of Steinitz.

It is easy to mould the theory of Steinitz into mathematical symbols by inventing a kind of Chess, the rules and regulations of which are themselves expressed by mathematical symbols. T h e Japanese game of Go is very nearly what I mean. In such a game the question, whether thorough analysis would confirm the theory of Steinitz or not, presumably could be quickly solved because the power of modern mathematics is exceedingly great.

The instant that this solution is worked out, humanity stands before the gate of an immense new science which prophetic philosophers have called the mathematics or the physics of contest.

T h e contests fought nowadavs by men—war, d i p l o m a t i c negotiation, competition in manufacture, disputes in the press, to name just a few—are conducted very amateurishly. That wars should appear to us a necessity is proof of our stupidity. T r u e, humanity has need of a test for progress, for right, for soundness of ethics in human affairs, but that need can be satisfied in other and more efficient ways than by war. To make this evident is difficult only because men do not *want* to know the truth. But this task will be an easy one as soon as the science of contest attains recognition.

To outlaw war will be possible because humanity has a wealth of efficient and useful means to fill the gap that would be left. The competition b e t w e e n research workers, inventors, discoverers, artists, statesmen causes the flow of blood in the body of culture. And this competition will retain its vigour till many centuries after the time that V i c t o r Hugo pictures, when cannons will have been stored in museums alongside of the instruments of torture to serve as memorials of a vanished barbaric epoch.

T h e mathematics of Chess does not, it is true, solve the problem of comprehending the contests of Life, but it sets that problem in precise terms and points to a solution. There the leverage will be supported whence investigators will set scientific research into motion. The first step is always the essential one. With the law of the lever by Archimedes came statics, with the law of the falling stone by Galileo arose dynamics, and their course, though their entry into the world was so modest, led them to revolutionise all science and all modes of living irrespective of the obstacles that hatred a n d stupidity heaped into their path. The science of contest will progress irresistibly, as soon as its first modest success has been scored.

It is desirable that institutes to further these ends should be erected. Such institutes would have to work upon a mass of material already extant: theory of mathematical games, of organisation, of the conduct of business, of dispute, of negotiation; they would have to breed teachers capable of elevating the multitude from its terrible dilettantism in matters of contest; they would have to produce books of instruction and for reading as plain, as intelligible, as va l u a b l e as Knigge's *Social Intercourse Amongst Mankind*. (*Umgang mit Menschen*) or Labruyère's *Characters*.

Such an institute should be founded by every people who want to make themselves fit for a sturdier future and at the same time to aid the progress and the happiness of all humankind.

These plans are not at all fantastic; they will certainly be realised at some time. Why not now? Let us hope that also in these days of all-round mediocrity Reason is not wholly without partisans.

THE END.

INDICES.

INDICES.—(Continued).

II.—INDEX TO GAMES WITH THE OPENINGS EMPLOYED.

The player whose name appears first had the move.

INDICES.—(Continued).

* Where heavy type is used the player of White is given first.
Where lighter type is used the player of Black is given first.

A CATALOGUE OF SELECTED DOVER BOOKS
IN ALL FIELDS OF INTEREST

A CATALOGUE OF SELECTED DOVER BOOKS
IN ALL FIELDS OF INTEREST

WHAT IS SCIENCE?, *N. Campbell*

The role of experiment and measurement, the function of mathematics, the nature of scientific laws, the difference between laws and theories, the limitations of science, and many similarly provocative topics are treated clearly and without technicalities by an eminent scientist. "Still an excellent introduction to scientific philosophy," H. Margenau in *Physics Today*. "A first-rate primer . . . deserves a wide audience," *Scientific American*. 192pp. 5⅜ x 8.

60043-2 Paperbound $1.25

THE NATURE OF LIGHT AND COLOUR IN THE OPEN AIR, *M. Minnaert*

Why are shadows sometimes blue, sometimes green, or other colors depending on the light and surroundings? What causes mirages? Why do multiple suns and moons appear in the sky? Professor Minnaert explains these unusual phenomena and hundreds of others in simple, easy-to-understand terms based on optical laws and the properties of light and color. No mathematics is required but artists, scientists, students, and everyone fascinated by these "tricks" of nature will find thousands of useful and amazing pieces of information. Hundreds of observational experiments are suggested which require no special equipment. 200 illustrations; 42 photos. xvi + 362pp. 5⅜ x 8.

20196-1 Paperbound $2.00

THE STRANGE STORY OF THE QUANTUM, AN ACCOUNT FOR THE GENERAL READER OF THE GROWTH OF IDEAS UNDERLYING OUR PRESENT ATOMIC KNOWLEDGE, *B. Hoffmann*

Presents lucidly and expertly, with barest amount of mathematics, the problems and theories which led to modern quantum physics. Dr. Hoffmann begins with the closing years of the 19th century, when certain trifling discrepancies were noticed, and with illuminating analogies and examples takes you through the brilliant concepts of Planck, Einstein, Pauli, Broglie, Bohr, Schroedinger, Heisenberg, Dirac, Sommerfeld, Feynman, etc. This edition includes a new, long postscript carrying the story through 1958. "Of the books attempting an account of the history and contents of our modern atomic physics which have come to my attention, this is the best," H. Margenau, Yale University, in *American Journal of Physics*. 32 tables and line illustrations. Index. 275pp. 5⅜ x 8.

20518-5 Paperbound $2.00

GREAT IDEAS OF MODERN MATHEMATICS: THEIR NATURE AND USE, *Jagjit Singh*

Reader with only high school math will understand main mathematical ideas of modern physics, astronomy, genetics, psychology, evolution, etc. better than many who use them as tools, but comprehend little of their basic structure. Author uses his wide knowledge of non-mathematical fields in brilliant exposition of differential equations, matrices, group theory, logic, statistics, problems of mathematical foundations, imaginary numbers, vectors, etc. Original publication. 2 appendixes. 2 indexes. 65 ills. 322pp. 5⅜ x 8.

20587-8 Paperbound $2.25

THE MUSIC OF THE SPHERES: THE MATERIAL UNIVERSE — FROM ATOM TO QUASAR, SIMPLY EXPLAINED, *Guy Murchie*
Vast compendium of fact, modern concept and theory, observed and calculated data, historical background guides intelligent layman through the material universe. Brilliant exposition of earth's construction, explanations for moon's craters, atmospheric components of Venus and Mars (with data from recent fly-by's), sun spots, sequences of star birth and death, neighboring galaxies, contributions of Galileo, Tycho Brahe, Kepler, etc.; and (Vol. 2) construction of the atom (describing newly discovered sigma and xi subatomic particles), theories of sound, color and light, space and time, including relativity theory, quantum theory, wave theory, probability theory, work of Newton, Maxwell, Faraday, Einstein, de Broglie, etc. "Best presentation yet offered to the intelligent general reader," *Saturday Review*. Revised (1967). Index. 319 illustrations by the author. Total of xx + 644pp. 5⅜ x 8½.
21809-0, 21810-4 Two volume set, paperbound $5.00

FOUR LECTURES ON RELATIVITY AND SPACE, *Charles Proteus Steinmetz*
Lecture series, given by great mathematician and electrical engineer, generally considered one of the best popular-level expositions of special and general relativity theories and related questions. Steinmetz translates complex mathematical reasoning into language accessible to laymen through analogy, example and comparison. Among topics covered are relativity of motion, location, time; of mass; acceleration; 4-dimensional time-space; geometry of the gravitational field; curvature and bending of space; non-Euclidean geometry. Index. 40 illustrations. x + 142pp. 5⅜ x 8½.   61771-8 Paperbound $1.35

HOW TO KNOW THE WILD FLOWERS, *Mrs. William Starr Dana*
Classic nature book that has introduced thousands to wonders of American wild flowers. Color-season principle of organization is easy to use, even by those with no botanical training, and the genial, refreshing discussions of history, folklore, uses of over 1,000 native and escape flowers, foliage plants are informative as well as fun to read. Over 170 full-page plates, collected from several editions, may be colored in to make permanent records of finds. Revised to conform with 1950 edition of Gray's Manual of Botany. xlii + 438pp. 5⅜ x 8½.   20332-8 Paperbound $2.50

MANUAL OF THE TREES OF NORTH AMERICA, *Charles Sprague Sargent*
Still unsurpassed as most comprehensive, reliable study of North American tree characteristics, precise locations and distribution. By dean of American dendrologists. Every tree native to U.S., Canada, Alaska; 185 genera, 717 species, described in detail—leaves, flowers, fruit, winterbuds, bark, wood, growth habits, etc. plus discussion of varieties and local variants, immaturity variations. Over 100 keys, including unusual 11-page analytical key to genera, aid in identification. 783 clear illustrations of flowers, fruit, leaves. An unmatched permanent reference work for all nature lovers. Second enlarged (1926) edition. Synopsis of families. Analytical key to genera. Glossary of technical terms. Index. 783 illustrations, 1 map. Total of 982pp. 5⅜ x 8.
20277-1, 20278-X Two volume set, paperbound $6.00

IT'S FUN TO MAKE THINGS FROM SCRAP MATERIALS,
Evelyn Glantz Hershoff
What use are empty spools, tin cans, bottle tops? What can be made from
rubber bands, clothes pins, paper clips, and buttons? This book provides
simply worded instructions and large diagrams showing you how to make
cookie cutters, toy trucks, paper turkeys, Halloween masks, telephone sets,
aprons, linoleum block- and spatter prints — in all 399 projects! Many are easy
enough for young children to figure out for themselves; some challenging
enough to entertain adults; all are remarkably ingenious ways to make things
from materials that cost pennies or less! Formerly "Scrap Fun for Everyone."
Index. 214 illustrations. 373pp. 5⅜ x 8½.   21251-3 Paperbound $1.75

SYMBOLIC LOGIC and THE GAME OF LOGIC, *Lewis Carroll*
"Symbolic Logic" is not concerned with modern symbolic logic, but is instead
a collection of over 380 problems posed with charm and imagination, using
the syllogism and a fascinating diagrammatic method of drawing conclusions.
In "The Game of Logic" Carroll's whimsical imagination devises a logical game
played with 2 diagrams and counters (included) to manipulate hundreds of
tricky syllogisms. The final section, "Hit or Miss" is a lagniappe of 101 additional puzzles in the delightful Carroll manner. Until this reprint edition,
both of these books were rarities costing up to $15 each. Symbolic Logic:
Index. xxxi + 199pp. The Game of Logic: 96pp. 2 vols. bound as one. 5⅜ x 8.
                                                          20492-8 Paperbound $2.50

MATHEMATICAL PUZZLES OF SAM LOYD, PART I
selected and edited by M. Gardner
Choice puzzles by the greatest American puzzle creator and innovator. Selected
from his famous collection, "Cyclopedia of Puzzles," they retain the unique
style and historical flavor of the originals. There are posers based on arithmetic,
algebra, probability, game theory, route tracing, topology, counter and sliding
block, operations research, geometrical dissection. Includes the famous "14-15"
puzzle which was a national craze, and his "Horse of a Different Color" which
sold millions of copies. 117 of his most ingenious puzzles in all. 120 line
drawings and diagrams. Solutions. Selected references. xx + 167pp. 5⅜ x 8.
                                                          20498-7 Paperbound $1.35

STRING FIGURES AND HOW TO MAKE THEM, *Caroline Furness Jayne*
107 string figures plus variations selected from the best primitive and modern
examples developed by Navajo, Apache, pygmies of Africa, Eskimo, in Europe,
Australia, China, etc. The most readily understandable, easy-to-follow book in
English on perennially popular recreation. Crystal-clear exposition; step-by-
step diagrams. Everyone from kindergarten children to adults looking for
unusual diversion will be endlessly amused. Index. Bibliography. Introduction
by A. C. Haddon. 17 full-page plates, 960 illustrations. xxiii + 401pp. 5⅜ x 8½.
                                                          20152-X Paperbound $2.25

PAPER FOLDING FOR BEGINNERS, *W. D. Murray and F. J. Rigney*
A delightful introduction to the varied and entertaining Japanese art of
origami (paper folding), with a full, crystal-clear text that anticipates every
difficulty; over 275 clearly labeled diagrams of all important stages in creation.
You get results at each stage, since complex figures are logically developed
from simpler ones. 43 different pieces are explained: sailboats, frogs, roosters,
etc. 6 photographic plates. 279 diagrams. 95pp. 5⅜ x 8⅜.
                                                          20713-7 Paperbound $1.00

PRINCIPLES OF ART HISTORY,
H. Wölfflin

Analyzing such terms as "baroque," "classic," "neoclassic," "primitive," "picturesque," and 164 different works by artists like Botticelli, van Cleve, Dürer, Hobbema, Holbein, Hals, Rembrandt, Titian, Brueghel, Vermeer, and many others, the author establishes the classifications of art history and style on a firm, concrete basis. This classic of art criticism shows what really occurred between the 14th-century primitives and the sophistication of the 18th century in terms of basic attitudes and philosophies. "A remarkable lesson in the art of seeing," *Sat. Rev. of Literature*. Translated from the 7th German edition. 150 illustrations. 254pp. 6⅛ x 9¼. 20276-3 Paperbound $2.25

PRIMITIVE ART,
Franz Boas

This authoritative and exhaustive work by a great American anthropologist covers the entire gamut of primitive art. Pottery, leatherwork, metal work, stone work, wood, basketry, are treated in detail. Theories of primitive art, historical depth in art history, technical virtuosity, unconscious levels of patterning, symbolism, styles, literature, music, dance, etc. A must book for the interested layman, the anthropologist, artist, handicrafter (hundreds of unusual motifs), and the historian. Over 900 illustrations (50 ceramic vessels, 12 totem poles, etc.). 376pp. 5⅜ x 8. 20025-6 Paperbound $2.50

THE GENTLEMAN AND CABINET MAKER'S DIRECTOR,
Thomas Chippendale

A reprint of the 1762 catalogue of furniture designs that went on to influence generations of English and Colonial and Early Republic American furniture makers. The 200 plates, most of them full-page sized, show Chippendale's designs for French (Louis XV), Gothic, and Chinese-manner chairs, sofas, canopy and dome beds, cornices, chamber organs, cabinets, shaving tables, commodes, picture frames, frets, candle stands, chimney pieces, decorations, etc. The drawings are all elegant and highly detailed; many include construction diagrams and elevations. A supplement of 24 photographs shows surviving pieces of original and Chippendale-style pieces of furniture. Brief biography of Chippendale by N. I. Bienenstock, editor of *Furniture World*. Reproduced from the 1762 edition. 200 plates, plus 19 photographic plates. vi + 249pp. 9⅛ x 12¼. 21601-2 Paperbound $3.50

AMERICAN ANTIQUE FURNITURE: A BOOK FOR AMATEURS,
Edgar G. Miller, Jr.

Standard introduction and practical guide to identification of valuable American antique furniture. 2115 illustrations, mostly photographs taken by the author in 148 private homes, are arranged in chronological order in extensive chapters on chairs, sofas, chests, desks, bedsteads, mirrors, tables, clocks, and other articles. Focus is on furniture accessible to the collector, including simpler pieces and a larger than usual coverage of Empire style. Introductory chapters identify structural elements, characteristics of various styles, how to avoid fakes, etc. "We are frequently asked to name some book on American furniture that will meet the requirements of the novice collector, the beginning dealer, and . . . the general public. . . . We believe Mr. Miller's two volumes more completely satisfy this specification than any other work," *Antiques*. Appendix. Index. Total of vi + 1106pp. 7⅞ x 10¾. 21599-7, 21600-4 Two volume set, paperbound $7.50

THE BAD CHILD'S BOOK OF BEASTS, MORE BEASTS FOR WORSE CHILDREN, and A MORAL ALPHABET, *H. Belloc*
Hardly and anthology of humorous verse has appeared in the last 50 years without at least a couple of these famous nonsense verses. But one must see the entire volumes — with all the delightful original illustrations by Sir Basil Blackwood — to appreciate fully Belloc's charming and witty verses that play so subacidly on the platitudes of life and morals that beset his day — and ours. A great humor classic. Three books in one. Total of 157pp. 5⅜ x 8.
20749-8 Paperbound $1.00

THE DEVIL'S DICTIONARY, *Ambrose Bierce*
Sardonic and irreverent barbs puncturing the pomposities and absurdities of American politics, business, religion, literature, and arts, by the country's greatest satirist in the classic tradition. Epigrammatic as Shaw, piercing as Swift, American as Mark Twain, Will Rogers, and Fred Allen, Bierce will always remain the favorite of a small coterie of enthusiasts, and of writers and speakers whom he supplies with "some of the most gorgeous witticisms of the English language" (H. L. Mencken). Over 1000 entries in alphabetical order. 144pp. 5⅜ x 8.
20487-1 Paperbound $1.00

THE COMPLETE NONSENSE OF EDWARD LEAR.
This is the only complete edition of this master of gentle madness available at a popular price. *A Book of Nonsense, Nonsense Songs, More Nonsense Songs and Stories* in their entirety with all the old favorites that have delighted children and adults for years. The Dong With A Luminous Nose, The Jumblies, The Owl and the Pussycat, and hundreds of other bits of wonderful nonsense: 214 limericks, 3 sets of Nonsense Botany, 5 Nonsense Alphabets, 546 drawings by Lear himself, and much more. 320pp. 5⅜ x 8. 20167-8 Paperbound $1.75

THE WIT AND HUMOR OF OSCAR WILDE, *ed. by Alvin Redman*
Wilde at his most brilliant, in 1000 epigrams exposing weaknesses and hypocrisies of "civilized" society. Divided into 49 categories—sin, wealth, women, America, etc.—to aid writers, speakers. Includes excerpts from his trials, books, plays, criticism. Formerly "The Epigrams of Oscar Wilde." Introduction by Vyvyan Holland, Wilde's only living son. Introductory essay by editor. 260pp. 5⅜ x 8.
20602-5 Paperbound $1.50

A CHILD'S PRIMER OF NATURAL HISTORY, *Oliver Herford*
Scarcely an anthology of whimsy and humor has appeared in the last 50 years without a contribution from Oliver Herford. Yet the works from which these examples are drawn have been almost impossible to obtain! Here at last are Herford's improbable definitions of a menagerie of familiar and weird animals, each verse illustrated by the author's own drawings. 24 drawings in 2 colors; 24 additional drawings. vii + 95pp. 6½ x 6. 21647-0 Paperbound $1.00

THE BROWNIES: THEIR BOOK, *Palmer Cox*
The book that made the Brownies a household word. Generations of readers have enjoyed the antics, predicaments and adventures of these jovial sprites, who emerge from the forest at night to play or to come to the aid of a deserving human. Delightful illustrations by the author decorate nearly every page. 24 short verse tales with 266 illustrations. 155pp. 6⅝ x 9¼.
21265-3 Paperbound $1.50

THE PRINCIPLES OF PSYCHOLOGY,
William James
The full long-course, unabridged, of one of the great classics of Western literature and science. Wonderfully lucid descriptions of human mental activity, the stream of thought, consciousness, time perception, memory, imagination, emotions, reason, abnormal phenomena, and similar topics. Original contributions are integrated with the work of such men as Berkeley, Binet, Mills, Darwin, Hume, Kant, Royce, Schopenhauer, Spinoza, Locke, Descartes, Galton, Wundt, Lotze, Herbart, Fechner, and scores of others. All contrasting interpretations of mental phenomena are examined in detail—introspective analysis, philosophical interpretation, and experimental research. "A classic," *Journal of Consulting Psychology.* "The main lines are as valid as ever," *Psychoanalytical Quarterly.* "Standard reading . . . a classic of interpretation," *Psychiatric Quarterly.* 94 illustrations. 1408pp. 5⅜ x 8.

20381-6, 20382-4 Two volume set, paperbound $6.00

VISUAL ILLUSIONS: THEIR CAUSES, CHARACTERISTICS AND APPLICATIONS,
M. Luckiesh
"Seeing is deceiving," asserts the author of this introduction to virtually every type of optical illusion known. The text both describes and explains the principles involved in color illusions, figure-ground, distance illusions, etc. 100 photographs, drawings and diagrams prove how easy it is to fool the sense: circles that aren't round, parallel lines that seem to bend, stationary figures that seem to move as you stare at them — illustration after illustration strains our credulity at what we see. Fascinating book from many points of view, from applications for artists, in camouflage, etc. to the psychology of vision. New introduction by William Ittleson, Dept. of Psychology, Queens College. Index, Bibliography. xxi + 252pp. 5⅜ x 8½. 21530-X Paperbound $1.50

FADS AND FALLACIES IN THE NAME OF SCIENCE,
Martin Gardner
This is the standard account of various cults, quack systems, and delusions which have masqueraded as science: hollow earth fanatics. Reich and orgone sex energy, dianetics, Atlantis, multiple moons, Forteanism, flying saucers, medical fallacies like iridiagnosis, zone therapy, etc. A new chapter has been added on Bridey Murphy, psionics, and other recent manifestations in this field. This is a fair, reasoned appraisal of eccentric theory which provides excellent inoculation against cleverly masked nonsense. "Should be read by everyone, scientist and non-scientist alike," R. T. Birge, Prof. Emeritus of Physics, Univ. of California; Former President, American Physical Society. Index. x + 365pp. 5⅜ x 8. 20394-8 Paperbound $2.00

ILLUSIONS AND DELUSIONS OF THE SUPERNATURAL AND THE OCCULT,
D. H. Rawcliffe
Holds up to rational examination hundreds of persistent delusions including crystal gazing, automatic writing, table turning, mediumistic trances, mental healing, stigmata, lycanthropy, live burial, the Indian Rope Trick, spiritualism, dowsing, telepathy, clairvoyance, ghosts, ESP, etc. The author explains and exposes the mental and physical deceptions involved, making this not only an expose of supernatural phenomena, but a valuable exposition of characteristic types of abnormal psychology. Originally titled "The Psychology of the Occult." 14 illustrations. Index. 551pp. 5⅜ x 8. 20503-7 Paperbound $3.50

FAIRY TALE COLLECTIONS, *edited by Andrew Lang*
Andrew Lang's fairy tale collections make up the richest shelf-full of traditional children's stories anywhere available. Lang supervised the translation of stories from all over the world—familiar European tales collected by Grimm, animal stories from Negro Africa, myths of primitive Australia, stories from Russia, Hungary, Iceland, Japan, and many other countries. Lang's selection of translations are unusually high; many authorities consider that the most familiar tales find their best versions in these volumes. All collections are richly decorated and illustrated by H. J. Ford and other artists.

THE BLUE FAIRY BOOK. 37 stories. 138 illustrations. ix + 390pp. 5⅜ x 8½.
21437-0 Paperbound $1.95

THE GREEN FAIRY BOOK. 42 stories. 100 illustrations. xiii + 366pp. 5⅜ x 8½.
21439-7 Paperbound $1.75

THE BROWN FAIRY BOOK. 32 stories. 50 illustrations, 8 in color. xii + 350pp. 5⅜ x 8½.
21438-9 Paperbound $1.95

THE BEST TALES OF HOFFMANN, *edited by E. F. Bleiler*
10 stories by E. T. A. Hoffmann, one of the greatest of all writers of fantasy. The tales include "The Golden Flower Pot," "Automata," "A New Year's Eve Adventure," "Nutcracker and the King of Mice," "Sand-Man," and others. Vigorous characterizations of highly eccentric personalities, remarkably imaginative situations, and intensely fast pacing has made these tales popular all over the world for 150 years. Editor's introduction. 7 drawings by Hoffmann. xxxiii + 419pp. 5⅜ x 8½.
21793-0 Paperbound $2.25

GHOST AND HORROR STORIES OF AMBROSE BIERCE,
edited by E. F. Bleiler
Morbid, eerie, horrifying tales of possessed poets, shabby aristocrats, revived corpses, and haunted malefactors. Widely acknowledged as the best of their kind between Poe and the moderns, reflecting their author's inner torment and bitter view of life. Includes "Damned Thing," "The Middle Toe of the Right Foot," "The Eyes of the Panther," "Visions of the Night," "Moxon's Master," and over a dozen others. Editor's introduction. xxii + 199pp. 5⅜ x 8½.
20767-6 Paperbound $1.50

THREE GOTHIC NOVELS, *edited by E. F. Bleiler*
Originators of the still popular Gothic novel form, influential in ushering in early 19th-century Romanticism. Horace Walpole's *Castle of Otranto*, William Beckford's *Vathek*, John Polidori's *The Vampyre*, and a *Fragment* by Lord Byron are enjoyable as exciting reading or as documents in the history of English literature. Editor's introduction. xi + 291pp. 5⅜ x 8½.
21232-7 Paperbound $2.00

BEST GHOST STORIES OF LEFANU, *edited by E. F. Bleiler*
Though admired by such critics as V. S. Pritchett, Charles Dickens and Henry James, ghost stories by the Irish novelist Joseph Sheridan LeFanu have never become as widely known as his detective fiction. About half of the 16 stories in this collection have never before been available in America. Collection includes "Carmilla" (perhaps the best vampire story ever written), "The Haunted Baronet," "The Fortunes of Sir Robert Ardagh," and the classic "Green Tea." Editor's introduction. 7 contemporary illustrations. Portrait of LeFanu. xii + 467pp. 5⅜ x 8.
20415-4 Paperbound $2.50

EASY-TO-DO ENTERTAINMENTS AND DIVERSIONS WITH COINS, CARDS, STRING, PAPER AND MATCHES, *R. M. Abraham*

Over 300 tricks, games and puzzles will provide young readers with absorbing fun. Sections on card games; paper-folding; tricks with coins, matches and pieces of string; games for the agile; toy-making from common household objects; mathematical recreations; and 50 miscellaneous pastimes. Anyone in charge of groups of youngsters, including hard-pressed parents, and in need of suggestions on how to keep children sensibly amused and quietly content will find this book indispensable. Clear, simple text, copious number of delightful line drawings and illustrative diagrams. Originally titled "Winter Nights' Entertainments." Introduction by Lord Baden Powell. 329 illustrations. v + 186pp. 5⅜ x 8½.   20921-0 Paperbound $1.00

AN INTRODUCTION TO CHESS MOVES AND TACTICS SIMPLY EXPLAINED, *Leonard Barden*

Beginner's introduction to the royal game. Names, possible moves of the pieces, definitions of essential terms, how games are won, etc. explained in 30-odd pages. With this background you'll be able to sit right down and play. Balance of book teaches strategy — openings, middle game, typical endgame play, and suggestions for improving your game. A sample game is fully analyzed. True middle-level introduction, teaching you all the essentials without oversimplifying or losing you in a maze of detail. 58 figures. 102pp. 5⅜ x 8½.   21210-6 Paperbound $1.25

LASKER'S MANUAL OF CHESS, *Dr. Emanuel Lasker*

Probably the greatest chess player of modern times, Dr. Emanuel Lasker held the world championship 28 years, independent of passing schools or fashions. This unmatched study of the game, chiefly for intermediate to skilled players, analyzes basic methods, combinations, position play, the aesthetics of chess, dozens of different openings, etc., with constant reference to great modern games. Contains a brilliant exposition of Steinitz's important theories. Introduction by Fred Reinfeld. Tables of Lasker's tournament record. 3 indices. 308 diagrams. 1 photograph. xxx + 349pp. 5⅜ x 8. 20640-8 Paperbound $2.50

COMBINATIONS: THE HEART OF CHESS, *Irving Chernev*

Step-by-step from simple combinations to complex, this book, by a well-known chess writer, shows you the intricacies of pins, counter-pins, knight forks, and smothered mates. Other chapters show alternate lines of play to those taken in actual championship games; boomerang combinations; classic examples of brilliant combination play by Nimzovich, Rubinstein, Tarrasch, Botvinnik, Alekhine and Capablanca. Index. 356 diagrams. ix + 245pp. 5⅜ x 8½.   21744-2 Paperbound $2.00

HOW TO SOLVE CHESS PROBLEMS, *K. S. Howard*

Full of practical suggestions for the fan or the beginner — who knows only the moves of the chessmen. Contains preliminary section and 58 two-move, 46 three-move, and 8 four-move problems composed by 27 outstanding American problem creators in the last 30 years. Explanation of all terms and exhaustive index. "Just what is wanted for the student," Brian Harley. 112 problems, solutions. vi + 171pp. 5⅜ x 8.   20748-X Paperbound $1.50

SOCIAL THOUGHT FROM LORE. TO SCIENCE,
H. E. Barnes and H. Becker
An immense survey of sociological thought and ways of viewing, studying, planning, and reforming society from earliest times to the present. Includes thought on society of preliterate peoples, ancient non-Western cultures, and every great movement in Europe, America, and modern Japan. Analyzes hundreds of great thinkers: Plato, Augustine, Bodin, Vico, Montesquieu, Herder, Comte, Marx, etc. Weighs the contributions of utopians, sophists, fascists and communists; economists, jurists, philosophers, ecclesiastics, and every 19th and 20th century school of scientific sociology, anthropology, and social psychology throughout the world. Combines topical, chronological, and regional approaches, treating the evolution of social thought as a process rather than as a series of mere topics. "Impressive accuracy, competence, and discrimination . . . easily the best single survey," *Nation*. Thoroughly revised, with new material up to 1960. 2 indexes. Over 2200 bibliographical notes. Three volume set. Total of 1586pp. 5⅜ x 8.
20901-6, 20902-4, 20903-2 Three volume set, paperbound $9.00

A HISTORY OF HISTORICAL WRITING, *Harry Elmer Barnes*
Virtually the only adequate survey of the whole course of historical writing in a single volume. Surveys developments from the beginnings of historiography in the ancient Near East and the Classical World, up through the Cold War. Covers major historians in detail, shows interrelationship with cultural background, makes clear individual contributions, evaluates and estimates importance; also enormously rich upon minor authors and thinkers who are usually passed over. Packed with scholarship and learning, clear, easily written. Indispensable to every student of history. Revised and enlarged up to 1961. Index and bibliography. xv + 442pp. 5⅜ x 8½.
20104-X Paperbound $2.75

JOHANN SEBASTIAN BACH, *Philipp Spitta*
The complete and unabridged text of the definitive study of Bach. Written some 70 years ago, it is still unsurpassed for its coverage of nearly all aspects of Bach's life and work. There could hardly be a finer non-technical introduction to Bach's music than the detailed, lucid analyses which Spitta provides for hundreds of individual pieces. 26 solid pages are devoted to the B minor mass, for example, and 30 pages to the glorious St. Matthew Passion. This monumental set also includes a major analysis of the music of the 18th century: Buxtehude, Pachelbel, etc. "Unchallenged as the last word on one of the supreme geniuses of music," John Barkham, *Saturday Review Syndicate*. Total of 1819pp. Heavy cloth binding. 5⅜ x 8.
22278-0, 22279-9 Two volume set, clothbound $15.00

BEETHOVEN AND HIS NINE SYMPHONIES, *George Grove*
In this modern middle-level classic of musicology Grove not only analyzes all nine of Beethoven's symphonies very thoroughly in terms of their musical structure, but also discusses the circumstances under which they were written, Beethoven's stylistic development, and much other background material. This is an extremely rich book, yet very easily followed; it is highly recommended to anyone seriously interested in music. Over 250 musical passages. Index. viii + 407pp. 5⅜ x 8.
20334-4 Paperbound $2.25

THREE SCIENCE FICTION NOVELS,
John Taine

Acknowledged by many as the best SF writer of the 1920's, Taine (under the name Eric Temple Bell) was also a Professor of Mathematics of considerable renown. Reprinted here are *The Time Stream*, generally considered Taine's best, *The Greatest Game*, a biological-fiction novel, and *The Purple Sapphire*, involving a supercivilization of the past. Taine's stories tie fantastic narratives to frameworks of original and logical scientific concepts. Speculation is often profound on such questions as the nature of time, concept of entropy, cyclical universes, etc. 4 contemporary illustrations. v + 532pp. 5⅜ x 8⅜.

21180-0 Paperbound $2.50

SEVEN SCIENCE FICTION NOVELS,
H. G. Wells

Full unabridged texts of 7 science-fiction novels of the master. Ranging from biology, physics, chemistry, astronomy, to sociology and other studies, Mr. Wells extrapolates whole worlds of strange and intriguing character. "One will have to go far to match this for entertainment, excitement, and sheer pleasure . . ."*New York Times*. Contents: The Time Machine, The Island of Dr. Moreau, The First Men in the Moon, The Invisible Man, The War of the Worlds, The Food of the Gods, In The Days of the Comet. 1015pp. 5⅜ x 8.

20264-X Clothbound $5.00

28 SCIENCE FICTION STORIES OF H. G. WELLS.

Two full, unabridged novels, *Men Like Gods* and *Star Begotten*, plus 26 short stories by the master science-fiction writer of all time! Stories of space, time, invention, exploration, futuristic adventure. Partial contents: *The Country of the Blind, In the Abyss, The Crystal Egg, The Man Who Could Work Miracles, A Story of Days to Come, The Empire of the Ants, The Magic Shop, The Valley of the Spiders, A Story of the Stone Age, Under the Knife, Sea Raiders*, etc. An indispensable collection for the library of anyone interested in science fiction adventure. 928pp. 5⅜ x 8.

20265-8 Clothbound $5.00

THREE MARTIAN NOVELS,
Edgar Rice Burroughs

Complete, unabridged reprinting, in one volume, of Thuvia, Maid of Mars; Chessmen of Mars; The Master Mind of Mars. Hours of science-fiction adventure by a modern master storyteller. Reset in large clear type for easy reading. 16 illustrations by J. Allen St. John. vi + 490pp. 5⅜ x 8½.

20039-6 Paperbound $2.50

AN INTELLECTUAL AND CULTURAL HISTORY OF THE WESTERN WORLD,
Harry Elmer Barnes

Monumental 3-volume survey of intellectual development of Europe from primitive cultures to the present day. Every significant product of human intellect traced through history: art, literature, mathematics, physical sciences, medicine, music, technology, social sciences, religions, jurisprudence, education, etc. Presentation is lucid and specific, analyzing in detail specific discoveries, theories, literary works, and so on. Revised (1965) by recognized scholars in specialized fields under the direction of Prof. Barnes. Revised bibliography. Indexes. 24 illustrations. Total of xxix + 1318pp.

21275-0, 21276-9, 21277-7 Three volume set, paperbound $8.25

HEAR ME TALKIN' TO YA, *edited by Nat Shapiro and Nat Hentoff*
In their own words, Louis Armstrong, King Oliver, Fletcher Henderson, Bunk Johnson, Bix Beiderbecke, Billy Holiday, Fats Waller, Jelly Roll Morton, Duke Ellington, and many others comment on the origins of jazz in New Orleans and its growth in Chicago's South Side, Kansas City's jam sessions, Depression Harlem, and the modernism of the West Coast schools. Taken from taped conversations, letters, magazine articles, other first-hand sources. Editors' introduction. xvi + 429pp. 5⅜ x 8½.   21726-4 Paperbound $2.00

THE JOURNAL OF HENRY D. THOREAU
A 25-year record by the great American observer and critic, as complete a record of a great man's inner life as is anywhere available. Thoreau's Journals served him as raw material for his formal pieces, as a place where he could develop his ideas, as an outlet for his interests in wild life and plants, in writing as an art, in classics of literature, Walt Whitman and other contemporaries, in politics, slavery, individual's relation to the State, etc. The Journals present a portrait of a remarkable man, and are an observant social history. Unabridged republication of 1906 edition, Bradford Torrey and Francis H. Allen, editors. Illustrations. Total of 1888pp. 8⅜ x 12¼.
20312-3, 20313-1 Two volume set. clothbound $30.00

A SHAKESPEARIAN GRAMMAR, *E. A. Abbott*
Basic reference to Shakespeare and his contemporaries, explaining through thousands of quotations from Shakespeare, Jonson, Beaumont and Fletcher, North's *Plutarch* and other sources the grammatical usage differing from the modern. First published in 1870 and written by a scholar who spent much of his life isolating principles of Elizabethan language, the book is unlikely ever to be superseded. Indexes. xxiv + 511pp. 5⅜ x 8½. 21582-2 Paperbound $3.00

FOLK-LORE OF SHAKESPEARE, *T. F. Thistelton Dyer*
Classic study, drawing from Shakespeare a large body of references to supernatural beliefs, terminology of falconry and hunting, games and sports, good luck charms, marriage customs, folk medicines, superstitions about plants, animals, birds, argot of the underworld, sexual slang of London, proverbs, drinking customs, weather lore, and much else. From full compilation comes a mirror of the 17th-century popular mind. Index. ix + 526pp. 5⅜ x 8½.
21614-4 Paperbound $2.75

THE NEW VARIORUM SHAKESPEARE, *edited by H. H. Furness*
By far the richest editions of the plays ever produced in any country or language. Each volume contains complete text (usually First Folio) of the play, all variants in Quarto and other Folio texts, editorial changes by every major editor to Furness's own time (1900), footnotes to obscure references or language, extensive quotes from literature of Shakespearian criticism, essays on plot sources (often reprinting sources in full), and much more.

HAMLET, *edited by H. H. Furness*
Total of xxvi + 905pp. 5⅜ x 8½.
21004-9, 21005-7 Two volume set, paperbound $5.25

TWELFTH NIGHT, *edited by H. H. Furness*
Index. xxii + 434pp. 5⅜ x 8½.   21189-4 Paperbound $2.75

LA BOHEME BY GIACOMO PUCCINI,
translated and introduced by Ellen H. Bleiler
Complete handbook for the operagoer, with everything needed for full enjoyment except the musical score itself. Complete Italian libretto, with new, modern English line-by-line translation—the only libretto printing all repeats; biography of Puccini; the librettists; background to the opera, Murger's La Boheme, etc.; circumstances of composition and performances; plot summary; and pictorial section of 73 illustrations showing Puccini, famous singers and performances, etc. Large clear type for easy reading. 124pp. 5⅜ x 8½.
20404-9 Paperbound $1.25

ANTONIO STRADIVARI: HIS LIFE AND WORK (1644-1737),
W. Henry Hill, Arthur F. Hill, and Alfred E. Hill
Still the only book that really delves into life and art of the incomparable Italian craftsman, maker of the finest musical instruments in the world today. The authors, expert violin-makers themselves, discuss Stradivari's ancestry, his construction and finishing techniques, distinguished characteristics of many of his instruments and their locations. Included, too, is story of introduction of his instruments into France, England, first revelation of their supreme merit, and information on his labels, number of instruments made, prices, mystery of ingredients of his varnish, tone of pre-1684 Stradivari violin and changes between 1684 and 1690. An extremely interesting, informative account for all music lovers, from craftsman to concert-goer. Republication of original (1902) edition. New introduction by Sydney Beck, Head of Rare Book and Manuscript Collections, Music Division, New York Public Library. Analytical index by Rembert Wurlitzer. Appendixes. 68 illustrations. 30 full-page plates. 4 in color. xxvi + 315pp. 5⅜ x 8½.
20425-1 Paperbound $2.25

MUSICAL AUTOGRAPHS FROM MONTEVERDI TO HINDEMITH,
Emanuel Winternitz
For beauty, for intrinsic interest, for perspective on the composer's personality, for subtleties of phrasing, shading, emphasis indicated in the autograph but suppressed in the printed score, the mss. of musical composition are fascinating documents which repay close study in many different ways. This 2-volume work reprints facsimiles of mss. by virtually every major composer, and many minor figures—196 examples in all. A full text points out what can be learned from mss., analyzes each sample. Index. Bibliography. 18 figures. 196 plates. Total of 170pp. of text. 7⅞ x 10¾.
21312-9, 21313-7 Two volume set, paperbound $5.00

J. S. BACH,
Albert Schweitzer
One of the few great full-length studies of Bach's life and work, and the study upon which Schweitzer's renown as a musicologist rests. On first appearance (1911), revolutionized Bach performance. The only writer on Bach to be musicologist, performing musician, and student of history, theology and philosophy, Schweitzer contributes particularly full sections on history of German Protestant church music, theories on motivic pictorial representations in vocal music, and practical suggestions for performance. Translated by Ernest Newman. Indexes. 5 illustrations. 650 musical examples. Total of xix + 928pp. 5⅜ x 8½.
21631-4, 21632-2 Two volume set, paperbound $4.50

THE METHODS OF ETHICS, *Henry Sidgwick*
Propounding no organized system of its own, study subjects every major methodological approach to ethics to rigorous, objective analysis. Study discusses and relates ethical thought of Plato, Aristotle, Bentham, Clarke, Butler, Hobbes, Hume, Mill, Spencer, Kant, and dozens of others. Sidgwick retains conclusions from each system which follow from ethical premises, rejecting the faulty. Considered by many in the field to be among the most important treatises on ethical philosophy. Appendix. Index. xlvii + 528pp. 5⅜ x 8½.
21608-X Paperbound $2.50

TEUTONIC MYTHOLOGY, *Jakob Grimm*
A milestone in Western culture; the work which established on a modern basis the study of history of religions and comparative religions. 4-volume work assembles and interprets everything available on religious and folkloristic beliefs of Germanic people (including Scandinavians, Anglo-Saxons, etc.). Assembling material from such sources as Tacitus, surviving Old Norse and Icelandic texts, archeological remains, folktales, surviving superstitions, comparative traditions, linguistic analysis, etc. Grimm explores pagan deities, heroes, folklore of nature, religious practices, and every other area of pagan German belief. To this day, the unrivaled, definitive, exhaustive study. Translated by J. S. Stallybrass from 4th (1883) German edition. Indexes. Total of lxxvii + 1887pp. 5⅜ x 8½.
21602-0, 21603-9, 21604-7, 21605-5 Four volume set, paperbound $11.00

THE I CHING, *translated by James Legge*
Called "The Book of Changes" in English, this is one of the Five Classics edited by Confucius, basic and central to Chinese thought. Explains perhaps the most complex system of divination known, founded on the theory that all things happening at any one time have characteristic features which can be isolated and related. Significant in Oriental studies, in history of religions and philosophy, and also to Jungian psychoanalysis and other areas of modern European thought. Index. Appendixes. 6 plates. xxi + 448pp. 5⅜ x 8½.
21062-6 Paperbound $2.75

HISTORY OF ANCIENT PHILOSOPHY, *W. Windelband*
One of the clearest, most accurate comprehensive surveys of Greek and Roman philosophy. Discusses ancient philosophy in general, intellectual life in Greece in the 7th and 6th centuries B.C., Thales, Anaximander, Anaximenes, Heraclitus, the Eleatics, Empedocles, Anaxagoras, Leucippus, the Pythagoreans, the Sophists, Socrates, Democritus (20 pages), Plato (50 pages), Aristotle (70 pages), the Peripatetics, Stoics, Epicureans, Sceptics, Neo-platonists, Christian Apologists, etc. 2nd German edition translated by H. E. Cushman. xv + 393pp. 5⅜ x 8.
20357-3 Paperbound $2.25

THE PALACE OF PLEASURE, *William Painter*
Elizabethan versions of Italian and French novels from *The Decameron*, Cinthio, Straparola, Queen Margaret of Navarre, and other continental sources — the very work that provided Shakespeare and dozens of his contemporaries with many of their plots and sub-plots and, therefore, justly considered one of the most influential books in all English literature. It is also a book that any reader will still enjoy. Total of cviii + 1,224pp.
21691-8, 21692-6, 21693-4 Three volume set, paperbound $6.75

THE WONDERFUL WIZARD OF OZ, *L. F. Baum*
All the original W. W. Denslow illustrations in full color—as much a part of "The Wizard" as Tenniel's drawings are of "Alice in Wonderland." "The Wizard" is still America's best-loved fairy tale, in which, as the author expresses it, "The wonderment and joy are retained and the heartaches and nightmares left out." Now today's young readers can enjoy every word and wonderful picture of the original book. New introduction by Martin Gardner. A Baum bibliography. 23 full-page color plates. viii + 268pp. 5⅜ x 8.
20691-2 Paperbound $1.95

THE MARVELOUS LAND OF OZ, *L. F. Baum*
This is the equally enchanting sequel to the "Wizard," continuing the adventures of the Scarecrow and the Tin Woodman. The hero this time is a little boy named Tip, and all the delightful Oz magic is still present. This is the Oz book with the Animated Saw-Horse, the Woggle-Bug, and Jack Pumpkinhead. All the original John R. Neill illustrations, 10 in full color. 287pp. 5⅜ x 8.
20692-0 Paperbound $1.75

ALICE'S ADVENTURES UNDER GROUND, *Lewis Carroll*
The original *Alice in Wonderland*, hand-lettered and illustrated by Carroll himself, and originally presented as a Christmas gift to a child-friend. Adults as well as children will enjoy this charming volume, reproduced faithfully in this Dover edition. While the story is essentially the same, there are slight changes, and Carroll's spritely drawings present an intriguing alternative to the famous Tenniel illustrations. One of the most popular books in Dover's catalogue. Introduction by Martin Gardner. 38 illustrations. 128pp. 5⅜ x 8½.
21482-6 Paperbound $1.00

THE NURSERY "ALICE," *Lewis Carroll*
While most of us consider *Alice in Wonderland* a story for children of all ages, Carroll himself felt it was beyond younger children. He therefore provided this simplified version, illustrated with the famous Tenniel drawings enlarged and colored in delicate tints, for children aged "from Nought to Five." Dover's edition of this now rare classic is a faithful copy of the 1889 printing, including 20 illustrations by Tenniel, and front and back covers reproduced in full color. Introduction by Martin Gardner. xxiii + 67pp. 6⅛ x 9¼.
21610-1 Paperbound $1.75

THE STORY OF KING ARTHUR AND HIS KNIGHTS, *Howard Pyle*
A fast-paced, exciting retelling of the best known Arthurian legends for young readers by one of America's best story tellers and illustrators. The sword Excalibur, wooing of Guinevere, Merlin and his downfall, adventures of Sir Pellias and Gawaine, and others. The pen and ink illustrations are vividly imagined and wonderfully drawn. 41 illustrations. xviii + 313pp. 6⅛ x 9¼.
21445-1 Paperbound $2.00

Prices subject to change without notice.

Available at your book dealer or write for free catalogue to Dept. Adsci, Dover Publications, Inc., 180 Varick St., N.Y., N.Y. 10014. Dover publishes more than 150 books each year on science, elementary and advanced mathematics, biology, music, art, literary history, social sciences and other areas.